Microsoft®
Training &
Certification

ILKEY

2BCK - KJG2E -
4FKJ

MIKE VESCHI

2274

CIRCLE VERED
@ PND.NET

2274: Managing a Microsoft® Windows® Server 2003 Environment

Released: 04/2003

Microsoft®

Course Number: 2274B
Part Number: X09-90415
Released: 04/2003

END-USER LICENSE AGREEMENT FOR MICROSOFT OFFICIAL CURRICULUM COURSEWARE –STUDENT EDITION

PLEASE READ THIS END-USER LICENSE AGREEMENT ("EULA") CAREFULLY. BY USING THE MATERIALS AND/OR USING OR INSTALLING THE SOFTWARE THAT ACCOMPANIES THIS EULA (COLLECTIVELY, THE "LICENSED CONTENT"), YOU AGREE TO THE TERMS OF THIS EULA. IF YOU DO NOT AGREE, DO NOT USE THE LICENSED CONTENT.

1.　　　**GENERAL.** This EULA is a legal agreement between you (either an individual or a single entity) and Microsoft Corporation ("Microsoft"). This EULA governs the Licensed Content, which includes computer software (including online and electronic documentation), training materials, and any other associated media and printed materials. This EULA applies to updates, supplements, add-on components, and Internet-based services components of the Licensed Content that Microsoft may provide or make available to you unless Microsoft provides other terms with the update, supplement, add-on component, or Internet-based services component. Microsoft reserves the right to discontinue any Internet-based services provided to you or made available to you through the use of the Licensed Content. This EULA also governs any product support services relating to the Licensed Content except as may be included in another agreement between you and Microsoft. An amendment or addendum to this EULA may accompany the Licensed Content.

2.　　　**GENERAL GRANT OF LICENSE.** Microsoft grants you the following rights, conditioned on your compliance with all the terms and conditions of this EULA. Microsoft grants you a limited, non-exclusive, royalty-free license to install and use the Licensed Content solely in conjunction with your participation as a student in an Authorized Training Session (as defined below). You may install and use one copy of the software on a single computer, device, workstation, terminal, or other digital electronic or analog device ("Device"). You may make a second copy of the software and install it on a portable Device for the exclusive use of the person who is the primary user of the first copy of the software. A license for the software may not be shared for use by multiple end users. An "Authorized Training Session" means a training session conducted at a Microsoft Certified Technical Education Center, an IT Academy, via a Microsoft Certified Partner, or such other entity as Microsoft may designate from time to time in writing, by a Microsoft Certified Trainer (for more information on these entities, please visit www.microsoft.com). WITHOUT LIMITING THE FOREGOING, COPYING OR REPRODUCTION OF THE LICENSED CONTENT TO ANY SERVER OR LOCATION FOR FURTHER REPRODUCTION OR REDISTRIBUTION IS EXPRESSLY PROHIBITED.

3.　　　**DESCRIPTION OF OTHER RIGHTS AND LICENSE LIMITATIONS**

　　　3.1　　　*Use of Documentation and Printed Training Materials.*

　　　　　3.1.1　　　The documents and related graphics included in the Licensed Content may include technical inaccuracies or typographical errors. Changes are periodically made to the content. Microsoft may make improvements and/or changes in any of the components of the Licensed Content at any time without notice. The names of companies, products, people, characters and/or data mentioned in the Licensed Content may be fictitious and are in no way intended to represent any real individual, company, product or event, unless otherwise noted.

　　　　　3.1.2　　　Microsoft grants you the right to reproduce portions of documents (such as student workbooks, white papers, press releases, datasheets and FAQs) (the "Documents") provided with the Licensed Content. You may not print any book (either electronic or print version) in its entirety. If you choose to reproduce Documents, you agree that: (a) use of such printed Documents will be solely in conjunction with your personal training use; (b) the Documents will not republished or posted on any network computer or broadcast in any media; (c) any reproduction will include either the Document's original copyright notice or a copyright notice to Microsoft's benefit substantially in the format provided below; and (d) to comply with all terms and conditions of this EULA. In addition, no modifications may made to any Document.

　　　　　Form of Notice:

　　　　　© 2003. Reprinted with permission by Microsoft Corporation. All rights reserved.

　　　　　Microsoft and Windows are either registered trademarks or trademarks of Microsoft Corporation in the US and/or other countries. Other product and company names mentioned herein may be the trademarks of their respective owners.

　　　3.2　　　*Use of Media Elements.* The Licensed Content may include certain photographs, clip art, animations, sounds, music, and video clips (together "Media Elements"). You may not modify these Media Elements.

　　　3.3　　　*Use of Sample Code.* In the event that the Licensed Content includes sample code in source or object format ("Sample Code"), Microsoft grants you a limited, non-exclusive, royalty-free license to use, copy and modify the Sample Code; if you elect to exercise the foregoing rights, you agree to comply with all other terms and conditions of this EULA, including without limitation Sections 3.4, 3.5, and 6.

　　　3.4　　　*Permitted Modifications.* In the event that you exercise any rights provided under this EULA to create modifications of the Licensed Content, you agree that any such modifications: (a) will not be used for providing training where a fee is charged in public or private classes; (b) indemnify, hold harmless, and defend Microsoft from and against any claims or lawsuits, including attorneys' fees, which arise from or result from your use of any modified version of the Licensed Content; and (c) not to transfer or assign any rights to any modified version of the Licensed Content to any third party without the express written permission of Microsoft.

3.5   *Reproduction/Redistribution Licensed Content.* Except as expressly provided in this EULA, you may not reproduce or distribute the Licensed Content or any portion thereof (including any permitted modifications) to any third parties without the express written permission of Microsoft.

4.   **RESERVATION OF RIGHTS AND OWNERSHIP.** Microsoft reserves all rights not expressly granted to you in this EULA. The Licensed Content is protected by copyright and other intellectual property laws and treaties. Microsoft or its suppliers own the title, copyright, and other intellectual property rights in the Licensed Content. You may not remove or obscure any copyright, trademark or patent notices that appear on the Licensed Content, or any components thereof, as delivered to you. **The Licensed Content is licensed, not sold.**

5.   **LIMITATIONS ON REVERSE ENGINEERING, DECOMPILATION, AND DISASSEMBLY.** You may not reverse engineer, decompile, or disassemble the Software or Media Elements, except and only to the extent that such activity is expressly permitted by applicable law notwithstanding this limitation.

6.   **LIMITATIONS ON SALE, RENTAL, ETC. AND CERTAIN ASSIGNMENTS.** You may not provide commercial hosting services with, sell, rent, lease, lend, sublicense, or assign copies of the Licensed Content, or any portion thereof (including any permitted modifications thereof) on a stand-alone basis or as part of any collection, product or service.

7.   **CONSENT TO USE OF DATA.** You agree that Microsoft and its affiliates may collect and use technical information gathered as part of the product support services provided to you, if any, related to the Licensed Content. Microsoft may use this information solely to improve our products or to provide customized services or technologies to you and will not disclose this information in a form that personally identifies you.

8.   **LINKS TO THIRD PARTY SITES.** You may link to third party sites through the use of the Licensed Content. The third party sites are not under the control of Microsoft, and Microsoft is not responsible for the contents of any third party sites, any links contained in third party sites, or any changes or updates to third party sites. Microsoft is not responsible for webcasting or any other form of transmission received from any third party sites. Microsoft is providing these links to third party sites to you only as a convenience, and the inclusion of any link does not imply an endorsement by Microsoft of the third party site.

9.   **ADDITIONAL LICENSED CONTENT/SERVICES.** This EULA applies to updates, supplements, add-on components, or Internet-based services components, of the Licensed Content that Microsoft may provide to you or make available to you after the date you obtain your initial copy of the Licensed Content, unless we provide other terms along with the update, supplement, add-on component, or Internet-based services component. Microsoft reserves the right to discontinue any Internet-based services provided to you or made available to you through the use of the Licensed Content.

10.   **U.S. GOVERNMENT LICENSE RIGHTS.** All software provided to the U.S. Government pursuant to solicitations issued on or after December 1, 1995 is provided with the commercial license rights and restrictions described elsewhere herein. All software provided to the U.S. Government pursuant to solicitations issued prior to December 1, 1995 is provided with "Restricted Rights" as provided for in FAR, 48 CFR 52.227-14 (JUNE 1987) or DFAR, 48 CFR 252.227-7013 (OCT 1988), as applicable.

11.   **EXPORT RESTRICTIONS.** You acknowledge that the Licensed Content is subject to U.S. export jurisdiction. You agree to comply with all applicable international and national laws that apply to the Licensed Content, including the U.S. Export Administration Regulations, as well as end-user, end-use, and destination restrictions issued by U.S. and other governments. For additional information see <http://www.microsoft.com/exporting/>.

12.   **TRANSFER.** The initial user of the Licensed Content may make a one-time permanent transfer of this EULA and Licensed Content to another end user, provided the initial user retains no copies of the Licensed Content. The transfer may not be an indirect transfer, such as a consignment. Prior to the transfer, the end user receiving the Licensed Content must agree to all the EULA terms.

13.   **"NOT FOR RESALE" LICENSED CONTENT.** Licensed Content identified as "Not For Resale" or "NFR," may not be sold or otherwise transferred for value, or used for any purpose other than demonstration, test or evaluation.

14.   **TERMINATION.** Without prejudice to any other rights, Microsoft may terminate this EULA if you fail to comply with the terms and conditions of this EULA. In such event, you must destroy all copies of the Licensed Content and all of its component parts.

15.   <u>DISCLAIMER OF WARRANTIES.</u> **TO THE MAXIMUM EXTENT PERMITTED BY APPLICABLE LAW, MICROSOFT AND ITS SUPPLIERS PROVIDE THE LICENSED CONTENT AND SUPPORT SERVICES (IF ANY)** *AS IS AND WITH ALL FAULTS,* **AND MICROSOFT AND ITS SUPPLIERS HEREBY DISCLAIM ALL OTHER WARRANTIES AND CONDITIONS, WHETHER EXPRESS, IMPLIED OR STATUTORY, INCLUDING, BUT NOT LIMITED TO, ANY (IF ANY) IMPLIED WARRANTIES, DUTIES OR CONDITIONS OF MERCHANTABILITY, OF FITNESS FOR A PARTICULAR PURPOSE, OF RELIABILITY OR AVAILABILITY, OF ACCURACY OR COMPLETENESS OF RESPONSES, OF RESULTS, OF WORKMANLIKE EFFORT, OF LACK OF VIRUSES, AND OF LACK OF NEGLIGENCE, ALL WITH REGARD TO THE LICENSED CONTENT, AND THE PROVISION OF OR FAILURE TO PROVIDE SUPPORT OR OTHER SERVICES, INFORMATION, SOFTWARE, AND RELATED CONTENT THROUGH THE LICENSED CONTENT, OR OTHERWISE ARISING OUT OF THE USE OF THE LICENSED CONTENT. ALSO, THERE IS NO WARRANTY OR CONDITION OF TITLE, QUIET ENJOYMENT, QUIET POSSESSION, CORRESPONDENCE TO DESCRIPTION OR NON-INFRINGEMENT WITH REGARD TO THE LICENSED CONTENT. THE ENTIRE RISK AS TO THE QUALITY, OR ARISING OUT OF THE USE OR PERFORMANCE OF THE LICENSED CONTENT, AND ANY SUPPORT SERVICES, REMAINS WITH YOU.**

16.   <u>EXCLUSION OF INCIDENTAL, CONSEQUENTIAL AND CERTAIN OTHER DAMAGES.</u> **TO THE MAXIMUM EXTENT PERMITTED BY APPLICABLE LAW, IN NO EVENT SHALL MICROSOFT OR ITS SUPPLIERS BE LIABLE FOR ANY SPECIAL, INCIDENTAL, PUNITIVE, INDIRECT, OR CONSEQUENTIAL DAMAGES WHATSOEVER (INCLUDING, BUT NOT**

LIMITED TO, DAMAGES FOR LOSS OF PROFITS OR CONFIDENTIAL OR OTHER INFORMATION, FOR BUSINESS INTERRUPTION, FOR PERSONAL INJURY, FOR LOSS OF PRIVACY, FOR FAILURE TO MEET ANY DUTY INCLUDING OF GOOD FAITH OR OF REASONABLE CARE, FOR NEGLIGENCE, AND FOR ANY OTHER PECUNIARY OR OTHER LOSS WHATSOEVER) ARISING OUT OF OR IN ANY WAY RELATED TO THE USE OF OR INABILITY TO USE THE LICENSED CONTENT, THE PROVISION OF OR FAILURE TO PROVIDE SUPPORT OR OTHER SERVICES, INFORMATION, SOFTWARE, AND RELATED CONTENT THROUGH THE LICENSED CONTENT, OR OTHERWISE ARISING OUT OF THE USE OF THE LICENSED CONTENT, OR OTHERWISE UNDER OR IN CONNECTION WITH ANY PROVISION OF THIS EULA, EVEN IN THE EVENT OF THE FAULT, TORT (INCLUDING NEGLIGENCE), MISREPRESENTATION, STRICT LIABILITY, BREACH OF CONTRACT OR BREACH OF WARRANTY OF MICROSOFT OR ANY SUPPLIER, AND EVEN IF MICROSOFT OR ANY SUPPLIER HAS BEEN ADVISED OF THE POSSIBILITY OF SUCH DAMAGES. BECAUSE SOME STATES/JURISDICTIONS DO NOT ALLOW THE EXCLUSION OR LIMITATION OF LIABILITY FOR CONSEQUENTIAL OR INCIDENTAL DAMAGES, THE ABOVE LIMITATION MAY NOT APPLY TO YOU.

17. **LIMITATION OF LIABILITY AND REMEDIES.** NOTWITHSTANDING ANY DAMAGES THAT YOU MIGHT INCUR FOR ANY REASON WHATSOEVER (INCLUDING, WITHOUT LIMITATION, ALL DAMAGES REFERENCED HEREIN AND ALL DIRECT OR GENERAL DAMAGES IN CONTRACT OR ANYTHING ELSE), THE ENTIRE LIABILITY OF MICROSOFT AND ANY OF ITS SUPPLIERS UNDER ANY PROVISION OF THIS EULA AND YOUR EXCLUSIVE REMEDY HEREUNDER SHALL BE LIMITED TO THE GREATER OF THE ACTUAL DAMAGES YOU INCUR IN REASONABLE RELIANCE ON THE LICENSED CONTENT UP TO THE AMOUNT ACTUALLY PAID BY YOU FOR THE LICENSED CONTENT OR US$5.00. THE FOREGOING LIMITATIONS, EXCLUSIONS AND DISCLAIMERS SHALL APPLY TO THE MAXIMUM EXTENT PERMITTED BY APPLICABLE LAW, EVEN IF ANY REMEDY FAILS ITS ESSENTIAL PURPOSE.

18. **APPLICABLE LAW.** If you acquired this Licensed Content in the United States, this EULA is governed by the laws of the State of Washington. If you acquired this Licensed Content in Canada, unless expressly prohibited by local law, this EULA is governed by the laws in force in the Province of Ontario, Canada; and, in respect of any dispute which may arise hereunder, you consent to the jurisdiction of the federal and provincial courts sitting in Toronto, Ontario. If you acquired this Licensed Content in the European Union, Iceland, Norway, or Switzerland, then local law applies. If you acquired this Licensed Content in any other country, then local law may apply.

19. **ENTIRE AGREEMENT; SEVERABILITY.** This EULA (including any addendum or amendment to this EULA which is included with the Licensed Content) are the entire agreement between you and Microsoft relating to the Licensed Content and the support services (if any) and they supersede all prior or contemporaneous oral or written communications, proposals and representations with respect to the Licensed Content or any other subject matter covered by this EULA. To the extent the terms of any Microsoft policies or programs for support services conflict with the terms of this EULA, the terms of this EULA shall control. If any provision of this EULA is held to be void, invalid, unenforceable or illegal, the other provisions shall continue in full force and effect.

Should you have any questions concerning this EULA, or if you desire to contact Microsoft for any reason, please use the address information enclosed in this Licensed Content to contact the Microsoft subsidiary serving your country or visit Microsoft on the World Wide Web at http://www.microsoft.com.

Si vous avez acquis votre Contenu Sous Licence Microsoft au CANADA :

DÉNI DE GARANTIES. Dans la mesure maximale permise par les lois applicables, le Contenu Sous Licence et les services de soutien technique (le cas échéant) sont fournis *TELS QUELS ET AVEC TOUS LES DÉFAUTS* par Microsoft et ses fournisseurs, lesquels par les présentes dénient toutes autres garanties et conditions expresses, implicites ou en vertu de la loi, notamment, mais sans limitation, (le cas échéant) les garanties, devoirs ou conditions implicites de qualité marchande, d'adaptation à une fin usage particulière, de fiabilité ou de disponibilité, d'exactitude ou d'exhaustivité des réponses, des résultats, des efforts déployés selon les règles de l'art, d'absence de virus et d'absence de négligence, le tout à l'égard du Contenu Sous Licence et de la prestation des services de soutien technique ou de l'omission de la 'une telle prestation des services de soutien technique ou à l'égard de la fourniture ou de l'omission de la fourniture de tous autres services, renseignements, Contenus Sous Licence, et contenu qui s'y rapporte grâce au Contenu Sous Licence ou provenant autrement de l'utilisation du Contenu Sous Licence. PAR AILLEURS, IL N'Y A AUCUNE GARANTIE OU CONDITION QUANT AU TITRE DE PROPRIÉTÉ, À LA JOUISSANCE OU LA POSSESSION PAISIBLE, À LA CONCORDANCE À UNE DESCRIPTION NI QUANT À UNE ABSENCE DE CONTREFAÇON CONCERNANT LE CONTENU SOUS LICENCE.

EXCLUSION DES DOMMAGES ACCESSOIRES, INDIRECTS ET DE CERTAINS AUTRES DOMMAGES. DANS LA MESURE MAXIMALE PERMISE PAR LES LOIS APPLICABLES, EN AUCUN CAS MICROSOFT OU SES FOURNISSEURS NE SERONT RESPONSABLES DES DOMMAGES SPÉCIAUX, CONSÉCUTIFS, ACCESSOIRES OU INDIRECTS DE QUELQUE NATURE QUE CE SOIT (NOTAMMENT, LES DOMMAGES À L'ÉGARD DU MANQUE À GAGNER OU DE LA DIVULGATION DE RENSEIGNEMENTS CONFIDENTIELS OU AUTRES, DE LA PERTE D'EXPLOITATION, DE BLESSURES CORPORELLES, DE LA VIOLATION DE LA VIE PRIVÉE, DE L'OMISSION DE REMPLIR TOUT DEVOIR, Y COMPRIS D'AGIR DE BONNE FOI OU D'EXERCER UN SOIN RAISONNABLE, DE LA NÉGLIGENCE ET DE TOUTE AUTRE PERTE PÉCUNIAIRE OU AUTRE PERTE

DE QUELQUE NATURE QUE CE SOIT) SE RAPPORTANT DE QUELQUE MANIÈRE QUE CE SOIT À L'UTILISATION DU CONTENU SOUS LICENCE OU À L'INCAPACITÉ DE S'EN SERVIR, À LA PRESTATION OU À L'OMISSION DE LA 'UNE TELLE PRESTATION DE SERVICES DE SOUTIEN TECHNIQUE OU À LA FOURNITURE OU À L'OMISSION DE LA FOURNITURE DE TOUS AUTRES SERVICES, RENSEIGNEMENTS, CONTENUS SOUS LICENCE, ET CONTENU QUI S'Y RAPPORTE GRÂCE AU CONTENU SOUS LICENCE OU PROVENANT AUTREMENT DE L'UTILISATION DU CONTENU SOUS LICENCE OU AUTREMENT AUX TERMES DE TOUTE DISPOSITION DE LA U PRÉSENTE CONVENTION EULA OU RELATIVEMENT À UNE TELLE DISPOSITION, MÊME EN CAS DE FAUTE, DE DÉLIT CIVIL (Y COMPRIS LA NÉGLIGENCE), DE RESPONSABILITÉ STRICTE, DE VIOLATION DE CONTRAT OU DE VIOLATION DE GARANTIE DE MICROSOFT OU DE TOUT FOURNISSEUR ET MÊME SI MICROSOFT OU TOUT FOURNISSEUR A ÉTÉ AVISÉ DE LA POSSIBILITÉ DE TELS DOMMAGES.

<u>LIMITATION DE RESPONSABILITÉ ET RECOURS.</u>   MALGRÉ LES DOMMAGES QUE VOUS PUISSIEZ SUBIR POUR QUELQUE MOTIF QUE CE SOIT (NOTAMMENT, MAIS SANS LIMITATION, TOUS LES DOMMAGES SUSMENTIONNÉS ET TOUS LES DOMMAGES DIRECTS OU GÉNÉRAUX OU AUTRES), LA SEULE RESPONSABILITÉ 'OBLIGATION INTÉGRALE DE MICROSOFT ET DE L'UN OU L'AUTRE DE SES FOURNISSEURS AUX TERMES DE TOUTE DISPOSITION DEU LA PRÉSENTE CONVENTION EULA ET VOTRE RECOURS EXCLUSIF À L'ÉGARD DE TOUT CE QUI PRÉCÈDE SE LIMITE AU PLUS ÉLEVÉ ENTRE LES MONTANTS SUIVANTS : LE MONTANT QUE VOUS AVEZ RÉELLEMENT PAYÉ POUR LE CONTENU SOUS LICENCE OU 5,00 $US. LES LIMITES, EXCLUSIONS ET DÉNIS QUI PRÉCÈDENT (Y COMPRIS LES CLAUSES CI-DESSUS), S'APPLIQUENT DANS LA MESURE MAXIMALE PERMISE PAR LES LOIS APPLICABLES, MÊME SI TOUT RECOURS N'ATTEINT PAS SON BUT ESSENTIEL.

À moins que cela ne soit prohibé par le droit local applicable, la présente Convention est régie par les lois de la province d'Ontario, Canada. Vous consentez Chacune des parties à la présente reconnaît irrévocablement à la compétence des tribunaux fédéraux et provinciaux siégeant à Toronto, dans de la province d'Ontario et consent à instituer tout litige qui pourrait découler de la présente auprès des tribunaux situés dans le district judiciaire de York, province d'Ontario.

Au cas où vous auriez des questions concernant cette licence ou que vous désiriez vous mettre en rapport avec Microsoft pour quelque raison que ce soit, veuillez utiliser l'information contenue dans le Contenu Sous Licence pour contacter la filiale de succursale Microsoft desservant votre pays, dont l'adresse est fournie dans ce produit, ou visitez écrivez à : Microsoft sur le World Wide Web à http://www.microsoft.com

Contents

Module 9: Managing the User Environment by Using Group Policy

Module 10: Implementing Administrative Templates and Audit Policy

About This Course

This section provides you with a brief description of the course, audience, suggested prerequisites, and course objectives.

Description

This five-day instructor-led course provides students with the knowledge and skills to manage accounts and resources in a Microsoft® Windows® Server 2003 environment. The course is intended for systems administrator and systems engineer candidates who are responsible for managing accounts and resources. These tasks include managing user, computer, and group accounts; managing access to network resources; managing printers; managing an organizational unit in a network based on Active Directory® directory service; and implementing Group Policy to manage users and computers.

Audience

This is the first course in the systems administrator and systems engineer tracks for Windows Server 2003 and serves as the entry point for other courses in the Windows Server 2003 curriculum.

Student prerequisites

This course requires that students meet the following prerequisites:

- A+ certification, or equivalent knowledge and skills
- Network+ certification, or equivalent knowledge and skills

Course objectives

After completing this course, the student will be able to:

- Create and populate organizational units with user and computer accounts.
- Manage user and computer accounts.
- Create and manage groups.
- Manage access to resources.
- Implement printing.
- Manage printing.
- Manage access to objects by using organizational units.
- Implement Group Policy.
- Manage the user and computer environment by using Group Policy.
- Implement administrative templates and audit policy in Windows Server 2003.

Student Materials Compact Disc Contents

The Student Materials compact disc contains the following files and folders:

- *Autorun.exe*. When the compact disc is inserted into the CD-ROM drive, or when you double-click the **Autorun.exe** file, this file opens the compact disc and allows you to browse the Student Materials compact disc.

- *Autorun.inf*. When the compact disc is inserted into the compact disc drive, this file opens Autorun.exe.

- *Default.htm*. This file opens the Student Materials Web page. It provides you with resources pertaining to this course, including additional reading, review and lab answers, lab files, multimedia presentations, and course-related Web sites.

- *Readme.txt*. This file explains how to install the software for viewing the Student Materials compact disc and its contents and how to open the Student Materials Web page.

- *Appendix*. This folder contains appendix files for this course.

- *Flash*. This folder contains the installer for the Macromedia Flash 6.0 browser plug-in.

- *Fonts*. This folder contains fonts that may be required to view the Microsoft Word documents that are included with this course.

- *Labfiles*. This folder contains files that are used in the hands-on labs. These files may be used to prepare the student computers for the hands-on labs.

- *Media*. This folder contains files that are used in multimedia presentations for this course.

- *Mplayer*. This folder contains the setup file to install Microsoft Windows Media® Player.

- *Sampcode*. This folder contains sample code that is accessible through the Web pages on the Student Materials compact disc.

- *Webfiles*. This folder contains the files that are required to view the course Web page. To open the Web page, open Windows Explorer, and in the root directory of the compact disc, double-click **Default.htm** or **Autorun.exe**.

- *Wordview*. This folder contains the Word Viewer that is used to view any Word document (.doc) files that are included on the compact disc.

Document Conventions

The following conventions are used in course materials to distinguish elements of the text.

Convention	Use
Bold	Represents commands, command options, and syntax that must be typed exactly as shown. It also indicates commands on menus and buttons, dialog box titles and options, and icon and menu names.
Italic	In syntax statements or descriptive text, indicates argument names or placeholders for variable information. Italic is also used for introducing new terms, for book titles, and for emphasis in the text.
Title Capitals	Indicate domain names, user names, computer names, directory names, and folder and file names, except when specifically referring to case-sensitive names. Unless otherwise indicated, you can use lowercase letters when you type a directory name or file name in a dialog box or at a command prompt.
ALL CAPITALS	Indicate the names of keys, key sequences, and key combinations—for example, ALT+SPACEBAR.
`monospace`	Represents code samples or examples of screen text.
[ ]	In syntax statements, enclose optional items. For example, [*filename*] in command syntax indicates that you can choose to type a file name with the command. Type only the information within the brackets, not the brackets themselves.
{ }	In syntax statements, enclose required items. Type only the information within the braces, not the braces themselves.
|	In syntax statements, separates an either/or choice.
▶	Indicates a procedure with sequential steps.
...	In syntax statements, specifies that the preceding item may be repeated.
. . .	Represents an omitted portion of a code sample.

Microsoft®
Training &
Certification

Introduction

Contents

Microsoft®

Introduction

- Name
- Company affiliation
- Title/function
- Job responsibility
- Systems administration experience
- Windows server operating systems experience
- Expectations for the course

Course Materials

- Name card
- Student workbook
- Student Materials compact disc
- Course evaluation

The following materials are included with your kit:

- *Name card*. Write your name on both sides of the name card.

- *Student workbook*. The student workbook contains the material covered in class, in addition to the hands-on lab exercises.

- *Student Materials compact disc*. The Student Materials compact disc contains the Web page that provides you with links to resources pertaining to this course, including additional readings, review and lab answers, lab files, multimedia presentations, and course-related Web sites.

> **Note**   To open the Web page, insert the Student Materials compact disc into the CD-ROM drive, and then in the root directory of the compact disc, double-click **Autorun.exe** or **Default.htm**.

- *Assessments*. There are assessments for each lesson, located on the Student Materials compact disc. You can use them as pre-assessments to identify areas of difficulty, or you can use them as post-assessments to validate learning.

- *Course evaluation*. To provide feedback on the course, training facility, and instructor, you will have the opportunity to complete an online evaluation near the end of the course.

To provide additional comments or feedback on the course, send e-mail to support@mscourseware.com. To inquire about the Microsoft® Certified Professional program, send e-mail to mcphelp@microsoft.com.

Additional Reading from Microsoft Press

Microsoft Windows® Server 2003 books from Microsoft Press can help you do your job—from the planning and evaluation stages through deployment and ongoing support—with solid technical information to help you get the most out of the Windows Server 2003 key features and enhancements. The following titles supplement the skills taught in this course:

Title	ISBN
Microsoft® Windows® Server 2003 Security Administrator's Companion	0-7356-1354-8
Microsoft® Windows® Server 2003 Administrator's Companion	0-7356-1367-2
Microsoft® Windows® Server 2003 Admin Pocket Consultant	0-7356-1574-0

Prerequisites

- A+ Certification, or equivalent knowledge and skills
- Network+ Certification, or equivalent knowledge and skills

This course requires that you meet the following prerequisites:

- A+ Certification, or equivalent knowledge and skills
- Network+ Certification, or equivalent knowledge and skills

Course Outline

- **Module 1: Introduction to Administering Accounts and Resources**
- **Module 2: Managing User and Computer Accounts**
- **Module 3: Managing Groups**
- **Module 4: Managing Access to Resources**
- **Module 5: Implementing Printing**

Module 1, "Introduction to Administering Accounts and Resources," introduces the Microsoft Windows Server 2003 family of operating systems and the tasks and tools for administering accounts and resources on computers running Windows Server 2003 in a networked environment.

Module 2, "Managing User and Computer Accounts," explains how to create and modify user and computer accounts on computers running Windows Server 2003 in a networked environment.

Module 3, "Managing Groups," explains how to use groups to simplify domain administration.

Module 4, "Managing Access to Resources," explains how permissions enable resource access. You also learn how to manage access to files and folders by using NTFS permissions, manage access to files and folders by using special permissions, and manage permission inheritance.

Module 5, "Implementing Printing," explains how to install, configure, and manage printers.

Course Outline *(continued)*

- Module 6: Managing Printing
- Module 7: Managing Access to Objects in Organizational Units
- Module 8: Implementing Group Policy
- Module 9: Managing the User Environment by Using Group Policy
- Module 10: Implementing Administrative Templates and Audit Policy

Module 6, "Managing Printing," explains how to set up a network-wide printing strategy to meet the needs of users and troubleshoot installation or configuration problems.

Module 7, "Managing Access to Objects in Organizational Units," explains the permissions available for managing access to objects in Active Directory® directory service. You also learn how to move objects between organizational units in the same domain and delegate control of an organizational unit.

Module 8, "Implementing Group Policy," explains the purpose and function of Group Policy in a Windows Server 2003 environment. It also explains how to implement and manage Group Policy objects (GPOs).

Module 9, "Managing the User Environment by Using Group Policy," explains how to use Group Policy to configure Folder Redirection, Microsoft Internet Explorer connectivity, and the desktop.

Module 10, "Implementing Administrative Templates and Audit Policy," explains how to manage security in an Active Directory domain and how to audit events to ensure the effectiveness of a security strategy.

Appendix A, "Differences Between the Microsoft Windows Server 2003 and Microsoft Windows 2000", explains the differences between the operating systems in the context of the tasks in each module. This appendix is provided for students who are familiar with Windows 2000 Server.

Appendix B, "References for Exam Preparation", provides references for further study for Exam 70-290, *Managing and Maintaining a Microsoft Windows Server 2003 Environment*.

Appendix C, "Administering Microsoft Windows Server 2003 by Using Scripts", provides information on using scripts to perform the administration tasks taught in this course.

Setup

- Classroom is configured as one Windows Server 2003 domain: nwtraders.msft
- London is a domain controller and the instructor computer
- Glasgow is a member server and is used as a remote computer for student labs
- Student computers are running Windows Server 2003, Enterprise Edition
- Each student computer has an organizational unit
- Students are administrators for their server and organizational unit

Course files

There are files associated with the labs and practices in this course. The lab files are located in the C:\MOC\2274 folder on the student computers.

Classroom setup

The classroom configuration consists of one domain controller and multiple student computers. Each computer is running Windows Server 2003, Enterprise Edition.

The name of the domain is nwtraders.msft. It is named after Northwind Traders, a fictitious company that has offices worldwide. The names of the computers correspond with the names of the cities where the fictitious offices are located.

The domain controller is named London, and the instructor also has a member server called Glasgow. The student computers are named after various cities, such as Acapulco, Bonn, and Casablanca. The name of each computer corresponds with an organizational unit of the same name. For example, the Acapulco computer is part of the Acapulco organizational unit.

The domain has been prepopulated with users, groups, and computer accounts for each administrator to manage.

Microsoft Official Curriculum

Introduction

Microsoft Training and Certification develops Microsoft Official Curriculum (MOC), including MSDN® Training, for computer professionals who design, develop, support, implement, or manage solutions by using Microsoft products and technologies. These courses provide comprehensive skills-based training in instructor-led and online formats.

Additional recommended courses

Each course relates in some way to another course. A related course may be a prerequisite, a follow-up course in a recommended series, or a course that offers additional training.

It is recommended that you take the following courses in this order:

- Course 2274 *Managing a Microsoft Windows Server 2003 Environment*
- Course 2275, *Maintaining a Microsoft Windows Server 2003 Environment*
- Course, 2276, *Implementing a Microsoft Windows Server 2003 Network Infrastructure: Network Hosts*
- Course 2277, *Implementing, Managing, and Maintaining a Microsoft Windows Server 2003 Network Infrastructure: Network Services*
- Course 2278, *Planning and Maintaining a Microsoft Windows Server 2003 Network Infrastructure*
- Course 2279, *Planning, Implementing, and Maintaining a Microsoft Windows Server 2003 Active Directory Infrastructure*

Other related courses may become available in the future, so for up-to-date information about recommended courses, visit the Training and Certification Web site.

Microsoft Training and Certification information

For more information, visit the Microsoft Training and Certification Web site at http://www.microsoft.com/traincert/.

Microsoft Certified Professional Program

Exam number and title	Core exam for the following track	Elective exam for the following track
70-290: *Managing and Maintaining a Microsoft Windows Server 2003 Environment*	MCSA	n/a

Microsoft
C E R T I F I E D
Professional

http://www.microsoft.com/traincert/

Introduction

Microsoft Training and Certification offers a variety of certification credentials for developers and IT professionals. The Microsoft Certified Professional program is the leading certification program for validating your experience and skills, keeping you competitive in today's changing business environment.

Related certification exams

This course, in combination with Course 2275, *Maintaining a Microsoft Windows Server 2003 Environment*, helps students to prepare for Exam 70-290: *Managing and Maintaining a Microsoft Windows Server 2003 Environment*. To prepare for the exam, you should complete both courses and study Appendix B, "References for Exam Preparation," on the Student Materials Web page.

Exam 70-290 is a core exam for the Microsoft Certified Systems Administrator certification.

MCP certifications

The Microsoft Certified Professional program includes the following certifications.

- MCSA on Microsoft Windows Server 2003

  The Microsoft Certified Systems Administrator (MCSA) certification is designed for professionals who implement, manage, and troubleshoot existing network and system environments based on Microsoft Windows 2000 platforms, including the Windows Server 2003 family. Implementation responsibilities include installing and configuring parts of the systems. Management responsibilities include administering and supporting the systems.

- MCSE on Microsoft Windows Server 2003

  The Microsoft Certified Systems Engineer (MCSE) credential is the premier certification for professionals who analyze the business requirements and design and implement the infrastructure for business solutions based on the Microsoft Windows 2000 platform and Microsoft server software, including the Windows Server 2003 family. Implementation responsibilities include installing, configuring, and troubleshooting network systems.

- MCAD

  The Microsoft Certified Application Developer (MCAD) for Microsoft .NET credential is appropriate for professionals who use Microsoft technologies to develop and maintain department-level applications, components, Web or desktop clients, or back-end data services or work in teams developing enterprise applications. The credential covers job tasks ranging from developing to deploying and maintaining these solutions.

- MCSD

  The Microsoft Certified Solution Developer (MCSD) credential is the premier certification for professionals who design and develop leading-edge business solutions with Microsoft development tools, technologies, platforms, and the Microsoft Windows DNA architecture. The types of applications MCSDs can develop include desktop applications and multi-user, Web-based, N-tier, and transaction-based applications. The credential covers job tasks ranging from analyzing business requirements to maintaining solutions.

- MCDBA on Microsoft SQL Server™ 2000

  The Microsoft Certified Database Administrator (MCDBA) credential is the premier certification for professionals who implement and administer Microsoft SQL Server databases. The certification is appropriate for individuals who derive physical database designs, develop logical data models, create physical databases, create data services by using Transact-SQL, manage and maintain databases, configure and manage security, monitor and optimize databases, and install and configure SQL Server.

- MCP

  The Microsoft Certified Professional (MCP) credential is for individuals who have the skills to successfully implement a Microsoft product or technology as part of a business solution in an organization. Hands-on experience with the product is necessary to successfully achieve certification.

- MCT

  Microsoft Certified Trainers (MCTs) demonstrate the instructional and technical skills that qualify them to deliver Microsoft Official Curriculum through Microsoft Certified Technical Education Centers (Microsoft CTECs).

Certification requirements

The certification requirements differ for each certification category and are specific to the products and job functions addressed by the certification. To become a Microsoft Certified Professional, you must pass rigorous certification exams that provide a valid and reliable measure of technical proficiency and expertise.

For More Information   See the Microsoft Training and Certification Web site at http://www.microsoft.com/traincert/.

You can also send e-mail to mcphelp@microsoft.com if you have specific certification questions.

Acquiring the skills tested by an MCP exam

Microsoft Official Curriculum (MOC) and MSDN Training can help you develop the skills that you need to do your job. They also complement the experience that you gain while working with Microsoft products and technologies. However, no one-to-one correlation exists between MOC and MSDN Training courses and MCP exams. Microsoft does not expect or intend for the courses to be the sole preparation method for passing MCP exams. Practical product knowledge and experience is also necessary to pass the MCP exams.

To help prepare for the MCP exams, use the preparation guides that are available for each exam. Each Exam Preparation Guide contains exam-specific information, such as a list of the topics on which you will be tested. These guides are available on the Microsoft Training and Certification Web site at http://www.microsoft.com/traincert/.

Multimedia: Job Roles in Today's Information Systems Environment

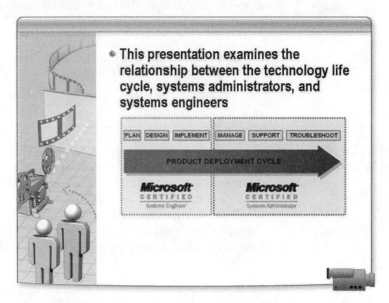

File location

To view the *Job Roles in Today's Information Systems Environment* presentation, open the Web page on the Student Materials compact disc, click **Multimedia**, and then click the title of the presentation. Do not open this presentation unless your instructor tells you to.

Facilities

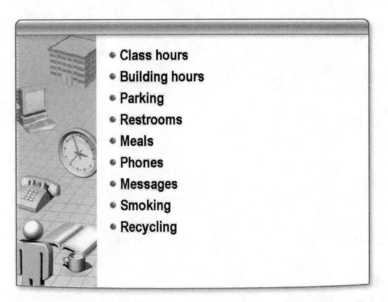

- Class hours
- Building hours
- Parking
- Restrooms
- Meals
- Phones
- Messages
- Smoking
- Recycling

Microsoft®
Training &
Certification

Module 1: Introduction to Administering Accounts and Resources

Contents

Overview

- Multimedia: Introduction to Managing a Microsoft Windows Server 2003 Environment
- The Windows Server 2003 Environment
- Logging on to Windows Server 2003
- Installing and Configuring Administrative Tools
- Creating an Organizational Unit
- Moving Domain Objects

Introduction

In this module, you will learn the skills and knowledge that you need to administer accounts and resources on computers running Microsoft® Windows® Server 2003 software in a networked environment. These lessons provide information and procedures that you will use throughout the course.

Objectives

After completing this module, you will be able to:

- Describe the Windows Server 2003 environment.
- Log on to a computer running Windows Server 2003.
- Install and configure the administrative tools.
- Create an organizational unit.
- Move objects within a domain.

Multimedia: Introduction to Managing a Microsoft Windows Server 2003 Environment

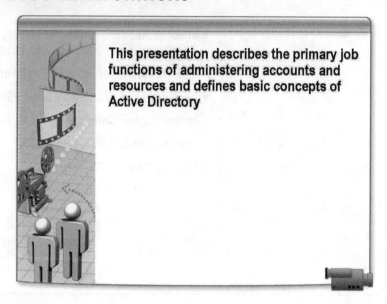

This presentation describes the primary job functions of administering accounts and resources and defines basic concepts of Active Directory

Introduction

In this presentation, you are introduced to the primary job functions of administering accounts and resources in a Windows Server 2003 environment. The tasks and concepts in this presentation are explained in more detail throughout the course.

File location

To view the *Introduction to Administering Accounts and Resources* presentation, open the Web page on the Student Materials compact disc, click **Multimedia**, and then click the title of the presentation. Do not open this presentation unless the instructor tells you to.

Objective

After completing this lesson, you will be able to describe some common tasks for administering accounts and resources.

Lesson: The Windows Server 2003 Environment

- Computer Roles
- The Windows Server 2003 Family
- What Is a Directory Service?
- Active Directory Terms
- Classroom Setup Review

Introduction

To manage a Windows Server 2003 environment, you must understand which operating system edition is appropriate for different computer roles. You must also understand the purpose of a directory service and how Active Directory® directory service provides a structure for the Windows Server 2003 environment.

Lesson objectives

After completing this lesson, you will be able to:

- Describe the different computer roles in a Windows Server 2003 environment.
- Describe the uses of the different editions of Windows Server 2003.
- Explain the purpose of a directory service.
- Differentiate between the components of an Active Directory structure.

Computer Roles

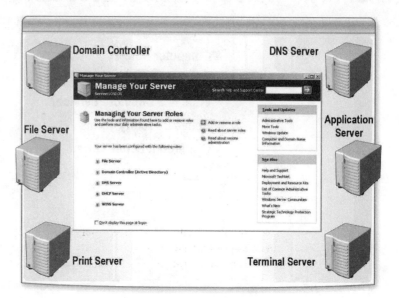

Introduction	Servers play many roles in the client/server networking environment. Some servers are configured to provide authentication, and others are configured to run applications. Some provide network services that enable users to communicate or find other servers and resources in the network. As a systems administrator, you are expected to know the primary types of servers and what functions they perform in your network.
Domain controller (Active Directory)	Domain controllers store directory data and manage communication between users and domains, including user logon processes, authentication, and directory searches. When you install Active Directory on a computer running Windows Server 2003, the computer becomes a domain controller.

Note In a Windows Server 2003 network, all servers in the domain that are not domain controllers are called *member servers*. Servers not associated with a domain are called *workgroup servers*.

File server	A file server provides a central location on your network where you can store and share files with users across your network. When users require an important file such as a project plan, they can access the file on the file server instead of passing the file between their separate computers.
Print server	A print server provides a central location on your network where users can print. The print server provides clients with updated printer drivers and handles all print queuing and security.
DNS server	Domain Name System (DNS) is an Internet and TCP/IP standard name service. The DNS service enables client computers on your network to register and resolve DNS domain names. A computer configured to provide DNS services on a network is a DNS server. You must have a DNS server on your network to implement Active Directory.

Application server

An application server provides key infrastructure and services to applications hosted on a system. Typical application servers include the following services:

- Resource pooling (for example, database connection pooling and object pooling)
- Distributed transaction management
- Asynchronous program communication, typically through message queuing
- A just-in-time object activation model
- Automatic Extensible Markup Language (XML) Web Service interfaces to access business objects
- Failover and application health detection services
- Integrated security

Microsoft Internet Information Services (IIS) provides the tools and features necessary to easily manage a secure Web server. If you plan to host Web and File Transfer Protocol (FTP) sites with IIS, configure the server as an application server.

Terminal server

A terminal server provides remote computers with access to Windows-based programs running on Windows Server 2003, Standard Edition; Windows Server 2003, Enterprise Edition; or Windows Server 2003, Datacenter Edition. With a terminal server, you install an application at a single point on a single server. Multiple users then can access the application without installing it on their computers. Users can run programs, save files, and use network resources all from a remote location, as if these resources were installed on their own computer.

The Manage Your Server tool

When Windows Server 2003 is installed and a user logs on for the first time, the Manage Your Server tool starts automatically. You use this tool to add or remove server roles. When you add a server role to the computer, the Manage Your Server tool adds this server role to the list of available, configured server roles. After the server role is added to the list, you can use various wizards that help you manage the specific server role. The Manage Your Server tool also provides Help files specific to the server role that have checklists and troubleshooting recommendations.

The Windows Server 2003 Family

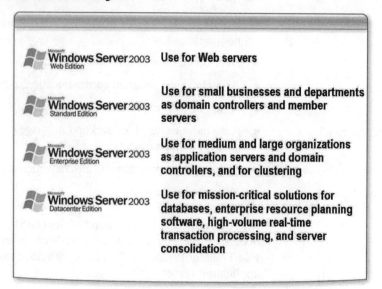

Introduction

Windows Server 2003 is available in five editions. Each edition is developed to be used in a specific server role. This enables you to select the operating system edition that provides only the functions and capabilities that your server needs.

Web Edition

Windows Server 2003, Web Edition, is designed to be used specifically as a Web server. It is available only through selected partner channels and is not available for retail. Although computers running Windows Server 2003, Web Edition, can be members of an Active Directory domain, you cannot run Active Directory on Windows Server 2003, Web Edition.

Standard Edition

Windows Server 2003, Standard Edition, is a reliable network operating system that delivers business solutions quickly and easily. This flexible server is the ideal choice for small businesses and departmental use. Use Windows Server 2003, Standard Edition, when your server does not require the increased hardware support and clustering features of Windows Server 2003, Enterprise Edition.

Enterprise Edition

Windows Server 2003, Enterprise Edition, has all the features in Windows Server 2003, Standard Edition. However, it also has features not included in Standard Edition that enhance availability, scalability, and dependability.

Windows Server 2003, Enterprise Edition, is designed for medium to large businesses. It is the recommended operating system for applications, XML Web services, and infrastructure, because it offers high reliability, performance, and superior business value.

The major difference between Windows Server 2003, Enterprise Edition, and Windows Server 2003, Standard Edition, is that Enterprise Edition supports high-performance servers. Windows Server 2003, Enterprise Edition, is recommended for servers running applications for networking, messaging, inventory and customer service systems, databases, and e-commerce Web sites. Also, you can cluster servers running Enterprise Edition together to handle larger loads.

Datacenter Edition

Windows Server 2003, Datacenter Edition, is designed for business-critical and mission-critical applications that demand the highest levels of scalability and availability.

The major difference between Windows Server 2003, Datacenter Edition, and Windows Server 2003, Enterprise Edition, is that Datacenter Edition supports more powerful multiprocessing and greater memory. In addition, Windows Server 2003, Datacenter Edition, is available only through the Windows Datacenter Program offered to Original Equipment Manufacturers (OEMs).

Additional reading

For detailed information about each edition's capabilities, see the product overviews on the Windows Server 2003 page at http://www.microsoft.com/windowsserver2003/default.mspx.

What Is a Directory Service?

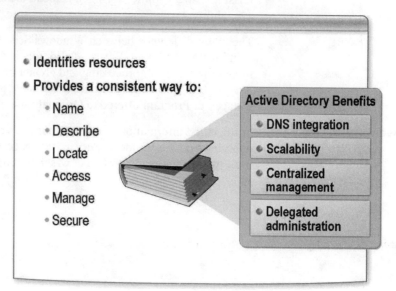

Introduction

As a user logged on to a network, you might need to connect to a shared folder or send a print job to a printer on the network. How do you find that folder and printer and other network resources?

Definition

A directory service is a network service that identifies all resources on a network and makes that information available to users and applications. Directory services are important, because they provide a consistent way to name, describe, locate, access, manage, and secure information about these resources.

When a user searches for a shared folder on the network, it is the directory service that identifies the resource and provides that information to the user.

Active Directory

Active Directory is the directory service in the Windows Server 2003 family. It extends the basic functionality of a directory service to provide the following benefits:

- DNS integration

   Active Directory uses DNS naming conventions to create a hierarchical structure that provides a familiar, orderly, and scalable view of network connections. DNS is also used to map host names, such as microsoft.com, to numeric TCP/IP addresses, such as 192.168.19.2.

- Scalability

   Active Directory is organized into sections that permit storage for a very large number of objects. As a result, Active Directory can expand as an organization grows. An organization that has a single server with a few hundred objects can grow to thousands of servers and millions of objects.

- Centralized management

    Active Directory enables administrators to manage distributed desktops, network services, and applications from a central location, while using a consistent management interface. Active Directory also provides centralized control of access to network resources by enabling users to log on only once to gain full access to resources throughout Active Directory.

- Delegated administration

    The hierarchical structure of Active Directory enables administrative control to be delegated for specific segments of the hierarchy. A user authorized by a higher administrative authority can perform administrative duties in their designated portion of the structure. For example, users may have limited administrative control over their workstation's settings, and a department manager may have the administrative rights to create new users in an organizational unit.

Additional reading   For more information on Active Directory, see *Technical Overview of Windows Server 2003 Active Directory* at http://www.microsoft.com/windowsserver2003/techinfo/overview/activedirectory.mspx.

Active Directory Terms

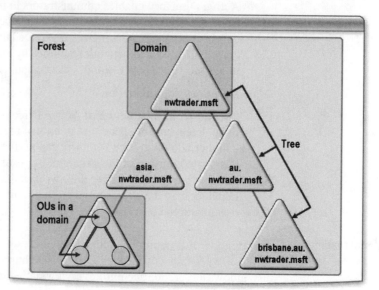

Introduction

The logical structure of Active Directory is flexible and provides a method for designing a hierarchy within Active Directory that is comprehensible to both users and administrators.

Logical components

The logical components of the Active Directory structure include the following:

- *Domain*. The core unit of the logical structure in Active Directory is the domain. A domain is a collection of computers, defined by an administrator, that share a common directory database. A domain has a unique name and provides access to the centralized user accounts and group accounts maintained by the domain administrator.

- *Organizational unit*. An organizational unit is a type of container object that you use to organize objects within a domain. An organizational unit may contain objects, such as user accounts, groups, computers, printers, and other organizational units.

- *Forest*. A forest is one or more domains that share a common configuration, schema, and global catalog.

- *Tree*. A tree consists of domains in a forest that share a contiguous DNS namespace.

Additional reading

For more information about Active Directory domains, see:

- Article 310996, "Active Directory Services and Windows 2000 or Windows Server 2003 Domains (Part 1)" in the Microsoft Knowledge Base at http://support.microsoft.com/?kbid=310996.

- Article 310997, "Active Directory Services and Windows 2000 or Windows Server 2003 Domains (Part 2)" in the Microsoft Knowledge Base at http://support.microsoft.com/?kbid=310997.

Classroom Setup Review

- The classroom is configured as one Windows Server 2003 domain: nwtraders.msft
- London is a domain controller and the instructor computer
- Glasgow is a member server and is used as a remote computer for student labs
- Student computers are running Windows Server 2003, Enterprise Edition
- Each student computer has an organizational unit
- Students are administrators for their server and organizational unit

Introduction

Now that you have been introduced to the basic components of an Active Directory structure, you can understand the setup of the classroom better.

Classroom setup

The classroom configuration consists of one domain controller and multiple student computers. Each computer is running Windows Server 2003, Enterprise Edition.

The name of the domain is nwtraders.msft. It is named after Northwind Traders, a fictitious company that has offices worldwide. The names of the computers correspond with the names of the cities where the fictitious offices are located.

The domain controller is named London, and the instructor also has a member server called Glasgow. The student computers are named after various cities, such as Acapulco, Bonn, and Casablanca. The name of each computer corresponds with an organizational unit of the same name. For example, the Acapulco computer is part of the Acapulco organizational unit.

The domain has been prepopulated with users, groups, and computer accounts for each administrator to manage.

Lesson: Logging on to Windows Server 2003

- Multimedia: Logon and Authentication
- Logon Dialog Box Options

Introduction

Windows Server 2003 authenticates a user during the logon process to verify the identity of the user. This mandatory process ensures that only valid users can access resources and data on a computer or the network.

Lesson objectives

After completing this lesson, you will be able to:

- Log on locally.
- Log on to a domain.

Practice: Logging on Using a Local Computer Account

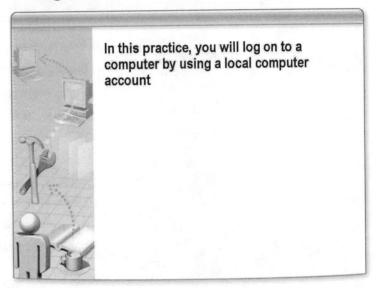

In this practice, you will log on to a computer by using a local computer account

Objective

In this practice, you will log on to a computer by using a local computer account.

Scenario

You have just been hired by Northwind Traders to help with the administration of computers, users, and resources for a city location in the Northwind Traders global network. You will also be responsible for a member server in your city and will occasionally log on with the local Administrator account on the member server.

Practice

▶ **Log on to your member server by using the local Administrator account**

1. Press CTRL+ALT+DEL.

2. In the **Log On to Windows** dialog box, in the **User name** box, type **Administrator**

3. In the **Password** box, type **P@ssw0rd** (The 0 is a zero).

4. In the **Log on to** box, click the name of your computer.

   The name of your computer has **(this computer)** after your computer name.

5. Click **OK**.

6. Log off the computer by doing the following:

   a. On the **Start** menu, click **Log Off**.

   b. In the message box, click **Log Off**.

Multimedia: Logon and Authentication

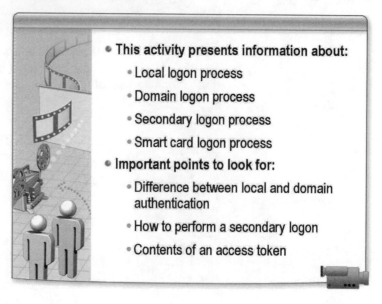

This activity presents information about:
- Local logon process
- Domain logon process
- Secondary logon process
- Smart card logon process

Important points to look for:
- Difference between local and domain authentication
- How to perform a secondary logon
- Contents of an access token

File location

To start the *Logon and Authentication* activity, open the Web page on the Student Materials compact disc, click **Multimedia**, and then click the title of the activity.

Questions

Review the information and processes in *Logon and Authentication*, and then answer the following questions.

1. What is the difference between authentication of a local logon and authentication of a domain logon?

   _____

   _____

   _____

2. How do you perform a secondary logon?

   _____

   _____

   _____

3.   What type of information is contained in an access token?

       _____

       _____

       _____

Logon Dialog Box Options

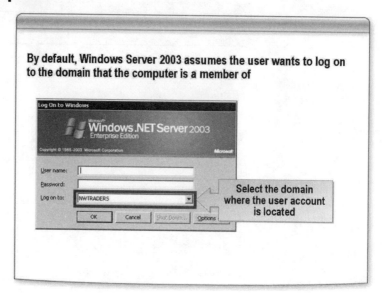

By default, Windows Server 2003 assumes the user wants to log on to the domain that the computer is a member of

Select the domain where the user account is located

Introduction

Windows Server 2003 provides two options when a user logs on to a domain. Windows Server 2003 enables the user to specify the domain that contains their user account from a computer that is located in a different domain. By default, Windows Server 2003 assumes that the user wants to log on to the domain that the computer is a member of and does not provide a way to specify a domain.

The logon dialog box   The following table describes all the options in the logon dialog box.

Option	Description
User name	A unique user logon name that is assigned by an administrator. To log on to a domain, this user account must reside in the directory database in Active Directory.
Password	The password that is assigned to the user account. Users must enter a password to prove their identity. Passwords are case sensitive. The password appears on the screen as asterisks (*) to protect it from onlookers. To prevent unauthorized access to resources and data, users must keep passwords secret.
Log on to	Determines whether a user logs on to a domain or logs on locally. A user can choose one of the following: • **Domain name**: The user must select the domain that their user account is in. This list contains all of the domains in a domain tree. • **Computer name**: The name of the computer that the user is logging on to. The user must have the Log on Locally user right for the computer. The option to log on locally is not available on a domain controller.
Log on using dial-up connection	Permits a user to connect to a server in the domain by using a dial-up network connection. Dial-up networking enables a user to log on and perform work from a remote location.
Shutdown	Closes all files, saves all operating system data, and prepares the computer so that a user can safely turn it off. On a computer running Windows Server 2003, the **Shutdown** button is not active. This prevents an unauthorized user from using this dialog box to shut down the server. To shut down a server, a user must be able to log on to it.
Options	Switches between the two versions of the **Enter Password** dialog box. One of these two dialog boxes provides the **Log on to** option, which enables the user to select a domain or the local computer.

Practice: Logging on Using a Domain Account

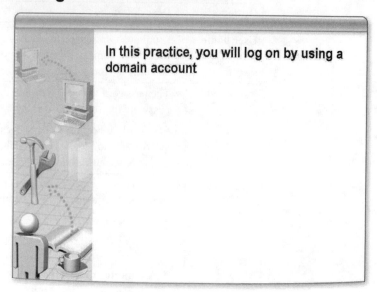

In this practice, you will log on by using a domain account

Objective

In this practice, you will log on to a local computer with a domain account.

Scenario

You have just been hired by Northwind Traders to help with the administration of computers, users, and resources for a city location in the Northwind Traders global network. You need to make sure you can successfully log on with your domain Administrator account.

Practice

▶ **Log on to your member server by using your domain Administrator account**

1. Press CTRL+ALT+DEL.

2. In the **Log On to Windows** box, in the **User name** dialog box, type *ComputerName***Admin** (Example: LondonAdmin).

3. In the **Password** box, type **P@ssw0rd** (The 0 is a zero).

4. In the **Log on to** box, click **NWTraders**, and then click **OK**.

5. Log off the computer by doing the following:

   a. On the **Start** menu, click **Log Off**.

   b. In the message box, click **Log Off**.

Lesson: Installing and Configuring Administrative Tools

- What Are Administrative Tools?
- How to Install Administrative Tools
- What Is MMC?
- How to Create a Custom MMC
- How to Resolve Problems with Installing and Configuring Administrative Tools

Introduction

In this lesson, you will learn how to install and configure administrative tools. This lesson also introduces the different types of user accounts and how to create them.

Lesson objectives

After completing this lesson, you will be able to:

- List the most commonly used administrative tools.
- Install administrative tools.
- Describe the Microsoft Management Console (MMC).
- Create a custom MMC.
- Resolve problems with installing and configuring administrative tools.

What Are Administrative Tools?

- **Commonly used administrative tools:**
  - Active Directory Users and Computers
  - Active Directory Sites and Services
  - Active Directory Domains and Trusts
  - Computer Management
  - DNS
  - Remote Desktops
- **Install to perform remote administration**

Introduction

Administrative tools enable network administrators to add, search, and change computer and network settings and Active Directory objects. You can install the administrative tools for managing a Windows Server 2003 environment on computers running Microsoft Windows XP Professional and Windows Server 2003 to remotely administer Active Directory and network settings.

Administrative tools

Some of the more commonly used tools include the following:

- Active Directory Users and Computers
- Active Directory Sites and Services
- Active Directory Domains and Trusts
- Computer Management
- DNS
- Remote Desktops

Installing administrative tools

You will need to install administrative tools on Windows XP Professional when you want to remotely manage network resources such as Active Directory, or network services such as Windows Internet Name Service (WINS) or Dynamic Host Configuration Protocol (DHCP), from a workstation. If you want to install the administrative tools on a computer running Windows XP Professional, Service Pack 1 and a hot fix from Microsoft Knowledge Base article 329357 must be installed.

Windows Server 2003 includes all the administrative tools as snap-ins that can be added to a custom MMC. This includes all the tools for managing Active Directory, but does not include management tools for services that are not installed on the server, such as WINS or DHCP. If you must remotely manage a network service from a computer running Windows Server 2003, and the service is not installed on the computer, you must install the administrative tools.

Note Uninstall the Windows Server 2003 Administration Tools Pack if someone who is not an administrator is going to use the computer running Windows XP Professional.

How to Install Administrative Tools

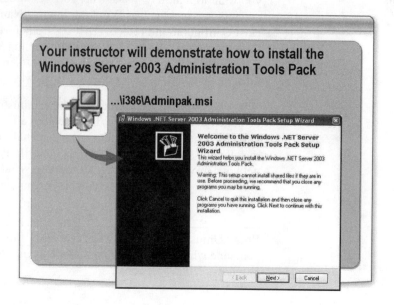

Introduction

To install the Windows Server 2003 Administration Tools Pack on a computer running Windows XP Professional, you must have administrative permissions on the local computer. If the computer is joined to a domain, members of the Domain Administrator group might be able to perform this procedure.

Procedure

To install or reinstall the Windows Server 2003 Administration Tools Pack from the Windows Server 2003 compact disc (CD):

1. Put your Windows Server 2003 CD into the CD tray of a computer running Windows XP Professional.

2. The CD installation setup runs automatically. If it does not:

   a. Click **Start**, and then click **Run**.

   b. In the **Run** dialog box, click **Browse**.

   c. In the **Browse** dialog box, click **My Computer**.

   d. Double-click the CD drive, and then double-click **setup.exe**.

   e. In the **Run** dialog box, click **OK**.

3. In the **Welcome to Microsoft Windows Server 2003** dialog box, click **Perform additional tasks**.

4. In the **What do you want to do?** dialog box, click **Browse this CD**.

5. Double-click the **i386** folder.

6. Double-click the **Adminpak.msi** icon.

7. Specify the installation location or drive where you want to install the Windows Server 2003 Administration Tools Pack.

What Is MMC?

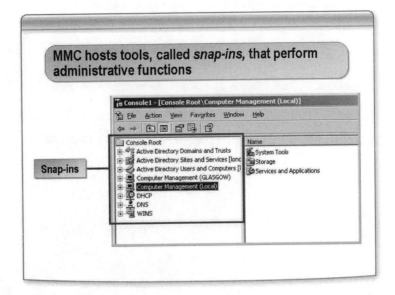

Definition	You use Microsoft Management Console (MMC) to create, save, and open administrative tools, called consoles, which manage the hardware, software, and network components of your Windows operating system. MMC runs on all client operating systems that are currently supported.
What are snap-ins?	A snap-in is a tool that is hosted in MMC. MMC offers a common framework in which various snap-ins can run so that you can manage several services with a single interface. MMC also enables you to customize the console. By picking and choosing specific snap-ins, you can create management consoles that include only the administrative tools that you need. For example, you can add tools to manage your local computer and remote computers.
Additional reading	For more information about MMC, see *Step-by-Step Guide to the Microsoft Management Console* at http://www.microsoft.com/technet/treeview/ default.asp?url=/technet/prodtechnol/windows2000serv/howto/mmcsteps.asp.

How to Create a Custom MMC

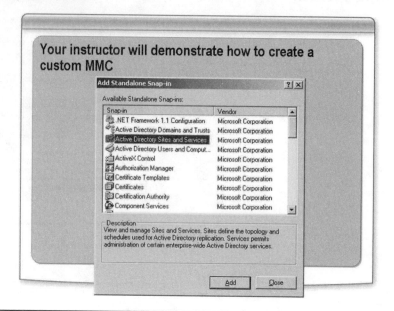

Introduction

You can use MMC to create custom tools and distribute these tools to users. With both Windows XP Professional and Windows Server 2003, you can save these tools so that they are available in the Administrative Tools folder on the Programs menu. To create a custom MMC, you will use the **Run as** command.

Procedure

1. Click **Start**, click **Run**, type **MMC** and then click **OK**.

2. In the console, on the **File** menu, click **Add/Remove Snap-in**.

3. In the **Add/Remove Snap-in** dialog box, click **Add**.

4. In the **Add Standalone Snap-in** dialog box, double-click the item that you want to add.

5. If a wizard appears, follow the instructions in the wizard.

6. To add another item to the console, repeat step 4.

7. In the **Add Standalone Snap-in** dialog box, click **Close**.

8. Click **OK** when you are finished.

9. On the **File** menu, click **Save**.

Practice: Configuring the Administrative Tools

- **In this practice, you will:**
  - Create a custom MMC that contains the following:
    - Computer Management (Local)
    - Computer Management (Glasgow)
    - Active Directory Users and Computers
  - Save the MMC as C:\MOC\CustomMMC.msc

Objective

In this practice, you will:

- Create a custom MMC.
- Add MMC snap-ins.
- Save a custom MMC.

Instructions

Before you begin this practice:

- Log on to the domain by using the *ComputerName*Admin account.
- Review the procedures in this lesson that describe how to perform this task.

Scenario

Your manager instructs you that you will be adding domain user accounts on the member server that supports your city and an additional server called Glasgow. Configure the support tools so that you have one administrative console that gives you quick access to the tools that you need to do the most common tasks for your job.

Practice

▶ **Configure a custom MMC**

1. Open a blank MMC.

2. Add a Computer Management snap-in for the local computer.

3. Add a Computer Management snap-in for Glasgow.

4. Add the Active Directory Users and Computers snap-in.

5. Save the MMC as C:\MOC\CustomMMC.msc.

Note   This practice focuses on the concepts in this lesson and as a result may not comply with Microsoft security recommendations. For example, this practice does not comply with the recommendation that users log on with domain user account and use the **Run as** command when performing administrative tasks.

How to Resolve Problems with Installing and Configuring Administrative Tools

Symptom	Cause	Resolution
Cannot install the administrative tools	Insufficient permissions	You must have administrative permissions on the local computer
	Incorrect operating system	You can install the Windows Server 2003 Administration Tools Pack only on currently supported operating systems
Broken links in Help files	Both server and client Help systems are required	Use both Help systems for the Windows Server 2003 Administration Tools Pack by installing the server Help on currently supported client operating systems

Introduction

Two common problems you might encounter when installing and configuring administrative tools are that you cannot install the administrative tools properly and that there are broken links in the Help files.

Cannot install

If you have problems installing or configuring administrative tools in Windows Server 2003, verify that you have administrative permissions on the local computer.

Another reason you may not be able to install the administrative tools is that the incorrect operating system is installed. You can only install the Windows Server 2003 Administration Tools Pack on computers running Windows XP Professional or Windows Server 2003.

Broken Help links

When the Windows Server 2003 Administration Tools Pack is installed on Windows XP Professional, some Help links might appear to be broken. The reason this happens is that you must have both server and client Help files for the Windows Server 2003 Administration Tools Pack on Windows XP Professional.

To resolve the problem, you must integrate the server and client Help files for the Windows Server 2003 Administration Tools Pack by installing the server Help files on Windows XP Professional. This is fairly easy to do and should be done after the Windows Server 2003 Administration Tools Pack is installed on Windows XP Professional.

To install Help files from another Windows computer, CD, or disk image:

1. On the **Start** menu, click **Help and Support**.

2. In the Help and Support window, in the navigation bar, click **Options**.

3. In the left pane, click **Install and share Windows Help**.

4. In the right pane, depending on where you want to install Help from, click **Install Help content from another Windows computer** or **Install Help content from a CD or disk image**.

5. Type the location of the computer, CD, or disk image, and then click **Find**.

   If you are installing from a CD or disk image, you can click **Browse** to locate the disk containing Help files.

6. When available Help files appear, click the version of Help you want, and then click **Install**.

   When the installation is complete, you can switch to the new Help files.

Lesson: Creating an Organizational Unit

- What Is an Organizational Unit?
- Organizational Unit Hierarchical Models
- Names Associated with Organizational Units
- How to Create an Organizational Unit

Introduction

In this lesson, you will learn how to create an organizational unit.

Lesson objectives

After completing this lesson, you will be able to create an organizational unit, including:

- Explain the purpose of an organizational unit.
- Describe organizational unit hierarchical models.
- Identify the names associated with organizational units.
- Create an organizational unit.

What Is an Organizational Unit?

- Organizes objects in a domain
- Allows you to delegate administrative control
- Simplifies the management of commonly grouped resources

Definition

An organizational unit is a particularly useful type of Active Directory object contained in a domain. Organizational units are useful, because you can use them to organize hundreds of thousands of objects in the directory into manageable units. You use an organizational unit to group and organize objects for administrative purposes, such as delegating administrative rights and assigning policies to a collection of objects as a single unit.

Benefits of using organizational units

You can use organizational units to:

- Organize objects in a domain.

    Organizational units contain domain objects, such as user and computer accounts and groups. File and printer shares that are published to Active Directory are also found in organizational units.

- Delegate administrative control.

    You can assign either complete administrative control, such as the Full Control permission, over all objects in the organizational unit, or you can assign limited administrative control, such as the ability to modify e-mail information, over user objects in the organizational unit. To delegate administrative control, you assign specific permissions on the organizational unit and the objects that the organizational unit contains for one or more users and groups.

- Simplify the management of commonly grouped resources.

    You can delegate administrative authority over individual attributes on individual objects in Active Directory, but you will usually use organizational units to delegate administrative authority. A user can have administrative authority for all organizational units in a domain or for a single organizational unit. Using organizational units, you can create containers in a domain that represent the hierarchical or logical structures in your organization. You can then manage the configuration and use of accounts and resources based on your organizational model.

Organizational Unit Hierarchical Models

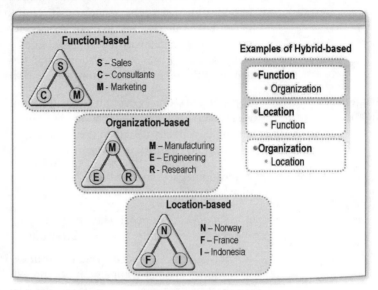

Introduction

As a systems administrator, you do not select the design of the Active Directory structure for your organization. However, it is important to know the characteristics and ramifications of each structure. This knowledge may be critical to you when performing systems administrator tasks within the Active Directory structure. This topic describes the four basic hierarchy designs.

Function-based hierarchy

The function-based hierarchy is based on only the business functions of the organization, without regard to geographical location or departmental or divisional barriers. Choose this approach only if the IT function is not based on location or organization.

When deciding whether to organize the Active Directory structure by function, consider the following characteristics of function-based designs:

- *Not affected by reorganizations.* A function-based hierarchy is not affected by corporate or organizational reorganizations.

- *May require additional layers.* When using this structure, it may be necessary to create additional layers in the organizational unit hierarchy to accommodate the administration of users, printers, servers, and network shares.

- *May impact replication.* Structures that are used to create domains may not result in efficient use of the network, because the domain naming context may replicate across one or more areas of low bandwidth.

This structure is only appropriate in small organizations because functional departments in medium and large organizations are often very diverse and cannot be effectively grouped into broad categories.

Organization-based hierarchy

The organization-based hierarchy is based on the departments or divisions in your organization. If the Active Directory structure is organized to reflect the organizational structure, it may be difficult to delegate administrative authority, because the objects in Active Directory, such as printers and file shares, may not be grouped in a way that facilitates delegation of administrative authority. Because users never see the Active Directory structure, the design should accommodate the administrator instead of the user.

Location-based hierarchy

If the organization is centralized, and network management is geographically distributed, then using a location-based hierarchy is recommended. For example, you may decide to create organizational units for New England, Boston, and Hartford in the same domain, such as contoso.msft.

A location-based organizational units or domain hierarchy has the following characteristics:

- *Not affected by reorganizations*. Although divisions and departments may change frequently, location rarely does change in most organizations.

- *Accommodates mergers and expansions*. If an organization merges with or acquires another company, it is simple to integrate the new locations into the existing organizational units and domain hierarchy structure.

- *Takes advantage of network strengths*. Typically, an organization's physical network topology resembles a location-based hierarchy. If you create domains with a location-based hierarchy, you can take advantage of areas where the network has high bandwidth and limit the amount of data replicated across low bandwidth areas.

- *May cause compromise security*. If a location includes multiple divisions or departments, an individual or group with administrative authority over that domain or over organizational units may also have authority over any child domains or organizational units.

Hybrid-based hierarchy

A hierarchy based on location and then by organization, or any other combination of structure types, is called a hybrid-based hierarchy. The hybrid-based hierarchy combines strengths from several areas to meet the needs of the organization. This type of hierarchy has the following characteristics:

- Accommodates additional growth in geographic, departmental, or divisional areas.

- Creates distinct management boundaries according to department or division.

- Requires cooperation between administrators to ensure the completion of administrative tasks if they are in the same location but in different divisions or departments.

Names Associated with Organizational Units

Name	Example
LDAP relative distinguished name	OU=MyOrganizationalUnit
LDAP distinguished name	OU=MyOrganizationalUnit, DC=microsoft, DC=com
Canonical name	Microsoft.com/MyOrganizationalUnit

Introduction

Each object in Active Directory can be referenced by several different types of names that describe the location of the object. Active Directory creates a relative distinguished name, a canonical name, and a relative distinguished name for each object, based on information that is provided when the object is created or modified.

LDAP relative distinguished name

The Lightweight Directory Access Protocol (LDAP) relative distinguished name uniquely identifies the object in its parent container. For example, the LDAP relative distinguished name of an organizational unit named MyOrganizational Unit is OU=MyOrganizationalUnit. Relative distinguished names must be unique in an organizational unit. It is important to understand the syntax of the LDAP relative distinguished name when using scripts to query and manage Active Directory.

LDAP distinguished name

Unlike the LDAP relative distinguished name, the LDAP distinguished name is globally unique. An example of the LDAP distinguished name of an organizational unit named MyOganizationalUnit in the microsoft.com domain is OU=MyOrganizationalUnit, DC=microsoft, DC=com. Systems administrators use the LDAP relative distinguished name and the LDAP distinguished name only when writing administrative scripts or during command-line administration.

Canonical name

The canonical name syntax is constructed in the same way as the LDAP distinguished name, but it is represented by a different notation. The canonical name of the organizational unit named myOrganizationalUnit in the microsoft.com domain is Microsoft.com/MyOrganizationalUnit. Administrators use canonical names through some administrative tools. It is used to represent a hierarchy in the administrative tools.

How to Create an Organizational Unit

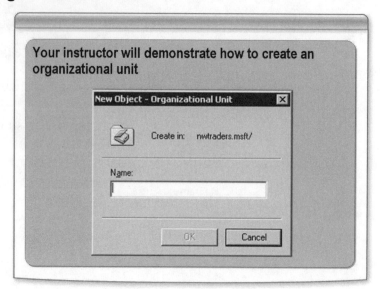

Introduction

You can create organizational units to represent a hierarchy or to manage the objects that go into organizational units.

Procedure

To create a new organizational unit:

1. Open Active Directory Users and Computers.

2. In the console tree, double-click the domain node.

3. Right-click the domain node or the folder in which you want to add the organizational unit, point to **New**, and then click **organizational unit**.

4. In the **New Object – Organizational Unit** dialog box, in the **Name** box, type the name of the organizational unit, and then click **OK**.

Note To perform this procedure, you must be a member of the Domain Admins group or the Enterprise Admins group in Active Directory, or you must be delegated the appropriate authority. As a security best practice, consider using **Run as** to perform this procedure.

Using a command line

To create an organizational unit by using **dsadd**:

1. Open a command prompt.

2. Type **dsadd ou** *OrganizationalUnitDomainName* [**-desc** *Description*] [{**-s** *Server* | **-d** *Domain*}] [**-u** *UserName*] [**-p** {*Password* | *}] [**-q**] [{**-uc** | **-uco** | **-uci**}]

Practice: Creating an Organizational Unit

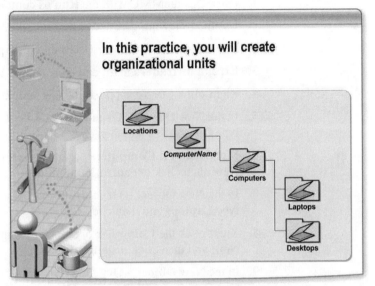

Objective	In this practice, you will create three organizational units.
Instructions	Before you begin this practice:

- Log on to the domain by using the *ComputerName*Admin account.
- Review the procedures in this lesson that describe how to perform this task.

Scenario

As a systems administrator for Northwind Traders, you are given the task of creating an organizational unit hierarchy designed by the Northwind Traders design team. The organizational unit hierarchy will use a location-based design that separates laptop computers from desktop computers. You will create a hierarchy of organizational units in your city organizational unit to separate computer types.

The following graphic is a representation of what you need to create for the NWTraders domain. The Locations organizational unit and the *ComputerName* organizational unit have already been created.

Practice

▶ **Create the computers, laptops, and desktops organizational units**

1. Open CustomMMC with the **Run as** command.

   Use the following user account: *ComputerName*Admin@nwtraders.msft

2. Expand **Active Directory Users and Computers**.

3. Expand **nwtraders.msft**, and then expand **Locations**.

4. Right-click *CityName*, point to **New**, and then click **organizational unit**.

5. In the **New Object – Organizational Unit** dialog box, in the **Name** box, type **Computers** and then click **OK**.

6. Right-click the **Computers** organizational unit that you just created, point to **New**, then click **organizational unit**.

7. In the **New Object – Organizational Unit** dialog box, in the **Name** box, type **Laptops** and then click **OK**.

8. Right-click the **Computer** organizational unit that you just created, point to **New**, and then click **organizational unit**.

9. In the **New Object – Organizational Unit** dialog box, in the **Name** box, type **Desktops** and then click **OK**.

10. Close and save CustomMMC.

    Your organizational unit hierarchy should look like the preceding diagram.

Scenario

The systems engineers want to test some advanced features of Active Directory. They want your team to create some organizational units in the IT Test organizational unit.

The IT Test organizational unit has already been created. You must add an additional organizational unit that matches your city, as shown in the following graphic.

        IT Test
           City

Practice: Using a command line

▶ **Create an organizational unit by using dsadd**

1. Click **Start**, and then click **Run**.

2. In the **Open** box, type **runas /user:nwtraders**ComputerName**Admin cmd** and then click **OK**

3. When prompted for the password, type **P@ssw0rd** and then press ENTER.

4. At the command prompt, type the following command:

   dsadd ou *OrganizationalUnitDomainName*

   Example: dsadd ou "ou=London,ou=IT Test, dc=nwtraders,dc=msft"

Lesson: Moving Domain Objects

- When Do You Move a Domain Object?
- How to Move a Domain Object

Introduction

The information in this lesson presents the skills and knowledge that you need to move domain objects.

Lesson objectives

After completing this lesson, you will be able to:

- List reasons for moving a domain object.
- Move a domain object.

When Do You Move a Domain Object?

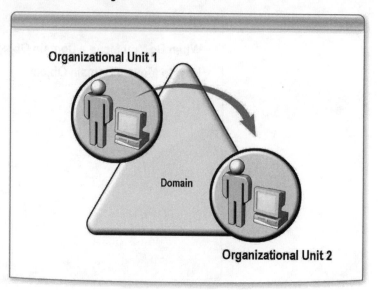

Introduction

You can move objects between organizational units in Active Directory when organizational or administrative functions change, for example, when an employee moves from one department to another. As a systems administrator, it is your task to maintain the Active Directory structure as business needs change.

The following items can be moved within the Active Directory structure:

- User account
- Contact account
- Group
- Shared folder
- Printer
- Computer
- Domain controller
- Organizational unit

Change locations

One reason to move a domain object is when your business physically moves from one location to another. If the Active Directory structure is based on geopolitical boundaries, such as city or country, you may need to move objects from one location to another location as objects are physically moved.

Organizational unit restructuring

Another reason to move a domain object is if your Active Directory structure is based on an organizational chart. You may need to move objects if the organizational structure changes.

For example, suppose the Sales team is represented by an organizational unit, the Marketing team is represented by another organizational unit, and both teams are merged into one Sales and Marketing team. In Active Directory, the objects are merged into one organizational unit. To make this process easier, you can select and move multiple domain objects at the same time.

How to Move a Domain Object

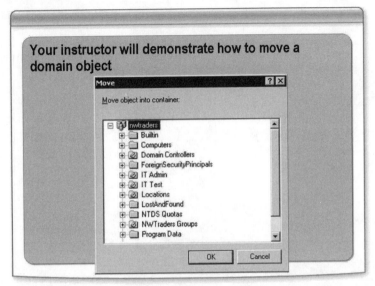

Your instructor will demonstrate how to move a domain object

Introduction

You can move domain objects either by using the menu option or by dragging the object from one organizational unit to another.

Procedure

To move a domain object:

1. In Active Directory Users and Computers, right-click the object you want to move, and then click **Move**.

   You can also drag the object to the new location.

2. In the **Move** dialog box, browse to the container that you want to move the object to, and then click **OK**.

Practice: Moving Active Directory Domain Objects

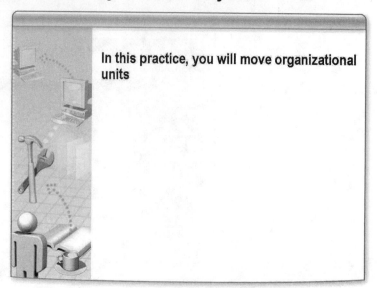

In this practice, you will move organizational units

Objective

In this practice, you will move domain objects from one organizational unit to another.

Instructions

Before you begin this practice:

- Log on to the domain by using the *ComputerName*User account.
- Open CustomMMC with the **Run as** command.

  Use the user account Nwtraders*ComputerName*Admin (Example: LondonAdmin).

- Ensure that CustomMMC contains Active Directory Users and Computers.
- Review the procedures in this lesson that describe how to perform this task.

Scenario

The systems engineers are testing some advanced reporting functionalities in Active Directory. They want you to create some domain objects and move them from the IT Test organizational unit to an organizational unit named IT Test Move.

Practice

▶ **Create and move organizational units**

1. Create the following organizational units in the IT Test organizational unit:
   - OU*ComputerName*1
   - OU*ComputerName*2
2. Move them to the IT Test Move organizational unit.

Lab A: Creating Organizational Units

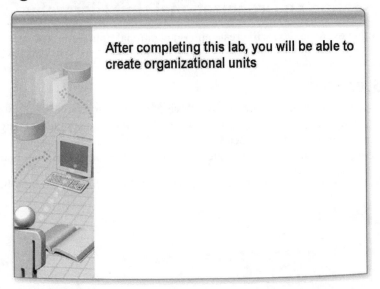

After completing this lab, you will be able to create organizational units

Introduction

After completing this lab, you will be able to create organizational units.

Prerequisites

Before working on this lab, you must have:

- Experience navigating an organizational unit structure in Active Directory Users and Computers.
- Experience creating organizational units.

Lab setup

The Lab Setup section lists the tasks that you must perform before you begin the lab. To complete this lab, you must have reviewed the procedures in the module and successfully completed each practice.

Before you begin this lab:

- Log on to the domain by using the *ComputerName*User account.
- Open CustomMMC with the **Run as** command.

  Use the user account Nwtraders*ComputerName*Admin (Example: LondonAdmin).

- Ensure that CustomMMC contains the following snap-ins:
  - Computer Management (Glasgow)
  - Computer Management (Local)
  - Active Directory Users and Computers

Review the procedures in this lesson that describe how to perform this task.

Estimated time to complete this lab: 30 minutes

Exercise 1
Creating an Organizational Unit Hierarchy

In this exercise, you will create an organizational unit hierarchy.

Scenario

As a systems administrator for Northwind Traders, you have been given the task of creating an organizational unit hierarchy designed by the Northwind Traders design team. The organizational unit hierarchy will use a location-based design that separates user and group accounts. You will create the organizational unit hierarchy in your city organizational unit.

At the end of this lab your organizational unit hierarchy should look like the following diagram:

Note You created the Computers, Laptops, and Desktops organizational units that are shown in the graphic in practices.

Tasks	Specific Instructions
1. Open CustomMMC by using the **Run as** command.	▪ User name: **NWTraders***ComputerName***Admin** ▪ Password: **P@ssw0rd**
2. Find the organizational unit that matches your computer name.	▪ Find the Nwtraders/Locations/*ComputerName* organizational unit.
3. Create an organizational unit in your *ComputerName* organizational unit named Users.	▪ Create the Nwtraders/Locations/*ComputerName*/Users organizational unit.
4. Create an organizational unit in your *ComputerName* organizational unit named Groups.	▪ Create the Nwtraders/Locations/*ComputerName*/Groups organizational unit.

Microsoft®
Training &
Certification

Module 2: Managing User and Computer Accounts

Contents

Overview

- Creating User Accounts
- Creating Computer Accounts
- Modifying User and Computer Account Properties
- Creating a User Account Template
- Enabling and Unlocking User and Computer Accounts
- Resetting User and Computer Accounts
- Locating User and Computer Accounts in Active Directory
- Saving Queries

Introduction

One of your functions as a systems administrator is to manage user and computer accounts. These accounts are Active Directory objects, and you use these accounts to enable individuals to log on to the network and access resources. In this module, you will learn the skills and knowledge that you need to modify user and computer accounts on computers running Microsoft® Windows® Server 2003 in a networked environment.

Objectives

After completing this module, you will be able to:

- Create user accounts.
- Create computer accounts.
- Modify user and computer account properties.
- Create a user account template.
- Enable and unlock user and computer accounts.
- Reset user and computer accounts.
- Locate user and computer accounts in the Active Directory® directory service.
- Save queries.

Lesson: Creating User Accounts

- What Is a User Account?
- Names Associated with Domain User Accounts
- Guidelines for Creating a User Account Naming Convention
- User Account Placement in a Hierarchy
- User Account Password Options
- When to Require Password Changes
- How to Create User Accounts
- Best Practices for Creating User Accounts

Introduction

As a systems administrator, you give users access to various network resources. Therefore, you must create user accounts to identify and authenticate the users so that they can gain access to the network.

Lesson objectives

After completing this lesson, you will be able to:

- Explain the purpose of user accounts.
- Describe the types of names associated with domain user accounts.
- Explain guidelines for creating a convention for naming user accounts.
- Describe user account placement in an Active Directory hierarchy.
- Describe user account password options.
- Determine when to require password changes on domain user accounts.
- Create local and domain user accounts.

What Is a User Account?

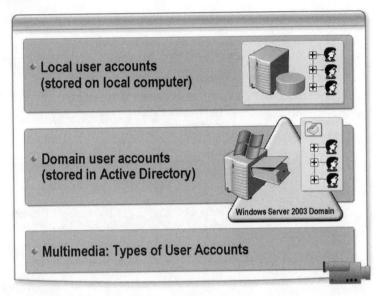

Definition

A user account is an object that consists of all the information that defines a user in Windows Server 2003. The account can be either a local or domain account. A user account includes the user name and password with which the user logs on, the groups that the user account is a member of, and the user rights and permissions the user has for gaining access to computer and network resources.

You can use a user account to:

- Enable someone to log on to a computer based on a user account's identity.

- Enable processes and services to run under a specific security context.

- Manage a user's access to resources such as Active Directory objects and their properties, shared folders, files, directories, and printer queues.

Multimedia: Types of User Accounts

To view the *Types of User Accounts* presentation, open the Web page on the Student Materials compact disc, click **Multimedia**, and then click the title of the presentation.

The *Types of User Accounts* presentation explains how using accounts that grant different levels of access to the network satisfy the needs of network users.

Names Associated with Domain User Accounts

Name	Example
User logon name	Jayadams
Pre-Windows 2000 logon name	Nwtraders\jayadams
User principal logon name	Jayadams@nwtraders.msft
LDAP relative distinguished name	CN=jayadams,CN=users,dc=nwtraders,dc=msft

Introduction

There are four types of names associated with domain user accounts. In Active Directory, each user account consists of a user logon name, a pre-Windows 2000 user logon name (Security Accounts Manager account name), a user principal logon name, and a Lightweight Directory Access Protocol (LDAP) relative distinguished name.

User logon name

When creating a user account, an administrator types a user logon name. The full name must be unique in the container in which you create the user account. It is used as the relative distinguished name. Users use this name only during the logon process. The user enters the user logon name, a password, and the domain name in separate fields on the logon screen.

User logon names can:

- Contain up to 20 uppercase and lowercase characters (the field accepts more than 20 characters, but Windows Server 2003 recognizes only 20).

- Include a combination of special and alphanumeric characters, except the following: " / \ [ ] : ; | = , + * ? < >.

An example of a user logon name is Jayadams or Jadams.

Pre-Windows 2000 logon name

You can use the pre-Windows 2000 network basic input/output system (NetBIOS) user account to log on to a Windows domain from computers running pre-Windows 2000 operating systems by using a name with the *DomainName\UserName* format. You can also use this name to log on to Windows domains from computers running Microsoft Windows 2000 or Microsoft Windows XP or servers running Windows Server 2003. The Pre-Windows 2000 logon name must be unique in the domain. Users can use this logon name with the **Run as** command or on a secondary logon screen.

An example of a Pre-Windows 2000 logon name is nwtraders\jayadams.

User principal logon name

The user principal name (UPN) consists of the user logon name and the user principal name suffix, joined by the at sign (@). The UPN must be unique in the forest.

The second part of the UPN is the user principal name suffix. The user principal name suffix can be the Domain Name System (DNS) domain name, the DNS name of any domain in the forest, or an alternative name that an administrator creates only for logon purposes. Users can use this name to log on with the **Run as** command or on a secondary logon screen.

An example of a UPN is Jayadams@nwtraders.msft.

LDAP relative distinguished name

The LDAP relative distinguished name uniquely identifies the object in its parent container. Users never use this name, but administrators use this name to add users to the network from a script or command line. All objects use the same LDAP naming convention, so all LDAP relative distinguished names must be unique in an organizational unit.

The following are examples of an LDAP relative distinguished name:

- CN=jayadams,CN=users,dc=nwtraders,dc=msft
- CN=computer1,CN=users,dc=nwtraders,dc=msft

Guidelines for Creating a User Account Naming Convention

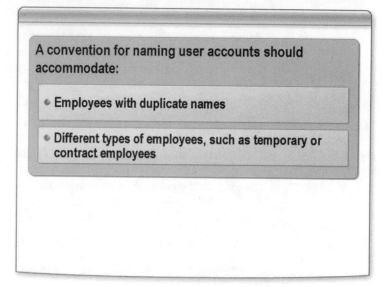

A convention for naming user accounts should accommodate:

- Employees with duplicate names

- Different types of employees, such as temporary or contract employees

Introduction

A naming convention establishes how user accounts are identified in the domain. A consistent naming convention makes it easier for you to remember user logon names and locate them in lists. It is a good practice to adhere to the naming convention already in use in an existing network that supports a large number of users.

Guidelines

Consider the following guidelines for creating a naming convention:

- If you have a large number of users, your naming convention for user logon names should accommodate employees with duplicate names. A method to accomplish this is to use the first name and the last initial, and then add additional letters from the last name to accommodate duplicate names. For example, for two users named Judy Lew, one user logon name can be Judyl and the other can be Judyle.

- In some organizations, it is useful to identify temporary employees by their user accounts. To do so, you can add a prefix to the user logon name, such as a T and a hyphen. An example is T-Judyl.

- User logon names for domain user accounts must be unique in Active Directory. Full names for domain user accounts must be unique in the domain in which you create the user account.

User Account Placement in a Hierarchy

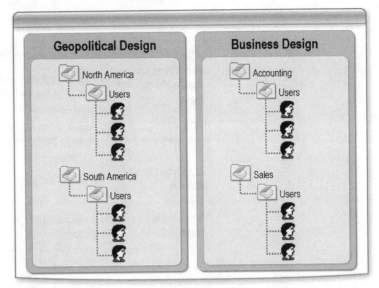

Introduction

You can place domain user accounts in any domain in the forest and any organizational unit in the domain. Typically, account hierarchies are based on geopolitical boundaries or business models. By structuring the Active Directory hierarchy and then managing the permissions on the objects and properties in Active Directory, you can precisely specify the accounts that can access information in Active Directory and the level of permissions that they can have.

Place user accounts in an Active Directory hierarchy based on the way the user accounts are managed.

Geopolitical design

In a geopolitical design, you place users in domains that match their physical location. Geopolitical domain structures place domain controllers that support users of the domain close to the users. This reduces logon times for users and enables users to log on if the wide area network (WAN) is down.

Business design

When the hierarchy of domains is based on business models, you place your sales personnel in a Sales domain and manufacturing personnel in a Manufacturing domain. This model ensures that there are enough domain controllers to support all the users in the WAN.

Note In many cases, one domain will work for a corporate environment. You can still separate administrative control of users by placing them into organizational units.

User Account Password Options

Account options	Description
User must change password at next logon	Users must change their passwords the next time they log on to the network
User cannot change password	A user does not have the permissions to change their own password
Password never expires	A user password is prevented from expiring
Account is disabled	A user cannot log on by using the selected account

Introduction

As a systems administrator, you can manage user account password options. These options can be set when the user account is created or in the **Properties** dialog box of a user account.

Password options

The administrator can choose from the following password options to protect access to the domain or a computer:

- **User must change password at the next logon**. This is used when a new user logs on to a system for the first time or when the administrator resets forgotten passwords for users.

- **User cannot change password**. Use this option when you want to control when a user account password can be changed.

- **Password never expires**. This option prevents the password from expiring. As a security best practice, do not use this option.

- **Account is disabled**. This option prevents the user from logging on by using the selected account.

When to Require or Restrict Password Changes

Option	Use this option when you:
Require password changes	• Create new domain accounts • Reset passwords
Restrict password changes	• Create local and domain service accounts • Create new local accounts that will not log on locally

Introduction

To create a more secure environment, require password changes on user accounts and restrict password changes on service accounts. The following table lists when you need to restrict or require password changes.

Password modifications options

Option	Use this option when you:
Require password changes	• Create new domain user accounts. Select the check box that requires the user to change the password the first time the user logs on to the domain. • Reset passwords. This option enables the administrator to reset a password when the password expires or if the user forgets it.
Restrict password changes	• Create local or domain service accounts. Service accounts typically have many dependencies on them. As a result, you may want to restrict the password change policy so that service account passwords are changed by the administrator who is responsible for the applications that depend on the service account. • Create new local accounts that will not log on locally.

Additional Readings

For more information about service accounts, see "Services permissions" at http://www.microsoft.com/technet/treeview/default.asp?url=/technet/prodtechn ol/windowsserver2003/proddocs/server/sys_srv_permissions.asp.

Form more information about changing passwords, see:

- Article 324744, "HOW TO: Prevent Users from Changing a Password Except When Required in Windows Server 2003," in the Microsoft Knowledge Base at http://support.microsoft.com/?kbid=324744.

- Article 320325, "User May Not Be Able to Change Their Password If You Configure the 'User Must Change Password at Next Logon' Setting," in the Microsoft Knowledge Base at http://support.microsoft.com/?kbid=320325.

For more information about preventing passwords of service accounts from being changed, see article 324744, "HOW TO: Prevent Users from Changing a Password Except When Required in Windows Server 2003," in the Microsoft Knowledge Base at http://support.microsoft.com/?kbid= 324744.

How to Create User Accounts

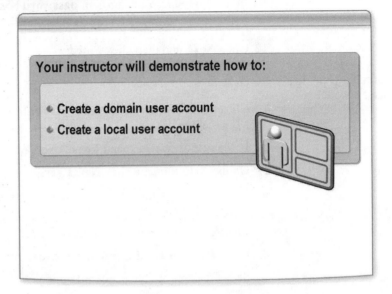

Your instructor will demonstrate how to:

- Create a domain user account
- Create a local user account

Introduction

Domain user accounts enable users to log on to a domain and access resources anywhere on the network, and local user accounts enable users to log on and access resources only on the computer on which you create the local user account. As a systems administrator, you must create domain and local user accounts to manage your network environment.

Important   You cannot create local user accounts on a domain controller.

Procedure for creating a domain user account

To create a domain user account:

1. Click **Start**, point to **Administrative Tools**, and then click **Active Directory Users and Computers**.

2. In the console tree, double-click the domain node.

3. In the details pane, right-click the organizational unit where you want to add the user, point to **New**, and then click **User**.

4. In the **New Object - User** dialog box, in the **First name** box, type the user's first name.

5. In the **Initials** box, type the user's initials.

6. In the **Last name** box, type the user's last name.

7. In the **User logon name** box, type the name that the user will log on with.

8. From the drop-down list, click the UPN suffix that must be appended to the user logon name after the at sign (@).

9. Click **Next**.

10. In the **Password** and **Confirm password** boxes, type the user's password.

11. Select the appropriate password options.

12. Click **Next**, and then click **Finish**.

Procedure for creating a local user account

To create a local user account:

1. Click **Start**, point to Administrative Tools, and then click **Computer Management**.

2. In the console tree, expand **Local Users and Groups**, and then click **Users**.

3. On the **Action** menu, click **New User**.

4. In the **New User** dialog box, in the **User name** box, type the name that the user will log on with.

5. Modify the full name as desired.

6. In the **Password** and **Confirm password** boxes, type the user's password.

7. Select the appropriate password options.

8. Click **Create**, and then click **Close**.

Note   A user name cannot be identical to any other user or group name on the computer being administered. It can contain up to 20 uppercase or lowercase characters, except for the following:

" / \ [ ] : ; | = , + * ? < >

A user name cannot consist solely of periods or spaces.

Using a command line

Another way to create a domain user account is to use the **dsadd** command. The **dsadd user** command adds a single user to the directory from a command prompt or batch file.

To create a user account by using **dsadd user**:

1. Open a command prompt.

2. Type **dsadd user** *UserDomainName* [**-samid** *SAMName*] [**-upn** *UPN*] [**-fn** *FirstName*] [**-ln** *LastName*] [**-display** *DisplayName*] [**-pwd** {*Password*|*}] Use " " if there is a space in any variable.

Note   For the complete syntax of the dsadd user command, at a command prompt, type **dsadd user /?**.

Example of **dsadd user**:

```
dsadd user "cn=testuser,cn=users,dc=nwtraders,dc=msft" -samid
testuser -upn testuser@nwtraders.msft -fn test -ln user -
display "test user" -pwd P@ssw0rd
```

Practice: Creating User Accounts

In this practice, you will:

- Create a local user account by using Computer Management

- Create a domain account by using Active Directory Users and Computers

- Create a domain user account by using Run as

- Create a domain user account by using dsadd

Objective

In this practice, you will:

- Create a local user account by using Computer Management.

- Create a domain account by using Active Directory Users and Computers.

- Create a domain user account by using **Run as**.

- Create a domain user account by using **dsadd**.

Instructions

Before you begin this practice:

- Log on to the student computer by using the *ComputerName*User account.

- Open CustomMMC with the **Run as** command.

    Use the user account Nwtraders*ComputerName*Admin (Example: LondonAdmin).

- Ensure that CustomMMC contains the following snap-ins:

    - Computer Management (local)

    - Active Directory Users and Computers

- Review the procedures in this lesson that describe how to perform this task.

Scenario

Your manager asks you to create a local user account that will be used to back up your company's software. Another department in your organization will install the software and give the account the user rights needed to back up the server. You must create a local user account to be used as a service account.

Practice: Creating a local user account

▶ **Create a local user account**

1. Open Computer Management for your local server.

2. Create an account by using the following parameters:

   a. User name: **Service_Backup**

   b. Description: **Service Account for Backup Software**

   c. Password: **P@ssw0rd**

3. Clear the **User must change password at next logon** check box.

Scenario

You will use the Administrator account to perform management tasks. Your company's security practices require that you create a personal user account that you will use to log on to the domain, read and send e-mail, and other nonadministrative tasks.

You must set up a domain user account for yourself. When you need to perform administrative tasks, you will either log on as a different user or use secondary logon credentials. This new account should be created in the nwtraders.msft/IT Admin/IT Users container.

Practice: Creating a domain user account

▶ **Create a domain user account**

1. Open Active Directory Users and Computers.

2. Add a user account to the IT Users container with the following parameters:

   a. First name: Your first name (Example: Misty)

   b. Last name: Your last name (Example: Shock)

   c. Full name: Your full name (Example: Misty Shock)

   d. User logon name: The first three letters of your first name and the first three letters of your last name (Example: MisSho)

   e. Password: Use a password that:

      • Is at least seven characters long.

      • Does not contain your user name, real name, or company name.

      • Does not contain a complete word that is found in the dictionary.

      • Contains characters from each of the following four groups.

Group	Examples
Uppercase letters	A, B, C ..
Lowercase letters	a, b, c ..
Numerals	0, 1, 2, 3, 4, 5, 6, 7, 8, 9
Symbols found on the keyboard (all keyboard characters not defined as letters or numerals)	~ ! @ # $ % ^ & * ( ) _ + - = { }	[ ] / : " ; ' < > ? , . \

An example of a strong password is J*p2leO4>F.

3. Log off.

4. Test the user account that you just created by logging on by using the user account.

5. Log off.

Scenario

Northwind Traders is in the process of testing advanced features of Active Directory. Your team has the task of creating user accounts in the IT Test organizational unit. The test team will use these accounts. Each member of your team must create five accounts.

Practice: Creating a domain user account using Run as

▶ **Create a domain user account by using Run as**

1. Log on to the student computer by using the *ComputerName*User account.

2. Open CustomMMC with the **Run as** command.

   - Use the user account Nwtraders*ComputerName*Admin (Example: LondonAdmin).

3. In Active Directory Users and Computers, expand **nwtraders.msft**.

4. Right-click the **IT Test** organizational unit, point to **New**, and then click **User**.

5. Add a user account to the IT Test organizational unit with the following parameters:

   a. First name: **User1**

   b. Last name: Your last name (Example: Shock)

   c. User logon name: **User1** followed by the first three letters of your last name (Example: User1Sho)

   d. Password: **P@ssw0rd**

6. Repeat step 5 and create four more user accounts.

   Example: User2Sho, User3Sho, User4Sho, User5Sho

7. Close all windows.

Scenario

Northwind Traders is in the process of testing advanced features of Active Directory. Your team has the task of creating user accounts in the IT Test organizational unit. The test team will use these accounts. Each member of your team must create five accounts.

Practice: Using a command line

▶ **Create a domain user account by using dsadd**

1. Click **Start**, click **Run**, and then type **runas /user:nwtraders*ComputerName*Admin cmd** and then click **OK**.

2. When prompted for the password, type **P@ssw0rd** and then press **ENTER**.

3. At the command prompt, type the following command:

   dsadd user "cn=User6*FirstThreeLettersOfLastName***,ou=it test,dc=nwtraders,dc=msft" -samid User6***FirstThreeLettersOfLastName* **-pwd** *P@ssw0rd*

Best Practices for Creating User Accounts

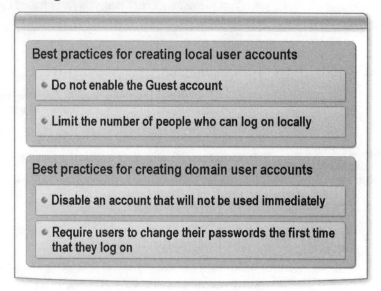

Best practices for creating local user accounts

- Do not enable the Guest account
- Limit the number of people who can log on locally

Best practices for creating domain user accounts

- Disable an account that will not be used immediately
- Require users to change their passwords the first time that they log on

Introduction

There are several best practices for creating user accounts that reduce security risks in the network environment. While software products change, review current best practices at www.microsoft.com/security.

Local user accounts

Consider the following best practices when creating local user accounts:

- Do not enable the Guest account.
- Rename the Administrator account.
- Limit the number of people who can log on locally.
- Use strong passwords.

Domain user accounts

Consider the following best practices when creating domain user accounts:

- Disable any account that will not be used immediately.
- Require users to change their passwords the first time that they log on.
- As a security best practice, it is recommended that you do not log on to your computer with administrative credentials.
- When you are logged on to your computer without administrative credentials, it is recommended that you use the **Run as** command to accomplish administrative tasks.
- Rename or disable the Administrator and Guest accounts in each domain to reduce the attacks on your domain.
- By default, all traffic on Active Directory administrative tools is signed and encrypted while in transit on the network. Do not disable this feature.

Lesson: Creating Computer Accounts

- What Is a Computer Account?
- Why Create a Computer Account?
- Where Computer Accounts Are Created in a Domain
- Computer Account Options
- How to Create a Computer Account

Introduction

The information in this lesson presents the skills and knowledge that you need to create a computer account.

Lesson objectives

After completing this lesson, you will be able to:

- Define computer account.
- Describe the purpose of computer accounts.
- Describe where computer accounts are created in a domain.
- Describe the various computer account options.
- Create a computer account.

What Is a Computer Account?

- Identifies a computer in a domain
- Provides a means for authenticating and auditing computer access to the network and to domain resources
- Is required for every computer running:
  - Windows Server 2003
  - Windows XP Professional
  - Windows 2000
  - Windows NT

Introduction

Every computer running Microsoft Windows NT®, Windows 2000, Windows XP, or Windows Server 2003 that joins a domain has a computer account. Similar to user accounts, computer accounts provide a means for authenticating and auditing computer access to the network and to domain resources.

What does a computer account do?

In Active Directory, computers are security principles, just like users. This means that computers must have accounts and passwords. To be fully authenticated by Active Directory, a user must have a valid user account, and the user must also log on to the domain from a computer that has a valid computer account.

Note   You cannot create computer accounts for computers running Microsoft Windows 95, Microsoft Windows 98, Microsoft Windows Millennium Edition, and Windows XP Home Edition, because their operating systems do not adhere to Active Directory security requirements.

Why Create a Computer Account?

- Security
  - Authentication
  - IPSec
  - Auditing
- Management
  - Active Directory features:
    Software deployment
    Desktop management
  - Hardware and software inventory through SMS

Introduction

Computers are responsible for performing key tasks, such as authenticating user logons, distributing Internet Protocol (IP) addresses, maintaining the integrity of Active Directory, and enforcing security policies. To have full access to these network resources, computers must have valid accounts in Active Directory. The two main functions of a computer account are performing security and management activities.

Security

A computer account must be created in Active Directory for users to take full advantage of Active Directory features. When a computer account is created, the computer can use advanced authentication processes such as Kerberos authentication and IP security (IPSec) to encrypt IP traffic. The computer also needs a computer account to dictate how auditing is applied and recorded.

Management

Computer accounts help the systems administrator manage the network structure. The systems administrator uses computer accounts to manage the functionality of the desktop environment, automate the deployment of software by using Active Directory, and maintain a hardware and software inventory by using Microsoft Systems Management Server (SMS). Computer accounts in the domain are also used to control access to resources.

Where Computer Accounts Are Created in a Domain

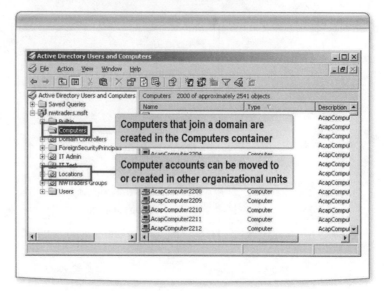

Introduction	When the systems administrator creates a computer account, they can choose the organizational unit in which to create that account. If a computer joins a domain, the computer account is created in the Computers container, and the administrator can move the account to its proper organizational unit as necessary.
Administrators designate the location of computer accounts	By default, Active Directory users can add up to 10 computers to the domain with their user account credentials. This default configuration can be changed. If the systems administrator adds a computer account directly to Active Directory, a user can join a computer to the domain without using any of the 10 allocated computer accounts.
Pre-staged computer accounts	Adding a computer to the domain with a previously created account is called pre-staging, which means that computers are added to any organizational unit where the systems administrator has permissions to add computer accounts. Usually, users do not have the appropriate permissions to pre-stage a computer account, so as an alternative they join a computer to the domain by using a pre-staged account.
Users designate the location of computer accounts	When a user joins a computer to the domain, the computer account is added to the Computers container in Active Directory. This is accomplished through a service that adds the computer account on behalf of the user. The system account also records how many computers each user has added to the domain. By default, any authenticated user has the user right to add workstations to a domain and can create up to 10 computer accounts in the domain.
Additional reading	For more information about users adding computer accounts to a domain, see article 251335, "Domain Users Cannot Join Workstation or Server to a Domain," in the Microsoft Knowledge Base at http://support.microsoft.com/?kbid=251335.

Computer Account Options

Introduction

There are two optional features that you can enable when creating a computer account. You can assign a computer account as a Pre-Windows 2000 computer or as a backup domain controller (BDC).

Pre-Windows 2000

Select the **Assign this computer account as a pre-Windows 2000 computer** check box to assign a password based on the computer name. If you do not select this check box, a random password is assigned as the initial password for the computer account. The password automatically changes every five days between the computer and the domain where the computer account is located. This option guarantees that a pre-Windows 2000 computer will be able to interpret whether the password meets the password requirements.

Backup domain controller

Select the **Assign this computer as a backup domain controller** check box if you intend to use the computer as a backup domain controller. You should use this feature if you are still in a mixed environment with a Window Server 2003 domain controller and Windows NT 4.0 BDC. After the account is created in Active Directory, you can then join the BDC to the domain during the installation of Windows NT 4.0.

Additional Reading

For more information about delegating authentication, see "Delegating authentication" at http://www.microsoft.com/technet/treeview/ default.asp?url=/technet/prodtechnol/windowsserver2003/proddocs/server/ SE_constrained_delegation.asp.

How to Create a Computer Account

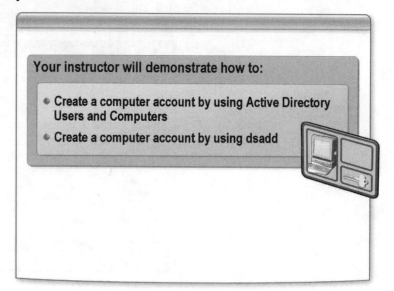

Introduction

By default, members of the Account Operators group can create computer accounts in the Computers container and in new organizational units. However, they cannot create computer accounts in the Builtin, Domain Controllers, ForeignSecurityPrincipals, LostAndFound, Program Data, System, or Users containers.

Procedure

To create a computer account:

1. In Active Directory Users and Computers, in the console tree, right-click **Computers** or the container in which you want to add the computer, point to **New**, and then click **Computer**.

2. In the **New Object – Computer** dialog box, in the **Computer name** box, type the computer name.

3. Select the appropriate options, and then click **Next**.

4. In the **Managed** dialog box, click **Next**.

5. Click **Finish**.

Note   To perform this procedure, you must be a member of the Account Operators group, Domain Admins group, or the Enterprise Admins group in Active Directory, or you must be delegated the appropriate authority. As a security best practice, consider using **Run as** to perform this procedure.

Using a command line   To create a computer account by using **dsadd computer**:

1. Open a command prompt.

2. Type **dsadd computer** *ComputerDomainName* [**-samid** *SAMName*] [**-desc** *Description*] [**-loc** *Location*] [**-memberof** *GroupDomainName* ..] [{**-s** *Server* | **-d** *Domain*}] [**-u** *UserName*] [**-p** {*Password* | ***}] [**-q**] [{**-uc** | **-uco** | **-uci**}]

Note   For the complete syntax of the dsadd user command, at a command prompt, type **dsadd computer /?**.

Practice: Creating a Computer Account

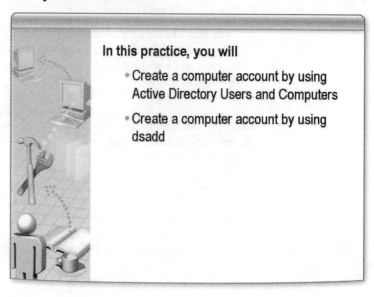

In this practice, you will

- Create a computer account by using Active Directory Users and Computers

- Create a computer account by using dsadd

Objective

In this practice, you will create computer accounts.

Instructions

Before you begin this practice:

- Log on to the domain by using the *ComputerName*User account.

- Open CustomMMC with the **Run as** command.

  Use the user account Nwtraders*ComputerName*Admin (Example: LondonAdmin).

- Ensure that CustomMMC contains Active Directory Users and Computers.

- Review the procedures in this lesson that describe how to perform this task.

Scenario

The systems engineers for Northwind Traders are testing some advanced features of Active Directory. Each member of your team must create five computer accounts in the IT Test organizational unit.

Practice: Creating a computer account

▶ **Create a computer account**

1. In Active Directory Users and Computers, expand **nwtraders.msft**, and then click the **IT Test** organizational unit.

2. Create a computer account with the following parameters:

   a. Computer name: *ComputerName***001**

   b. Computer name (pre-Windows 2000): *ComputerName***001**

3. Repeat step 2 for the following computer names: *ComputerName***002**, *ComputerName***003**, *ComputerName***004**

4. Close all windows.

Scenario

The systems engineers for Northwind Traders are testing some advanced features of Active Directory. Each member of your team must create five computer accounts in the IT Test organizational unit.

Practice: Using a command line

▶ **Create a computer account by using dsadd**

1. Click **Start**, click **Run**, and then type **runas /user:nwtraders***ComputerName***Admin cmd**

2. When prompted for the password, type **P@ssw0rd** and then press **ENTER**.

3. At the command prompt, type the following command:

   ```
   dsadd computer "cn=ComputerName005,ou=IT
   Test,dc=nwtraders,dc=msft"
   ```

Lesson: Modifying User and Computer Account Properties

- When to Modify User and Computer Account Properties
- Properties Associated with User Accounts
- Properties Associated with Computer Accounts
- How to Modify User and Computer Account Properties

Introduction

This lesson presents the skills and knowledge that you need to modify user and computer accounts.

Lesson objectives

After completing this lesson, you will be able to:

- Determine when to modify user and computer account properties.
- Describe properties associated with user accounts.
- Describe properties associated with computer accounts.
- Modify user and computer account properties.

When to Modify User and Computer Account Properties

Modify user account properties to:

- Make it easier to use search capabilities to find users
- Match a company's organizational hierarchy
- Determine the group membership of a user account

Modify computer account properties to:

- Assist in asset tracking (Location property)
- Document who manages a computer (Managed By property)

Introduction

As a systems administrator, you may be responsible for creating user and computer accounts in Active Directory. You also may be responsible for maintaining those user and computer accounts. To complete these tasks, you must be very familiar with the various properties for each user and computer account.

User account properties

It is critical that systems administrators are familiar with user account properties so that they can manage the network structure. Users may use the user account properties as a single source of information about users, like a telephone book, or to search for users based on items such as office location, supervisor, or department name. The systems administrator can use the properties of a user account to determine how the user account behaves in a terminal server session or how the user can gain access to the network through a dial-up connection.

Computer account properties

To maintain computer accounts, you must find the physical location of the computer. The most commonly used properties for computer accounts in Active Directory are the **Location** and **Managed by** properties. The **Location** property is useful, because you can document the computer's physical location in your network. The **Managed By** tab lists the individual responsible for the server. This can be useful when you have a data center with servers for different departments and you need to perform maintenance on the server. You can call or send e-mail to the person who is responsible for the server before you perform maintenance on the server.

Properties Associated with User Accounts

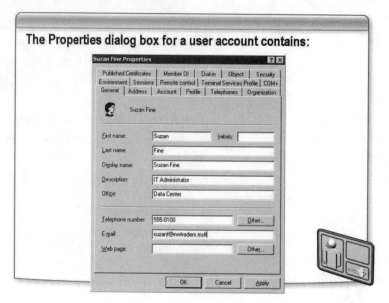

Introduction

The **Properties** dialog box for a user account contains information about each user account that is stored in Active Directory. The more complete the information in the **Properties** dialog box, the easier it is to search for users in Active Directory.

User account properties

The following table lists the most commonly used property options for user accounts.

Tab	Properties
General	Name, description, office location, telephone number, e-mail address, and home page information
Address	Street address, post office box, city, state or province, postal zip code, and country
Account	Logon name, account options, unlock account, and account expiration
Profile	Profile path and home folder
Telephone	Home, pager, mobile phone, fax, and IP telephone numbers
Organization	Title, department, manager, and direct reports
Member Of	Groups to which the user belongs
Dial-in	Remote access permissions, callback options, and static IP address and routes
Environment	One or more applications to start and the devices to connect to when a Terminal Services user logs on
Sessions	Terminal Services settings
Remote control	Terminal Services remote control settings
Terminal Services Profile	The user's Terminal Services profile

Properties Associated with Computer Accounts

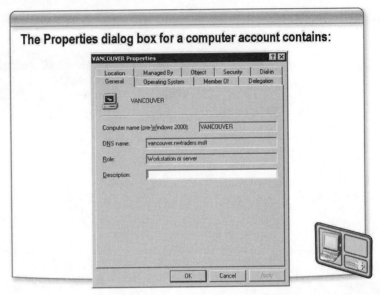

The Properties dialog box for a computer account contains:

Introduction

The **Properties** dialog box for a computer account contains unique information about each computer account that is stored in Active Directory. The more complete the information in the **Properties** dialog box, the easier it is to search for computers in Active Directory.

Computer account properties

The following table lists the most commonly used property options for computer accounts.

Tab	Properties
General	Computer name, DNS name, description, and role
Operating System	Name and version of the operating system running on the computer and the latest service pack installed
Member Of	The groups in the local domain and any groups to which the computer belongs
Location	The location of the computer
Managed By	Name, office location, street, city, state or province, country or region, telephone number, and fax number of the person that manages the computer
Object	The canonical name of the object, object class, the date it was created, the date it was last modified, and update sequence numbers (USNs)
Security	The users and groups who have permissions for the computer
Dial-in	Remote access permission, callback options, and routing options

How to Modify User and Computer Account Properties

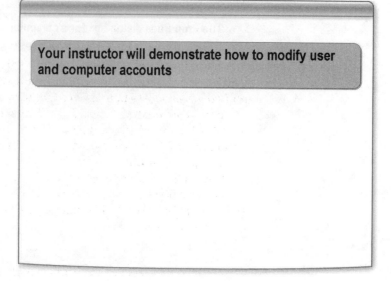

Your instructor will demonstrate how to modify user and computer accounts

Introduction

As a systems administrator, you must be able to modify user and computer account properties to manage the network efficiently.

Procedure

To modify user and computer accounts:

1. In Active Directory Users and Computers, in the console tree, navigate to the container that contains the user or computer account that you want to modify.

2. In the details pane, select the user or computer account that you want to modify, right-click the selection, and then click **Properties**.

3. In the **Properties** dialog box, modify the properties of the account as necessary.

Note To perform this procedure, you must be a member of the Account Operators, Domain Admins, or Enterprise Admins group in Active Directory, or you must be delegated the appropriate authority. As a security best practice, consider using **Run as** to perform this procedure.

Using a command line   You can use the **dsmod** command to modify attributes of one or more existing users or computers in Active Directory. To modify the attributes of a user account:

1. Open a command prompt.

2. For a user account, type **dsmod user** *UserDN* ... [**-upn** *UPN*] [**-fn** *FirstName*] [**-mi** *Initial*] [**-ln** *LastName*] [**-display** *DisplayName*] [**-empid** *EmployeeID*] [**-pwd** (*Password* | *)] [**-desc** *Description*] [**-office** *Office*] [**-tel** *PhoneNumber*] [**-email** *E-mailAddress*] [**-hometel** *HomePhoneNumber*] [**-pager** *PagerNumber*] [**-mobile** *CellPhoneNumber*] [**-fax** *FaxNumber*] [**-iptel** *IPPhoneNumber*] [**-webpg** *WebPage*] [**-title** *Title*] [**-dept** *Department*] [**-company** *Company*] [**-mgr** *Manager*] [**-hmdir** *HomeDirectory*] [**-hmdrv** *DriveLetter:*] [**-profile** *ProfilePath*] [**-loscr** *ScriptPath*] [**-mustchpwd** {yes | no}] [**-canchpwd** {yes | no}] [**-reversiblepwd** {yes | no}] [**-pwdneverexpires** {yes | no}] [**-acctexpires** *NumberOfDays*] [**-disabled** {yes | no}] [{**-s** *Server* | **-d** *Domain*}] [**-u** *UserName*] [**-p** {*Password* | *}] [**-c**] [**-q**] [{**-uc** | **-uco** | **-uci**}]

   –or–

   For a computer account, type **dsmod computer** *ComputerDN* ... [**-desc** *Description*] [**-loc** *Location*] [**-disabled** {yes | no}] [**-reset**] [{**-s** *Server* | **-d** *Domain*}] [**-u** *UserName*] [**-p** {*Password* | *}] [**-c**] [**-q**] [{**-uc** | **-uco** | **-uci**}]

Note   For the complete syntax of the dsmod command, at a command prompt, type **dsmod user /?** or **dsmod computer /?**.

Practice: Modifying User and Computer Account Properties

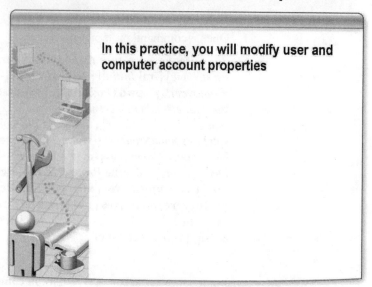

In this practice, you will modify user and computer account properties

Objective

In this practice, you will modify user and computer account properties.

Instructions

Before you begin this practice:

- Log on to the domain by using the *ComputerName*User account.

- Open CustomMMC with the **Run as** command.

  Use the user account Nwtraders*ComputerName*Admin (Example: LondonAdmin).

- Ensure that CustomMMC contains Active Directory Users and Computers.

- Review the procedures in this lesson that describe how to perform this task.

Scenario

The systems engineers for Northwind Traders are working on integrating Active Directory with the payroll system. You must create a user in the IT Test organizational unit and set user account properties that the payroll system will use to identify the user. Because this is a test account, you will not mandate the user to change the password. Also, because the systems engineers will use this account later, you should disable the account.

Practice: Modify user account properties

▶ **Create a user account**

- In Active Directory Users and Computers, create a user account with the following parameters:

  - First name: *ComputerName* (Example: London)

  - Last name: **Payroll**

  - Full name: *ComputerName* **Payroll** (Example: London Payroll)

  - User logon name: *ComputerName***Payroll** (Example: LondonPayroll)

  - User logon name [pre-Windows 2000]: *ComputerName***Payroll** (Example: LondonPayroll)

  - Password: **P@ssw0rd**

▶ **Modify the user account**

- In Active Directory Users and Computers, modify the following parameters of the *ComputerName*Payroll user account:

  - Description: **Account for AD and Payroll Test**

  - Office: **Payroll**

  - Telephone number: **973-555-0198**

  - E-mail: *ComputerName***Payroll@nwtraders.msft**

  - Title: **Payroll Test Account**

  - Department: **Payroll Test**

  - Company: **Payroll Test**

  - Manager: **User0002**

  - Home Telephone number: **555-0101**

Scenario

The systems engineers for Northwind Traders want to test your ability to track and search for computer assets by using the **Location** property of a computer account. You must create a computer account in the IT Test organizational unit and edit the **Location** property to match your city location.

Practice: Modifying computer account properties

▶ **Create a computer account**

- In Active Directory Users and Computers, create a computer account whose computer name is **Server***ComputerName* (Example: ServerLondon).

▶ **Modify the computer account**

- In Active Directory Users and Computers, change the **Location** property of the Server*ComputerName* computer account to *ComputerName*.

Scenario

The systems engineers for Northwind Traders are modifying user accounts with command-line tools. You must create a user and modify its properties.

Practice: Using a command line to modify user accounts

▶ **Add a user account**

- Using **dsadd**, add a user account with a user name of *ComputerName***Dsmod**.

  Example: dsadd user "cn=londonDsmod,ou=it test,dc=nwtraders,dc=msft"

► **Modify the user account**

- Using **dsmod**, modify the following parameters of the user account:

  - First name: *ComputerName*

  - Last name: **Dsmod**

  - Full name: *ComputerName* **Dsmod**

  - User logon name: *ComputerName***Dsmod**

  - Password: **P@ssw0rd**

  - Description: **Account for AD and Dsmod Test**

  - Office: **DataCenter**

  - Telephone number: **555-0101**

  - E-mail: *ComputerName***Dsmod@nwtraders.msft**

  - Title: **Dsmod Test Account**

  - Department: **Data Center**

  - Company: **NWTraders**

  - Home Telephone number: **555-0101**

  Example: dsmod user "cn=Londondsmod,ou=it test,dc=nwtraders,dc=msft" -upn Londondsmod@nwtraders.msft -fn London -ln dsmod -display Londondsmod -office DataCenter -tel 555-0101 -title Title ITAdmin -dept DataCenter -company NWTraders -hometel 555-0101

Scenario

The systems engineers for Northwind Traders want to test your ability to track and search for computer assets by using the **Location** property of the Active Directory computer account. You need to create a computer account in the IT Test organizational unit and edit the **Location** property to match your city location.

Practice: Using a command line to modify computer accounts

► **Add a computer account**

1. Click **Start**, click **Run**, and then type **runas /user:nwtraders***ComputerName***Admin cmd**

2. When prompted for the password, type **P@ssw0rd** and then press **ENTER**.

3. In the command prompt, using **dsadd**, add a computer account with the following parameters:

   - Computer name: **dsmod***ComputerName*

   - Organizational unit: IT Test

Example: dsadd computer "cn=dsmodlondon,ou=it test,dc=nwtraders,dc=msft"

► **Modify the location attribute for a computer account**

- Using **dsmod**, modify the computer account **dsmod***ComputerName* with the following attribute:

  - Location: *ComputerName*

Example: dsmod computer "cn=serverlondon,ou=it test,dc=nwtraders,dc=msft" -loc London

Lesson: Creating a User Account Template

- What Is a User Account Template?
- What Properties Are in a Template?
- Guidelines for Creating User Account Templates
- How to Create a User Account Template

Introduction

The information in this lesson presents the skills and knowledge that you need to create a user account template.

Lesson objectives

After completing this lesson, you will be able to:

- Explain the purpose of a user account template.
- Describe the properties of a user account template.
- Create a user account template.

What Is a User Account Template?

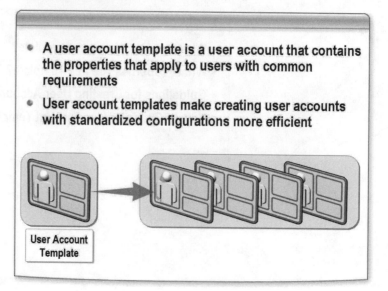

- A user account template is a user account that contains the properties that apply to users with common requirements

- User account templates make creating user accounts with standardized configurations more efficient

User Account
Template

Definition

You can simplify the process of creating domain user accounts by creating a user account template. A user account template is an account that has commonly used settings and properties already configured.

Using account templates

For each new user account, you only need to add the information that is unique to that user account. For example, if all sales personnel must be a member of 15 sales groups and have the same manager, you can create a template that includes membership to all the groups and the reporting manager. When the template is copied for a new salesperson, it retains the group memberships and manager that were in the template.

What Properties Are in a Template?

Tab	Properties copied
Address	All properties except **Street Address**
Account	All properties except **Logon Name**
Profile	All properties, except **Profile path** and **Home folder**, reflect new user's logon name
Organization	All properties except **Title**
Member Of	All properties

Properties

There are numerous properties associated with each account. However, only a limited number of properties can be copied in a template. The following table lists the user properties that can be copied from an existing domain user account to a new domain user account.

Properties tab	Properties copied to new domain user account
Address	All properties, except **Street Address**, are copied.
Account	All properties, except **Logon Name**, which is copied from the **Copy Object – User** dialog box, are copied.
Profile	All properties, except the **Profile path** and **Home folder** entries, are modified to reflect the new user's logon name.
Organization	All properties, except **Title**, are copied.
Member Of	All properties are copied.

Additional reading

For more information about profiles, see article 324749, "HOW TO: Create a Roaming User Profile in Windows Server 2003" in the Microsoft Knowledge Base at http://support.microsoft.com/?kbid=324749.

Form more information about home folders, see article 325853, "HOW TO: Use Older Roaming User Profiles with Windows Server 2003" in the Microsoft Knowledge Base at http://support.microsoft.com/?kbid=325853.

Guidelines for Creating User Account Templates

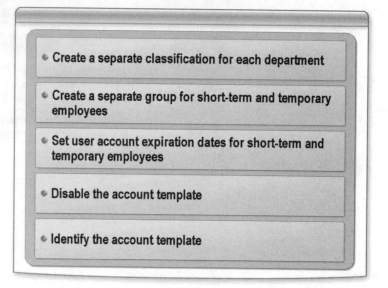

Guidelines

Consider the following best practices for creating user account templates:

- Create a separate classification for each department in your business group.
- Create a separate group for short-term and temporary employees with logon and workstation restrictions.
- Set user account expiration dates for short-term and temporary employees to prevent them from accessing the network when their contracts expire.
- Disable the account template.
- Identify the account template. For example, place a T_ before the name of the account to identify the account as an account template.

How to Create a User Account Template

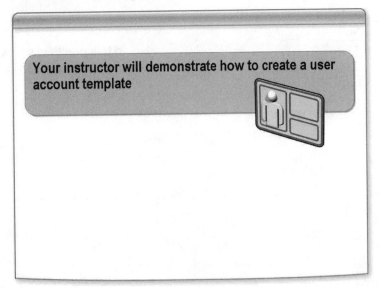

Introduction

To create an account that you can use as a template, you create a user account, configure the settings that you want, disable the account, and then copy the account when you need to create a new user.

Procedure

To create a new user account template:

1. Create a new domain user account, or copy an existing domain user account.

2. Type the user name and user logon name information for the new user account, and then click **Next**.

3. Type and confirm the password, set the password requirements, select the **Account is disabled** check box, if necessary, and then click **Next**.

4. Verify the new user account information, and then click **Finish**.

Practice: Creating a User Account Template

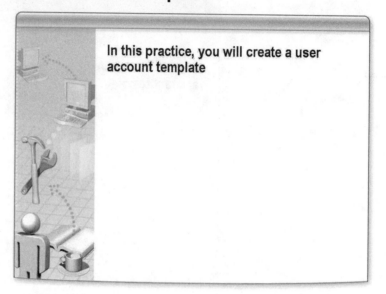

In this practice, you will create a user account template

Objective

In this practice, you will create and copy a user account template.

Instructions

Before you begin this practice:

- Log on to the domain by using the *ComputerName*User account.
- Open CustomMMC with the **Run as** command.

    Use the user account Nwtraders*ComputerName*Admin (Example: LondonAdmin).

- Ensure that CustomMMC contains Active Directory Users and Computers.
- Review the procedures in this lesson that describe how to perform this task.

Scenario

Your manager asks you to research the values to be copied from an account template. You must create an account template with the following parameters, copy the account to a user account, and document the variables that were copied and the variables that were not copied.

Practice: creating a user account template

▶ **Create a user account template**

- Create a user account template with the following parameters.

Parameter	Properties	Example
First name	*ComputerName*	London
Last name	**Template**	
Full name	*ComputerName* **Template**	London Template
User logon name	_*ComputerName***Template**	_LondonTemplate
Password	**P@ssw0rd**	

► **Modify the user account template**

- Modify the following parameters of the *ComputerName*Template user account.

Parameter	Properties	Example
Description	**Telemarketing User**	
Office	**Telemarketing**	
Telephone number	**555-1000**	
E-mail	*ComputerName***Template@ nwtraders.msft**	LondonTemplate@ nwtraders.msft
City	**Redmond**	
Street	**One Microsoft Way**	
State	**Washington**	
Zip	**98052**	
Country/region	**United States**	
Home Telephone number	**555-0101**	
Title	**Telemarketing User**	
Department	**Telemarketing**	
Company	**NWTraders**	
Manager	**User 0001**	
Member (group membership)	**G NWTraders Telemarketing Personnel**	
Account is disabled		

Scenario

You must create accounts for the Telemarketing team at Northwind Traders. The Telemarketing team has a high turnover of employees. For security reasons, Northwind Traders does not want to rename and reuse user accounts. You must create a user account template that meets the needs of the Telemarketing team.

Practice: copying a user account template

► **Copy the user account template**

- Copy the *ComputerName*Template account that has the following parameters.

Parameter	Properties	Example
First name	*ComputerName*	London
Last name	**User**	
Full name	*ComputerName* **User**	London User
User logon name	*ComputerName***Template**	LondonTemplate
Password	**P@ssw0rd**	

Lesson: Enabling and Unlocking User and Computer Accounts

- Why Enable and Disable User and Computer Accounts?
- How to Enable and Disable User and Computer Accounts
- What Are Locked-out User Accounts?
- How to Unlock User Accounts

Introduction

The information in this lesson presents the skills and knowledge that you need to enable and disable user and computer accounts.

Lesson objectives

After completing this lesson, you will be able to:

- Explain why you enable and disable user and computer accounts.
- Enable and disable user and computer accounts.
- Explain how user accounts can become locked-out.
- Unlock user accounts.

Why Enable or Disable User and Computer Accounts?

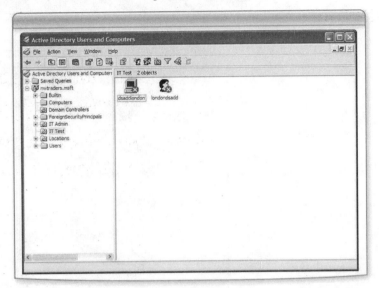

Introduction

After creating user accounts, you perform frequent administrative tasks to ensure that the network continues to meet the organization's needs. These administrative tasks include enabling and disabling user and computer accounts. When you enable or disable an account, you give or restrict access to the account.

Scenarios for enabling and disabling accounts

To provide a secure network environment, a systems administrator must disable user accounts when users do not need their accounts for an extended period, but need to use them later. The following are examples of when you need to enable or disable user accounts:

- If the user takes a two-month leave of absence from work, you disable the account when the user leaves and then enable the account when the user returns.

- When you add accounts in the network that will be used in the future or for security purposes, you disable the accounts until they are needed.

- Disable an account when you do not want users to be authenticated from a shared computer.

How to Enable and Disable User and Computer Accounts

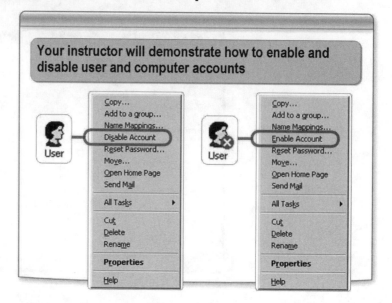

Introduction

When an account is disabled, the user cannot log on. The account appears in the details pane with an X on the account icon.

Procedure

To enable and disable a user or computer account by using Active Directory Users and Computers:

1. In Active Directory Users and Computers, in the console tree, select the container or the user that contains the account to be enabled or disabled.

2. In the details pane, right-click the user account.

3. To disable, click **Disable Account**.

4. To enable, click **Enable Account**.

To disable or enable a local user account by using Computer Management:

1. In Computer Management, expand **System Tools**.

2. In System Tools, expand **Local Users and Groups**, and then click **Users**.

3. Right-click the user account, and then click **Properties**.

4. In the **Properties** dialog box, to disable, select the **Account is Disabled** check box, and then click **OK**.

5. To enable, clear the **Account is Disabled** check box.

Note   To enable and disable user and computer accounts, you must be a member of the Account Operators group, Domain Admins group, or the Enterprise Admins group in Active Directory, or you must be delegated the appropriate authority. As a security best practice, consider using **Run as** to perform this procedure.

Using a command line

You can also enable or disable accounts by using the **dsmod** command. As a security best practice, consider using **runas** to perform this procedure.

To enable or disable accounts by using **dsmod**:

1. Open a command prompt with the **runas** command.

2. Type **dsmod user** *UserDN* **-disabled {yes|no}**

Value	Description
UserDN	Specifies the distinguished name of the user object to be disabled or enabled
{**yes**|**no**}	Specifies whether the user account is disabled for log on (**yes**) or enabled (**no**)

What Are Locked-out User Accounts?

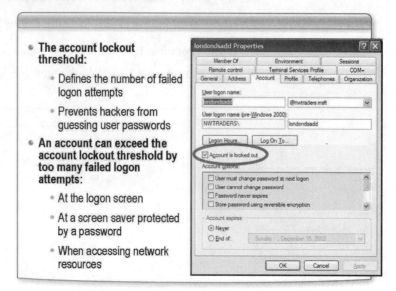

- **The account lockout threshold:**
  - Defines the number of failed logon attempts
  - Prevents hackers from guessing user passwords
- **An account can exceed the account lockout threshold by too many failed logon attempts:**
  - At the logon screen
  - At a screen saver protected by a password
  - When accessing network resources

Introduction

A user account is locked out because the account has exceeded the account lockout threshold for a domain. This may be because the user has attempted to access the account with an incorrect password too many times or because a computer hacker has attempted to guess users' passwords and invoked the lockout policy on the account.

Account lockout threshold

Authorized users can lock themselves out of an account by mistyping or forgetting their password or by changing their password on a computer while they are logged on to another computer. The computer with the incorrect password continuously tries to authenticate the user. Because the password it is using to authenticate is incorrect, the user account is eventually locked out.

A security setting in Active Directory determines the number of failed logon attempts that causes a user to be locked out. A user cannot use a locked-out account until an administrator resets the account or until the lockout duration for the account expires. When a user account is locked out, an error message appears, and the user is not allowed any further logon attempts.

What is a failed logon attempt?

A user can be locked out of an account if there are too many failed password attempts. Failed password attempts happen when:

- A user logs on at the logon screen and supplies a bad password.

- A user logs on with a local account and supplies a domain user account and a bad password while accessing network resources.

- A user logs on with a local account and supplies a domain user account and a bad password while accessing resources with the **runas** command.

By default, domain account lockout attempts are not recorded when unlocking a workstation (using a password protected screen saver). You can change this behavior by modifying the **Interactive logon: Require Domain controller authentication to unlock workstation** Group Policy setting.

How to Unlock User Accounts

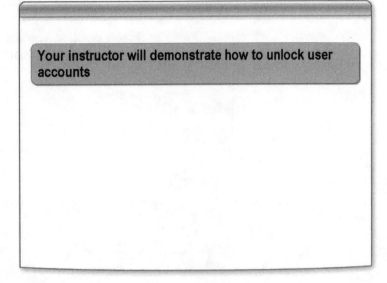

Introduction

After an account is locked out, you must unlock the account to maintain and manage the account.

Procedure

To unlock an account:

1. In Active Directory Users and Computers, in the console tree, select the organizational unit that contains the user account that you want to unlock.

2. In the details pane, select the user account you want to unlock.

3. Right-click the selected account and then click **Unlock**.

Practice: Enabling and Disabling User and Computer Accounts

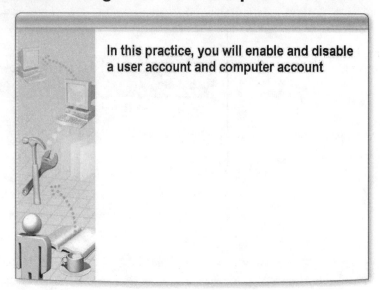

Objective

In this exercise, you will disable and enable a user account and a computer account.

Instructions

Before you begin this practice:

- Log on to the domain by using the *ComputerName*User account.
- Open CustomMMC with the **Run as** command.

    Use the user account Nwtraders*ComputerName*Admin (Example: LondonAdmin).

- Ensure that CustomMMC contains Active Directory Users and Computers.
- Review the procedures in this lesson that describe how to perform this task.

Scenario

The security policy of Northwind Traders states that the user accounts of employees going on extended leave must be disabled for the duration of their leave. This is one of your job tasks. You must create an account in the IT Test organizational unit, disable the account, and log on as the user to verify that the account is disabled.

Practice: Disabling a user account

▶ **Create a disabled user account**

- Create a user account with the following parameters:
    - Organizational Unit: **IT Test**
    - User name: *ComputerName***Disabled**
    - Password: **P@ssw0rd**
    - The account is disabled

▶ **Test the disabled user account**

- Try to log on as the new user to verify that you cannot log on.

Scenario

You have just disabled a user account and verified that the user cannot log on. You want to verify that there are no other problems with the account, so you must enable the user account and log on to verify that the user account is activated.

Practice: Enabling a user account

▶ **Enable the user account**

- Enable the user account that has the following parameters:
    - Organizational unit: IT Test
    - User name: *ComputerName*Disabled

▶ **Test the enabled user account**

1. Log on with the *ComputerName*Disabled user account to verify that you can log on.

2. Log on with a password of P@ssw0rd.

Scenario

A systems engineer is concerned that an unauthorized user is attempting to use a kiosk computer after business hours. The systems engineer asks you to disable the computer account until they can look at the log files on the computer. You must disable the computer account.

Practice: Disabling a computer account

▶ **Create a disabled computer account**

- Create a disabled computer account with the following parameters:
    - Organizational unit: IT Test
    - Computer name: *ComputerName***Kiosk**
    - The account is disabled

Scenario

The systems engineer discovers that the nightly security guard was trying to log on to the kiosk computer without a domain account. The security guard has been notified that they should not attempt to log on to the kiosk computer. The systems engineer wants you to enable the kiosk computer for your city location.

Practice: Enabling a computer account

▶ **Enable the computer account**

- Enable the computer account that has the following parameters:
    - Organizational unit: IT Test
    - Computer name: *ComputerName*Kiosk

Practice: Using a command line

▶ **Disable a user account by using dsmod**

- Disable a user account in the IT Test organizational unit by using **dsmod**.

    Example: Dsmod user "cn=London user,ou=it test,dc=nwtraders,dc=msft" -disabled yes

▶ **Enable a user account by using dsmod**

- Enable a user account in the IT Test organizational unit by using **dsmod**.

    Example: Dsmod user "cn=London user,ou=it test,dc=nwtraders,dc=msft" -disabled no

Lesson: Resetting User and Computer Accounts

- When to Reset Passwords
- How to Reset Passwords
- When to Reset Computer Accounts
- How to Reset Computer Accounts

Introduction

Resetting passwords and accounts are common administrative tasks. Be aware of the impact of performing these procedures.

Lesson objectives

After completing this lesson, you will be able to:

- Explain the situations that require you to reset passwords and the potential data loss resulting from resetting passwords.
- Reset passwords for domain and local accounts.
- Determine when to reset computer accounts.
- Reset computer accounts.

When to Reset User Passwords

- **Reset a password when a user forgets his or her password**
- **After resetting a password, a user can no longer access some types of information, including:**
  - E-mail that is encrypted with the user's public key
  - Internet passwords that are saved on the computer
  - Files that the user has encrypted

Introduction

People occasionally forget their passwords. Without their passwords, these people cannot access their user accounts. Administrators can reset users' passwords so that users can access their accounts again. Before attempting to reset local or domain passwords, verify that you have the appropriate level of authority.

Consequences of resetting passwords

After a user's password is reset, some types of information are no longer accessible, including the following:

- E-mail that is encrypted with the user's public key
- Internet passwords that are saved on the computer
- Files that the user has encrypted

Additional reading

For more information about resetting a domain controller account and resetting a computer account with a script, see article 325850, "HOW TO: Use Netdom.exe to Reset Machine Account Passwords of a Windows Server 2003 Domain Controller," in the Microsoft Knowledge Base at: http://support.microsoft.com/?kbid=325850.

For more information about how Windows data protection API handles stored passwords, see "Windows Data Protection" at http://msdn.microsoft.com/library/default.asp?url=/library/en-us/dnsecure/html/windataprotection-dpapi.asp.

How to Reset User Passwords

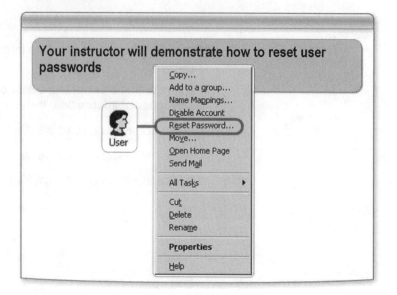

Introduction

When you need to reset a user password, you must remember that only local administrators are authorized to reset local user passwords and that only domain administrators are authorized to reset domain user passwords.

Procedure for resetting local user passwords

To reset local user passwords:

1. In Computer Management, in the console tree, double-click **Local Users and Groups**, and then click **Users**.

2. In the details pane, right-click the user name, and then click **Set Password**.

3. Read the warning message. If you want to continue, click **Proceed**.

4. In the **New password** and **Confirm password** boxes, type the new password, and then click **OK**.

Procedure for resetting domain user passwords

To reset domain user passwords:

1. In Active Directory Users and Computers, in the console tree, click **Users**.

2. In the details pane, right-click the user name, and then click **Reset Password**.

3. In the **New Password** and **Confirm New Password** boxes, type a new password, and then click **OK**.

When to Reset Computer Accounts

Reset computer accounts when:

- Computers fail to authenticate to the domain
- Passwords need to be synchronized

Introduction

As a systems administrator, you occasionally need to reset computer accounts. For example, suppose your network went through a full backup seven days ago. The computer relayed information to the domain controller that changed the password on the computer account. However, the computer's hard drive crashed, and the computer was restored from tape backup. The computer now has an outdated password, and the user cannot log on because the computer cannot authenticate to the domain. You now need to reset the computer account.

Considerations

There are two items that you must consider before resetting the computer account:

- To perform this procedure, you must be a member of the Account Operators group, Domain Admins group, or the Enterprise Admins group in Active Directory, or you must be delegated the appropriate authority. As a security best practice, consider using **Run as** to perform this procedure.

- When you reset a computer account, you break the computer's connection to the domain, and you must rejoin it to the domain.

How to Reset Computer Accounts

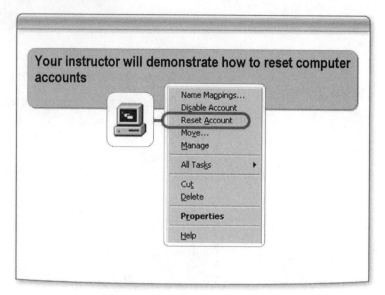

Introduction

To perform this procedure, you must be a member of the Account Operators group, Domain Admins group, or the Enterprise Admins group in Active Directory, or you must be delegated the appropriate authority. As a security best practice, consider using **Run as** to perform this procedure.

Procedure

To reset computer accounts:

1. In Active Directory Users and Computers, in the console tree, click **Computers** or the container that contains the computer that you want to reset.

2. In the details pane, right-click the computer, and then click **Reset Account**.

Using a command line

You can use the **dsmod** command to reset computer accounts. As a security best practice, consider using **runas** to perform this procedure.

1. Open a command prompt by using the **runas** command.

2. Type **dsmod computer** *ComputerDN* **–reset**

Value	Description
ComputerDN	Specifies the distinguished names of one or more computer objects that you want to reset

Practice: Resetting a User Account Password

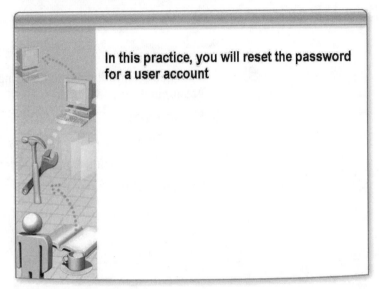

In this practice, you will reset the password for a user account

Objective

In this practice, you will reset a user account so that the user can log on to the domain.

Instructions

Before you begin this practice:

- Log on to the domain by using the *ComputerName*User account.
- Open CustomMMC with the **Run as** command.

  Use the user account Nwtraders*ComputerName*Admin (Example: LondonAdmin).

- Ensure that CustomMMC contains Active Directory Users and Computers.
- Review the procedures in this lesson that describe how to perform this task.

Scenario

You are notified that a user in your city recently forgot their password. You have followed company policy and verified the user is who they say they are. You must reset the password on their account and make them change their password at next logon.

Practice

▶ **Reset the user account**

1. In Active Directory Users and Computer, find the *ComputerName*User account in the Users organizational unit.

2. Reset the password to **P@ssw0rd1** and make the user change the password at next logon.

3. Close all programs and log off.

▶ **Test the new password**

1. Log on as *ComputerName*User with a password of P@ssw0rd1.

2. Change the password to **P@ssword2**

Lesson: Locating User and Computer Accounts in Active Directory

- Multimedia: Introduction to Locating User and Computer Accounts in Active Directory
- Search Types
- How to Search for Active Directory Objects
- How to Search Using Common Queries
- Using a Custom Query

Introduction

The information in this lesson presents the skills and knowledge that you need to use common and custom queries.

Lesson objectives

After completing this lesson, you will be able to:

- Explain the criteria for locating a user or computer account.
- Describe the types of common queries.
- Explain the uses of custom queries.
- Locate user and computer accounts in Active Directory.

Multimedia: Introduction to Locating User and Computer Accounts in Active Directory

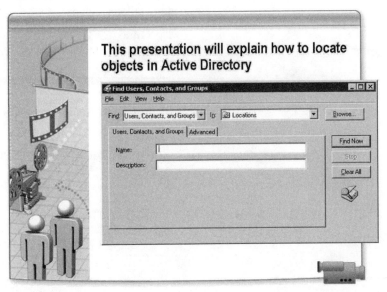

File location

To view the *Introduction to Locating User and Computer Accounts in Active Directory* presentation, open the Web page on the Student Materials compact disc, click **Multimedia**, and then click the title of the presentation. Do not open this presentation unless the instructor tells you to.

Search Types

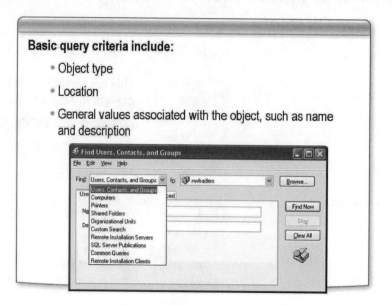

Basic query criteria include:

- Object type
- Location
- General values associated with the object, such as name and description

Introduction

Because all user accounts reside in Active Directory, administrators can search for the user account that they administer. By searching Active Directory for user accounts, you do not need to browse through hundreds or thousands of user accounts in Active Directory Users and Computers.

In addition to searching for user accounts, you can also search for other Active Directory objects, such as computers, printers, and shared folders. After locating these objects, you can administer these objects from the **Search Results** box.

Administering objects from Search Results

After a successful search, the results are displayed, and you can then perform administrative functions on the found objects. The administrative functions that are available depend on the type of object you find. For example, if you search for user accounts, you can rename and delete the user account, disable the user account, reset the password, move the user account to another organizational unit, or modify the user account's properties.

To administer an object from the **Search Results** box, right-click the object and select an action from the menu.

Find Users, Contacts and Groups

Active Directory provides information about all objects on a network, which includes people, groups, computers, printers, shared folders, and organizational units. It is easy to search for users, contacts, and groups by using the **Find Users, Contacts, and Groups** dialog box.

Find Computers

Use **Find Computers** to search for computers in Active Directory by using criteria such as the name assigned to the computer or the operating system on which the computer runs. After you find the computer you want, you can manage it by right-clicking the computer in the **Search Results** box, and then clicking **Manage**.

Find Printers

When a shared printer is published in Active Directory, you can use **Find Printers** to search for it by using criteria such as its asset number, the printer language it uses, or whether it supports double-sided printing. After you find the printer you want, you can easily connect to it by right-clicking the printer in the **Search Results** box, and then clicking **Connect**, or by double-clicking the printer.

Find Shared Folders

When a shared folder is published in Active Directory, you can use **Find Shared Folders** to search for it by using criteria such as keywords assigned to it, the name of the folder, or the name of the person managing the folder. After you find the folder you want, you can open Windows Explorer to view the files located in the folder by right-clicking the folder in the **Search Results** box, and then clicking **Explore**.

Find Custom Search

In Active Directory, you can search for familiar objects such as computers, printers, and users. You can also search for other objects, such as a specific organizational unit or certificate template. Use **Find Custom Search** to build custom search queries by using advanced search options or build advanced search queries by using LDAP, which is the primary access protocol for Active Directory.

Find Common Queries

You can use **Find Common Queries** to perform common administrative queries in Active Directory. For example, you can quickly search for user or computer accounts that have been disabled.

Advanced query options

For each search option except **Find Common Queries**, there is an **Advanced** tab that you can use to create a more detailed search. For example, you can search for all users in a city or zip code from the **Advanced** tab.

Additional reading

For more information about searching Active Directory see "Search Companion overview" at http://www.microsoft.com/technet/treeview/default.asp?url=/technet/prodtechnol/windowsserver2003/proddocs/server/find_overview.asp.

How to Search for Active Directory Objects

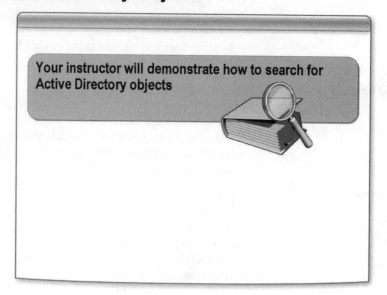

Your instructor will demonstrate how to search for Active Directory objects

Introduction

To perform administrative tasks on a user or computer account, you must first find the account in Active Directory. This may be difficult if your Active Directory structure is large.

Procedure

To find a user account:

1. Open Active Directory Users and Computers.

2. To search the entire domain, in the console tree, right-click the domain node, and then click **Find**.

   If you know which organizational unit the user is in, right-click the organizational unit, and then click **Find**.

3. In the **Find Users, Contacts, and Groups** dialog box, in the **Name** box, type the name of the user you want to find.

4. Click **Find Now**.

Using a command line

You can use the **dsquery** command to find users and computers in Active Directory that match the specified search criteria. If the predefined search criteria in this command are insufficient, use the more general version of the command, **dsquery ***.

To search for a user by using **dsquery**:

- In a command prompt, type the following:

  dsquery user [{*StartNode* | **forestroot** | **domainroot**}] [**-o** {**dn** | **rdn** | **upn** | **samid**}] [**-scope** {**subtree** | **onelevel** | **base**}] [**-name** *Name*] [**-desc** *Description*] [**-upn** *UPN*] [**-samid** *SAMName*] [**-inactive** *NumberOfWeeks*] [**-stalepwd** *NumberOfDays*] [**-disabled**] [{**-s** *Server* | **-d** *Domain*}] [**-u** *UserName*] [**-p** {*Password* | *****}] [**-q**] [**-r**] [**-gc**] [**-limit** *NumberOfObjects*] [{**-uc** | **-uco** | **-uci**}]

To search for a computer by using **dsquery**:

- In a command prompt, type the following:

  dsquery computer [{*StartNode* | **forestroot** | **domainroot**}] [**-o** {**dn** | **rdn** | **samid**}] [**-scope** {**subtree** | **onelevel** | **base**}] [**-name** *Name*] [**-desc** *Description*] [**-samid** *SAMName*] [**-inactive** *NumberOfWeeks*] [**-stalepwd** *NumberOfDays*] [**-disabled**] [{**-s** *Server* | **-d** *Domain*}] [**-u** *UserName*] [**-p** {*Password* | *****}] [**-q**] [**-r**] [**-gc**] [**-limit** *NumberOfObjects*] [{**-uc** | **-uco** | **-uci**}]

How to Search Using Common Queries

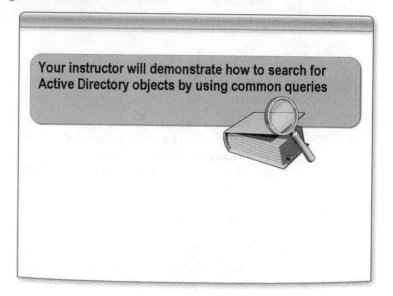

Introduction

The search functionality is one of the key features of Active Directory. A search operation enables you to find objects in Active Directory based on selection criteria and to retrieve specified properties for the objects that you find.

Procedure

To start a basic search operation:

1. In Active Directory Users and Computers, on the **Action** menu, click **Find**.

2. In the **Find Users, Contacts, and Groups** dialog box, in the **Find** box, select the type of object for which you want to search.

3. Enter the search text in the search criteria boxes.

   The types of search criteria that are available vary depending on the type of object that you selected.

Using a Custom Query

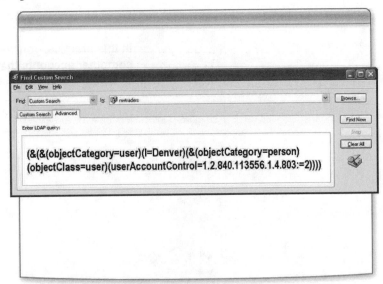

Introduction

In Active Directory, you can search for familiar objects, such as computers, printers, and users, and you can also search for other objects, such as a specific organizational units or certificate templates.

Custom Search

Use the **Find Custom Search** dialog box to build custom search queries using advanced search options and to build advanced search queries by using LDAP, which is the primary access protocol for Active Directory.

The LDAP query on the slide includes the following items:

- **l=Denver**

  The **l** is the city property or location attribute for a user account.

- **(ObjectClass=user)(ObjectCategory=person)**

  To query for a user, the query must contain the **(&(objectClass=user)(objectCategory=person))** search expression. This is because the computer class is a subclass of the user class. A query containing only **(objectClass=user)** returns user objects and computer objects.

- **UserAccountControl:**1.2.840.113556.1.4.803:=2

  This specifies the flags that control the password, lockout option, disable or enable option, script, and home directory behavior for the user. This property also contains a flag that indicates the account type of the object. The flag used here is for disabled accounts.

Additional reading

For more information about LDAP language, see "Listing Properties to Retrieve for Each Object Found" at http://msdn.microsoft.com/library/default.asp?url=/library/en-us/netdir/ad/listing_properties_to_retrieve_for_each_object_found.asp.

Practice: Locating User and Computer Accounts

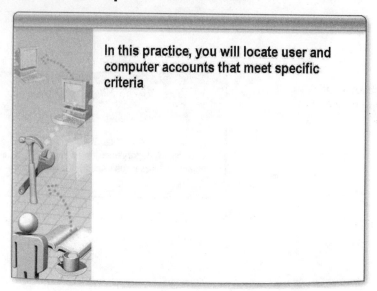

In this practice, you will locate user and computer accounts that meet specific criteria

Objective

In this exercise, you will locate:

- User accounts by name.
- Computer accounts by name.
- Disabled accounts.
- Computer accounts by city.
- User and computer accounts by using **dsquery**.

Instructions

Before you begin this practice:

- Log on to the domain by using the *ComputerName*User account.
- Open CustomMMC with the **Run as** command.

  Use the user account Nwtraders*ComputerName*Admin (Example: LondonAdmin).

- Ensure that CustomMMC contains Active Directory Users and Computers.
- Review the procedures in this lesson that describe how to perform this task.

Scenario

The systems engineers are bulk importing user accounts into the Users container. They need you to verify that all Sales Manager user accounts were successfully imported into Active Directory.

Practice: locating user accounts by name

▶ **Locate user accounts by name**

- Locate user accounts:
  - In the Users container in the NWTraders domain.
  - With a description of Sales Manager.

  Your search should produce approximately 24 Sales Manager user accounts.

Scenario

The systems engineers are bulk importing computer accounts into the Computers container. They need you to verify that all computer accounts from your city location were successfully imported into Active Directory. The naming convention used to bulk import computer accounts is the first three to four letters of the city location, followed by **Computer** and an incremental number, for example, CasaComputer2005.

Practice: locating computer accounts by name

▶ **Locate computer accounts by name**

- Locate a computer account:
  - In the Computers container in the NWTraders domain.
  - With a computer name that is the first three letters of your city location.

  Your search should produce approximately 101 computer accounts.

Scenario

The systems engineers are bulk importing computer accounts into the Computers container. They need you to verify that all computer accounts from your city location have been successfully imported into Active Directory. The naming convention used to bulk import computer accounts is to use the first three to four letters of the city location, followed by **Computer** and an incremental number, for example, CasaComputer2005.

Practice: locating disabled accounts

▶ **Locate disabled accounts**

- Locate user accounts:
  - In the NWTraders domain.
  - With a description that starts with Sales.
  - That are disabled (*Do not enable the accounts*).

  Your search should produce approximately 240 disabled user accounts.

Scenario

The systems engineers are bulk importing computer accounts into the Computers container. They need you to verify that all computer accounts from your city location were successfully imported into Active Directory. The naming convention used to bulk import computer accounts is to use the first three to four letters of the city location, followed by **Computer** and an incremental number, for example, CasaComputer2005.

Practice: locating computer accounts by city

▶ **Locate computer accounts by city**

- Locate computer accounts:
  - In the Computers container in the NWTraders domain.
  - With a computer name that is the first three letters of your city location.

  Your search should produce approximately 101 computer accounts.

Practice: locating user and computer accounts by using dsquery

▶ **Locate all users with the first name of user**

- From a command prompt, type **Dsquery user –name user***

▶ **Locate all computers with the first 3 letters lon**

- From a command prompt, type **Dsquery computer –name lon***

Lesson: Saving Queries

- What Is a Saved Query?
- How to Create a Saved Query

Introduction

You can use saved queries to quickly and consistently access a common set of Active Directory objects that you want to perform specific tasks on or monitor.

Lesson objectives

After completing this lesson, you will be able to:

- Explain what a saved query is.
- Create a saved query.

What Is a Saved Query?

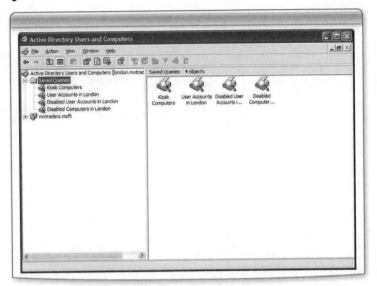

Introduction

Active Directory Users and Computers has a Saved Queries folder in which you can create, edit, save, and organize saved queries. Before saved queries, administrators were required to create custom Active Directory Services Interfaces (ADSI) scripts that performed a query on common objects. This was an often lengthy process that required knowledge of how ADSI uses LDAP search filters to resolve a query.

Definition

Saved queries use predefined LDAP strings to search only the specified domain partition. You can narrow searches to a single container object. You can also create a customized saved query that contains an LDAP search filter.

All queries are located in the Saved Queries folder called dsa.msc, which is stored in Active Directory Users and Computers. After you successfully create your customized set of queries, you can copy the .msc file to other Windows Server 2003 domain controllers that are in the same domain and reuse the same set of saved queries. You can also export saved queries to an Extensible Markup Language (XML) file. You can then import them into other Active Directory Users and Computers consoles located on Windows Server 2003 domain controllers that are in the same domain.

Additional Reading

For more information about saved queries see "Using saved queries" at: http://www.microsoft.com/technet/treeview/default.asp?url=/technet/ prodtechnol/windowsserver2003/proddocs/server/usingsavedqueries.asp.

How to Create a Saved Query

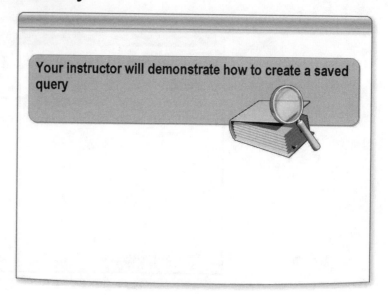

Introduction

You can save queries to search for disabled user or computer accounts, number of days since the last user logon, users with passwords that do not expire, and many other commonly used queries. After a saved query is executed and the desired objects are displayed, you can then modify each object directly in the **Query results** box.

Procedure

To create a saved query:

1. In Active Directory Users and Computers, in the console tree, right-click **Saved Queries** or any of its subfolders in which you want to save a query, point to **New**, and then click **Query**.

2. In the **New Query** dialog box, in the **Name** box , type a query name.

3. In the **Description** box, type a query description.

4. Click **Browse** to define the container from which to begin your search.

5. To search all subcontainers of the selected container, select the **Include subcontainers** check box.

6. Click **Define Query** to define your query.

Practice: Creating Saved Queries

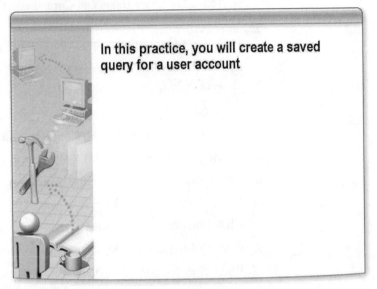

In this practice, you will create a saved query for a user account

Objectives

In this practice, you will create a saved query for a user account.

Instructions

Before you begin this practice:

- Log on to the domain by using the *ComputerName*User account.

- Open CustomMMC with the **Run as** command.

  Use the user account Nwtraders*ComputerName*Admin (Example: LondonAdmin).

- Ensure that CustomMMC contains Active Directory Users and Computers.

- Review the procedures in this lesson that describe how to perform this task.

Scenario

You discover that you often search for the same information. You want to save searches for future use. Create a saved query for a user account. The saved query must have the following properties:

- The saved query is named *ComputerName* User Account.

- The saved query is saved in the Users container in the NWTraders domain.

- The City value equals your computer name that equals your computer name.

Practice

▶ **Create a saved query**

1. In Active Directory Users and Computers, right-click **Saved Queries**, click **New**, and then click **Query**.

2. In the **New Query** dialog box, create a query with the following parameters:

   • Name: *ComputerName* **User Accounts**

   • Description: *ComputerName* **User Accounts**

3. Click **Define Query**.

4. In the **Find** box, click **Users, Contacts, and Groups**.

5. On the **Advanced** tab, click **Field**, point to **User**, and then click **City**.

6. Verify that **Starts with** is in the **Condition** box.

7. In the **Value** box, type *ComputerName* and then click **Add**.

8. Click **OK** to close the **Find Users, Contacts, and Groups** dialog box.

9. Click **OK** to close the **New Query** dialog box.

10. Right-click the query, and then click **Refresh** to refresh the saved query.

Lab A: Managing User and Computer Accounts

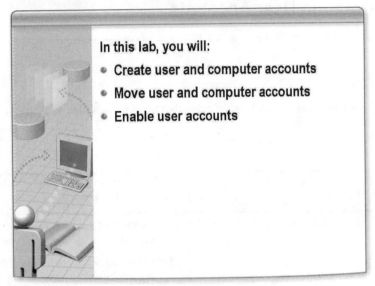

In this lab, you will:

- Create user and computer accounts
- Move user and computer accounts
- Enable user accounts

Objectives

After completing this lab, you will be able to:

- Create user and computer accounts.
- Move user and computer accounts to a new organizational unit.
- Enable user accounts.

Lab setup

This lab requires that your computer has:

- Log on to the domain by using the *ComputerName*User account.
- Open CustomMMC with the **Run as** command.

  Use the user account Nwtraders*ComputerName*Admin (Example: LondonAdmin).

- Ensure that CustomMMC contains Active Directory Users and Computers.
- Review the procedures in this lesson that describe how to perform this task.
- An organizational unit called Locations/*ComputerName*/Computers/Desktops.
- An organizational unit called Locations/*ComputerName*/Computers/Laptops.

Estimated time to complete this lab: 30 minutes

Exercise 1
Creating User Accounts

In this exercise, you will create two user accounts.

Scenario

You have been given a list of users that need to be added to Active Directory. Find the users on the list that have an office in your city location and add them to the appropriate organizational unit in your city organizational unit.

Tasks	Specific Instructions
1. Create user accounts.	▪ Create user accounts in the nwtraders.msft/Locations/*ComputerName*/Users organizational unit. ▪ Create the accounts for the users in the following table that match your organization's city location by using the following parameters: • First name: *FirstName* • Last name: *LastName* • User logon name: The first three letters of the first name and the first three letters of the last name • User logon name (pre-Windows 2000): The first three letters of the first name and the first three letters of the last name • Password: **P@ssw0rd** • Disable the user account
2. Modify the user accounts.	▪ City: *ComputerName* ▪ Telephone number: **555-2469** ▪ Manager: *ComputerName***User**

Last name, First name	City
Brown, Robert	Acapulco
Browne, Kevin F.	Acapulco
Byham, Richard A.	Auckland
Calafato, Ryan	Auckland
Berg, Karen	Bangalore
Berge, Karen	Bangalore
Barnhill, Josh	Bonn
Barr, Adam	Bonn
Altman, Gary E. III	Brisbane
Anderson, Nancy	Brisbane
Chapman, Greg	Caracas
Charles, Mathew	Caracas

(continued)

Last name, First name	City
Bonifaz, Luis	Casablanca
Boseman, Randall	Casablanca
Ackerman, Pilar	Denver
Adams, Jay	Denver
Connelly, Peter	Khartoum
Conroy, Stephanie	Khartoum
Barreto de Mattos, Paula	Lima
Bashary, Shay	Lima
Arthur, John	Lisbon
Ashton, Chris	Lisbon
Bankert, Julie	Manila
Clark, Brian	Manila
Burke, Brian	Miami
Burlacu, Ovidiu	Miami
Chor, Anthony	Montevideo
Ciccu, Alice	Montevideo
Casselman, Kevin A.	Moscow
Cavallari, Matthew J.	Moscow
Cornelsen, Ryan	Nairobi
Cox, Brian	Nairobi
Alberts, Amy E.	Perth
Alderson, Gregory F. (Greg)	Perth
Benshoof, Wanida	Santiago
Benson, Max	Santiago
Bezio, Marin	Singapore
Bischoff, Jimmy	Singapore
Carothers, Andy	Stockholm
Carroll, Matthew	Stockholm
Cannon, Chris	Suva
Canuto, Suzana De Abreu A.	Suva
Combel, Craig M.	Tokyo
Con, Aaron	Tokyo
Bradley, David M.	Tunis
Bready, Richard	Tunis
Abolrous, Sam	Vancouver
Acevedo, Humberto	Vancouver

Exercise 2
Creating Computer Accounts

In this exercise, you will create 10 computer accounts.

Scenario

You are expecting to receive four new laptop computers and five new desktop computers in your location. A consultant with a user account in the domain will add these computers to the domain. Northwind Traders policy states that the laptop and desktop computers will be managed by the administrators of the city organizational unit.

Tasks	Special instructions
1. Create five desktop computers.	▪ Create accounts in the nwtraders.msft/Locations/*ComputerName*/Computers/Desktops organizational unit. ▪ Add the following five computer accounts: 01*ComputerName*Desk, 02*ComputerName*Desk, 03*ComputerName*Desk, 04*ComputerName*Desk, 05*ComputerName*Desk
2. Create five laptop computers.	▪ Create accounts in the nwtraders.msft/Locations/*ComputerName*/Computers/Laptops organizational unit. ▪ Add the following five computer accounts: 01*ComputerName*Lap, 02*ComputerName*Lap, C03*omputerName*Lap, 04*ComputerName*Lap, 05*ComputerName*Lap

Exercise 3
Searching for and Moving Users Accounts

In this exercise, you will search for users in your city location and move them to the *ComputerName*/Users organizational unit.

Scenario

The system engineers at NorthWind Traders have imported user accounts for the entire nwtraders domain. The system administrators are responsible for searching for the user accounts that have a city location attribute of their *ComputerName* and move the account to the Users folder in their *ComputerName* organizational unit.

Tasks	Special instructions
1. Search for user accounts by using the following advanced search criteria.	<ul><li>Starting point for the search: nwtraders.msft</li><li>Find: **Users, Contacts, and Groups**</li><li>Field: **City**</li><li>Condition: **Is (exactly)**</li><li>Value: *ComputerName*</li></ul>
2. Move user accounts to the following location.	<ul><li>Nwtraders.msft/Locations/*ComputerName*/Users</li></ul>

Exercise 4
Searching for and Moving Computer Accounts

In this exercise, you will search for computer accounts whose names have the first three letters of your computer name and move them to your *ComputerName*/Computers organizational unit.

Scenario

The system engineers at NorthWind Traders have imported computer accounts for the entire nwtraders domain. The system administrators are responsible for searching for the computer accounts that have the first three letters of their *ComputerName* and move the account to the Computers folder in their *ComputerName* organizational unit.

Tasks	Special instructions
1. Search for computer accounts by using the following advanced search criteria.	<ul><li>Starting point for the search: nwtraders.msft</li><li>Find: **Computers**</li><li>Field: **Computer name (pre-Windows 2000)**</li><li>Condition: **Starts with**</li><li>Value: The first three letters of your computer name</li></ul>
2. Move computer accounts to the following location.	<ul><li>Nwtraders.msft/Locations/*ComputerName*/Computers</li></ul>

Exercise 5
Searching for and Enabling User Accounts

In this exercise, you will enable user and computer accounts in your city organizational unit.

Scenario

The system engineers at NorthWind Traders have imported user account for the entire nwtraders domain. The system administrators are responsible for searching user accounts that have a city location attribute of their *ComputerName* and then enabling the accounts so that the users can logon.

Tasks	Special instructions
1. Search for disabled user accounts in the following location.	■ Nwtraders.msft/Locations/*ComputerName*/Users
2. Enable all disabled user accounts.	

Microsoft®
Training &
Certification

Module 3: Managing Groups

Contents

Overview

- Creating Groups
- Managing Group Membership
- Strategies for Using Groups
- Modifying Groups
- Using Default Groups
- Best Practices for Managing Groups

Introduction

A group is a collection of user accounts. You can use groups to efficiently manage access to domain resources, which helps simplify network maintenance and administration. You can use groups separately, or you can place one group within another to further simplify administration.

Before you can effectively use groups, you must understand the function of groups and the types of groups that you can create. The Active Directory® directory service supports different types of groups and also provides options to determine the group's scope, which is how the group can be used in multiple domains.

Objectives

After completing this module, you will be able to:

- Create groups.
- Manage group membership.
- Apply strategies for using groups.
- Modify groups.
- Manage default groups.

Lesson: Creating Groups

- What Are Groups?
- What Are Domain Functional Levels?
- What Are Global Groups?
- What Are Universal Groups?
- What Are Domain Local Groups?
- What Are Local Groups?
- Where to Create Groups
- Naming Guidelines for Groups
- How to Create a Group

Introduction

The information in this lesson presents the skills and knowledge that you need to create groups.

Lesson objectives

After completing this lesson, you will be able to:

- Explain the purpose of groups, group types, and group scopes.
- Identify the domain functional levels.
- Describe global groups.
- Describe universal groups.
- Describe domain local groups.
- Describe local groups.
- Decide whether to create groups in a domain or organizational unit.
- Determine naming guidelines for groups.
- Create a group.

What Are Groups?

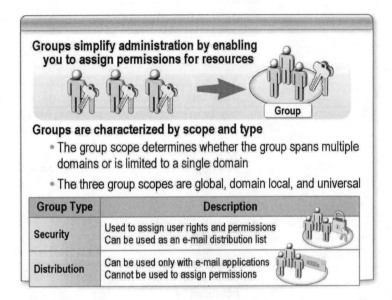

Groups simplify administration by enabling you to assign permissions for resources

Groups are characterized by scope and type
- The group scope determines whether the group spans multiple domains or is limited to a single domain
- The three group scopes are global, domain local, and universal

Group Type	Description
Security	Used to assign user rights and permissions Can be used as an e-mail distribution list
Distribution	Can be used only with e-mail applications Cannot be used to assign permissions

Definition

Groups are a collection of user and computer accounts that you can manage as a single unit. Groups:

- Simplify administration by enabling you to grant permissions for resources, once to a group rather than to each user account individually.
- Can be based on Active Directory or local to an individual computer.
- Are characterized by scope and type.
- Can be nested, which means that you can add a group to another group.

Group scopes

The group scope determines whether the group spans multiple domains or is limited to a single domain. Group scopes enable you to use groups to grant permissions. The group scope determines:

- The domains from which you can add members to the group.
- The domains in which you can use the group to grant permissions.
- The domains in which you can nest the group within other groups.

The group scope determines who the members of the group are. Membership rules govern the members that a group can contain and the groups of which a group can be a member. Group members consist of user accounts and other groups.

To assign the correct members to groups and to use nesting, it is important to understand the characteristics of the group scope. There are the following group scopes:

- Global
- Domain local
- Universal

Group types

You use groups to organize user accounts, computer accounts, and other group accounts into manageable units. Working with groups instead of individual users helps simplify network maintenance and administration. There are the following types of groups in Active Directory:

- Security groups

  You use security groups to assign user rights and permissions to groups of users and computers. Rights determine what members of a security group can do in a domain or forest, and permissions determine what resources a member of a group can access on the network.

  You can also use security groups to send e-mail messages to multiple users. Sending an e-mail message to the group sends the message to all members of the group. Therefore, security groups have the capabilities of distribution groups.

- Distribution groups

  You use distribution groups with e-mail applications, such as Microsoft® Exchange, to send e-mail messages to collections of users. The primary purpose of this type of group is to gather related objects, not to grant permissions.

  Distribution groups are not security-enabled, meaning that they cannot be used to assign permissions. If you need a group for controlling access to shared resources, create a security group.

  Even though security groups have all the capabilities of distribution groups, distribution groups are still required, because some applications can use only distribution groups.

Both distribution and security groups support one of the three group scopes.

What Are Domain Functional Levels?

	Windows 2000 mixed (default)	Windows 2000 native	Windows Server 2003
Domain controllers Supported	Windows NT® Server 4.0, Windows 2000, Windows Server 2003	Windows 2000, Windows Server 2003	Windows Server 2003
Group scopes supported	Global, domain local	Global, domain local, universal	Global, domain local, universal

Definition

The characteristics of groups in Active Directory depend on the domain functional level. Domain functionality enables features that will affect the entire domain and that domain only. Three domain functional levels are available: Microsoft Windows® 2000 mixed, Windows 2000 native, and Microsoft Windows Server 2003. By default, domains operate at the Windows 2000 mixed functional level. You can raise the domain functional level to either Windows 2000 native or Windows Server 2003.

The table above lists the domain functional levels and the domain controllers and group scopes they each support.

Note You can convert a group from a security group to a distribution group, and vice versa, at any time, but only if the domain functional level is set to Windows 2000 native or higher.

Additional Reading

For more information on raising functional levels see KB Article How To: Raise the Domain Functional Level in Windows Server 2003.

What Are Global Groups?

	Global group rules
Members	• **Mixed mode:** User accounts from same domain • **Native mode:** User accounts and global groups from same domain
Can be a member of	• **Mixed mode:** Domain local groups • **Native mode:** Universal and domain local groups in any domain and global groups in the same domain
Scope	Visible in its own domain and all trusted domains
Permissions	All domains in the forest

Definition

A global group is a security or distribution group that can contain users, groups, and computers that are from the same domain as the global group. You can use global security groups to assign user rights and permissions to resources in any domain in the forest.

Characteristics of global groups

The following summarizes the characteristics of global groups:

- Members

  - In domain mixed functional level, global groups can contain user and computer accounts that are from the same domain as the global group.

  - In native functional level, global groups can contain user accounts and global groups that are from the same domain as the global group.

- Can be a member of

  - In mixed mode, a global group can be a member of only domain local groups.

  - In native mode, a global group can be a member of universal and domain local groups in any domain and global groups that are from the same domain as the global group.

- Scope

  A global group is visible within its domain and all trusted domains, which include all of the domains in the forest.

- Permissions

  You can grant permissions to a global group for all domains in the forest.

When to use global groups

Because global groups have a forest-wide visibility, do not create them for domain-specific resource access. Use a global group to organize users who share the same job tasks and have similar network access requirements. A different group type is more appropriate for controlling access to resources within a domain.

What Are Universal Groups?

Universal group rules		
Members	• **Mixed mode:** Not applicable	
	• **Native mode:** User accounts, global groups, and other universal groups from any domain in the forest	
Can be a member of	• **Mixed mode:** Not applicable	
	• **Native mode:** Domain local and universal groups in any domain	
Scope	Visible in all domains in a forest	
Permissions	All domains in a forest	

Definition

A universal group is a security or distribution group that can contain users, groups, and computers from any domain in its forest. You can use universal security groups to assign user rights and permissions to resources in any domain in the forest.

Characteristics of universal groups

The following summarizes the characteristics of universal groups:

- Members

  - You cannot create universal groups in mixed mode.

  - In native mode, universal groups can contain user accounts, global groups, and other universal groups from any domain in the forest.

- Can be a member of

  - The universal group is not applicable in mixed mode.

  - In native mode, the universal group can be a member of domain local and universal groups in any domain.

- Scope

  Universal groups are visible in all domains in the forest.

- Permissions

  You can grant permissions to universal groups for all domains in the forest.

When to use universal groups

Use universal groups to nest global groups so that you can assign permissions to related resources in multiple domains. A Windows Server 2003 domain must be in Windows 2000 native mode or higher to use universal groups.

What Are Domain Local Groups?

Domain local group rules	
Members	• **Mixed mode:** User accounts and global groups from any domain • **Native mode:** User accounts, global groups, and universal groups from any domain in the forest, and domain local groups from the same domain
Can be a member of	• **Mixed mode:** None • **Native mode:** Domain local groups in the same domain
Scope	Visible only in its own domain
Permissions	Domain to which the domain local group belongs

Definition

A domain local group is a security or distribution group that can contain universal groups, global groups, other domain local groups that are from its own domain, and accounts from any domain in the forest. You can use domain local security groups to assign user rights and permissions to resources only in the same domain where the domain local group is located.

Characteristics of domain local groups

The following summarizes the characteristics of domain local groups:

- Members

  - In mixed mode, domain local groups can contain user accounts and global groups from any domain. Member servers cannot use domain local group in mixed mode.

  - In native mode, domain local groups can contain user accounts, global groups, and universal groups from any domain in the forest, and domain local groups that are from the same domain as the domain local group.

- Can be a member of

  - In mixed mode, a domain local group cannot be a member of any group.

  - In native mode, a domain local group can be a member of domain local groups that are from the same domain as the domain local group.

- Scope

  A domain local group is visible only in the domain that the domain local group belongs to.

- Permissions

  You can assign permissions to a domain local group for the domain that the domain local group belongs to.

When to use domain local groups

Use a domain local group to assign permissions to resources that are located in the same domain as the domain local group. You can place all global groups that need to share the same resources into the appropriate domain local group.

What Are Local Groups?

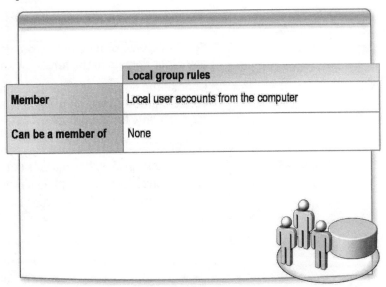

	Local group rules
Member	Local user accounts from the computer
Can be a member of	None

Definition

A local group is a collection of user accounts or domain groups created on a member server or a stand-alone server. You can create local groups to grant permissions for resources residing on the local computer. Windows 2000 or Windows Server 2003 creates local groups in the local security database. Local groups can contain users, computers, global groups, universal groups, and other domain local groups.

Because groups with a domain local scope are sometimes referred to as local groups, it is important to distinguish between a local group and a group with domain local scope. Local groups are sometimes referred to as machine local groups to distinguish them from domain local groups.

Characteristics of local groups

The following summarizes the characteristics of local groups:

- Local groups can contain local user accounts from the computer where you create the local group.
- Local groups cannot be members of any other group.

When to use local groups

The following are guidelines for using local groups:

- You can use local groups only on the computer where you create the local groups. Local group permissions provide access to resources only on the computer where you created the local group.
- You can use local groups on computers running currently supported Microsoft client operating systems and member servers running Windows Server 2003. You cannot create local groups on domain controllers, because domain controllers cannot have a security database that is independent of the database in Active Directory.
- Create local groups to limit the ability of local users and groups to access network resources when you do not want to create domain groups.

Where to Create Groups

- **You can create groups in the root domain of the forest, any other domain in the forest, or an organizational unit**
- **Choose the domain or organizational unit where you create a group based on the administration requirements for the group**
  - **For example:**

    If your directory has multiple organizational units, each of which has a different administrator, you can create global groups in those organizational units

Introduction

In Active Directory, groups are created in domains. You use Active Directory Users and Computers to create groups. If you have the necessary permissions, and by correctly associating users and computers with groups, you can create groups in any other domain in the forest, or an organizational unit.

Besides the domain in which it is created, a group is also characterized by its scope. The scope of a group determines:

- The domain from which members can be added.
- The domain in which the user rights and permissions assigned to the group are valid.

Choosing a domain or organizational unit

Choose the particular domain or organizational unit where you create a group based on the administration requirements for the group.

For example, suppose your directory has multiple organizational units, each of which has a different administrator. You may want to create global groups in those organizational units so that those administrators can manage group membership for users in their respective organizational units.

If groups are required to control access outside the organizational unit, you can nest the groups within the organizational unit into universal groups (or other groups with global scope) that can be used elsewhere in the forest. It may be more efficient to nest global groups if the domain functional level is set to Windows 2000 native or higher, the domain contains a hierarchy of organizational units, and administration is delegated to administrators at each organizational unit.

Naming Guidelines for Groups

For security groups:

- Incorporate the scope in the naming convention of the group name
- The name should reflect the ownership (division or team name)
- Place domain names or abbreviations at the beginning of the group name
- Use a descriptor to identify the maximum permissions a group can have, such as DL IT London OU Admins

For distribution groups:

- Use a short alias name
- Do not include a user's alias name as part of a display name
- Allow a maximum of five co-owners of a single distribution group

Introduction

In Active Directory, there are many security and distribution groups. The following naming conventions help you manage these groups. Organizations develop their own naming conventions for their security and distribution groups. A group name should identify the scope, type, who the group was created for, and what permissions the group can have.

Security group

Consider the following in defining a naming convention for security groups:

- Scope of security groups

  Although the group type and scope are displayed as the group type in Active Directory Users and Computers, organizations often incorporate the scope in the naming convention of the group name.

  For example, Northwind Traders identifies the scope of security groups by adding a first letter to the group name:

  - **G** IT Admins

    G for global groups

  - **U** All IT Admins

    U for universal groups

  - **DL** IT Admins Full Control

    DL for domain local groups

- Ownership of the security group

  The name for any domain-level security group, whether universal, global, or domain local, should clearly identify ownership by including the name of the division or team that owns the group.

  The following is an example of a naming convention that Northwind Traders might use to identify group ownership:

  - G **Marketing** Managers

  - DL **IT Admins** Full Control

- Domain name

  Upon client request, the domain name or abbreviation is placed at the beginning of the group name. For example:

  - G **NWTraders** Marketing

  - DL **S.N.MSFT** IT Admins Read

- Purpose of the security group

  Finally, in a name, you can include the business purpose of the group and maximum permissions the group should ever have on the network. This naming convention is more applicable to domain local or local groups.

  The following is an example of a naming convention that Northwind Traders might use to identify the purpose of the security group. Northwind Traders uses a descriptor to identify the maximum permissions a group should ever have on the network. For example:

  - DL IT London **OU Admins**

  - DL IT Admins **Full Control**

Distribution groups

Because security groups are mostly used for network administration, only the personnel administering the network must use the naming convention. End users use distribution groups, so the naming convention must be relevant to an end user.

When defining a naming convention for distribution groups consider the following:

- E-mail names

  - *Length*. Use a short alias name. To conform to current downstream data standards, the minimum length of this field is three characters, and the maximum length is eight characters.

  - *Offensive words*. Do not create distribution groups with words that may be considered offensive. If in doubt, do not use the word.

  - *Allowed characters*. You can use all ASCII characters. The only allowed special characters are the hyphen (-) and underscore (_).

  - *Special designations*. Do not use the following character combinations for distributions groups:

    - An underscore (_) as the beginning character of the group name of the alias name

    - A first name or combination of first name and last name that may easily be confused with a user account name

■ Display names

- *User alias names*. For standardization purposes, do not include a user's alias name as part of a display name (for example, Sfine Direct Reports). Include the full name (for example, Suzan Fine's Direct Reports).

- *Offensive words*. Do not create distribution groups with words that may be considered offensive.

- *Social discussions*. Distribution groups for social discussions should not be allowed, because public folders are a more efficient means of transmitting and storing high-volume communications associated with social discussions. Because a post is visible to multiple users, both network traffic and data storage are minimized if you use public folders instead of corporate distribution groups.

- *Length*. The maximum length of this field is 40 characters. Abbreviations are acceptable as long as the meaning is clear.

- *Style*. Do not capitalize the entire description, but capitalize the first letter in the display name. Use proper punctuation and spelling.

- *Top of the address book*. Do not use the word *A*, numbers, special characters (especially quotes), or a space to begin a description. This makes it appear at the top of the address book. The address book should begin with individual user names starting with A.

- *Special characters*. Slashes (/) are acceptable in display names, but do not use them in front of server names. Do not use more than one apostrophe (') and do not use the following special characters: " * @ # $ % | [ ] ; < > =

■ Ownership

There can be a maximum of five co-owners of a single distribution group.

Local groups

A local group name cannot be identical to any other group or user name on the local computer being administered. A local group name cannot consist solely of periods (.) or spaces. It can contain up to 256 uppercase or lowercase characters, except the following: " / \ [ ] : ; | = , + * ? < >

Note Your environment may not use these guidelines but will most likely use some group naming conventions.

How to Create a Group

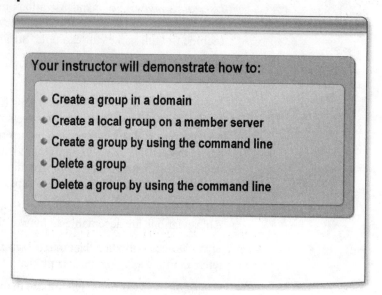

Your instructor will demonstrate how to:

- Create a group in a domain
- Create a local group on a member server
- Create a group by using the command line
- Delete a group
- Delete a group by using the command line

Introduction

In most corporate environments, you will create groups in domains. Active Directory has security and tracking features that limit the addition of users to groups. Active Directory also gives corporations the flexibility to use groups on member servers. Corporations often have servers that are exposed to the Internet and want to use local groups on member servers rather than domain local groups to limit the exposure of internal groups and group members.

Procedure for creating a group in a domain

To create a group in an Active Directory domain:

1. In Active Directory Users and Computers, in the console tree, right-click the folder to which you want to add the group, point to **New**, and then click **Group**.

2. In the **New Object – Group** dialog box, in the **Group name** box, type the name of the new group.

3. Under **Group scope**, click the group scope for the new group.

4. Under **Group type**, click the group type for the new group.

Note To perform this procedure, you must be a member of the Account Operators group, Domain Admins group, or the Enterprise Admins group in Active Directory, or you must be delegated the appropriate authority. As a security best practice, consider using **Run as** to perform this procedure.

Important If the domain in which you are creating the group is set to the domain functional level of Windows 2000 mixed, you can select only security groups with domain local or global scope.

Procedure for creating a local group on a member server

To create a local group on a member server:

1. In Computer Management, in the console tree, click **Groups**.

2. On the **Action** menu, click **New Group**.

3. In the **New Group** dialog box, in the **Group name** box, type a name for the new group.

4. In the **Description** box, type a description for the new group.

5. To add one or more users to a new group, click **Add**.

6. Click **Create**, and then click **Close**.

Note   To perform this procedure, you must be a member of the Power Users group or the Administrators group on the local computer, or you must be delegated the appropriate authority. If the computer is joined to a domain, members of the Domain Admins group might be able to perform this procedure. As a security best practice, consider using **Run as** to perform this procedure.

Using a command line

To create a group in an Active Directory domain by using **dsadd**:

1. Open a command prompt.

2. Type **dsadd group** *GroupDN* **-samid** *SAMName* **-secgrp** *yes | no* **-scope** *l | g | u*

Value	Description
GroupDN	Specifies the distinguished name of the group object that you want to add
SAMName	Specifies the Security Accounts Manager (SAM) name as the unique SAM account name for this group (for example, operators)
*yes	no*	Specifies whether the group you want to add is a security group (yes) or a distribution group (no)
*l	g	u*	Specifies whether the scope of the group you want to add is domain local (l), global (g), or universal (u)

Note   To view the complete syntax for this command, at a command prompt, type **dsadd group** **/?**

Procedure for deleting a group

To delete a group:

1. In Active Directory Users and Computers, in the console tree, click the folder that contains the group.

2. In the details pane, right-click the group, and then click **Delete**.

Note   To perform this procedure, you must be a member of the Account Operators group, Domain Admins group, or the Enterprise Admins group in Active Directory, or you must be delegated the appropriate authority. As a security best practice, consider using **Run as** to perform this procedure.

Using a command line

To delete a group by using **dsrm**:

1. Open a command prompt.

2. Type **dsrm** *GroupDN*

Value	Description
GroupDN	Specifies the distinguished name of the group object to be deleted.

Note   To view the complete syntax for this command, at a command prompt, type **dsrm /?**

Practice: Creating Groups

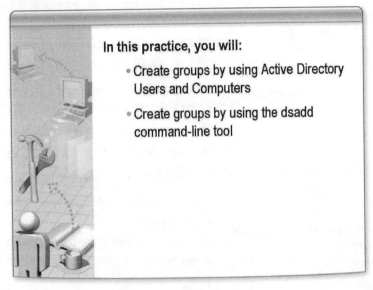

In this practice, you will:

- Create groups by using Active Directory Users and Computers

- Create groups by using the dsadd command-line tool

Objective

In this practice, you will create global and local groups by using Active Directory Users and Computers. You will also create global groups by using the **dsadd** command-line tool.

Instructions

Before you begin this practice:

- Log on to the domain by using the *ComputerName*User account.

- Open CustomMMC with the **Run as** command.

  Use the user account Nwtraders*ComputerName*Admin (Example: LondonAdmin).

- Ensure that CustomMMC contains Active Directory Users and Computers.

- Review the procedures in this lesson that describe how to perform this task.

Scenario

As a systems administrator, you must create multiple groups for the Accounting department. These groups will eventually be used for grouping accounts and assigning groups to resources.

Practice

▶ **Create groups by using Active Directory Users and Computers**

1. Create the following global groups in the organizational unit Locations/*ComputerName*/Groups:

   - G *ComputerName* Accounting Managers

   - G *ComputerName* Accounting Personnel

2. Create the following domain local groups in the organizational unit Locations/*ComputerName*/Groups:

   - DL *ComputerName* Accounting Managers Full Control

   - DL *ComputerName* Accounting Managers Read

   - DL *ComputerName* Accounting Personnel Full Control

   - DL *ComputerName* Accounting Personnel Read

Practice: Using the command line

▶ **Create groups by using the dsadd command-line tool**

1. Create the following global group in the IT Test organizational unit:

   - G *ComputerName*Test

   Example: C:\>dsadd group "cn=G London Test,ou=it test,dc=nwtraders,dc=msft" -secgrp yes -scope g -samid "G London Test"

2. Create the following domain local group in the IT Test organizational unit:

   - DL *ComputerName*Test

   Example: C:\>dsadd group "cn=DL London Test,ou=it test,dc=nwtraders,dc=msft" -secgrp yes -scope L -samid "DL London Test"

Lesson: Managing Group Membership

- The Members and Member Of Properties
- Demonstration: Members and Member Of
- How to Determine the Groups That a User Account Is a Member Of
- How to Add and Remove Members from a Group

Introduction

Because many users often require access to different resources throughout an organization, administrators may have to grant membership to groups that reside in Active Directory or on local computers.

When adding members to or removing members from groups in Active Directory, an administrator can open Active Directory Users and Computers, click on a user account, drag it to the desired group, and drop the user account onto the group. This action quickly adds the user account to the group.

When adding members to or removing members from groups on a local computer, an administrator can use Computer Management to change group membership on the local computer.

Lesson objectives

After completing this lesson, you will be able to:

- Distinguish between the **Members** and **Member Of** properties.
- Use the **Members** and **Member Of** properties by using the interface.
- Determine the groups that a user account is a member of.
- Add members to and remove members from a group.

The Members and Member Of Properties

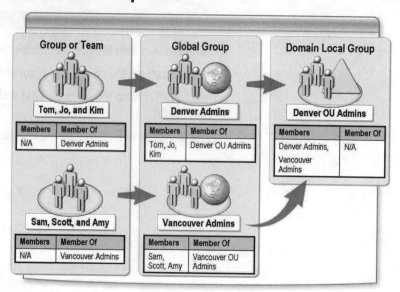

Introduction	The illustration in the slide describes the **Members** and **Member Of** properties.
Definition of Members and Member Of	Tom, Jo, and Kim are *members of* the Denver Admins global group. The global group Denver Admins is a *member of* the domain local group Denver OU Admins.

Sam, Scott, and Amy are *members of* the Vancouver Admins global group. The global group Vancouver Admins is a *member of* the domain local group Denver OU Admins.

The following table summarizes the information in the slide.

User or Group	Members	Members Of
Tom, Jo, Kim		Denver Admins
Denver Admins	Tom, Jo, Kim	Denver OU Admins
Sam, Scott, Amy		Vancouver Admins
Vancouver Admins	Sam, Scott, Amy	Denver OU Admins
Denver OU Admins	Denver Admins	
	Vancouver Admins	

By using the **Members** and **Member Of** properties, you can determine groups that the user belongs to and what groups that group belongs to.

Demonstration: Members and Member Of

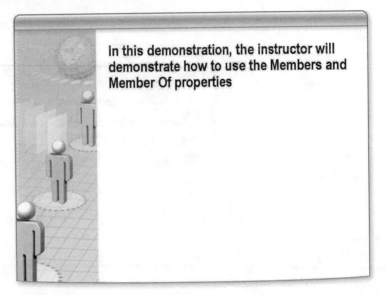

In this demonstration, the instructor will demonstrate how to use the Members and Member Of properties

Objective

In this demonstration, the instructor will demonstrate how to use the **Members** and **Member Of** properties.

Demonstration

To demonstrate how to use **Members** and **Member Of**:

1. Open Active Directory Users and Computers.

2. In the console tree, expand **NWTraders.msft**, and then expand the **IT Admin** organizational unit.

3. Click the **IT Users** organizational unit.

4. In the details pane double-click the **AcapulcoAdmin** user account.

5. In the **Properties** dialog box, on the **Member Of** tab, notice that the AcapulcoAdmin user account is a member of the following groups:

   - Domain Users

   - G Acapulco Admins

   - G IT Admins

6. Double-click the **G IT Admins** group.

7. In the **Properties** dialog box, on the **Members** tab, notice that the G IT Admins group has many members.

8. On the **Member Of** tab, notice the G IT Admins group is a member of the DL IT OU Administrators group.

9. Double-click the **DL IT OU Administrators** group.

10. In the **Properties** dialog box, on the **Members** tab, notice that the G IT Admins group is a member.

How to Determine the Groups That a User Account Is a Member Of

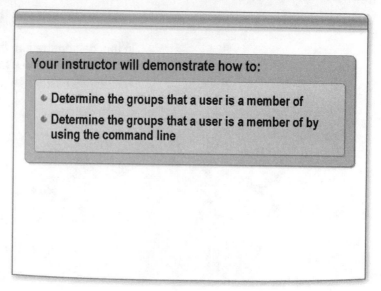

Introduction

After you add users to groups, Active Directory updates the **Member Of** property of their user accounts.

Procedure

To determine the groups that a user is a member of:

1. In Active Directory Users and Computers, in the console tree, click **Users** or click the folder that contains the user account.

2. In the details pane, right-click a user account, and then click **Properties**.

3. In the **Properties** dialog box, click the **Member Of** tab.

Note   You do not need administrative credentials to perform this task. Therefore, as a security best practice, consider performing this task as a user without administrative credentials.

Using a command line

To determine the groups a user is a member of by using **dsget**:

1. Open a command prompt.

2. Type **dsget user** *UserDN* **-memberof**

Value	Description
UserDN	Specifies the distinguished name of the user object for which you want to display group membership

Note   To view the complete syntax for this command, at the command prompt, type **dsget user /?**

How to Add and Remove Members from a Group

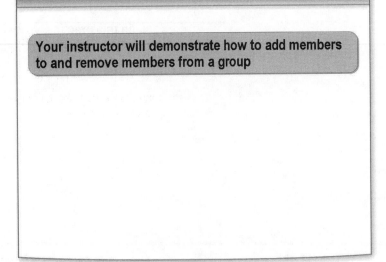

Your instructor will demonstrate how to add members to and remove members from a group

Introduction

After creating a group, you add members by using Active Directory Users and Computers. Members of groups can include user accounts, other groups, and computers.

Procedure

To add members to or remove members from a group:

1. In Active Directory Users and Computers, in the console tree, click the folder that contains the group to which you want to add a member.

2. In the details pane, right-click the group, and then click **Properties**.

3. In the **Properties** dialog box, on the **Members** tab, click **Add**.

   If you want to remove a member from the group, click the member, and then click **Remove**.

4. In the **Select Users, Contact, Computers, or Groups** dialog box, in the **Enter the object names to select** box, type the name of the user, group, or computer that you want to add to the group, and then click **OK**.

Tip   You can also add a user account or group by using the **Member Of** tab in the **Properties** dialog box for that user account or group. Use this method to quickly add the same user or group to multiple groups.

Practice: Managing Group Membership

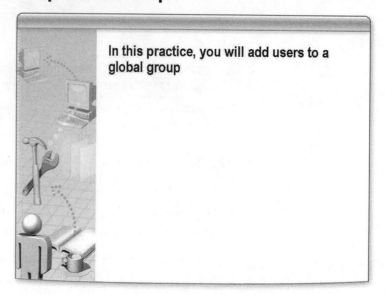

In this practice, you will add users to a global group

Objectives

In this practice, you will add users to a global group.

Instructions

Before you begin this practice:

- Log on to the domain by using the *ComputerName*User account.
- Open CustomMMC with the **Run as** command.

  Use the user account Nwtraders\ComputerNameAdmin (Example: LondonAdmin).
- Ensure that CustomMMC contains Active Directory Users and Computers.
- Ensure that the following groups are in the Locations/*ComputerName*/Groups organizational unit:
  - Global groups:
    - G *ComputerName* Accounting Managers
    - G *ComputerName* Accounting Personnel
- Review the procedures in this lesson that describe how to perform this task.

Scenario

Northwind Traders is starting to implement global groups. You will need to find all Accounting personnel in your city organizational unit and add them to the G *ComputerName* Accounting Personnel group.

Practice

▶ **Perform a custom search for Accounting personnel**

- Search for users with the City search attribute of *ComputerName* (Example: London) and the Department search attribute of Accounting.

  This search should produce approximately 10 users. One of the users is the Accounting manager.

▶ **Add the users to G *ComputerName* Accounting Personnel**

1. Select all users produced by the preceding search.

2. Right-click the selection, and then click **Add to a group**.

3. Add the users to G *ComputerName* Accounting Personnel.

Lesson: Strategies for Using Groups

- Multimedia: Strategy for Using Groups in a Single Domain
- What Is Group Nesting?
- Group Strategies

Introduction

To use groups effectively, you need strategies for applying different group scopes. This lesson covers skills and knowledge that you need to use groups optimally by employing different strategies with groups.

Lesson objectives

After completing this lesson, you will be able to:

- Explain the AGDLP strategy for using groups in a single domain.
- Describe group nesting.
- Describe the following strategies for using groups:
  - A G P
  - A DL P
  - A G DL P
  - A G U DL P
  - A G L P

Multimedia: Strategy for Using Groups in a Single Domain

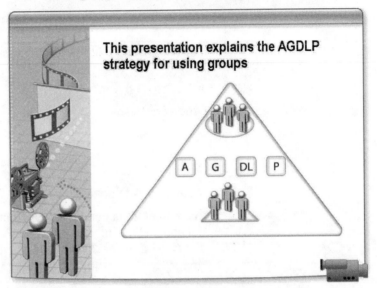

File location	To view the *Strategy for Using Groups in a Single Domain* presentation, open the Web page on the Student Materials compact disc, click **Multimedia**, and then click the title of the presentation. Do not open this presentation unless the instructor tells you to.
Key points	User accounts → Global groups → Domain Local groups ← Permissions
	(A) (G) (DL) (P)

What Is Group Nesting?

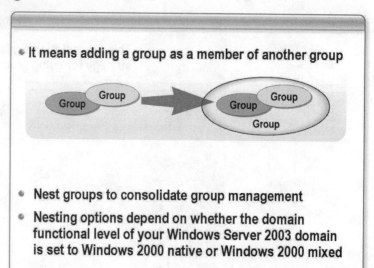

- It means adding a group as a member of another group

- Nest groups to consolidate group management
- Nesting options depend on whether the domain functional level of your Windows Server 2003 domain is set to Windows 2000 native or Windows 2000 mixed

---

Introduction

Using nesting, you can add a group as a member of another group. You can nest groups to consolidate group management. Nesting increases the member accounts that are affected by a single action and reduces replication traffic caused by the replication of changes in group membership.

Nesting options

Your nesting options depend on whether the domain functional level of your Windows Server 2003 domain is set to Windows 2000 native or Windows 2000 mixed. In domains where the domain functional level is set to Windows 2000 native, group membership is determined as follows:

- Universal groups can have as their members: user accounts, computer accounts, universal groups, and global groups from any domain.

- Global groups can have as their members: user accounts from the same domain and global groups from the same domain.

- Domain local groups can have as their members: user accounts, universal groups, and global groups, all from any domain. They can also have as members domain local groups from within the same domain.

You cannot create security groups with universal scope in domains where the domain functional level is set to Windows 2000 mixed. Universal scope is supported only in domains where the domain functional level is set to Windows 2000 native or Windows Server 2003.

Note   Minimize the levels of nesting. A single level of nesting is the most effective method, because tracking permissions is more complex with multiple levels.

Also, troubleshooting becomes difficult if you must trace permissions through multiple levels of nesting. Therefore, document group membership to keep track of permissions.

Group Strategies

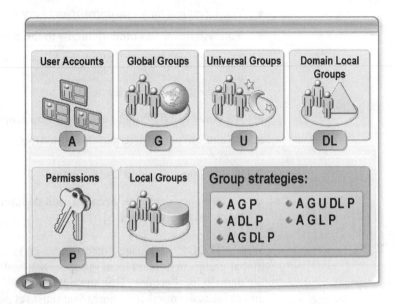

Introduction	To use groups effectively, you need strategies for applying the different group scopes. The strategy you choose depends on the Windows network environment of your organization. In a single domain, the common practice is to use global and domain local groups to grant permissions for network resources. In a network with multiple domains, you can incorporate global and universal groups into your strategy.
A G P	With A G P, you place user accounts (A) in global groups (G), and you grant permissions (P) to the global groups. The limitation of this strategy is that it complicates administration when you use multiple domains. If global groups from multiple domains require the same permissions, you must grant permissions to each global group individually.
When to use the A G P strategy	Use A G P for forests with one domain and very few users and to which you will never add other domains.

A G P has the following advantages:

- Groups are not nested and therefore troubleshooting may be easier.

- Accounts belong to a single group scope.

A G P has the following disadvantages:

- Every time a user authenticates with a resource, the server must check the global group membership to determine if the user is still a member of the group.

- Performance degrades, because a global group is not cached.

| A DL P | With A DL P, you place user accounts (A) in domain local groups (DL), and you grant permissions (P) to the domain local groups. One limitation of this strategy is that it does not allow you to grant permissions for resources outside of the domain. Therefore, it reduces flexibility as your network grows. |

When to use the A DL P strategy

Use A DL P for a forest where all of the following are true:

- The forest has only one domain and very few users.

- You will never add other domains to the forest.

- There are no Microsoft Windows NT 4.0 member servers in the domain.

A DL P has the following advantages:

- Accounts belong only to a single group scope.

- Groups are not nested, and therefore troubleshooting may be easier.

A DL P has the following disadvantage:

- Performance degrades, because each domain local group has many members that must be authenticated.

A G DL P

With A G DL P, you place user accounts (A) in global groups (G), place the global groups in domain local groups (DL), and then grant permissions (P) to the domain local groups. This strategy creates flexibility for network growth and reduces the number of times you must set permissions.

When to use the A G DL P strategy

Use A G DL P for a forest consisting of one or more domains and to which you might have to add future domains.

A G DL P has the following advantages:

- Domains are flexible.

- Resource owners require less access to Active Directory to flexibly secure their resources.

A G DL P has the following disadvantage:

- A tiered management structure is more complex to set up initially, but easier to manage over time.

A G U DL P

With A G U DL P, you place user accounts (A) in global groups (G), place the global groups in universal groups (U), place the universal groups in domain local groups (DL), and then grant permissions (P) to the domain local groups.

When to use the A G U DL P strategy

Use A G U DL P for a forest with more than one domain where administrators require centralized administration for many global groups.

A G U DL P has the following advantages:

- There is flexibility across the forest.

- It enables centralized administration.

Note Domain Local groups should not be used to assign Active Directory object permissions in a Forest with more than one Domain. For more information see Microsoft Knowledge Base Article 231273, Group Type and Scope Usage in Windows at http://support.microsoft.com/default.aspx?scid=kb%3Ben-us%3B231273.

A G U DL P has the following disadvantage:

- The membership of universal groups is stored in the global catalog.

Note The global catalog is a domain controller that stores a copy of all Active Directory objects in a forest. The global catalog stores a full copy of all objects in Active Directory for its host domain and a partial copy of all objects for all other domains in the forest.

- It may be necessary to add more global catalog servers.

- There may be global catalog replication latency. When referring to the global catalog, *latency* is the time it takes to replicate a change to each global catalog server in the forest.

There is a disadvantage to using universal groups only if the universal groups have a very dynamic membership with a lot of global catalog replication traffic as the membership changes) in a multidomain forest. With A G U DL P, this is less of an issue, because the membership of universal groups is relatively static (that is, the universal group has global groups, not individual users, as members).

A G L P

Use the A G L P strategy to place user accounts in a global group and grant permissions to the local group. One limitation of this strategy is that you cannot grant permissions for resources outside the local computer.

Therefore, place user accounts in a global group, add the global group to the local group, and then grant permissions to the local group. With this strategy, you can use the same global group on multiple local computers.

Note Use domain local groups whenever possible. Use local groups only when a domain local group has not been created for this purpose.

When to use the A G L P strategy

Use the A G L P strategy when your domain has the following characteristics:

- Upgrade from Windows NT 4.0 to Windows Server 2003
- Contain one domain
- Have few users
- Will never add other domains
- To maintain a Windows NT 4.0 group strategy
- To maintain centralized user management and decentralized resource management

It is recommended that you use A G L P with Windows Server 2003 Active Directory and Windows NT 4.0 member servers.

A G L P has the following advantages:

- It maintains the Windows NT 4.0 group strategy.
- Resource owners own membership to every group that needs access.

A G L P has the following disadvantages:

- Active Directory does not control access.
- You must create redundant groups across member servers.
- It does not enable centralized administration.

Class Discussion: Using Groups in a Single Domain

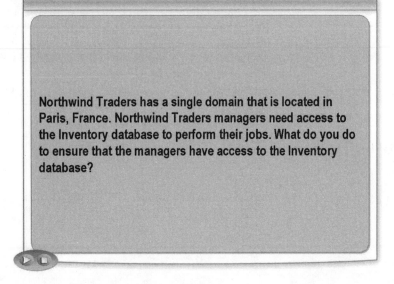

Northwind Traders has a single domain that is located in Paris, France. Northwind Traders managers need access to the Inventory database to perform their jobs. What do you do to ensure that the managers have access to the Inventory database?

Example 1

Northwind Traders has a single domain that is located in Paris, France. Northwind Traders managers need access to the Inventory database to perform their jobs.

What do you do to ensure that the managers have access to the Inventory database?

_____

_____

_____

_____

Example 2

Northwind Traders wants to react more quickly to market demands. It is determined that the accounting data must be available to all Accounting personnel. Northwind Traders wants to create the group structure for the entire Accounting division, which includes the Accounts Payable and Accounts Receivable departments.

What do you do to ensure that the managers have the required access and that there is a minimum of administration?

_____

_____

_____

_____

Practice: Adding Global Groups to Domain Local Groups

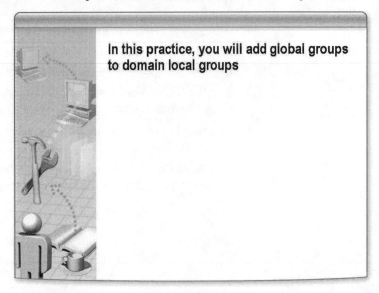

In this practice, you will add global groups to domain local groups

Objective

In this exercise, you will add a global group to a domain local group.

Instructions

Before you begin this practice:

- Log on to the domain by using the *ComputerName*User account.

- Open CustomMMC with the **Run as** command.

  Use the user account Nwtraders\ComputerNameAdmin (Example: LondonAdmin).

- Ensure that CustomMMC contains Active Directory Users and Computers.

- Ensure that the following groups are in the Locations/*ComputerName*/Groups organizational unit:

  - Global groups:

    - G *ComputerName* Accounting Managers

    - G *ComputerName* Accounting Personnel

  - Domain local groups:

    - DL *ComputerName* Accounting Managers Full Control

    - DL *ComputerName* Accounting Managers Read

    - DL *ComputerName* Accounting Personnel Full Control

    - DL *ComputerName* Accounting Personnel Read

- Review the procedures in this lesson that describe how to perform this task.

Scenario

Northwind Traders is implementing A G DL P and needs you to add global groups to domain local groups.

Practice

▶ **Add global groups to domain local groups**

1. Add the G *ComputerName* Accounting Managers global group to DL *ComputerName* Accounting Managers Full Control.

2. Add the G *ComputerName* Accounting Managers global group to DL *ComputerName* Accounting Managers Read.

3. Add the G *ComputerName* Accounting Personnel global group to DL *ComputerName* Accounting Personnel Full Control.

4. Add the G *ComputerName* Accounting Personnel global group to DL *ComputerName* Accounting Personnel Read.

Lesson: Modifying Groups

- What Is Modifying the Scope or Type of a Group?
- How to Change the Scope or Type of a Group
- Why Assign a Manager to a Group?
- How to Assign a Manager to a Group

Introduction

This lesson introduces you to the skills and knowledge that you need to modify groups.

Lesson objectives

After completing this lesson, you will be able to:

- Explain what it means to modify the scope or type of a group.
- Change the scope or type of a group.
- Explain why you assign a manager to a group.
- Assign a manager to a group.

What Is Modifying the Scope or Type of a Group?

- Changing group scope
  - Global to universal
  - Domain local to universal
  - Universal to global
  - Universal to domain local
- Changing group type
  - Security to distribution
  - Distribution to security

Introduction

When creating a new group, by default, the new group is configured as a security group with global scope, regardless of the current domain functional level.

Changing group scope

Although you cannot change group scope in domains with a domain functional level set to Windows 2000 mixed, you can make the following scope changes in domains with the domain functional level set to Windows 2000 native or Windows Server 2003:

- *Global to universal*. This is allowed only if the group you want to change is not a member of another global group.

  Note   You cannot change a group's scope from global to domain local directly. To do that, you must change the group's scope from global to universal and then from universal to domain local.

- *Domain local to universal*. This is allowed only if the group you want to change does not have another domain local group as a member.
- *Universal to global*. This is allowed only if the group you want to change does not have another universal group as a member.
- *Universal to domain local*. There are no restrictions for this change.

Changing group type

You can convert a group from a security group to a distribution group, and vice versa, at any time, but only if the domain functional level is set to Windows 2000 native or higher. You cannot convert a group while the domain functional level is set to Windows 2000 mixed.

You may convert groups from one type to the other in the following scenarios:

- Security to distribution

  A company splits into two companies. Users migrate from one domain to another domain, but they keep their old e-mail addresses. You want to send them e-mail messages by using old security groups, but you want to remove security context from the group.

- Distribution to security

  A distribution group gets very large, and the users want to use this group for security-related tasks. However, they still want to use the group for e-mail.

Note Although you can add a contact to a security group and to a distribution group, you cannot grant permissions to contacts. You can send contacts e-mail messages.

How to Change the Scope or Type of a Group

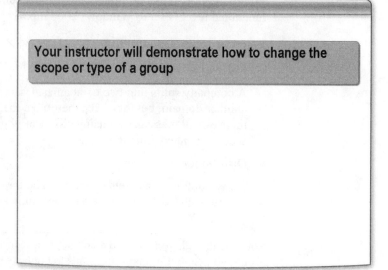

Introduction

To change the scope or type of a group, the domain functional level must be set to Windows 2000 native or higher. You cannot change the scope or type of groups if the domain functional level is set to Windows 2000 mixed.

Procedure

To change the scope or type of a group:

1. In Active Directory Users and Computers, in the console tree, click the folder that contains the group.
2. In the details pane, right-click the group, and then click **Properties**.
3. In the **Properties** dialog box, on the **General** tab, under **Group type**, click the group type to change it.
4. Under **Group scope**, click the group scope to change it.

Note   To perform this procedure, you must be a member of the Account Operators group, Domain Admins group, or Enterprise Admins group in Active Directory, or you must be delegated the appropriate authority. As a security best practice, consider using **Run as** to perform this procedure.

Practice: Changing the Scope and Type of a Group

In this practice, you will:

- Change the group scope from global to domain local

- Convert a security group into a distribution group

Objective

In this practice, you will:

- Change the group scope from global to a domain local.

- Convert a security group into a distribution group.

Instructions

Before you begin this practice:

- Log on to the domain by using the *ComputerName*User account.

- Open CustomMMC with the **Run as** command.

    Use the user account Nwtraders\ComputerNameAdmin (Example: LondonAdmin).

- Ensure that CustomMMC contains Active Directory Users and Computers.

Scenario

The IT managers at Northwind Traders want you to write a procedure for changing the scope of a security group from global to domain local. You must create all test groups in the IT Test organizational unit.

Practice: Changing group scope

▶ **Create a global security group**

- In the IT Test organizational unit, create a global security group named *ComputerName* Group Scope Test.

▶ **Document the procedure for converting the global group into a domain local group**

_____

_____

_____

_____

_____

_____

_____

Scenario

The IT managers at Northwind Traders want you to test the Active Directory feature that enables you to convert a security group into a distribution group. They want you to convert the security group you created into a distribution group.

Practice: Changing group type

▶ **Convert a global security group into a distribution group**

• Change the _ComputerName_ Group Scope group from a security group to a distribution group.

Why Assign a Manager to a Group?

- ● **To enable you to:**
  - ● Track who is responsible for groups
  - ● Delegate to the manager of the group the authority to add users to and remove users from the group
- ● **To distribute the administrative responsibility of adding users to groups to the people who request the group**

Advantages of assigning a manager to a group

Active Directory in Windows Server 2003 allows you to assign a manager to a group as a property of the group. This enables you to:

- ■ Track who is responsible for groups.
- ■ Delegate to the manager of the group the authority to add users to and remove users from the group.

Because people in large organizations are added to and removed from groups so often, some organizations distribute the administrative responsibility of adding users to groups to the people who request the group.

If you document who the manager of the group is, the contact information for that user account is recorded. If the group ever needs to be migrated to another domain or needs to be deleted, the network administrator has a record of who owns the group and their contact information. Therefore, the network administrator can call or send an e-mail message to the manager to notify the manager about the change that needs to be made to the group.

How to Assign a Manager to a Group

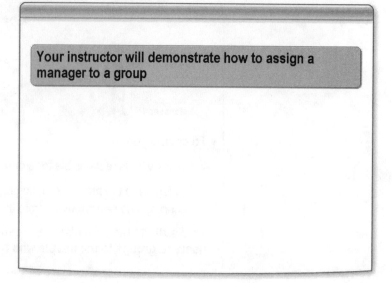

Your instructor will demonstrate how to assign a manager to a group

Introduction

Use the following procedure to assign a manager to a group.

Procedure

To assign a manager to a group:

1. In Active Directory Users and Computers, in the console tree, double-click the group that needs a manager.

2. In the **Properties** dialog box, on the **Managed By** tab, click **Change** to add a manager to a group or to change the manager of a group.

3. In the **Select User or Contact** dialog box, in the **Enter the object name to select** box, type the user name of the user who you want to manage the group, and then click **OK**.

4. Select the **Manager can update membership list** check box if you want the manager to add and remove users and groups.

5. In the **Properties** dialog box, click **OK**.

Practice: Assigning a Manager to a Group

In this practice, you will:

- Create a global group
- Assign a manager to a group
- Test the group manager properties

Objective

In this practice, you will:

- Create a global group.
- Assign a manager to the group who can modify group membership.
- Test the group manager properties.

Instructions

Before you begin this practice:

- Log on to the domain by using the *ComputerName*User account.
- Open CustomMMC with the **Run as** command.

    Use the user account Nwtraders\ComputerNameAdmin (Example: LondonAdmin).
- Ensure that CustomMMC contains Active Directory Users and Computers.

Scenario

You have been asked to create a group for the Sales department called G *ComputerName* Sales Strategy. The owner of the group will be the Sales manager for your city organizational unit.

Practice

▶ **Create a global group in your city organizational unit**

1. Create a global group called G *ComputerName* Sales Strategy in the organizational unit Locations/*ComputerName*
2. Log off.

▶ **Test the group manager properties**

1. Log on by using the *ComputerName*User account.

2. Open CustomMMC and try to add a user to G *ComputerName* Sales Strategy.

   You should not be able to add any users to this group.

3. Close CustomMMC.

4. Open CustomMMC (do not use the **Run as** command).

5. In Active Directory Users and Computers, navigate to your city organizational unit, and then double-click **G** *ComputerName***Sales Strategy**.

6. In the **Properties** dialog box, click the **Members** tab, and notice that you cannot add any users, because the **Add** button is unavailable.

7. Close CustomMMC.

▶ **Make *ComputerName*User a manager of G *ComputerName* Sales Strategy**

1. Open CustomMMC with the **Run as** command.

   Use the Nwtraders*ComputerName*Admin account.

2. In Active Directory Users and Computers, navigate to your city organizational unit, and then double-click **G** *ComputerName* **Sales Strategy**.

3. In the **Properties** dialog box, on the **Managed By** tab, add the *ComputerName*User user account.

4. Select the **Manager can update membership list** check box.

5. Close CustomMMC.

▶ **Test the group manager properties**

1. In Active Directory Users and Computers, navigate to your city organizational unit, and then double-click **G** *ComputerName* **Sales Strategy**.

2. In the **Properties** dialog box, on the **Members** tab, add the User0001 user account.

3. Close all windows and CustomMMC.

Lesson: Using Default Groups

- Default Groups on Member Servers
- Default Groups in Active Directory
- When to Use Default Groups
- Security Considerations for Default Groups
- System Groups

Introduction

This lesson introduces how default groups are used.

Lesson objectives

After completing this lesson, you will be able to:

- Explain how default groups are used on member servers.
- Explain how default groups are used in Active Directory.
- Identify when to use default groups.
- Identify the security considerations for default groups.
- Explain how system groups are used.

Default Groups on Member Servers

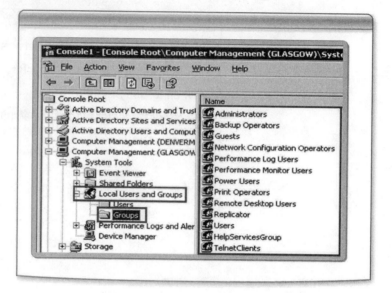

Definition

The Groups folder is located on a member server in the Local Users and Groups console, which displays all built-in default local groups and any local groups you create. The default local groups are created automatically when you install Windows Server 2003. The local groups can contain local user accounts, domain user accounts, computer accounts, and global groups.

Default local groups on member server

The following table describes some of the default local groups on a member or stand-alone server running Windows Server 2003.

Group	Description
Administrators	• Members have full control of the server and can assign user rights and access control permissions to users as necessary.
	• Administrators is a default member account and has full control of the server.
	• Users should be added with caution.
	• When joined to a domain, the Domain Admins group is automatically added to this group.
Guests	• A temporary profile is created for a member when the member logs on.
	• When the guest member logs off, the profile is deleted.
	• The Guest account is disabled by default.
Performance Log Users	• Members can manage performance counters, logs, and alerts on the server locally and from remote clients without being a member of the Administrators group.

(continued)

Group	Description
Performance Monitor Users	• Members can monitor performance counters on the server locally and from remote clients without being a member of the Administrators or Performance Log Users groups.
Power Users	• Members can create user accounts and then modify and delete the accounts they have created.
	• Members can create local groups and then add or remove users from the local groups they have created.
	• Members can add or remove users from the Power Users, Users, and Guests groups.
	• Members can create shared resources and administer the shared resources they have created.
	• Members cannot take ownership of files, back up or restore directories, load or unload device drivers, or manage security and auditing logs.
Print Operators	• Members can manage printers and print queues.
Users	• Members perform common tasks, such as running applications, using local and network printers, and locking the server.
	• Users cannot share directories or create local printers.
	• The Domain Users, Authenticated Users, and Interactive groups are members of this group. Therefore, any user account created in the domain becomes a member of this group.

The following additional groups are also default groups on a member server which are not commonly used.

- Network Configuration Operators
- Remote Desktop Users
- Replicator
- HelpServicesGroup
- Terminal Server Users

Note For more information about default groups on member servers, search for "default local groups" in Windows Server 2003 Help.

Default groups used by network services

The following table describes the default groups used by network services and installed only with the Dynamic Host Configuration Protocol (DHCP) service.

Group	Membership
DHCP Administrators	• Members have administrative access to the DHCP service.
	• The DHCP Administrators group provides security to assign limited administrative access to the DHCP server only, while not providing full access to the server.
	• Members can administer DHCP on a server by using the DHCP console or the **Netsh** command, but they cannot perform other administrative actions on the server.
DHCP Users	• Members have read-only access to the DHCP service.
	• Members can view information and properties stored at a specified DHCP server. This information is useful to support staff when they need to obtain DHCP status reports.
WINS Users	• Members are permitted read-only access to the Windows Internet Name Service (WINS).
	• Members can view information and properties stored at a specified WINS server. This information is useful to support staff when they need to obtain WINS status reports.

Default Groups in Active Directory

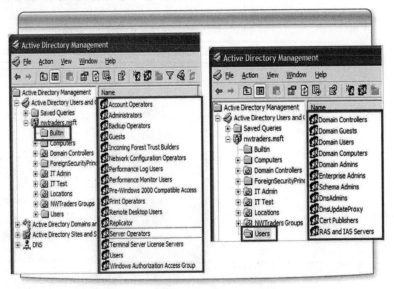

Definition

Default groups are security groups automatically created when you install an Active Directory domain. You can use these predefined groups to manage shared resources and delegate specific domain-wide administrative roles.

Many default groups are automatically assigned a set of user rights that determine what each group and their members can do within the scope of a domain or forest. User rights authorize members of a group to perform specific actions, such as log on to a local system or back up files and folders. For example, a member of the Backup Operators group has the right to perform backup operations for all domain controllers in the domain.

Several default groups are available in the Users and Builtin containers of Active Directory. The Builtin container contains domain local groups. The Users container contains global groups and domain local groups. You can move groups in the Users and Builtin containers to other group or organizational unit folders in the domain, but you cannot move them to other domains.

Groups in the Builtin container

The following table describes each default group in the Builtin container that is added to the default groups on a stand-alone or member server when Active Directory is installed. All of these default groups are added along with the user rights assigned to each group.

Group	Description
Account Operators	• Members can create, modify, and delete accounts for users, groups, and computers located in the Users or Computers containers and organizational units in the domain, except the Domain Controllers organizational unit. • Members do not have permission to modify the Administrators or the Domain Admins groups or accounts for members of those groups. • Members can log on locally to domain controllers in the domain and shut them down. • Because this group has significant power in the domain, add users with caution.
Incoming Forest Trust Builders	• Members can create one-way, incoming forest trusts to the forest root domain. • This group has no default members.
Pre-Windows 2000 Compatible Access	• Members have read access on all users and groups in the domain. • This group is provided for backward compatibility for computers running Windows NT 4.0 and earlier. • Add users to this group only if they are using Remote Access Service (RAS) on a computer running Windows NT 4.0 or earlier.
Server Operators	• Members can log on interactively, create and delete shared resources, start and stop some services, back up and restore files, format the hard disk, and shut down the computer. • This group has no default members. • Because this group has significant power on domain controllers, add users with caution.

Groups in the Users container

The following table describes each default group in the Users container and the user rights assigned to each group.

Group	Description
Domain Controllers	• This group contains all domain controllers in the domain.
Domain Guests	• This group contains all domain guests.
Domain Users	• This group contains all domain users.
	• Any user account created in the domain is a member of this group automatically.
Domain Computers	• This group contains all workstations and servers joined to the domain.
	• Any computer account created becomes a member of this group automatically.
Domain Admins	• Members have full control of the domain.
	• This group is a member of the Administrators group on all domain controllers, all domain workstations, and all domain member servers at the time they are joined to the domain.
	• The Administrator account is a member of this group. Because the group has full power in the domain, add users with caution.
Enterprise Admins	• Members have full control of all domains in the forest.
	• This group is a member of the Administrators group on all domain controllers in the forest.
	• The Administrator account is a member of this group. Because this group has full control of all domains in the forest, add users with caution.
Group Policy Creator Owners	• Members can modify Group Policy in the domain.
	• The Administrator account is a member of this group. Because this group has significant power in the domain, add users with caution.

The following list contains the additional Default groups that Systems Engineers would use to manage groups:

- Schema Admins
- DnsAdmins
- DnsUpdateProxy
- Cert Publishers
- RAS and IAS Servers

Note For more information about other groups in the Users container, search for "Active Directory default groups" in Windows Server 2003 Help.

When to Use Default Groups

- **Default groups are:**

  - Created during the installation of the operating system or when services are added such as Active Directory or DHCP

  - Automatically assigned a set of user rights

- **Use Default groups to:**

  - Control access to shared resources

  - Delegate specific domain-wide administration

Using default groups

Predefined groups help you to control access to shared resources and delegate specific domain-wide administrative roles. Many default groups are automatically assigned a set of user rights that authorize members of the group to perform specific actions in a domain, such as log on to a local system or back up files and folders.

When you add a user to a group, the user receives all the user rights assigned to the group and all the permissions assigned to the group for any shared resources.

As a security best practice, it is recommended that members of default groups with broad administrative access use **Run as** to perform administrative tasks.

Security Considerations for Default Groups

- Place a user in a default group only when you are sure you want to give the user all the user rights and permissions assigned to that group in Active Directory; otherwise, create a new security group

- As a security best practice, members of default groups should use Run as

---

Security considerations for default groups

Only place a user in a default group when you are sure you want to give the user:

- All the user rights assigned to that group in Active Directory.

- All of the permissions assigned to that group for any shared resources associated with that default group.

Otherwise, create a new security group and assign the group only those user rights or permissions that the user absolutely requires.

As a security best practice, members of default groups that have broad administrative access should not perform an interactive logon by using administrative credentials. Instead, users with this level of access should use **Run as**.

Warning   Only add members to default groups when members need all rights associated with the group. For example, if you need to add a service account to back up and restore files on a member server, you add the service account to the Backup Operators group. The Backup Operators group has the user rights to back up and restore files on the computer.

However, if your service account only needs to back up files and not restore them, it is better to create a new group. You can then grant the group the user right to back up files and not grant the group the right to restore files.

System Groups

- System groups represent different users at different times
- You can grant user rights and permissions to system groups, but you cannot modify or view the memberships
- Group scopes do not apply to system groups
- Users are automatically assigned to system groups whenever they log on or access a particular resource

Introduction

You cannot change the membership of system groups. The operating system creates them, and you cannot change or manage them. It is important to understand the system groups, because you can use them for security purposes.

Definition

Servers running Windows Server 2003 include several special identities in addition to the groups in the Users and Builtin containers. For convenience, these identities are generally referred to as system groups.

System groups represent different users at different times, depending on the circumstances. Although you can grant user rights and permissions to the system groups, you cannot modify or view their memberships.

Group scopes do not apply to system groups. Users are automatically assigned to system groups whenever they log on or access a particular resource.

System groups

The following table describes the system groups.

System group	Description
Anonymous Logon	The Anonymous Logon system group represents users and services that access a computer and its resources through the network without using an account name, password, or domain name.
	On computers running Windows NT and earlier, the Anonymous Logon group is a member of the Everyone group by default.
	On computers running a member of the Windows Server 2003 family, the Anonymous Logon group is not a member of the Everyone group by default. If you want to create a file share for an anonymous user, you grant permissions to the Anonymous Logon group.
Everyone	The Everyone system group represents all current network users, including guests and users from other domains. Whenever a user logs on to the network, the user is automatically added to the Everyone group.
	If security is not a concern for a specific group in your domain, you can grant permissions to the Everyone group. However, because the Anonymous Logon group can become a member of the Everyone group, it is not recommended that you use this group for permissions above read-only.
Network	The Network system group represents users currently accessing a given resource over the network, as opposed to users who access a resource by logging on locally at the computer where the resource is located. Whenever a user accesses a given resource over the network, the user is automatically added to the Network group.
Interactive	The Interactive system group represents all users currently logged on to a particular computer and accessing a given resource located on that computer, as opposed to users who access the resource over the network. Whenever a user accesses a resource on the computer to which they are currently logged on, the user is automatically added to the Interactive group.
Authenticated Users	The Authenticated Users system group represents all users within Active Directory. Always use the Authenticated Users group when granting permissions for a resource instead of using the Everyone group to prevent guests from accessing resources.
Creator Owner	The Creator Owner system group includes the user account for the user who created or took ownership of a resource. If a member of the Administrators group creates a resource, the Administrators group is the owner of the resource.

Class Discussion: Using Default Groups vs. Creating New Groups

Northwind Traders has over 100 servers across the world. You are attending a meeting to discuss the current tasks that administrators must perform and what minimum level of access the users need to perform specific tasks. You also must determine if you can use default groups or if you must create groups and assign specific user rights and permissions to the groups to perform the tasks.

Scenario

Northwind Traders has over 100 servers across the world. You are attending a meeting to discuss the current tasks that administrators must perform and what minimum level of access the users need to perform specific tasks. You also must determine if you can use default groups or if you must create groups and assign specific user rights and permissions to the groups to perform the tasks.

Discussion

You must assign default groups or create new groups for the following tasks. List the group that has the most restrictive user rights for performing the following actions or determine if you must create a new group.

1. Backing up and restoring domain controllers

   _____

   _____

   _____

2. Backing up member servers

   _____

   _____

   _____

3. Creating groups in the NWTraders Groups organizational unit

   _____

   _____

   _____

4. Logging on to the domain

   _____

   _____

   _____

5. Determining who needs read-only access to the DHCP servers

   _____

   _____

   _____

6. Determining what help desk employees need access to control the desktop remotely

   _____

   _____

   _____

7. Determining who needs administrative access to all computers in the entire domain

   _____

   _____

   _____

8. Determining who need access to a shared folder called Sales on a server called LonSrv2

   _____

   _____

   _____

Best Practices for Managing Groups

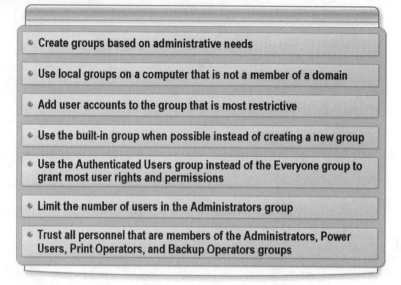

Best practices

Consider the following best practices for managing groups:

- Create groups based on administrative needs. When you create a group based on a job function and another person takes over that job, you only need to change the group membership. You do not need to change all permissions that are granted to the individual user account. Because of this, it is sometimes advantageous to create a group that has only one member.

- Use local groups to give users access to resources on local computers when the computer is not a member of a domain.

- If you have multiple groups to which you can add user accounts, add user accounts to the group that is most restrictive. However, ensure that you grant the appropriate user rights and permissions so that users can accomplish any required task.

- Whenever a default group enables users to accomplish a task, use the default group instead of creating a new group. Create groups only when there are no default groups that provide the required user rights and permissions.

- Use the Authenticated Users group instead of the Everyone group to grant most user rights and permissions. Using this group minimizes the risk of unauthorized access, because Windows Server 2003 adds only valid user accounts to members of the Authenticated Users system group.

- Limit the number of users in the Administrators group. Members of the Administrators group on a local computer have Full Control permissions for that computer. Add a user to the Administrators group if the user will perform only administrative tasks.

- Your organization must equally trust all personnel that are members of the Administrators, Power Users, Print Operators, and Backup Operators groups. Some default user rights assigned to specific default local groups may allow members of those groups to gain additional rights on your computer, including administrative rights.

Lab A: Creating and Managing Groups

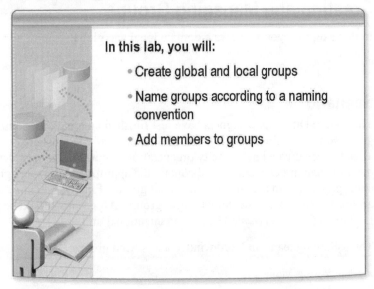

In this lab, you will:

- Create global and local groups
- Name groups according to a naming convention
- Add members to groups

Objectives

After completing this lab, you will be able to:

- Create global and domain local groups.
- Name groups according to a naming convention.
- Add members to groups.

Prerequisites

Before working on this lab, you must have knowledge of Active Directory, organizational units, organizational unit hierarchy, and accounts in Active Directory.

Before you begin this lab:

- Log on to the domain by using the *ComputerName*User account.
- Open CustomMMC with the **Run as** command.

  Use the user account Nwtraders\ComputerNameAdmin (Example: LondonAdmin).

- Ensure that CustomMMC contains Active Directory Users and Computers.

Estimated time to complete this lab: 60 minutes

Exercise 1
Creating and Managing Groups

In this exercise, you will create domain local and global groups, add members to groups, and nest groups.

Scenario

The Active Directory designers have just finished creating the group naming convention. They have given you a list of teams in Northwind Traders that you must create groups for. Some groups have already been created in your city organizational unit, so you must determine if the existing groups meet the naming convention and contain the appropriate users and groups. You then must add the appropriate user to the appropriate global groups. Finally, you must add the appropriate global groups to the appropriate domain local groups. All groups should be created in the Locations/*ComputerName*/Groups organizational unit.

The following teams in Northwind Traders need groups:

- Marketing Managers
- Marketing Personnel
- HR Managers
- HR Personnel

The Active Directory designers have created the following naming convention for groups:

- The first part of the group name defines the scope of the group (Example: **G** for global group and **DL** for domain local group).
- The second part of the group name defines the city organizational unit that the group belongs to (Example: London).
- The third part of the group name defines who the group is created for (Example: Sales Managers or Sales Personnel).
- If the group is a domain local group, the last part of the group name defines the maximum permissions the group will be used for (Example: Read or Full Control).

Tasks	Specific instructions
1. Create global groups for the following teams in the Locations/*ComputerName*/Groups organizational unit.	a. Marketing Managers (Example: G London Marketing Managers) b. Marketing Personnel c. HR Managers d. HR Personnel
2. Search for users who are managers and add them to the manager global groups.	a. Search for all Marketing Managers in the city called *ComputerName* and add them to the G *ComputerName* Marketing Managers group. b. Do the preceding step for the following groups: <ul><li>G ComputerName Marketing Personnel</li><li>G ComputerName HR Managers</li><li>G ComputerName HR Personnel</li></ul>
3. Search for users who are personnel and add them to the personnel global groups.	a. Search for all users in the city called *ComputerName* and in the Marketing department and add them to the G Marketing Personnel group. b. Do the preceding step for each global personnel group.
4. Create domain local groups that will be used for Read and Modify permissions for the following teams in the Locations/*ComputerName*/Groups organizational unit.	▪ Create the following Domain Local groups: <ul><li>DL ComputerName Marketing Managers Read</li><li>DL ComputerName Marketing Personnel Read</li><li>DL ComputerName HR Managers Read</li><li>DL ComputerName HR Personnel Read</li><li>DL ComputerName Marketing Managers Modify</li><li>DL *ComputerName* Marketing Personnel Modify</li><li>DL ComputerName HR Managers Modify</li><li>DL ComputerName HR Personnel Modify</li></ul>
5. Add members to the domain local groups for managers.	a. For each manager domain local group that was created, add the appropriate managers global group. For example: add G *ComputerName* Marketing Managers to DL ComputerName Marketing Managers Read and DL ComputerName Marketing Managers Modify. b. Do the preceding step for every manager's domain local group.
6. Add members to the domain local groups for personnel.	a. For each personnel domain local group that was created, add the appropriate global group for personnel. For example: add G *ComputerName* Marketing Personnel to DL *ComputerName* Marketing Personnel Read and DL *ComputerName* Marketing Personnel Modify. b. Do the preceding step for every personnel's domain local group.

Microsoft®
Training &
Certification

Module 4: Managing Access to Resources

Contents

Microsoft®

Overview

- Overview of Managing Access to Resources
- Managing Access to Shared Folders
- Managing Access to Files and Folders Using NTFS Permissions
- Determining Effective Permissions
- Managing Access to Shared Files Using Offline Caching

Introduction

This module introduces the job function of managing access to resources. Specifically, the module provides the skills and knowledge that you need to explain; manage access to files and folders by using shared folder permissions, NTFS permissions, or effective permissions; and manage access to shared files using offline caching.

Objectives

After completing this module, you will be able to:

- Manage access to resources.
- Manage access to shared folders.
- Manage access to files and folders by using NTFS permissions.
- Determine effective permissions.
- Managing access to shared files by using offline caching.

Lesson: Overview of Managing Access to Resources

- Multimedia: Access Control in Microsoft Windows Server 2003
- What Are Permissions?
- What Are Standard and Special Permissions?
- Multimedia: Permission States

Introduction

The information in this lesson presents the knowledge that you need to manage access to resources.

Lesson objectives

After completing this lesson, you will be able to:

- Describe the components of access control in Microsoft® Windows® Server 2003.
- Define permissions.
- Explain the differences between standard and special permissions.
- Explain the characteristics of implicit and explicit permission states.

Multimedia: Access Control in Microsoft Windows Server 2003

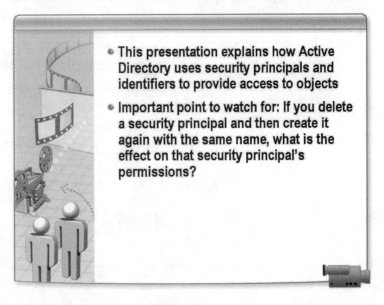

File location

To view the *Access Control in Microsoft Windows Server 2003* presentation, open the Web page on the Student Materials compact disc, click **Multimedia**, and then click the title of the presentation.

Key points

Key points from the presentation are summarized in the following list:

- Security principal

  A security principal is an account that can be authenticated.

- Security identifier (SID)

  A SID is an alphanumeric structure that is issued when an account is created and that uniquely identifies a security principal.

- Discretionary access control list (DACL)

  Each resource is associated with a DACL, which identifies the users and groups that are allowed or denied access to that resource.

- Access control entry (ACE)

  A DACL contains multiple ACEs. Each ACE specifies a SID, special permissions, inheritance information, and an Allow or Deny permission.

Additional reading

For more information about access control, see "Access Control Components" at http://msdn.microsoft.com/library/default.asp?url=/library/en-us/security/security/access_control_components.asp.

What Are Permissions?

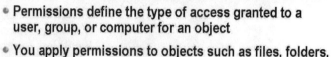

- Permissions define the type of access granted to a user, group, or computer for an object
- You apply permissions to objects such as files, folders, shared folders, and printers
- You assign permissions to users and groups in Active Directory or on a local computer

Definition

Permissions define the type of access granted to a user, group, or computer for an object. For example, you can let one user read the contents of a file, let another user make changes to the file, and prevent all other users from accessing the file. You can set similar permissions on printers so that certain users can configure the printer and other users can only print from it.

Permissions are also applied to any secured objects, such as files, objects in the Active Directory® directory service, and registry objects. Permissions can be granted to any user, group, or computer.

You can grant permissions for objects to:

- Groups, users, and special identities in the domain.
- Groups and users in any trusted domains.
- Local groups and users on the computer where the object resides.

Permission types

When you set permissions, you specify the level of access for groups and users. The permissions attached to an object depend on the type of object. For example, the permissions that are attached to a file are different from those that are attached to a registry key. Some permissions, however, are common to most types of objects. The following permissions are common permissions:

- Read permissions
- Write permissions
- Delete permissions

What Are Standard and Special Permissions?

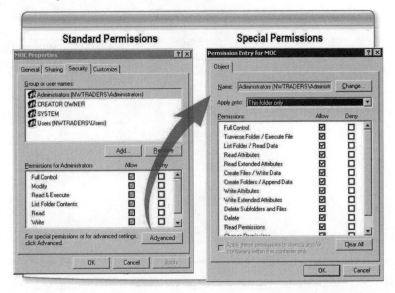

Introduction	You can grant standard and special permissions for objects. Standard permissions are the most frequently assigned permissions. Special permissions provide you with a finer degree of control for assigning access to objects.
Standard permissions	The system has a default level of security settings for a specific object. These are the most common set of permissions that a systems administrator uses on a daily basis. The list of standard permissions that are available varies depending on what type of object you are modifying the security for.
Special permissions	Special permissions are a more detailed list of permissions. A standard NFTS permission of Read is related to the following special permissions:

- List Folder/Read Data
- Read Attributes
- Read Extended Attributed
- Read Permissions

If the systems administrator removes a special permission that relates to a standard permission, the check box for the standard permission is no longer selected. The check box for the special permission under the standard permission list is selected.

Multimedia: Permission States

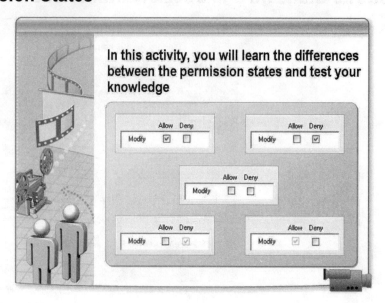

File location

To start the *Permission States* activity, open the Web page on the Student Materials compact disc, click **Multimedia**, and then click the title of the activity.

Lesson: Managing Access to Shared Folders

- What Are Shared Folders?
- What Are Administrative Shared Folders?
- Who Can Access Shared Folders?
- How to Create a Shared Folder
- What Are Published Shared Folders?
- How to Publish a Shared Folder
- Shared Folder Permissions
- How to Set Permissions on a Shared Folder
- How to Connect to Shared Folders

Introduction

The Windows Server 2003 family organizes files into directories that are graphically represented as folders. These folders contain all types of files and can contain subfolders. Some of these folders are reserved for operating system files and program files. Users should never place any data into the operating system folders or program file folders.

Shared folders give users access to files and folders over a network. Users can connect to the shared folder over the network to access the folders and files they contain. Shared folders can contain applications, public data, or a user's personal data. Using shared application folders centralizes administration by enabling you to install and maintain applications on a server instead of client computers. Using shared data folders provides a central location for users to access common files and makes it easier to back up data contained in those files.

Lesson objectives

After completing this lesson, you will be able to:

- Explain what shared folders are.
- Explain what administrative shared folders are.
- Identify the requirements for sharing folders.
- Create a shared folder.
- Explain what published shared folders are.
- Publish a shared folder.
- Explain what shared folder permissions are.
- Set permissions on a shared folder.
- Connect to shared folders.

What Are Shared Folders?

- **Copy a shared folder**
  - The original shared folder is still shared, but the copy of the folder is not shared
- **Move a shared folder**
  - The folder is no longer shared
- **Hide a shared folder**
  - Include a $ after the name of the shared folder
  - Users can access a hidden shared folder by typing the UNC, for example, \\server\secrets$

Introduction

Sharing a folder is when a folder is made accessible to multiple users simultaneously over the network. After a folder is shared, users can access all of the files and subfolders in the shared folder if they are granted permission.

You can place shared folders on a file server and also place them on any computer on the network. You can store files in shared folders according to categories or functions. For example, you can place shared data files in one shared folder and shared application files in another.

Characteristics of shared folders

Some of the most common characteristics of shared folders are as follows:

- A shared folder appears in Windows Explorer as an icon of a hand holding the folder.

- You can only share folders, not individual files. If multiple users need access to the same file, you must place the file in a folder and then share the folder.

- When a folder is shared, the Read permission is granted to the Everyone group as the default permission. Remove the default permission and grant the Change permission or Read permission to groups as needed.

- When users or groups are added to a shared folder, the default permission is Read.

- When you copy a shared folder, the original shared folder is still shared, but the copy is not shared. When a shared folder is moved to another location, the folder is no longer shared.

- You can hide a shared folder if you put a dollar sign ($) after the name of the shared folder. The user cannot see the shared folder in the user interface, but a user can access the shared folder by typing the Universal Naming Convention (UNC) name, for example, \\server\secrets$.

What Are Administrative Shared Folders?

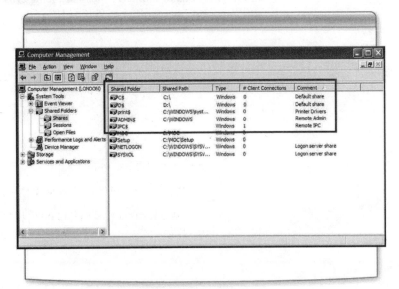

Introduction

Windows Server 2003 automatically shares folders that enable you to perform administrative tasks. They are designated by an appended dollar sign ($) at the end of the folder name. The dollar sign hides the shared folder from users who browse to the computer in My Network Places. Administrators can quickly administer files and folders on remote servers by using these hidden shared folders.

Types of administrative shared folders

By default, members of the Administrators group have the Full Control permission for administrative shared folders. You cannot modify the permissions for administrative shared folders. The following table describes the purpose of the administrative shared folders that Windows Server 2003 automatically provides.

Shared folder	Purpose
C$, D$, E$	You use these shared folders to remotely connect to a computer and perform administrative tasks. The root of each partition (that has a drive letter assigned to it) on a hard disk is automatically shared. When you connect to this folder, you have access to the entire partition.
Admin$	This is the systemroot folder, which is C:\Winnt by default. Administrators can access this shared folder to administer Windows Server 2003 without knowing the folder in which it is installed.
Print$	This folder provides access to printer driver files for client computers. When you install the first shared printer, the *Systemroot*\System32\ Spool\Drivers folder is shared as Print$. Only members of the Administrators, Server Operators, and Print Operators groups have Full Control permission for this folder. The Everyone group has Read permission for this folder.
IPC$	This folder is used during remote administration of a computer and when viewing a computer's shared resources.
FAX$	This shared folder is used to temporarily cache files and access cover pages on the server.

Additional reading   For more information on IPC$, see article 101150, "Operating Characteristics and Restrictions of Named Pipes" in the Microsoft Knowledge Base at http://support.microsoft.com/?kbid=101150.

Who Can Access Shared Folders?

- **Windows Server 2003 domain controller**
  - Administrators Group
  - Server Operators Group
- **A member server or stand-alone server running Windows Server 2003**
  - Administrators Group
  - Power Users Group

Introduction

In Windows Server 2003, the only groups that can access shared folders are the Administrators, Server Operators, and Power Users groups. These groups are built-in groups that are placed in the Group folder in Computer Management or the built-in folder in Active Directory Users and Groups.

Groups that can access shared folders

The following table describes who can access shared folders.

To share folders:	You must be a member of:
On a Windows Server 2003 domain controller	The Administrators or Server Operators group. Note that the Power Users group can share folders on a member server in a Windows Server 2003 domain.
On a stand-alone or member server running Windows Server 2003	The Administrators or Power Users group.

How to Create a Shared Folder

Your instructor will demonstrate how to:

- Create a shared folder by using Computer Management
- Create a shared folder by using Windows Explorer
- Create a shared folder by using net share

Introduction

When you create a shared folder, you give it a shared folder name and provide a comment that describes the folder and its contents. You can also limit the number of users who can access the folder, grant permissions, and share the same folder multiple times.

Procedure using Computer Management

To create a shared folder by using Computer Management:

1. In Computer Management, in the console tree, expand **Shared Folders** and then click **Shares**.

2. On the **Action** menu, click **New Share**.

3. Follow the steps in the Share a Folder Wizard.

Procedure using Windows Explorer

To create a shared folder by using Windows Explorer:

1. In Windows Explorer, right-click the folder, and then click **Sharing and Security**.

2. In the **Properties** dialog box, on the **Sharing** tab, configure the options described in the following table.

Option	Description
Share this folder	Click to share the folder.
Share name	Enter the name that users from remote locations use to connect to the shared folder. The default shared folder name is the folder name. This option is required.
	Note: Some client computers that connect to a shared folder only see a limited number of characters.
Description	Enter an optional description for the shared folder. You can use this comment to identify the contents of the shared folder.
User Limit	Enter the number of users who can concurrently connect to the shared folder. This option is not required if you click **Maximum Allowed**, current Windows client operating systems supports up to 10 concurrent connections.
Permissions	Click to set the shared folder permissions that apply only when the folder is accessed over the network. This option is not required. By default, the Everyone group is granted the Read permission for all new shared folders.

Using a command line

The **net share** command creates, deletes, or displays shared folders. To create a shared folder by using **net share**:

1. Open a command prompt.

2. Type **net share** *SharedFolderName=Drive:Path*

Value	Description
SharedFolderName=Drive:Path	This is the network name of the shared folder and the absolute path of its location.

What Are Published Shared Folders?

- A published shared folder is a shared folder object in Active Directory

- Clients can search Active Directory for shared folders that are published

- Clients do not need to know the name of the server to connect to a shared folder

Definition

Publishing resources and shared folders in Active Directory enables users to search Active Directory and locate resources on the network even if the physical location of the resources changes.

For example, if you move a shared folder to another computer, all shortcuts pointing to the Active Directory object that represents the published shared folder continue to work, as long as you update the reference to the physical location. Users do not have to update their connections.

Publishing the folder

You can publish any shared folder in Active Directory that can be accessed by using a UNC name. After a shared folder is published, a user at a computer running Windows Server 2003 can use Active Directory to locate the object representing the shared folder and then connect to the shared folder.

When the shared folder is published to Active Directory, the shared folder becomes a child object of the computer account. To view shared folders as an object, in Active Directory Users and Computers, on the **View** menu, click **Users, Group, and Computers as containers**. Then, in the console tree, click the computer account. On the details pane, you will see all the published shared folders that are associated with the computer account.

How to Publish a Shared Folder

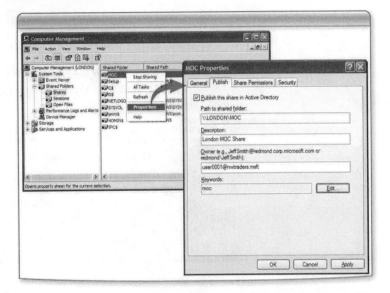

Introduction	Publishing information about network resources in Active Directory makes it easy for users to find them on the network. You can publish information about printers and shared folders by using Computer Management or Active Directory Users and Computers.

Procedure for publishing a shared folder as a server object

To publish a shared folder as a server object:

1. In Computer Management, in the console tree, expand **Shared Folders** and then click **Shares**.

2. Right-click a shared folder, and then click **Properties**.

3. In the **Properties** dialog box, on the **Publish** tab, select the **Publish this share in Active Directory** check box, and then click **OK**.

Procedure for publishing a shared folder to an organizational unit

To publish a shared folder to an organizational unit:

1. In Active Directory Users and Computers, in the console tree, right-click the folder in which you want to add the shared folder, point to **New**, and then click **Shared Folder**.

2. In the **New Object – Shared Folder** dialog box, in the **Name** box, type the name of the folder you want clients to use.

3. In the **Network path** box, type the UNC name that you want to publish in Active Directory, and then click **OK**.

Shared Folder Permissions

Permission	Allows the user to:
Read (Default, applied to the Everyone group)	• View data in files and attributes • View file names and subfolder names • Run program files
Change (Includes all Read permissions)	• Add files and subfolders • Change data in files • Delete subfolders and files
Full Control	• Includes all Read and Change permissions • Enables you to change NTFS files and folders permissions

Introduction

Shared folder permissions only apply to users who connect to the folder over the network. They do not restrict access to users who access the folder at the computer where the folder is stored. You can grant shared folder permissions to user accounts, groups, and computer accounts.

Permissions

Shared folder permissions include the following:

■ Read

Read is the default shared folder permission and is applied to the Everyone group. Read permission enables you to:

  • View file names and subfolder names.

  • View data in files and attributes.

  • Run program files.

■ Change

The Change permission includes all Read permissions and also enables you to:

  • Add files and subfolders.

  • Change data in files.

  • Delete subfolders and files.

■ Full Control

Full Control includes all Read and Change permissions and also enables you to change permissions for NTFS files and folders.

How to Set Permissions on a Shared Folder

Your instructor will demonstrate how to:

- Set permissions on a shared folder by using Computer Management
- Set permissions on a shared folder by using Windows Explorer

Introduction

Use the following procedure to set permissions on a shared folder.

Procedure using Computer Management

To set permissions on a shared folder by using Computer Management:

1. In Computer Management, in the console tree, expand **Shared Folders**, and then click **Shares**.

2. In the details pane, right-click the shared folder for which you want to set permissions, and then click **Properties**.

3. In the **Properties** dialog box, on the **Share Permissions** tab, do one of the following:

   - Click **Add** to grant a user or group permission for a shared folder. In the **Select Users, Computers, or Groups** dialog box, select or type the user or group name, and then click **OK**.

   - Click **Remove** to revoke access to a shared folder.

4. In the **Permissions** box, select the **Allow** or **Deny** check boxes to set individual permissions for the selected user or group, and then click **OK**.

Procedures using Windows Explorer

To set permissions on a shared folder by using Windows Explorer:

1. In Windows Explorer, right-click the shared folder for which you want to set permissions, and then click **Sharing and Security**.

2. In the **Properties** dialog box, on the **Sharing** tab, click **Permissions**.

3. In the **Permissions** dialog box, do one of the following:

   - Click **Add** to grant a user or group permission for a shared folder. In the **Select Users, Computers, or Groups** dialog box, select or type the user or group name, and then click **OK**.

   - Click **Remove** to revoke access to a shared resource.

4. In the **Permissions** box, select the **Allow** or **Deny** check boxes to set individual permissions for the selected user or group.

How to Connect to Shared Folders

Introduction

After you create a shared folder, users can access the folder across the network. Users can access a shared folder on another computer by using My Network Places, the **Map Network Drive** feature, or the **Run** command on the **Start** menu.

Procedure using My Network Places

To connect to a shared folder by using My Network Places:

1. Open My Network Places and double-click **Add a network place**.

2. In the Add Network Place Wizard, on the **Welcome** page, click **Next**.

3. On the **Where do you want to create this network place** page, click **Choose another network location**, and then click **Next**.

4. On the **What is the address of this network place** page, type the UNC path of the shared folder or click **Browse**.

   a. If you click **Browse**, expand **Entire Network**.

   b. Expand **Microsoft Windows Network**.

   c. Expand the domain and server you want to connect to.

   d. Click the shared folder that you want to add, and then click **OK**.

5. Click **Next**.

6. On the **What do you want to name this place** page, type the name of the network place, and then click **Next**.

7. On the **Completing the Add Network Place Wizard** page, click **Finish**.

Note   When you open a shared folder over the network, Windows Server 2003 automatically adds it to My Network Places.

Procedure using Map Network Drive

When you want a drive letter and icon associated with a specific shared folder, you must map to a network drive. This makes it easier to refer to the location of a file in a shared folder. You can also use drive letters to access shared folders for which you cannot use a UNC path, such as a folder for an older application.

To connect to a shared folder by using My Network Places:

1. Right-click **My Network Places**, and then click **Map Network Drive**.

2. In the **Map Network Drive** dialog box, in the **Drive** box, select the drive that you want to use.

3. In the **Folder** box, type the name of the shared folder you want to connect to or click **Browse**.

4. For a shared folder that you will use on a recurring basis, select the **Reconnect at logon** check box to connect automatically to the shared folder each time you log on.

Procedure using the Run command

When you use the **Run** command on the **Start** menu to connect to a network resource, a drive letter is not required. This enables you to connect to the shared folder an unlimited number of times, independent of available drive letters.

1. Click **Start**, and then click **Run**.

2. In the **Run** dialog box, enter a UNC path, and then click **OK**.

   When you enter the server name, a list of available shared folders appears. Windows Server 2003 gives you the option to choose one of the entries based on the shared folders that are available to you.

Practice: Managing Access to Shared Folders

In this practice, you will:

- Create shared folders
- Test Read permissions of the shared folder
- Test Full Control permissions of the shared folder

Objective

In this practice, you will create a shared folder, grant Read and Full Control permissions to two separate groups, and test the permissions.

Instructions

Before you begin this practice:

- Log on to the domain as *ComputerName*Admin.

   Note You cannot use the **Run as** command with Windows Explorer, so you must log on as *ComputerName*Admin to have the permissions that you need to complete this practice.

- Ensure that CustomMMC contains Computer Management (Local).
- Review the procedures in this lesson that describe how to perform this task.

Scenario

You have been asked to create a shared folder for the Human Resources department. The Human Resources department needs a shared folder for which Human Resources personnel will have Full Control permissions and all Accounting managers will have read access. You must create the shared folder with the proper permissions to meet the needs of the Human Resources personnel and Accounting managers.

Practice

▶ **Create a shared folder**

- Using Computer Management, create a shared folder on your student computer with the following parameters:
    - Folder location: D:\
    - Folder name: **HR Reports**
    - Security:
        - Grant Full Control permissions to DL NWTraders HR Personnel Full Control
        - Grant Read permissions to DL NWTraders Accounting Managers Read
        - Remove the Everyone group

▶ **Test Read permissions of the shared folder**

1. Log on as **AccountingManager** with a password of **P@ssw0rd**.
2. Connect to the shared folder *ComputerName*\HR Reports.
3. Try to create a text file in the HR Reports folder.

    You *should not* be able to create a text file in the shared folder.

▶ **Test Full Control permissions of the shared folder**

1. Log on as **HRUser** with a password of **P@ssw0rd**.
2. Connect to the shared folder *ComputerName*\HR Reports.
3. Try to create a text file in the HR Reports folder.

    You *should* be able to access the shared folder.

Lesson: Managing Access to Files and Folders Using NTFS Permissions

- What Is NTFS?
- NTFS File and Folder Permissions
- Effects on NTFS Permissions When Copying and Moving Files and Folders
- What Is NTFS Permissions Inheritance?
- How to Copy or Remove Inherited Permissions
- Best Practices for Managing Access to Files and Folders Using NTFS Permissions
- How to Manage Access to Files and Folders Using NTFS Permissions

Introduction

The information in this lesson presents the skills and knowledge that you need to manage access to files and folders by using NTFS permissions.

Lesson objectives

After completing this lesson, you will be able to:

- Explain what NTFS is.
- Explain what NTFS file and folder permissions are.
- Explain the effects on NTFS permissions of copying and moving files and folders.
- Explain what NTFS permissions inheritance is.
- Explain best practices for managing access to files and folders by using NTFS permissions.
- Copy or remove inherited permissions.
- Manage access to files and folders by using NTFS permissions.

What Is NTFS?

NTFS is a file system that provides:

- Reliability
- Security at the file level and folder level
- Improved management of storage growth
- Multiple user permissions

Introduction

NTFS is a file system that is available on Windows Server 2003. NTFS provides performance and features that are not found in either FAT (file allocation table) or FAT32.

Benefits of NTFS

NTFS provides the following benefits:

- Reliability

  NTFS uses log file and checkpoint information to restore the integrity of the file system when the computer is restarted. If there is a bad-sector error, NTFS dynamically remaps the cluster containing the bad sector and allocates a new cluster for the data. NTFS also marks the cluster as unusable.

- Greater security

  NTFS files use the Encrypting File System (EFS) to secure files and folders. If EFS is enabled, files and folders can be encrypted for use by single or multiple users. The benefits of encryption are data confidentiality and data integrity, which means that data is protected against malicious or accidental modification. NTFS also enables you to set access permissions on a file or folder. Permissions can be set to Read, Read and Write, or Deny.

  NTFS also stores an access control list (ACL) with every file and folder on an NTFS partition. The ACL contains a list of all user accounts, groups, and computers that are granted access for the file or folder and the type of access that they are granted. For a user to access a file or folder, the ACL must contain an entry, called an ACE, for the user account, group, or computer that the user is associated with. The ACE must specifically allow the type of access the user is requesting for the user to access the file or folder. If no ACE exists in the ACL, Windows Server 2003 denies the user access to the resource.

■ Improved management of storage growth

NTFS supports disk quotas, which enable you to specify the amount of disk space that is available to a user. By using disk quotas, you can track and control disk space usage and configure whether users are allowed to exceed a warning level or storage quota limit.

NTFS supports larger files and a larger number of files per volume than FAT or FAT32. NTFS also manages disk space efficiently by using smaller cluster sizes. For example, a 30-gigabyte (GB) NTFS volume uses four-kilobyte (KB) clusters. The same volume formatted with FAT32 uses 16-KB clusters. Using smaller clusters reduces wasted space on hard disks.

■ Multiple user permissions

If you grant NTFS permissions to an individual user account and to a group to which the user belongs, then you grant multiple permissions to the user. There are rules for how NTFS combines these multiple permissions to produce the user's effective permissions.

Additional reading

For more information on NTFS, see "NTFS" at http://www.microsoft.com/technet/treeview/default.asp?url=/technet/prodtechnol/windowsserver2003/proddocs/server/ntfs.asp.

For more information on FAT and NTFS, see "Choosing Between FAT and NTFS" at http://www.microsoft.com/technet/treeview/default.asp?url=/technet/ittasks/deploy/fat.asp.

NTFS File and Folder Permissions

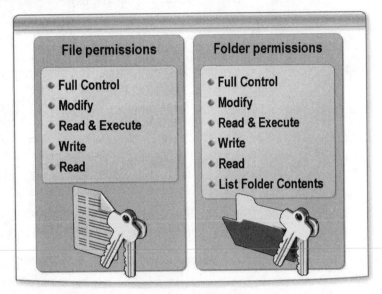

File permissions	Folder permissions
• Full Control	• Full Control
• Modify	• Modify
• Read & Execute	• Read & Execute
• Write	• Write
• Read	• Read
	• List Folder Contents

Introduction

NTFS permissions are used to specify which users, groups, and computers can access files and folders. NTFS permissions also dictate what users, groups, and computers can do with the contents of the file or folder.

NTFS file permissions

The following table lists the standard NTFS file permissions that you can grant and the type of access that each permission provides.

NTFS file permission	Allows the user to:
Full Control	Change permissions, take ownership, and perform the actions permitted by all other NTFS file permissions
Modify	Modify and delete the file and perform the actions permitted by the Write permission and the Read & Execute permission
Read & Execute	Run applications and perform the actions permitted by the Read permission
Write	Overwrite the file, change file attributes, and view file ownership and permissions
Read	Read the file and view file attributes, ownership, and permissions

NTFS folder permissions

Permissions control access to folders and the files and subfolders that are contained in those folders. The following table lists the standard NTFS folder permissions that you can grant and the type of access that each permission provides.

NTFS folder permission	Allows the user to:
Full Control	Change permissions, take ownership, delete subfolders and files, and perform actions permitted by all other NTFS folder permissions
Modify	Delete the folder and perform actions permitted by the Write permission and the Read & Execute permission
Read & Execute	Traverse folders and perform actions permitted by the Read permission and the List Folder Contents permission
Write	Create new files and subfolders in the folder, change folder attributes, and view folder ownership and permissions
Read	View files and subfolders in the folder, folder attributes, ownership, and permissions
List Folder Contents	View the names of files and subfolders in the folder

Additional reading

For more information about permissions, see "Permissions" at http://www.microsoft.com/technet/treeview/default.asp?url=/technet/prodtechnol/windowsserver2003/proddocs/server/sag_sfmhowworks_13.asp.

Effects on NTFS Permissions When Copying and Moving Files and Folders

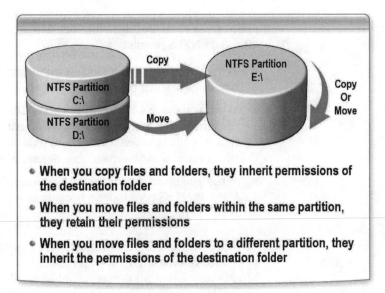

- When you copy files and folders, they inherit permissions of the destination folder
- When you move files and folders within the same partition, they retain their permissions
- When you move files and folders to a different partition, they inherit the permissions of the destination folder

Introduction

When you copy or move a file or folder, the permissions may change depending on where you move the file or folder. It is important to understand the changes that the permissions undergo when being copied or moved.

Effects of copying files and folders

When you copy files or folders from one folder to another folder, or from one partition to another partition, permissions for the files or folders may change. Copying a file or folder has the following effects on NTFS permissions:

- When you copy a folder or file within a single NTFS partition, the copy of the folder or file inherits the permissions of the destination folder.

- When you copy a folder or file to a different NTFS partition, the copy of the folder or file inherits the permissions of the destination folder.

- When you copy a folder or file to a non-NTFS partition, such as a FAT partition, the copy of the folder or file loses its NTFS permissions, because non-NTFS partitions do not support NTFS permissions.

Effects of moving files and folders

To copy files and folders within a single NTFS partition or between NTFS partitions, you must have Read permission for the source folder and Write permission for the destination folder.

When you move a file or folder, permissions may change, depending on the permissions of the destination folder. Moving a file or folder has the following effects on NTFS permissions:

- When you move a folder or file within an NTFS partition, the folder or file retains its original permissions.

- When you move a folder or file to a different NTFS partition, the folder or file inherits the permissions of the destination folder. When you move a folder or file between partitions, Windows Server 2003 copies the folder or file to the new location and then deletes it from the old location.

- When you move a folder or a file to a non-NTFS partition, the folder or file loses its NTFS permissions, because non-NTFS partitions do not support NTFS permissions.

To move files and folders within an NTFS partition or between NTFS partitions, you must have both Write permission for the destination folder and Modify permission for the source folder or file. The Modify permission is required to move a folder or file, because Windows Server 2003 removes the folder or file from the source folder after it copies it to the destination folder.

Effects of copying and moving within volumes

The following table lists the possible copy and move options and describes how Windows Server 2003 treats the compression state of a file or folder.

Action	Result
Copy a file or folder within a volume	Inherits compression state of the destination folder
Move a file or folder within a volume	Retains original compression state of the source
Copy a file or folder between volumes	Inherits compression state of the destination folder
Move a file or folder between volumes	Inherits compression state of source file or folder

What Is NTFS Permissions Inheritance?

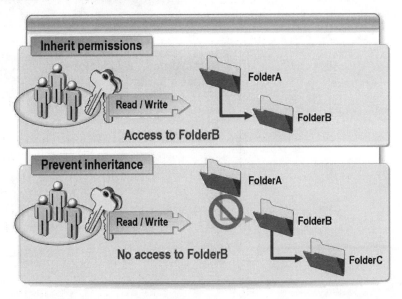

Definition	By default, permissions that you grant to a parent folder are inherited by the subfolders and files that are contained in the parent folder. When you create files and folders, and when you format a partition with NTFS, Windows Server 2003 automatically assigns default NTFS permissions.
Controlling permissions inheritance	You can prevent subfolders and files from inheriting permissions that are assigned to the parent folder. When you prevent permissions inheritance, you can either:

- Copy inherited permissions from the parent folder.

  - or -

- Remove the inherited permissions and retain only the permissions that were explicitly assigned.

The folder at which you prevent permissions inheritance becomes the new parent folder, and the subfolders and files that are contained in it inherit the permissions assigned to it.

Why prevent propagating permissions?	Permissions inheritance simplifies how permissions for parent folders, subfolders, and resources are assigned. However, you may want to prevent inheritance so that permissions do not propagate from a parent folder to subfolders and files.

For example, you may need to keep all Sales department files in one Sales folder for which everyone in the Sales department has Write permission. However, for a few files in the folder, you may need to limit the permissions to Read. To do so, prevent inheritance so that the Write permission does not propagate to the files contained in the folder.

How to Copy or Remove Inherited Permissions

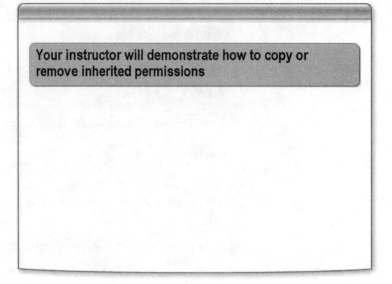

Your instructor will demonstrate how to copy or remove inherited permissions

Introduction   Use the following procedure to copy or remove inherited permissions.

Procedure   To copy or remove inherited permissions:

1. In Windows Explorer, right-click the file or folder you want to change inherited permissions on, and then click **Properties**.

2. In the **Properties** dialog box, on the **Security** tab, click **Advanced**.

3. In the **Advanced Security Settings** dialog box, clear the check box labeled **Allow inheritable permissions from the parent to propagate to this object and all child objects. Include these with entries explicitly defined here**.

4. In the **Security** dialog box, click one of the following:

   • Click **Copy** to copy the permission entries that were previously applied from the parent to this object.

   • Click **Remove** to remove permission entries that were previously applied from the parent and keep only those permissions explicitly assigned.

5. In the **Advanced Security Settings** dialog box, click **OK**.

6. In the **Properties** dialog box, click **OK**.

Best Practices for Managing Access to Files and Folders Using NTFS Permissions

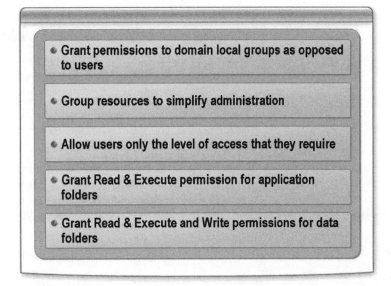

Best practices

When managing access to files and folders, consider the following best practices when granting NTFS permissions:

- Grant permissions to groups instead of users. Because it is inefficient to maintain user accounts directly, avoid granting permissions to individual users.

- Use Deny permissions in the following situations:

  - To exclude a subset of a group that has Allow permissions

  - To exclude one permission when you have already granted Full Control permissions to a user or group

- If possible, do not change the default permission entries for file system objects, particularly on system folders and root folders. Changing default permissions can cause unexpected access problems or reduce security.

- Never deny the Everyone group access to an object. If you deny everyone access to an object, you deny administrators access. Instead, it is recommended that you remove the Everyone group, as long as you grant permissions for the object to other users, groups, or computers.

- Grant permissions to an object that is as high on the tree as possible so that the security settings are propagated throughout the tree. You can quickly and effectively grant permissions to all children or a subtree of a parent object. By doing this, you affect the most objects with the least effort. Grant permissions that are adequate for the majority of users, groups, and computers.

- To simplify administration, group files according to function, for example:
  - Group program files into folders where commonly used applications are kept.
  - Group data folders containing home folders into one folder.
  - Group data files that are shared by multiple users into one folder.
- Grant the Read & Execute permission to the Users and Administrators groups for application folders. This prevents users or viruses from accidentally deleting or damaging data and application files.
- Only allow users the level of access that they require. For example, if a user only needs to read a file, grant the Read permission for the file to the user or group to which the user belongs.
- Grant the Read & Execute and Write permissions to the Users group and the Modify permission to the Creator Owner group for data folders. This enables users to read and modify documents that other users create and to read, modify, and delete the files and folders that they themselves create.

How to Manage Access to Files and Folders Using NTFS Permissions

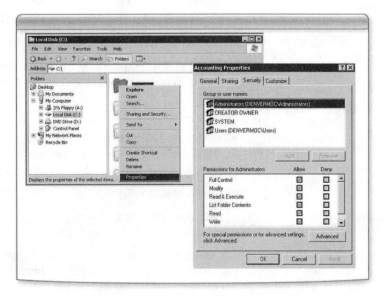

Introduction

Use the follow procedure to change standard and special permissions for files and folders.

Procedure for changing standard permissions

To change standard permissions:

1. In Windows Explorer, right-click the file or folder for which you want to grant permissions, and then click **Properties**.

2. In the **Properties** dialog box, on the **Security** tab, do one of the following:

   - To grant permissions to a group or user that does not appear in the **Group or user names** box, click **Add**. In the **Select users, computers, or groups** dialog box, in the **Enter object names to select** box, type the name of the group or user you want to grant permissions to, and then click **OK**.

   - To change or remove permissions from an existing group or user, in the **Group or user names** box, click the name of the group or user, and then do one of the following:

     - To allow or deny permission, in the **Permissions for** box, select the **Allow** or **Deny** check box.

     - To remove the group or user from the **Group or user names** box, click **Remove**.

Procedure for changing special permissions

To change special permissions:

1. In Windows Explorer, right-click the object for which you want to grant special permissions, and then click **Properties**.

2. In the **Properties** dialog box, on the **Security** tab, click **Advanced**.

3. In the **Advanced Security Settings** dialog box, do one of the following:

   • To grant special permissions to an additional group or user, click **Add**. In the **Select user, computer, or group** dialog box, in the **Enter object name to select** box, type the name of the user or group, and then click **OK**.

   • To view or change special permissions for an existing group or user, click the name of the group or user, and then click **Edit**.

4. In the **Permissions Entry** dialog box, select or clear the appropriate **Allow** or **Deny** check box.

5. In the **Apply onto** drop down list, click the folders or subfolders you want these permissions to be applied to.

6. To configure security so that the subfolders and files do not inherit these permissions, clear the **Apply these permissions to objects and/or containers within this container only** check box.

7. Click **OK** and then, in the **Advanced Security Settings** dialog box, click **OK**.

Note   To remove an existing group or user and its special permissions, click the name of the group or user, and then click **Remove**. If the **Remove** button is unavailable, clear the **Allow inheritable permissions from the parent to propagate to this object and all child objects. Include these with entries explicitly defined here** check box, and then click **Copy** or **Remove**.

Practice: Managing Access to Files and Folders Using NTFS Permissions

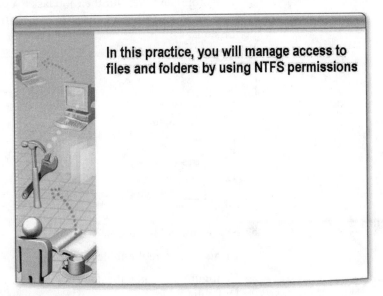

In this practice, you will manage access to files and folders by using NTFS permissions

Objective

In this practice, you will manage access to files and folders by using NTFS permissions.

Instructions

Before you begin this practice:

- Log on to the domain as *ComputerName*Admin.

  Note You cannot use the **Run as** command with Windows Explorer, so you must log on as *ComputerName*Admin to have the permissions that you need to complete this practice.

- Review the procedures in this lesson that describe how to perform this task.

Scenario

Northwind Traders wants you to create a shared folder called Public that is accessible to the Accounting department and the Human Resources department. All employees will need to access the same shared folder and will then navigate to the appropriate folder for their job tasks. You must create the folders represented in the following diagram and configure the shared folder and NTFS permissions:

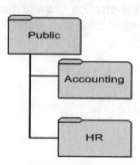

Practice

▶ **Share the Public folder**

1. Create and share the folder D:\Public.

2. Configure the Authenticated Users group to have Change permission for the D:\Public folder.

3. Remove the Everyone group.

▶ **Create folders according to the diagram**

1. Create the folder D:\Public\Accounting.

2. Create the folder D:\Public\HR.

▶ **Configure NTFS permissions**

- Remove all inherited permissions in the following folders and apply the permissions only to the folder. Do not let subfolders inherit permissions.

Folder	Group	NTFS Special Permissions
D:\Public	Authenticated Users	Traverse Folder / Execute File List Folder / Read Data Read Permissions
	ComputerName\Administrators	Full Control
D:\Public\Accounting	DL NWTraders Accounting Personnel Full Control	Full Control
	ComputerName\Administrator	Full Control
D:\Public\HR	DL NWTraders HR Personnel Full Control	Full Control
	ComputerName\Administrators	Full Control

▶ **Test the NTFS permissions**

1. Log on as **HRUser** with a password of **P@ssw0rd**.

2. Attempt to access *ComputerName*\Public\Accounting.

   You should *not* be able to access the Accounting folder. If you can access the folder, check that there are no NTFS permissions granted to Authenticated Users for the Accounting folder.

3. Attempt to Connect to D:\Public\Accounting.

   You should *not* be able to access the Accounting folder. If you can access the folder, check that there are no NTFS permissions granted to Authenticated Users for the Accounting folder.

4. Connect to *ComputerName*\Public\HR.

   You *should* be able to access the HR folder. If you cannot access the folder, check that the DL NWTraders HR Personnel Full Control group has NTFS Full Control permissions granted to the HR folder.

5. Connect to D:\Public\HR.

   You *should* be able to access the HR folder. If you cannot access the folder, check that the DL NWTraders HR Personnel Full Control group has NTFS Full Control permissions granted to the HR folder.

Lesson: Determining Effective Permissions

- **What Are Effective Permissions on NTFS Files and Folders?**
- **How to Determine Effective Permissions on NTFS Files and Folders**
- **Effects of Combined Shared Folder and NTFS Permissions**
- **How to Determine the Effective Permissions on Combined Shared Folder and NTFS Permissions**

Introduction

If you grant NTFS permissions to an individual user account and a group to which the user belongs, then you grant multiple permissions to the user. There are rules for how NTFS combines these multiple permissions to produce the user's effective permissions.

Lesson objectives

After completing this lesson, you will be able to:

- Explain what effective permissions on NTFS files and folders are.
- Determine effective permissions on NTFS files and folders.
- Explain the effects of combined shared folder and NTFS permissions.
- Determine effective permissions on combined shared folder and NTFS permissions.

What Are Effective Permissions on NTFS Files and Folders?

- **Permissions are cumulative**
- **File permissions are separate from folder permissions**
- **Deny overrides all permissions**
- **Take ownership**

Introduction

Windows Server 2003 provides a tool that shows effective permissions, which are cumulative permissions based on group membership. The information is calculated from the existing permissions entries and is displayed in a read-only format.

Characteristics

Effective permissions have the following characteristics:

- Cumulative permissions are the combination of the highest NTFS permissions granted to the user and all the groups the user is a member of.

- NTFS file permissions take priority over folder permissions.

- Deny permissions override all permissions.

- Every object is owned in an NTFS volume or Active Directory. The owner controls how permissions are set on the object and to whom permissions are granted.

Important An administrator who needs to repair or change permissions on a file must take ownership of the file.

Ownership

By default, in the Windows Server 2003 family, the owner is the Administrators group. The owner can always change permissions on an object, even when denied all access to the object.

Ownership can be taken by:

- An administrator. By default, the Administrators group is given the **Take ownership of files or other objects** user right.

- Anyone or any group who has the **Take ownership** permission for the object in question.

- A user who has the **Restore files and directories** privilege.

Ownership can be transferred in the following ways:

- The current owner can grant the **Take ownership** permission to another user. The user must actually take ownership to complete the transfer.

- An administrator can take ownership.

- A user who has the **Restore files and directories** privilege can double-click **Other users and groups** and choose any user or group to assign ownership to.

Important   Permissions on a shared folder are not part of the effective permissions calculation. Access to shared folders can be denied though shared folder permissions even when access is allowed through NTFS permissions.

Class Discussion: Applying NTFS Permissions

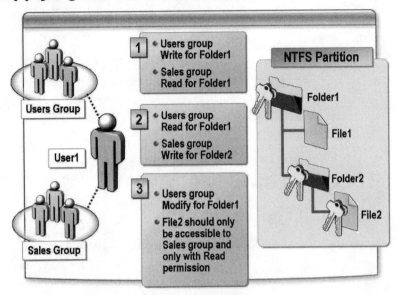

Introduction

In this exercise, you are presented with a scenario where you are asked to apply NTFS permissions. You and your classmates will discuss possible solutions to the scenario.

Discussion

User1 is a member of the Users group and the Sales group.

1. The Users group has Write permission and the Sales group has Read permission for Folder1. What permissions does User1 have for Folder1?

2. The Users group has Read permission for Folder1. The Sales group has Write permission for Folder2. What permissions does User1 have for File2?

3. The Users group has Modify permission for Folder1. File2 should only be accessible to the Sales group, and they should only be able to read File2. What do you do to ensure that the Sales group has only Read permission for File2?

    _____

    _____

How to Determine Effective Permissions on NTFS Files and Folders

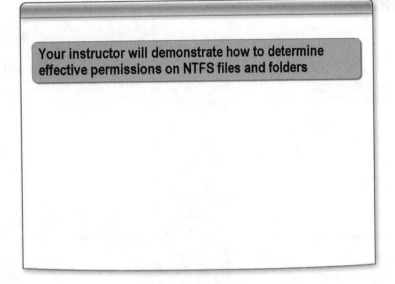

Your instructor will demonstrate how to determine effective permissions on NTFS files and folders

Introduction

Use the following procedure to view the effective permissions for files and folders.

Procedure

To view the effective permissions for files and folders:

1. In Windows Explorer, right-click the file or folder for which you want to view effective permissions, and then click **Properties**.

2. In the **Properties** dialog box, on the **Security** tab, click **Advanced**.

3. In the **Advanced Security Settings** dialog box, on the **Effective Permissions** tab, click **Select**.

4. In the **Select, User, Computer or Group** dialog box, in the **Enter the object name to select** box, type the name of a user or group, and then click **OK**.

   The selected check boxes in the **Advanced Security Settings** dialog box indicate the effective permissions of the user or group for that file or folder.

Additional reading

For more information about effective permissions, see "Effective Permission tool" at http://www.microsoft.com/technet/treeview/default.asp?url=/technet/prodtechnol/windowsserver2003/proddocs/server/acl_effective_perm.asp.

Practice: Determining Effective Permissions on NTFS Files and Folders

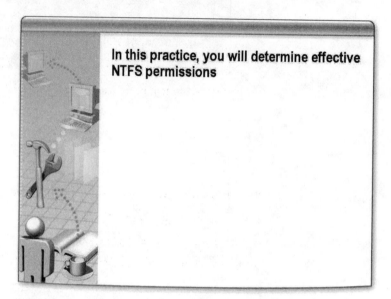

In this practice, you will determine effective NTFS permissions

Objective

In this practice, you will determine the effective NTFS permissions.

Instructions

Before you begin this practice:

- Log on to the domain as *ComputerName*Admin.

  Note You cannot use the **Run as** command with Windows Explorer, so you must log on as *ComputerName*Admin to have the permissions that you need to complete this practice.

- Review the procedures in this lesson that describe how to perform this task.

Scenario

The HR Manager for your city calls you and wants to know if they have the permissions to create documents in the *ComputerName*\Public\HR folder and what permissions a user called TelemarketingUser has for the HR folder.

Practice

▶ **Determine effective permissions for HRManager**

1. Navigate to *ComputerName*\Public\HR.

2. Determine effective permissions for the HRManager user account.

3. Write the highest permissions granted to HRManager

_____

_____

▶ **Determine effective permissions for TelemarketingUser**

1. Navigate to *ComputerName*\Public\HR.

2. Determine effective permissions for the Telemarketing user account.

3. Write the highest permissions granted to TelemarketingUser.

_____

_____

Effects of Combined Shared Folder and NTFS Permissions

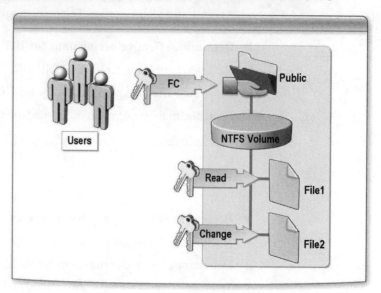

Introduction

When allowing access to network resources on an NTFS volume, it is recommended that you use the most restrictive NTFS permissions to control access to folders and files, combined with the most restrictive shared folder permissions that control network access.

What are combined permissions?

When you create a shared folder on a partition formatted with NTFS, both the shared folder permissions and the NTFS permissions combine to secure file resources. NTFS permissions apply whether the resource is accessed locally or over a network.

When you grant shared folder permissions on an NTFS volume, the following rules apply:

- NTFS permissions are required on NTFS volumes. By default, the Everyone groups has Read permission.

- Users must have the appropriate NTFS permissions for each file and subfolder in a shared folder, in addition to the appropriate shared folder permissions, to access those resources.

- When you combine NTFS permissions and shared folder permissions, the resulting permission is the most restrictive permission of the combined shared folder permissions or the combined NTFS permissions.

How to Determine the Effective Permissions on Combined Shared Folder and NTFS Permissions

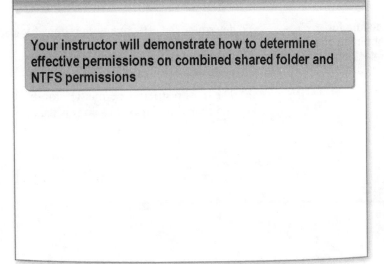

Your instructor will demonstrate how to determine effective permissions on combined shared folder and NTFS permissions

Introduction

Use Windows Explorer to view effective permissions on shared folders. To determine effective permissions, you need to first determine the maximum NTFS and the shared folder permissions and then compare the permissions.

Procedure for determining maximum NTFS permissions

To determine the maximum permissions a user has for a file on an NTFS volume:

1. In Windows Explorer, locate the file or folder for which you want to view effective permissions.

2. Right-click the file or folder, and then click **Properties**.

3. In the **Properties** dialog box, on the **Security** tab, click **Advanced**.

4. In the **Advanced Security Settings** dialog box, on the **Effective Permissions** tab, click **Select**.

5. In the **Select User, Computer, or Group** dialog box, in the **Enter the object name to select (examples)** box, enter the name of a user or group, and then click **OK**.

   The selected check boxes indicate the maximum NTFS permissions that a user or group has for a file or folder.

Procedure for determining maximum shared folder permissions

To determine the maximum permissions a user has for a shared folder:

1. Open the **Properties** dialog box for the shared folder.

2. Find the maximum permissions the user has to the share by determining what groups the user belongs to.

Procedure for determining effective permissions

To determine the effective permissions for a shared folder:

1. Compare the maximum NTFS permissions with the maximum shared folder permissions.

2. The most restrictive permission for the user between the maximum NTFS and shared folder permissions is the effective permissions.

Practice: Determining Effective NTFS and Shared Folder Permissions

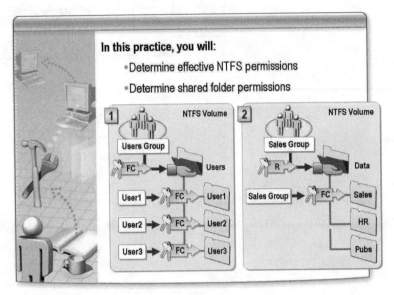

Objective

In this practice, you will determine the effective NTFS and shared folder permissions.

Class discussion

The graphic on this page illustrates two shared folders that contain folders or files that have been assigned NTFS permissions. Look at each example and determine a user's *effective* permissions.

1. In the first example, the Users folder has been shared, and the Users group has the shared folder permission Full Control. User1, User2, and User3 have been granted the NTFS permission Full Control to *only* their folder. These users are all members of the Users group.

   Do members of the Users group have Full Control to *all* home folders in the Users folder once they connect to the Users shared folder?

   _____

   _____

2. In the second example, the Data folder has been shared. The Sales group has
    been granted the shared folder permission Read for the Data shared folder
    and the NTFS permission Full Control for the Sales folder.

    What are the Sales group's effective permissions when they access the Sales
    folder by connecting to the Data shared folder?

    _____

    _____

Lesson: Managing Access to Shared Files Using Offline Caching

- What Is Offline Files?
- How Offline Files Are Synchronized
- Offline File Caching Options
- How to Use Offline Caching

Introduction

The information in this lesson presents the skills and knowledge that you need to manage access to shared files by using offline caching.

Lesson objectives

After completing this lesson, you will be able to:

- Explain what Offline Files is.
- Explain how offline files are synchronized.
- Explain the offline file caching modes.
- Use offline caching.

What Is Offline Files?

> - Offline Files is a document-management feature that provides the user with consistent online and offline access to files
> - Advantages of using Offline Files:
>   - Support for mobile users
>   - Automatic synchronization
>   - Performance advantages
>   - Backup advantages

Definition

Offline Files is an important document-management feature that provides the user with consistent online and offline access to files. When the client disconnects from the network, anything that has been downloaded to the local cache remains available. Users can continue working as though they were still connected to the network. They can continue editing, copying, deleting, and so forth.

From the user's perspective, the workspaces appear identical, whether they are on or off the network. Visual cues, such as icons, menus, and Active Directory, remain the same, including the view of the mapped network drives. Network files appear in the same network drive directory and can be accessed, copied, edited, printed, or deleted precisely as they are when they are online. When you reconnect to the network, client and server files are automatically resynchronized.

Advantages of using Offline Files

Using Offline Files has the following advantages:

- Support for mobile users

  When a mobile user views the shared folder while disconnected, the user can still browse, read, and edit files, because they have been cached on the client computer. When the user later connects to the server, the system reconciles the changes with the server.

- Automatic synchronization

  You can configure synchronization policy and behavior based on the time of day and network connection type by using Synchronization Manager. For example, you can configure synchronization so that it occurs automatically when the user logs on to a direct local area network (LAN) connection, but only at a user's request when he or she uses a dial-up connection.

- Performance advantages

  Offline Files provides performance advantages for networks. While connected to the network, clients can still read files from the local cache, reducing the amount of data transferred over the network.

- Backup advantages

  Offline Files solves a dilemma facing most enterprise organizations today. Many organizations implement a backup policy that requires all user data to be stored on managed servers. The organization's IT department often does not back up data stored on local disks. This becomes a problem for mobile users of portable computers.

  If you want to access data when offline, a mechanism is needed to replicate data between the portable computer and the servers. Some organizations use the Briefcase tool. Others use batch files or replicate data manually. With Windows Server 2003, replication between client and server is managed automatically. Files can be accessed while offline and are automatically synchronized with the managed server.

Additional reading

For more information about offline file security, see "Securing Offline Files" at http://www.microsoft.com/technet/treeview/default.asp?url=/technet/prodtechnol/winxppro/reskit/prdc_mcc_lvvu.asp.

How Offline Files Are Synchronized

- **Disconnected from the network**
  - Windows Server 2003 synchronizes the network files with a locally cached copy of the file
  - The user works with the locally cached copy
- **Logged on to the network**
  - Windows Server 2003 synchronizes offline files that the user has modified with the network version of the files
- **If a file has been modified in both locations**
  - The user is prompted to choose which version of the file to keep or to rename one file and keep both versions

Introduction

A user can configure a file on a network to be available offline, provided that Offline Files is enabled for the folder in which the file resides. When users configure files to be available offline, the users work with the network version of the files while they are connected to the network and then with a locally cached version of the files when they are not connected to the network.

Synchronization events

When a user configures a file to be available offline, the following synchronization events occur when the user disconnects from the network:

- When the user logs off the network, the Windows client operating system synchronizes the network files with a locally cached copy of the file.

- While the computer is disconnected from the network, the user works with the locally cached copy of the file.

- When the user again logs on to the network, the Windows client operating system synchronizes any offline file that the user has modified with the network version of the file. If the file has been modified on both the network and the user's computer, the Windows client operating system prompts the user to choose which version of the file to keep, or the user can rename one file and keep both versions.

Important   Using offline files is not a substitute for document version control. If two users work with the same offline file at the same time, and then synchronize the file with the network version, one of the versions may be lost.

Additional reading

For more information about how clients synchronize offline files, see "Offline Files overview" at http://www.microsoft.com/technet/treeview/default.asp?url=/technet/prodtechnol/windowsserver2003/proddocs/datacenter/csc_overview.asp.

Offline File Caching Options

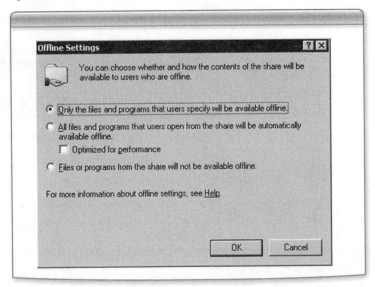

Introduction	Offline Files caches files that are often accessed from a shared folder. This is similar to the way in which a Web browser keeps a cache of recently visited Web sites. When you create shared folders on the network, you can specify the caching option for the files and programs in that folder. There are three different caching options.
Manual caching of documents	Manual caching of documents provides offline access for only the files and programs that the user specifies will be available. This caching option is ideal for a shared network folder containing files that several people will access and modify. This is the default option when you configure a shared folder to be available offline.
Automatic caching of documents	With automatic caching of documents, all files and programs that users open from the shared folder are automatically available offline. Files that the user does not open are not available offline. Older copies are automatically overwritten by newer versions of files.
Automatic caching of programs	When the **Optimized for performance** check box is selected, it provides automatic caching of programs, which provides offline access to shared folders containing files that are not to be changed. Automatic caching of programs reduces network traffic, because offline files are opened directly. The network versions are not accessed in any way, and the offline files generally start and run faster than the network versions.
	When you use automatic caching of programs, be sure to restrict permissions for the files contained in the shared folders to Read access.

How to Use Offline Caching

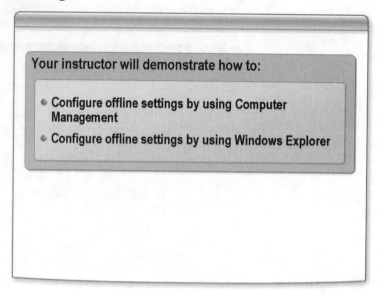

Your instructor will demonstrate how to:

- Configure offline settings by using Computer Management
- Configure offline settings by using Windows Explorer

Introduction

Use the following procedures to manage access to shared files by using offline caching.

Procedure using Computer Management

To configure offline settings by using Computer Management:

1. In Computer Management, in the console tree, expand **Shared Folders**, and then click **Shares**.

2. In the details pane, right-click the shared resource for which you want to configure offline settings, and then click **Properties**.

3. In the **Properties** dialog box, on the **General** tab, click **Offline Settings**.

4. In the **Offline Settings** dialog box, select the option that you want, and then click **OK**.

Procedure using Windows Explorer

To configure offline settings by using Windows Explorer:

1. In Windows Explorer, right-click the shared folder or drive for which you want to configure offline access, and then click **Sharing and Security**.

2. In the **Properties** dialog box, on the **Sharing** tab, click **Offline Settings**.

3. In the **Offline Settings** dialog box, select the option that you want, and then click **OK**.

Using a command line

To configure offline settings by using **net share**:

1. Open a command prompt.

2. To configure manual caching, type
   net share *SharedFolderName* **/cache:manual**

3. To configure caching of documents, type
   net share *SharedFolderName* **/cache:documents**

4. To configure caching of programs, type
   net share *SharedFolderName* **/cache:programs**

5. To configure a shared folder to not cache, type
   net share *SharedFolderName* **/cache:none**

Practice: Using Offline Caching

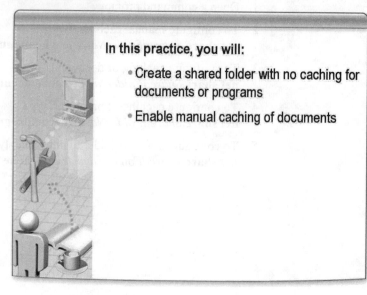

In this practice, you will:

- Create a shared folder with no caching for documents or programs

- Enable manual caching of documents

Objective

In this practice, you will create a shared folder and use different caching options.

Instructions

Before you begin this practice:

- Log on to the domain as *ComputerName*Admin.

    Note   You cannot use the **Run as** command with Windows Explorer, so you must log on as *ComputerName*Admin to have the permissions that you need to complete this practice.

- Review the procedures in this lesson that describe how to perform this task.

Scenario

The Human Resources department wants you to configure a shared folder that contains sensitive human resources data. Northwind Traders does not want this data to be cached on any desktop and laptop computer of Human Resources personnel.

Practice: Creating a shared folder with no caching

▶ **Create a shared folder with no caching for documents of programs**

1. Create a shared folder on the your student computer by using the following parameters:

   - Folder location: D:\

   - Folder name: **HR Confidential**

   - Share name: **HR Confidential**

2. Configure shared folder permissions as follows:

   - Grant Full Control permissions to DL NWTraders HR Personnel Full Control.

   - Remove the Everyone group.

3. Configure NTFS permissions as follows:

   - Remove all inherited NTFS permissions.

   - Grant Full Control permission to DL NWTraders HR Personnel Full Control.

   - Grant Full Control permission to *ComputerName*\Administrators.

4. Set the offline settings to **Files or programs from the share will not be available offline**.

Scenario

Corporate policy has changed and now states that all desktop and laptop computers must have only NTFS partitions, and all laptops of Human Resources personnel must use the EFS feature of NTFS. Your IT security team notifies the Human Resources department that they are now allowed to copy all sensitive Human Resources information for offline use.

Practice: Enabling manual caching of documents

▶ **Enable manual caching of documents**

- Enable manual caching of documents in the HR Confidential folder by changing the offline settings to **Only the files and programs that users specify will be available offline**.

Scenario

The Human Resources department uses a custom application based on Microsoft Visual Basic® that has a single executable file. For performance reasons, you want this file to run from the local hard drive. However, sometimes this application is updated, and you want this application to be automatically redeployed after it is updated. You decide to put this application on the server in your city organizational unit and use automatic caching for programs that is optimized for performance.

Practice: Enabling automatic caching of programs

▶ **Create a shared folder for the Human Resources department**

1. Create a share by using the following parameters:
   - Folder location: D:\
   - Folder name: **HR App**
   - Share name: **HR App**

2. Configure shared folder permissions as follows:
   - Grant Change permission to DL NWTraders HR Personnel Change.
   - Remove the Everyone group.

3. Configure NTFS permissions as follows:
   - Grant Change permission to DL NWTraders HR Personnel Change.
   - Grant Full Control permission to *ComputerName*\Administrators.

4. Set offline settings to **All files and programs that users open from the share will be automatically available offline** and **Optimized for performance**.

Lab A: Managing Access to Resources

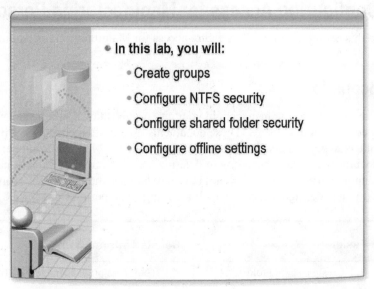

In this lab, you will:
- Create groups
- Configure NTFS security
- Configure shared folder security
- Configure offline settings

Objectives

After completing this lab, you will be able to:

- Create groups.
- Configure NTFS security.
- Configure shared folder security.
- Configure offline settings.

Instructions

Before you begin this practice:

- Log on to the domain as *ComputerName*Admin.

> **Note**   You cannot use the **Run as** command with Windows Explorer, so you must log on as *ComputerName*Admin to have the permissions that you need to complete this practice.

- Ensure that CustomMMC contains Computer Management (Glasgow).
- Review the procedures in this lesson that describe how to perform this task.

Estimated time to complete this lab: 30 minutes

Exercise 1
Configuring Access for Manufacturing Personnel

In this exercise, you will configure access for Manufacturing personnel.

Scenario

The Manufacturing managers in your city organizational unit need a shared folder for thousands of specification documents. These documents do not often change, but the managers need to be able to add, change, and delete documents. They want the Manufacturing personnel to only read the documents, without changing or deleting the files, and they want to have Change permission. Manufacturing personnel do not have any laptops and do require offline access to the documents. You must configure security, offline settings, and permissions for the Manufacturing personnel.

Tasks	Detailed Information
1. Create a shared folder.	▪ Tool: Computer Management (Glasgow) ▪ Server name: Glasgow ▪ Folder path: D:*ComputerName* Manufacturing ▪ Share name: *ComputerName* Manufacturing ▪ Shared folder permissions: 　• Grant Full Control to DL NWTraders Manufacturing Managers Full Control 　• Grant Read to DL NWTraders Manufacturing Personnel Read 　• Remove Everyone
2. Set the NTFS permissions.	▪ Grant Modify to DL Manufacturing Managers Full Control ▪ Grant Read to DL Manufacturing Personnel Read ▪ Grant Full Control to GLASGOW\\Administrators ▪ Copy all NTFS permissions inheritance
3. Set the offline caching settings.	▪ Clear the offline caching settings

Exercise 2
Configuring Access for Marketing Personnel

In this exercise, you will configure access for Marketing personnel.

Scenario

The Marketing department at Northwind Traders needs you to create a shared folder that will contain electronic catalog files. There will be hundreds of electronic catalog files that change quarterly, and the Marketing personnel need offline access to all catalog files. You must create a shared folder, configure security, offline settings, and permissions for Marketing personnel.

Tasks	Detailed Information

1. Create a shared folder.	▪ Tool: Computer Management (Glasgow)
	▪ Server name: Glasgow
	▪ Folder path: D:*ComputerName* Marketing
	▪ Share name: *ComputerName* Marketing
	▪ Shared folder permissions:
	  • Grant Full Control to DL NWTraders Marketing Personnel Full Control
	  • Grant Full Control GLASGOW\Administrators

2. Set the NTFS permissions.	▪ Grant Modify to DL Marketing Personnel Full Control ▪ Grant Full Control to GLASGOW\Administrators ▪ Copy all NTFS permissions inheritance
3. Set the offline caching settings.	▪ Enable automatic caching for documents

Exercise 3
Configure Access for Accounting Personnel

In this exercise, you will configure access for Accounting personnel.

Scenario

The Accounting department at Northwind Traders needs a shared folder for accounting policies and procedures so that everyone in the department can change the shared documents. Most of the Accounting personnel use laptops. They only need offline access to the policy and procedures that they open from the shared folder. You must create groups and configure security, offline settings, and permissions for the Accounting personnel.

Tasks	Detailed Information
1. Create a shared folder.	<ul><li>Tool: Computer Management (Glasgow)</li><li>Server name: Glasgow</li><li>Folder path: D:\ComputerName Accounting</li><li>Share name: ComputerName Accounting</li><li>Shared folder permissions:<ul><li>Grant Full Control to DL NWTraders Accounting Personnel Full Control</li><li>Grant Full Control to GLASGOW\Administrators</li></ul></li></ul>
2. Set NTFS permissions.	<ul><li>Grant Modify to DL ComputerName Accounting Personnel Full Control</li><li>Grant Full Control to GLASGOW\Administrators</li><li>Copy all NTFS permissions inheritance</li></ul>
3. Set the offline caching settings.	<ul><li>Enable caching for files that the users opens from the shared folder</li></ul>

Microsoft®
Training &
Certification

Module 5: Implementing Printing

Contents

Overview

- Introduction to Printing in the Windows Server 2003 Family
- Installing and Sharing Printers
- Managing Access to Printers Using Shared Printer Permissions
- Managing Printer Drivers
- Implementing Printer Locations

Introduction

Printers are common resources that are shared by multiple users on a network. As a systems administrator, you should set up a network-wide printing strategy that meets the needs of users. To set up an efficient network of printers, you must know how to install and share network printers and how to mange printer drivers and printer locations. The Microsoft® Windows® Server 2003 family helps you to perform these tasks efficiently though an easy-to-use interface.

Objectives

After completing this module, you will be able to:

- Explain the printing process in the Windows Server 2003 family.
- Install and share printers.
- Manage access to printers by using shared printer permissions.
- Manage printer drivers.
- Implement printer locations.

Lesson: Introduction to Printing in the Windows Server 2003 Family

- Multimedia: Printing Terminology
- Types of Clients That Can Print to Servers Running Windows Server 2003
- How Printing Works in a Windows Server 2003 Environment

Introduction

The Windows Server 2003 family makes it easy for an administrator to set up network printing and configure the print resources from a central location. You can also configure client computers running Microsoft Windows 95, Microsoft Windows 98, or Microsoft Windows NT® to print from the network print devices.

Before you set up printing in Windows Server 2003, you should be aware of the terms used and how printing works in a Windows Server 2003 environment.

Lesson objectives

After completing this lesson, you will be able to:

- Explain printing terminology.
- Describe the client computers that can print to servers running Windows Server 2003.
- Explain how printing works in a Windows Server 2003 environment.

Multimedia: Printing Terminology

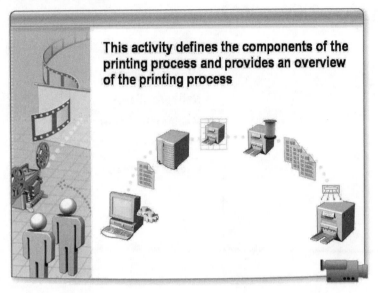

This activity defines the components of the printing process and provides an overview of the printing process

File location

To start the *Printing Terminology* activity, open the Web page on the Student Materials compact disc, click **Multimedia**, and then click the title of the activity.

Component definitions

In the first part of the activity, you drag labels to components of the printing process. When you drop a label on the correct component, the definition of that component is displayed. You can also click **Show me** to have all definitions displayed.

Printing process

After all component definitions are displayed, click **Play** to view an animation of the basic printing process.

Types of Clients That Can Print to Servers Running Windows Server 2003

* Microsoft clients
* NetWare clients
* Macintosh clients
* UNIX clients
* Clients that supports IPP 1.0

Introduction

Client computers can access a printer immediately after a systems administrator adds the printer to a print server running Windows Server 2003.

Client computers that can print to Windows Server 2003

A print server running Windows Server 2003 supports the following clients:

- Microsoft clients

  All 16-bit clients running Windows and clients running Microsoft MS-DOS® require 16-bit printer drivers on each client. Necessary drivers are downloaded to 32- and 64-bit Windows clients.

- NetWare clients

  NetWare clients require that Microsoft File and Print Services for NetWare is installed on the print server running Windows Server 2003. They also require that transport compatible with Internetwork Packet Exchange/ Sequenced Packed Exchange (IPX/SPX) is installed on the print server and on each client.

- Macintosh clients

  Macintosh clients require that Microsoft Print Services for Macintosh is installed on the print server running Windows Server 2003. They also require that the Appletalk networking protocol transport is installed on the print server and on each client.

- UNIX clients

    UNIX clients require that Microsoft Print Services for UNIX is installed on the print server running Windows Server 2003. UNIX clients that support the Line Printer Remote (LPR) specification connect to a print server by using the Line Printer Daemon (LPD) service.

- Client that support Internet Printing Protocol (IPP) 1.0

    Any client that supports IPP 1.0 can print to a print server running Windows Server 2003 by using Hypertext Transfer Protocol (HTTP). The clients that support IPP are clients running Windows 95, Windows 98, or Windows Server 2003. You must first install Microsoft Internet Information Services (IIS) or Microsoft Peer Web Services (PWS) on the computer running Windows Server 2003.

Additional reading   For more information about IPP, see article 323428 "How To: Configure Internet Printing in Windows Server 2003" in the Microsoft Knowledge Base at http://support.microsoft.com/?kbid=323428.

How Printing Works in a Windows Server 2003 Environment

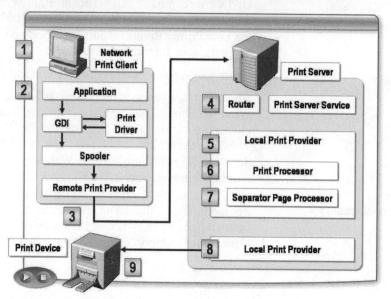

Introduction

When you add a printer that is connected to a network through a network adapter, you can implement printing in the following ways:

- Add a printer directly to each user's computer without using a print server computer.

- Add the printer once to a print server computer and then connect each user to the printer through the print server computer.

Printing without using a print server

Suppose that a small workgroup has only a few computers and a printer that is connected directly to the network. Each user on the network adds the printer to their Printers and Faxes folder without sharing the printer and sets their own driver setting.

This configuration has the following disadvantages:

- The users do not know the actual state of the printer.

- Each computer has its own print queue that displays only those print jobs sent from that computer.

- You cannot determine where your print job is in relation to all the print jobs from other computers.

- Error messages, such as paper jams or empty paper trays, appear only on the print queue for the current print job.

- All the processes on a document submitted for printing are done on that one computer.

Printing with a print server

A computer running Windows Server 2003 functions as a print server. The computer adds the printer and shares it with the other users. A computer running Microsoft Windows XP Professional can also function as a print server. However, it cannot support Macintosh or NetWare services, and it is limited to only 10 connections in the same local area network (LAN).

Printing with a print server has the following advantages:

- The print server manages the printer driver settings.

- A single print queue appears on every computer connected to the printer, enabling each user to see where their print job is in relation to others waiting to print.

- Because error messages appear on all computers, everyone knows the actual state of the printer.

- Some processing is passed from the client computer to the print server.

- You can have a single log for administrators wanting to audit the printer events.

Note   Typically, print servers are implemented on servers that also perform other functions.

Additional reading

For more information about the printing process, see:

- "Printing overview" at http://www.microsoft.com/technet/treeview/ default.asp?url=/technet/prodtechnol/windowsserver2003/proddocs/ entserver/sag_PRINTconcepts_01.asp?frame=true.

- "Printing and print servers" at http://www.microsoft.com/technet/treeview/ default.asp?url=/technet/prodtechnol/windowsserver2003/proddocs/ entserver/sag_PRINTconcepts_ps_queue_spooler.asp?frame=true.

Lesson: Installing and Sharing Printers

- What Is a Local Printer and a Network Printer?
- Hardware Requirements for Configuring a Print Server
- How to Install and Share a Local Printer
- How to Install and Share a Network Printer

Introduction

Users in a home environment mostly print to a local printer attached to their client computer. In a businesses environment, client computers print to a centralized print server that redistributes the print jobs to a print device. By using a print server, the network administrators can centrally manage all printers and print devices.

Lesson objectives

After completing this lesson, you will be able to:

- Explain the differences between printing to a local printer and printing to a network printer.
- Explain the requirements for configuring a print server.
- Install and share local printers.
- Install and share network printers.

What Is a Local Printer and a Network Printer?

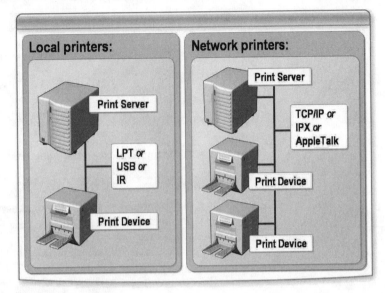

Introduction

As a systems administrator, you will be asked to create two types of printers: a local printer and a network printer. You must create both types of printers before sharing them for others to use.

Definition

Local printers are created to print to a locally attached print device by using parallel (LPT), Universal Serial Bus (USB), or infrared (IR). Local printers also print to a network print device that uses Internet Protocol (IP) or IPX. They also support Plug and Play.

Network printers print to a network printer by using IP, IPX or Appletalk. Network printers also print to a printer that redirects the print job to a print device.

Advantages and disadvantages

The following table lists the advantages and disadvantages of printing to a local printer or a network printer.

	Local printer	**Network printer**
Advantages	• The print device is in close proximity to the user's computer • Plug and Play can detect local printers and automatically install drivers	• Many users can access print devices
Disadvantages	• A print device is needed for every computer • Drivers must be manually installed to every local printer • A local printer takes more processor clock cycles to print	• Security is limited on the physical security of the print device • Network printers support distributing updated printer drivers to multiple clients • The local computer takes more processor clock cycles to print

Hardware Requirements for Configuring a Print Server

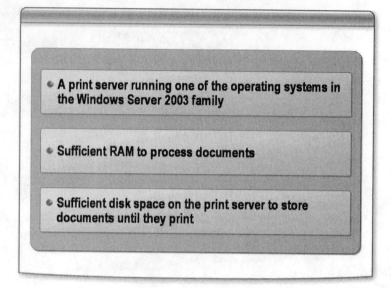

Introduction

There are certain hardware requirements for setting up an efficient printing environment. Whether you are using a local printer or a network printer, if the minimum hardware requirements are not met, network printing may be highly inefficient.

Hardware requirements

Setting up printing on a Windows Server 2003 network requires the following:

- At least one computer to function as the print server that is running one of the operating systems in the Windows Server 2003 family

  If the print server is expected to manage many print jobs, it is recommended that you dedicate a server for printing. The print server can run any operating system in the Windows Server 2003 family. Use one of these products when you need to support a large number of connections in addition to Macintosh, UNIX, and NetWare clients.

- Sufficient RAM to process documents

  If a print server manages many printers or many large documents, the server may require additional RAM beyond what Windows Server 2003 requires for other tasks. If a print server does not have sufficient RAM for its workload, printing performance may decline.

- Sufficient disk space on the print server to store documents

  You must have enough disk space to ensure that Windows Server 2003 can store documents that are sent to the print server until the print server sends the documents to the print device. This is critical when documents are large or when documents accumulate. For example, if 10 users each send one large document to print at the same time, the print server must have enough disk space to hold all of the documents until the print server sends them to the print device.

How to Install and Share a Local Printer

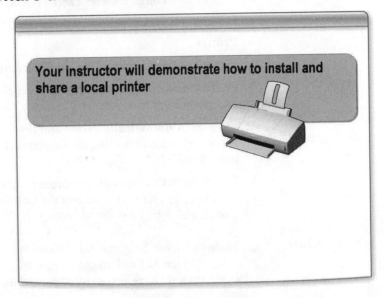

Your instructor will demonstrate how to install and share a local printer

Introduction

To install and share a local printer, you use the Add Printer Wizard, located in the Printers and Faxes folder. You can also add and configure printer ports in the Add Printer Wizard. The Add Printer Wizard prompts you to install a printer driver if one is needed or to replace the existing driver.

The Add Printer Wizard also enables you to connect to a remote shared printer and install its software interface on your computer, assuming that you want local control and have the correct permissions. If you do this, the printing process bypasses the print server for the remote printer by processing print jobs locally and redirecting the output to a remote printer.

Install a printer attached to your computer with a parallel port (LPT):

Connect the printer to the appropriate port on your computer according to the printer manufacturer's documentation, and verify that it is ready to print.

1. Connect the printer to your computer.

2. In Control Panel, in the Printers and Faxes folder, double-click **Add Printer**.

3. In the Add Printer Wizard, on the **Welcome** page, click **Next**.

4. On the **Local or Network Printer** page, click **Local printer attached to this computer**.

5. Select the **Automatically detect and install my Plug and Play printer** check box, and then click **Next**.

6. Depending on the printer you are installing, a Found New Hardware message or the Found New Hardware Wizard appears to notify you that the printer has been detected and that installation has begun.

7. Follow the instructions on the screen to complete the printer installation.

8. The printer icon is added to your Printers and Faxes folder.

Installation without using Plug and Play

If you could not install your printer by using Plug and Play, or if the printer is attached to your computer with a serial (COM) port:

1. In Control Panel, in the Printers and Faxes folder, double-click **Add Printer**.

2. In the Add Printer Wizard, on the **Welcome** page, click **Next**.

3. On the **Local or Network Printer** page, click **Local printer attached to this computer**.

4. Clear the **Automatically detect and install my Plug and Play printer** check box to avoid waiting for the completion of another printer search, and then click **Next**.

5. Follow the instructions on the screen to finish installing the printer by selecting a printer port, selecting the manufacturer and model of your printer, and typing a name for your printer.

Sharing a local printer

In Windows Server 2003, the Add Printer Wizard shares the printer and publishes it in the Active Directory® directory service by default, unless you select the **Do not share this printer** check box on the **Printer Sharing** page of the Add Printer Wizard.

How to Install and Share a Network Printer

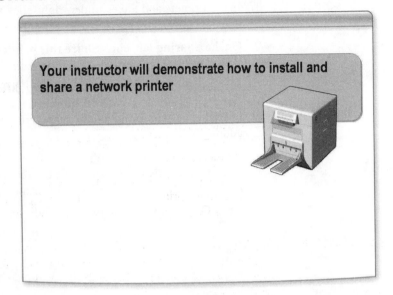

Introduction

In larger organizations, most print devices have a network interface. Using these print devices has several advantages. There is greater flexibility in where you locate your printers. In addition, network connections transfer data quicker than printer cable connections.

Procedure for installing a network printer

To install a network printer:

1. In the Printers and Faxes folder, double-click **Add Printer**.

2. In the Add Printer Wizard, on the **Welcome** page, click **Next**.

3. On the **Local or Network Printer** page, click **Local printer attached to this computer**.

4. Clear the **Automatically detect and install my Plug and Play printer** check box, and then click **Next**.

5. When the Add Printer Wizard prompts you to select the printer port, click **Create a new port**.

6. From the list, click the appropriate port type and follow the instructions.

   By default, only **Local Port** and **Standard TCP/IP Port** appear in the list.

**Procedure for sharing a
network printer**

To share a network printer:

1. In the Printers and Faxes folder, right-click the printer you want to share,
    and then click **Sharing**.

2. On the **Sharing** tab, click **Share this printer**, and then type a name for the
    shared printer.

    If you share the printer with users using different hardware or different
    operating systems, click **Additional Drivers**. Click the environment and
    operating system for the other computers, and then click **OK** to install the
    additional drivers.

    If you are logged on to a Windows 2000 or Windows Server 2003 domain,
    you can make the printer available to other users on the domain by clicking
    List in the Directory to publish the printer in Active Directory.

3. Click **OK**, or if you have installed additional drivers, click **Close**.

Practice: Installing and Sharing Printers

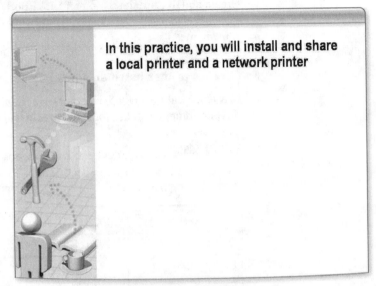

In this practice, you will install and share a local printer and a network printer

Objective

In this practice, you will install and share a local printer and a network printer.

Instructions

Before you begin this practice:

- Log on to the domain as *ComputerName*Admin.

Note This practice focuses on the concepts in this lesson and as a result may not comply with Microsoft security recommendations. For example, this practice does not comply with the recommendation that users log on with domain user account and use the **Run as** command when performing administrative tasks. When using the Printers and Faxes interface, you cannot use the **Run as** command.

- Review the procedures in this lesson that describe how to perform this task.

Scenario

As a network administrator, you must configure your server running Windows Server 2003 Server as a print server for a print device attached locally and a print device attached to the network. The Sales department in your city organizational unit is located in Building 1 on the first floor and has a network print device that must be configured. The IT department has a print device attached to the local LPT1 port of your server.

Note Your student computer is not actually attached to a print server. This practice simulates the creation of a print server. A test page will not print, so you will receive a test page print error if you attempt to print a test page.

Practice

▶ **Create a printer attached to an LPT1 port**

- Create an HP LaserJet 5si on an LPT1 port, name the printer *ComputerName* IT Datacenter Printer, and then share the printer with the same name.

▶ **Create a printer based on a print device on a subnet**

- Create a local LaserJet 5si printer on a Standard TCP/IP port. Find the name of your computer in the following table and use the port and shared printer name next to it.

The LaserJet 5si print device uses a Generic Network Card and a LaserJet 5si driver.

City	IP address	Shared printer name
Vancouver	192.168.11.50	Vancouver Sales Printer
Denver	192.168.21.50	Denver Sales Printer
Perth	192.168.31.50	Perth Sales Printer
Brisbane	192.168.41.50	Brisbane Sales Printer
Lisbon	192.168.51.50	Lisbon Sales Printer
Bonn	192.168.61.50	Bonn Sales Printer
Lima	192.168.71.50	Lima Sales Printer
Santiago	192.168.169.50	Santiago Sales Printer
Bangalore	192.168.179.50	Bangalore Sales Printer
Singapore	192.168.189.50	Singapore Sales Printer
Casablanca	192.168.199.50	Casablanca Sales Printer
Tunis	192.168.209.50	Tunis Sales Printer
Acapulco	192.168.219.50	Acapulco Sales Printer
Miami	192.168.229.50	Miami Sales Printer
Auckland	192.168.239.50	Auckland Sales Printer
Suva	192.168.9.50	Suva Sales Printer
Stockholm	192.168.19.50	Stockholm Sales Printer
Moscow	192.168.29.50	Moscow Sales Printer
Caracas	192.168.39.50	Caracas Sales Printer
Montevideo	192.168.49.50	Montevideo Sales Printer
Manila	192.168.59.50	Manila Sales Printer
Tokyo	192.168.69.50	Tokyo Sales Printer
Khartoum	192.168.79.50	Khartoum Sales Printer
Nairobi	192.168.89.50	Nairobi Sales Printer

Lesson: Managing Access to Printers Using Shared Printer Permissions

- What Are Shared Printer Permissions?
- Why Modify Shared Printer Permissions?
- How to Manage Access to Printers

Introduction

Most corporate printers do not enforce security on printers, because limiting who can print to a printer may be counterproductive in a work environment. However, strict security should be enabled for some printers, such as printers that print payroll checks or high-capacity printers that print bound booklets or photo-quality print jobs. You must configure printer security to enable the correct people to use the printers with the level of access they need to do their job.

Lesson objectives

After completing this lesson, you will be able to:

- Explain the different types of shared printer permissions.
- Explain why you modify shared printer permissions.
- Manage access to printers by setting and removing permissions for a printer.

What Are Shared Printer Permissions?

Permission	Allows the user to:
Print	Connect to a printer and send documents to the printer.
Manage Printers	Perform the tasks associated with the Print permission. The user also has complete administrative control of the printer. The user can pause and restart the printer, change spooler settings, share a printer, adjust printer permissions, and change printer properties.
Manage Documents	Pause, resume, restart, cancel, and rearrange the order of documents that all other users submit. The user cannot send documents to the printer or control the status of the printer.

Introduction

Windows provides the following levels of shared printer permissions:

- Print

- Manage Printers

- Manage Documents

When multiple permissions are granted to a group of users, the least restrictive permission applies. However, when a Deny permission is applied, it takes precedence over any permission.

Tasks that can be performed at each permission level

The following is a brief explanation of the types of tasks a user can perform at each permission level:

- Print

  The user can connect to a printer and send documents to the printer. By default, the Print permission is granted to all members of the Everyone group.

- Manage Printers

  The user can perform the tasks associated with the Print permission and has complete administrative control of the printer. The user can pause and restart the printer, change spooler settings, share a printer, adjust printer permissions, and change printer properties. By default, the Manage Printers permission is granted to members of the Administrators and Power Users groups.

  By default, members of the Administrators and Power Users groups have full access, which means that the users are granted the Print, Manage Documents, and Manage Printers permissions.

- Manage Documents

  The user can pause, resume, restart, cancel, and rearrange the order of documents submitted by all other users. The user cannot, however, send documents to the printer or control the status of the printer. By default, the Manage Documents permission is granted to members of the Creator Owner group.

  When a user is granted the Manage Documents permission, the user cannot access existing documents currently waiting to be printed. They can only access documents sent to the printer after they are granted the permission.

Printer permissions assigned to default groups

Windows assigns printer permissions to six groups of users. These groups include Administrators, Creator Owner, Everyone, Power Users, Print Operators, and Server Operators. By default, each group is granted a combination of the Print, Manage Documents, and Manage Printers permissions, as shown in the following table.

Group	Print	Manage Documents	Manage Printers
Administrators	X	X	X
Creator Owner		X	
Everyone	X		
Power Users	X	X	X
Print Operators	X	X	X
Server Operators	X	X	X

Caution Add a minimum number of trusted users to the Administrators, Power Users, Print Operators, and Server Operators groups.

Why Modify Shared Printer Permissions?

- **Limit access to a printer for selected users**
  - Example: Give all nonadministrative users in a department a low-level permission and give all managers a higher-level permission. This enables both users and managers to print documents, but managers can change the print status of any document sent to the printer.
- **Deny access to a printer for selected users**
  - Example: Give selected members of a group the ability to print documents, and deny other group members access to the printer to force them to use another printer.

Introduction	When a shared printer is installed on a network, default printer permissions are assigned that enable all users to print. You can also enable selected groups to manage documents sent to the printer and enable selected groups to mange the printer. You can explicitly deny access to the printer through user or group membership.
Limit access to a printer for selected users	You might want to limit access for some users by granting specific printer permissions. For example, you can grant the Print permission to all nonadministrative users in a department and grant the Print and Manage Documents permissions to all managers. As a result, all users and managers can print documents, but managers can also change the print status of any document sent to the printer.
Deny access to a printer for selected users	In some cases, you may need to give access to a printer to a group of users. However, there may be a few users in the group whom you do not want to access the printer. In this case, you can grant permissions to the group and deny permission to specific users in the group. For example, you can give selected members of a group the ability to print documents and deny other group members access to the printer to force them to use another printer.

How to Manage Access to Printers

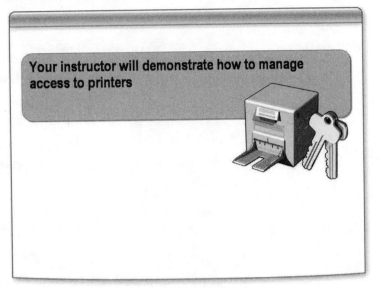

Introduction

You must change shared printer permissions as your networking environment changes.

Procedure

To manage access to printers by allowing or denying permissions for a printer:

1. In the Printers and Faxes folder, right-click the printer for which you want to set permissions, and then click **Properties**.

2. In the **Properties** dialog box, on the **Security** tab, do one of the following:

   - To change or remove permissions of an existing user or group, under **Group or User names**, click the name of the user or group.

   - To grant permissions to a new user or group, click **Add**. In the **Select Users, Computers, or Groups** dialog box, type the name of the user or group you want to grant permissions to, and then click **OK**.

3. Under **Permissions for Administrators**, select the **Allow** or **Deny** check box for each permission you want to allow or deny.

Note   To view or change the underlying permissions that make up the Print, Manage Printers, and Manage Documents permissions, click **Advanced**.

Practice: Managing Access to Printers Using Shared Printer Permissions

In this practice, you will:

- Set printer permissions that enable one group to manage printer documents

- Set printer permissions that give one group printer operator permissions

Objective

In this practice, you will:

- Set printer permissions that enable one group to manage printer documents.

- Set printer permissions that give one group printer operator permissions.

Instructions

Before you begin this practice:

- Log on to the domain by using the *ComputerName*Admin account.

Note   This practice focuses on the concepts in this lesson and as a result may not comply with Microsoft security recommendations. For example, this practice does not comply with the recommendation that users log on with domain user account and use the **Run as** command when performing administrative tasks. When using the Printers and Faxes interface, you cannot use the **Run as** command.

- Ensure that you have a printer called *ComputerName* Sales Printer.

- Review the procedures in this lesson that describe how to perform this task.

Scenario   A systems engineer asks you to modify printer permissions for the printer used by the Sales department. You must configure printer permissions so that only users in the Sales department can print to the printer and that IT personnel can manage the printer.

Practice   ▶ **Modify printer permissions**

- Configure permissions for *ComputerName* Sales Printer as follows:

  - Grant Print permission to the group DL NWTraders Sales Personnel Print.

  - Grant Manage Printers permissions to the group DL NWTraders IT Personnel Print.

  - Remove the Everyone group.

Lesson: Managing Printer Drivers

- What Is a Printer Driver?
- How to Install Printer Drivers
- How to Add Printer Drivers for Other Client Operating Systems

Introduction

This lesson introduces you to the skills and knowledge that you need to manage printer drivers.

Lesson objectives

After completing this lesson, you will be able to:

- Explain what a printer driver is.
- Install new or updated printer drivers.
- Add printer drivers for other client operating systems.

What Is a Printer Driver?

- **Software that computer programs use to communicate with printers and plotters**
- **Translates the information you send from the computer into commands that the printer understands**
- **Consists of the following types of files:**

Configuration or printer interface file	• Displays the Properties and Preferences dialog boxes when you configure a printer • Has a .dll extension
Data file	• Provides information about the capabilities of a specific printer • Can have a .dll, .pcd, .gpd, or .ppd extension
Printer graphics driver file	• Translates DDI commands into commands that a printer can understand • Has a .dll extension

Definition

A printer driver is software used by computer programs to communicate with printers and plotters.

What is the purpose of printer drivers?

Printer drivers translate the information you send from the computer into commands that the printer understands. Usually, printer drivers are not compatible across platforms, so various drivers must be installed on the print server to support different hardware and operating systems. For example, if your computer is running Windows XP and you share a printer with users with computers running Microsoft Windows 3.1, you might need to install multiple printer drivers.

Printer driver files

Printer drivers consist of the following three types of files:

- Configuration or printer interface file

  - This file displays the **Properties** and **Preferences** dialog boxes when you configure a printer.

  - This file has a .dll extension.

- Data file

  - This file provides information about the capabilities of a specific printer, including its resolution capability, whether it can print on both sides of the page, and what size paper it can accept.

  - This file can have a .dll, .pcd, .gpd, or .ppd extension.

- Printer graphics driver file

  - This file translates device driver interface (DDI) commands into commands that a printer can understand. Each driver translates a different printer language. For example, the file Pscript.dll translates the PostScript printer language.

  - This file has a .dll extension.

Example of how printer driver files works

Printer driver files, which are usually accompanied by a Help file, work together to make printing possible. For example, when you install a new printer, the configuration file reads the data file and displays the available printer options. When you print, the printer graphics driver file queries the configuration file about your selections so that it can create the proper printer commands.

Signed print drivers

It is strongly recommended that you use only device drivers with the **Designed for Microsoft Windows XP** or **Designed for Microsoft Windows 2003 Server** logos. Installing device drivers that Microsoft has not digitally signed might disable the system, allow viruses on to your computer, or otherwise impair the correct operation of your computer either immediately or in the future.

How to Install Printer Drivers

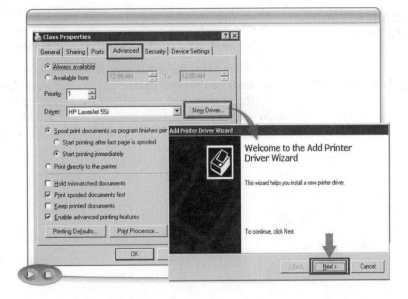

Introduction

If you are managing a print server, you occasionally receive updated printer drivers from print device manufacturers. These updated drivers often have hot fixes, but they should be thoroughly tested before you install them on your print server.

Procedure for installing new or updated printer drivers

To install new or updated printer drivers:

1. In the Printers and Faxes folder, right-click the printer for which you want to change drivers, and then click **Properties**.

2. In the **Properties** dialog box, on the **Advanced** tab, click **New Driver**.

3. In the Add Printer Driver Wizard, on the **Welcome** page, click **Next**.

4. Do one of the following:

   • Select the appropriate printer manufacturer and printer model if the new or updated driver is in the list.

   • Click **Have Disk** if the printer driver is not included in the list or if you have received a new or updated driver on CD or diskette from the printer manufacturer. Type the path where the driver is located, and then click **OK**.

5. Click **Next**, and then follow the instructions on the screen to finish installing the printer driver.

Note   To install new or updated printer drivers, you must be logged on to your computer as a member of the Administrators group. When using Windows 2000 Professional, you may be able to install new or updated printer drivers when you are logged on as a member of the Power Users group, depending on the components required by the printer driver.

If the printer driver you want to use already exists on the print server, you can install it by selecting it in the **Driver** list.

Procedure for removing printer drivers

To remove printer drivers:

1. In the Printers and Faxes folder, on the **File** menu, click **Server Properties**.

2. In the **Print Server Properties** dialog box, on the **Drivers** tab, under **Installed printer drivers**, select the driver you want to remove, click **Remove**.

3. In the message box, click **Yes**.

How to Add Printer Drivers for Other Client Operating Systems

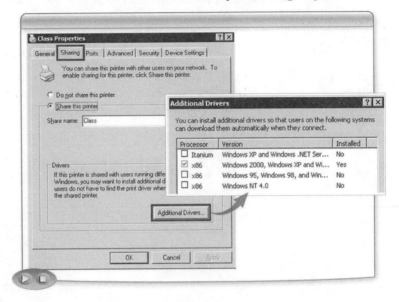

Introduction

If you share a printer with users running Windows 95, Windows 98, or Windows NT 4.0, you can install additional printer drivers on your computer so that those users can connect to your printer without being prompted to install the drivers missing from their systems. The drivers are located on the Windows Server 2003 Support CD. Printer drivers for Microsoft Windows NT version 3.1 and Microsoft Windows NT version 3.5 are not included but might be available from the print device manufacturer.

Procedure

To add printer drivers for other versions of Windows:

1. In the Printers and Faxes folder, right-click the printer for which you want to install additional drivers, and then click **Properties**.

2. In the **Properties** dialog box, on the **Sharing** tab, click **Additional Drivers**.

3. In the **Additional Drivers** dialog box, select the check boxes for the additional environments and operating systems, and then click **OK**.

Additional reading

For more information about downloading print drivers to clients, see "Managing printer drivers" at http://www.microsoft.com/technet/treeview/default.asp?url=/technet/prodtechnol/windowsserver2003/proddocs/entserver/sag_printconcepts_20.asp?frame=true.

Practice: Managing Printer Drivers

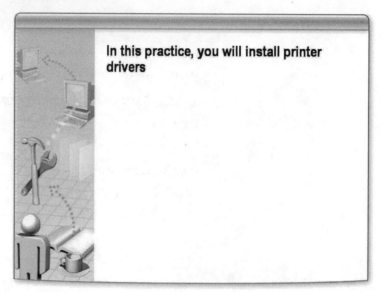

Objective

In this practice, you will install printer drivers.

Instructions

Before you begin this practice:

- Log on to the domain by using the *ComputerName*Admin account.

- Ensure that you have a printer called *ComputerName* Sales Printer.

- Review the procedures in this lesson that describe how to perform this task.

Note   This practice focuses on the concepts in this lesson and as a result may not comply with Microsoft security recommendations. For example, this practice does not comply with the recommendation that users log on with domain user account and use the **Run as** command when performing administrative tasks. When using the Printers and Faxes interface, you cannot use the **Run as** command.

Scenario

You have discovered that the Sales department for your city organizational unit uses clients running Windows 98 and Windows NT 4.0. The Sales manager informs you that the Sales staff keeps asking for printer drivers when they connect to printers on your print server. You must add Windows 98 and Windows NT 4.0 drivers to the *ComputerName* Sales Printer so that clients can automatically install the appropriate drivers.

Practice

▶ **Install printer drivers for other client operating systems**

- Install printer drivers for *ComputerName* Sales Printer for the following operating systems:

  - Windows 98

  - Windows NT 4.0

Lesson: Implementing Printer Locations

- What Are Printer Locations?
- Requirements for Implementing Printer Locations
- Naming Conventions for Printer Locations
- How Printer Locations Are Configured
- How to Set the Location of Printers
- How to Locate Printers

Introduction
This lesson introduces you to skills and knowledge that you need to implement printer locations.

Lesson objectives
After completing this lesson, you will be able to:

- Explain the purpose of printer locations.
- Explain the requirements for implementing printer locations.
- Explain the naming conventions for printer locations.
- Explain the tasks involved in configuring printer locations.
- Set the location of the printers.
- Locate printers.

What Are Printer Locations?

- Printer locations enable users to search and connect to print devices that they are in close physical proximity to
- In Active Directory, an IP subnet is represented by a subnet object, which contains a Location attribute that is used during a search for printers
- Active Directory uses the value of the Location attribute as the text string to display printer location

Definition

Printer locations enable users to search and connect to print devices that they are in close physical proximity to.

Why implement printer locations?

Implementing printer locations:

- Enables you to install printers easily in a prepopulated query.

- Enables users to use a hierarchy to find printers in other locations by clicking **Browse**.

Active Directory and printer locations

When you implement printer locations, a search for published printers in Active Directory returns a list of printers that are located in the same physical location (for example, in the same building or on the same floor) as the client computer the user is using to perform the search.

This printer location tracking capability is based on the assumption that print devices that are physically located near a user reside on the same Internet IP subnet as the user's client computer. Subnets are subdivisions of an IP network. Each subnet possesses its own unique network address.

In Active Directory, an IP subnet is represented by a subnet object, which contains a Location attribute that is used during a search for printers. Active Directory uses the value of the Location attribute as the text string to display printer location. Therefore, when a user searches for a printer and a printer location is implemented, Active Directory:

- Finds the subnet object that corresponds to the subnet on which the user's computer is located.

- Uses the value in the Location attribute of the subnet object as the text string for a search for all published printers that have the same Location attribute value.

- Returns to the user a list of printers whose Location attribute value matches the one that is defined for the subnet object. The user can then connect to the nearest printer.

Additionally, users can also search for printers in any location. This is useful if they need to find and connect to a printer in a physical location different from the one in which they normally work.

Requirements for Implementing Printer Locations

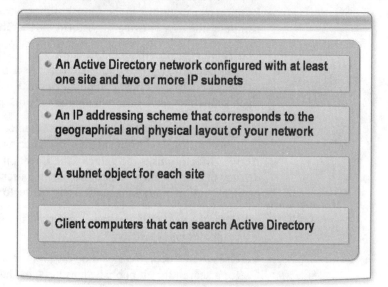

Requirements

Before you can implement printer locations, your Windows Server 2003 network must have the following:

- An Active Directory network configured with at least one site and two or more IP subnets

  Networks with one subnet do not need printer location tracking. Because IP subnets are used to identify the physical location of a printer, a network with only one subnet will generally have all printers in close proximity to users.

- An IP addressing scheme that corresponds to the geographical and physical layout of your network

  Computers and printers that reside on the same IP subnet must also reside in approximately the same physical location. If this is not the case with your network, you cannot implement printer locations.

- A subnet object for each site

  The subnet object, which represents an IP subnet in Active Directory, contains a Location attribute that is used during a search for printers. The value of this Location attribute is used during a search in Active Directory to locate printers that reside near the physical location of the user's client computer.

- Client computers that can search Active Directory

  Users with client computers running Windows 2000 Professional, or previous versions of Windows on which Active Directory client software is installed, can use printer locations when searching for printers.

When printer location is disabled

You can add information to the **Location** box on the **General** tab of the printer's **Properties** dialog box even if printer location is disabled. However, this may make printers difficult for users to locate. When users search for printers on the tenth floor and printer location is disabled, they need to know exactly what to type in the **Find Printers** dialog box. When printer location is enabled, the **Location** box in the **Find Printers** dialog box is filled in automatically.

Naming Conventions for Printer Locations

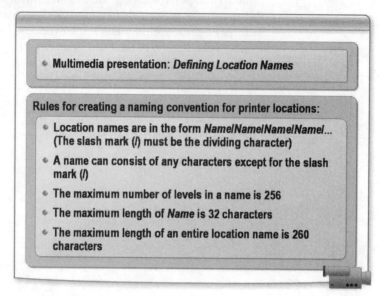

Introduction

The key to implementing printer locations is developing a naming convention for printer locations that corresponds to the physical layout of your network. Printer location names must correspond to an IP subnet. You use a naming convention to determine the values of the Location attributes for both the subnet object and the printer object.

Multimedia: Defining Location Names

The *Defining Location Names* presentation explains the relationship between the Location attributes of subnets and printers. To start the presentation, open the Web page on the Student Materials compact disc, click **Multimedia**, and then click **Defining Location Names**. Do not open the presentation unless the instructor tells you to.

Rules for creating a naming convention for printer locations

To enable printer locations, create a naming convention for printer locations by using the following rules:

- Location names are in the form *Name/Name/Name/Name/...* (The slash mark (/) must be the dividing character).

- A name can consist of any characters except for the slash mark (/).

- The maximum number of levels in a name is 256.

- The maximum length of *Name* is 32 characters.

- The maximum length of an entire location name is 260 characters.

Because location names are used by end users, they should be simple and easy to recognize. Avoid using special names that only facilities management knows. To make the name easier to read, avoid using special characters in a name, and keep names to a maximum of 32 characters so that the whole name string is visible in the user interface.

Example

Note that the tree varies in depth depending on the complexity of the organization and the amount of detail available in the IP network. The naming convention for this example includes more levels than for a smaller organization located in a single city or a single building. The full name for Floor1 of Building1 in London is London/Building1/Floor1, and the full name for RemoteOffice1 in Vancouver is Vancouver/RemoteOffice1.

How Printer Locations Are Configured

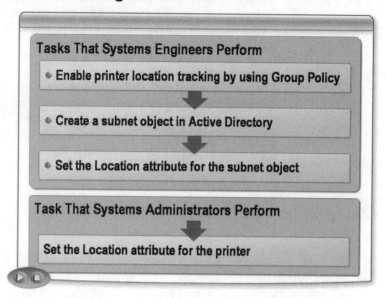

Tasks That Systems Engineers Perform
- Enable printer location tracking by using Group Policy
- Create a subnet object in Active Directory
- Set the Location attribute for the subnet object

Task That Systems Administrators Perform
- Set the Location attribute for the printer

Introduction

To initially set up printer locations, you must have read/write access to Active Directory Sites and Subnet Objects so that you can create subnet objects, give the subnet object a location, and associate the subnet object with a site. When assigning locations to a printer, you must match the location for the printer with the location for the subnet object.

Tasks that systems engineers perform

After a systems engineer ensures that the network meets the requirements for implementing printer locations and a naming convention is created, the systems engineer performs the following tasks to configure printer locations:

1. Enable printer location tracking by using Group Policy. Printer location tracking prepopulates the Location search field when a user searches for a printer in Active Directory. The value used to prepopulate the search field is the same value that is specified in the Location attribute of the subnet object that corresponds to the IP subnet in which the user's computer is located.

2. Create a subnet object in Active Directory. If a subnet object does not already exist, use Active Directory Sites and Services to create a subnet object.

3. Set the Location attribute of the subnet object. Use the naming convention that you developed for printer location names as the value of this attribute.

Note To set the Location attribute for the subnet object, in Active Directory Sites and Services, right-click the subnet object, and then click **Properties**. On the **Location** tab, type the location name that corresponds to the subnet object, and then click **OK**.

Tasks that systems administrators perform

The following task is the only task that a systems administrator performs to configure printer locations:

- Set the Location attribute of printers. For each printer, add the Location attribute of the IP subnet in which the printer resides to the printer's properties. Use the same printer location name that you used for the location of the subnet object.

  When installing a new printer, you can specify the Location attribute by using the Add Printer Wizard.

How to Set the Location of Printers

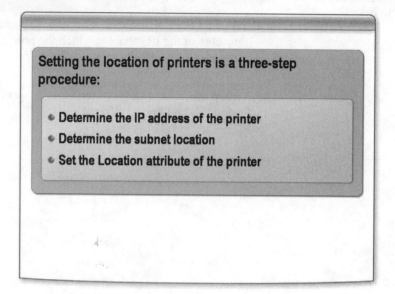

Setting the location of printers is a three-step procedure:

- Determine the IP address of the printer
- Determine the subnet location
- Set the Location attribute of the printer

Introduction

Before setting the Location attribute of a printer, you must determine the following two things:

- The IP address of the printer to determine the Location attribute of the subnet object

  After you determine the proper location name, you can then add the name to the Location attribute of the printer. If you are configuring a new printer, the systems engineer gives you a printout from the print device that tells you the IP address and the appropriate driver to use. If you are adding the location name to an existing printer, you can determine the IP address of the print device by looking at the TCP/IP port that the printer is printing to.

- Subnet location

Procedure for determining the IP address of an existing printer

To determine the IP address of an existing printer:

1. In the Printers and Faxes folder, right-click the printer whose Location attribute you want to set, and then click **Properties**.

2. In the **Properties** dialog box, on the **Ports** tab, click the TCP/IP port used for the printer, and then click **Configure Port**.

3. In the **Configure Standard TCP/IP Port Monitor** dialog box, write down the IP address found in the Printer Name or IP Address, and then click **OK**.

4. In the **Properties** dialog box, click **Close**.

Procedure for determining the subnet location

To determine the subnet location:

1. In Active Directory Sites and Services, in the console tree, expand **Sites**, and then expand **Subnets**.

2. Right-click the network that matches the IP address of the print device, and then click **Properties**.

3. Look on the **Location** tab, and then write down the Location attribute of the subnet object.

4. Click **OK**.

Procedure for setting the Location attribute of the printer

To set the Location attribute of the printer:

1. In the Printers and Faxes folder, right-click the printer whose Location attribute you want to set, and then click **Properties**.

2. In the **Properties** dialog box, on the **General** tab, in the **Location** box, type the printer location, or click **Browse** to find it.

   It is recommended that you are more precise when you describe the printer location than the subnet location. For example, for the subnet location US/NYC, you might enter the printer location as US/NYC/Floor42/Room4207.

How to Locate Printers

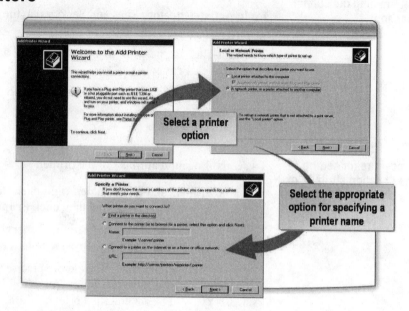

Select a printer option

Select the appropriate option for specifying a printer name

Introduction

Location tracking is used whenever a user queries Active Directory. To start the query, a user clicks **Start**, clicks **Search**, and then clicks **Find Printers**. Users can also click **Find a printer in the directory** in the Add Printer Wizard to launch the **Find Printers** dialog box.

If location tracking is enabled, the system first determines where the client computer is physically located in the organization. While this is in progress, the **Location** box of the **Find Printers** dialog box displays **Checking**. After the location is determined, it is entered into **Location** box. If the location cannot be determined, the **Location** box is left blank.

When the user clicks **Find Now**, Active Directory lists all printers matching the user's query that are located in the location of the user. Users can change the value in the **Location** box by clicking **Browse**.

For example, suppose an organization is located in a building with several floors, and each floor is configured as a subnet. If a user located on the first floor fails to locate a color printer on Floor 1, then the user can change the location to **Organization 1/Floor 2** or even to **Organization 1** to increase the scope of the search.

Note   The **Location** box is not automatically available for users running Windows 95, Windows 98, or Windows NT 4.0 without a directory service client.

Procedure

To locate a printer:

1. In the Printers and Faxes folder, double-click **Add Printer**.

2. In the Add Printer Wizard, on the **Welcome** page, click **Next**.

3. On the **Local or Network Printer** page, click **A network printer, or a printer attached to another computer**, and then click **Next**.

4. On the **Specify a Printer** page, connect to the desired printer by using one of the following three methods:

   - Search for it in Active Directory by doing the following:

Note   If the user is not logged on to a domain running Active Directory, this method is not available.

---

   i. Click **Find a printer in the directory**, and then click **Next**.

   If needed, change the default printer location listed in the **Location** box by clicking **Browse** and then choosing the appropriate location.

   ii. In the **Find Printers** dialog box, click **Find Now**.

   iii. In the list that appears, click the printer you want to connect to, and then click **OK**.

   - Type the printer name or browse for it by doing the following:

   i. Click **Connect to this printer**.

   ii. In the **Name** box, type the printer name by using the *PrintServerName**SharedPrinterName* format, and then click **Next**.

   - or -

   Browse for it on the network by clicking **Next**. On the **Browse for Printer** page, in the **Shared printers** box, locate the printer, and then click **Next**.

   - Connecting to a printer on the Internet or intranet by doing the following:

   i. Click **Connect to a printer on the Internet or on a home or office network**.

   ii. In the **URL** box, type the URL to the printer by using the **http:**//*PrintServerName*/**Printers** format, and then click **Next**.

5. Follow the instructions on the screen to finish connecting to the printer.

   The icon for the printer appears in your Printers and Faxes folder.

Practice: Implementing Printer Locations

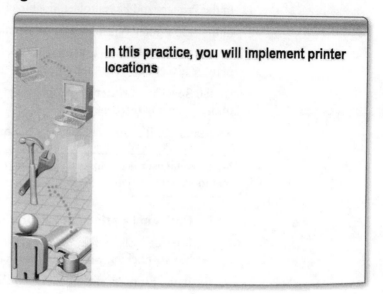

In this practice, you will implement printer locations

Objective

In this practice, you will implement printer locations.

Instructions

Before you begin this practice:

- Log on to the domain by using the *ComputerName*Admin account.
- Ensure that you have a printer called *ComputerName* Sales Printer.
- Ensure that you have a printer called *ComputerName* IT Datacenter Printer.
- Review the procedures in this lesson that describe how to perform this task.

Note   This practice focuses on the concepts in this lesson and as a result may not comply with Microsoft security recommendations. For example, this practice does not comply with the recommendation that users log on with domain user account and use the **Run as** command when performing administrative tasks. When using the Printers and Faxes interface, you cannot use the **Run as** command.

Scenario

You have learned that the Northwind Traders systems administrators have finished testing printer location tracking. They want you to set the value of the Location attributes for the printers in your city.

Practice

▶ **Determine the Location attribute of your printers**

1. In the Printer Subnet table below, write down the printer share name and the subnet number for each printer in your city. (Example: Bonn Sales Printer, 192.168.61.0/24)

Printer Share Name	Subnet

2. Open Active Directory Sites and Services.

3. In the console tree, expand **Sites**, and then click **Subnets**.

4. Take the subnet number from step 1. Write down the Location attribute for each subnet in your city by using the Location attribute of the subnet object for each printer in your city.

Printer Share Name	Subnet	Location

5. Close Active Directory Sites and Services.

▶ **Set the location of the printers on your student computer**

- Set the Location attribute of the Sales and IT Datacenter Printer on your student computer found in step 4.

Printer Subnet Table

City	Printer Share Name	Subnet
Acapulco	Acapulco Sales Printer	192.168.131.0/24
Acapulco	Acapulco IT Datacenter Printer	192.168.129.0/24
Auckland	Auckland Sales Printer	192.168.151.0/24
Auckland	Auckland IT Datacenter Printer	192.168.149.0/24
Bangalore	Bangalore Sales Printer	192.168.91.0/24
Bangalore	Bangalore IT Datacenter Printer	192.168.89.0/24
Bonn	Bonn Sales Printer	192.168.61.0/24
Bonn	Bonn IT Datacenter Printer	192.168.59.0/24
Brisbane	Brisbane Sales Printer	192.168.41.0/24
Brisbane	Brisbane IT Datacenter Printer	192.168.39.0/24
Caracas	Caracas Sales Printer	192.168.191.0/24
Caracas	Caracas IT Datacenter Printer	192.168.189.0/24
Casablanca	Casablanca Sales Printer	192.168.111.0/24
Casablanca	Casablanca IT Datacenter Printer	192.168.109.0/24
Denver	Denver Sales Printer	192.168.21.0/24
Denver	Denver IT Datacenter Printer	192.168.19.0/24
Khartoum	Khartoum Sales Printer	192.168.231.0/24

(continued)

City	Printer Share Name	Subnet
Khartoum	Khartoum IT Datacenter Printer	192.168.229.0/24
Lima	Lima Sales Printer	192.168.71.0/24
Lima	Lima IT Datacenter Printer	192.168.69.0/24
Lisbon	Lisbon Sales Printer	192.168.51.0/24
Lisbon	Lisbon IT Datacenter Printer	192.168.49.0/24
Manila	Manila Sales Printer	192.168.59.0/24
Manila	Manila IT Datacenter Printer	192.168.211.0/24
Miami	Miami Sales Printer	192.168.141.0/24
Miami	Miami IT Datacenter Printer	192.168.139.0/24
Montevideo	Montevideo Sales Printer	192.168.201.0/24
Montevideo	Montevideo IT Datacenter Printer	192.168.199.0/24
Moscow	Moscow Sales Printer	192.168.181.0/24
Moscow	Moscow IT Datacenter Printer	192.168.179.0/24
Nairobi	Nairobi Sales Printer	192.168.241.0/24
Nairobi	Nairobi IT Datacenter Printer	192.168.239.0/24
Perth	Perth Sales Printer	192.168.31.0/24
Perth	Perth IT Datacenter Printer	192.168.29.0/24
Santiago	Santiago Sales Printer	192.168.81.0/24
Santiago	Santiago IT Datacenter Printer	192.168.79.0/24
Singapore	Singapore Sales Printer	192.168.101.0/24
Singapore	Singapore IT Datacenter Printer	192.168.99.0/24
Stockholm	Stockholm Sales Printer	192.168.171.0/24
Stockholm	Stockholm IT Datacenter Printer	192.168.169.0/24
Suva	Suva Sales Printer	192.168.161.0/24
Suva	Suva IT Datacenter Printer	192.168.159.0/24
Tokyo	Tokyo Sales Printer	192.168.221.0/24
Tokyo	Tokyo IT Datacenter Printer	192.168.219.0/24
Tunis	Tunis Sales Printer	192.168.121.0/24
Tunis	Tunis IT Datacenter Printer	192.168.119.0/24
Vancouver	Vancouver Sales Printer	192.168.11.0/24
Vancouver	Vancouver IT Datacenter Printer	192.168.9.0/24

Lab A: Implementing Printing

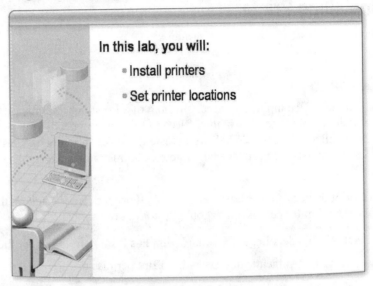

In this lab, you will:
- Install printers
- Set printer locations

Objectives

After completing this lab, you will be able to:

- Install printers.
- Set printer locations.

Instructions

Before you begin this lab, log on to the domain by using the *ComputerName*Admin account.

Note This practice focuses on the concepts in this lesson and as a result may not comply with Microsoft security recommendations. For example, this practice does not comply with the recommendation that users log on with domain user account and use the **Run as** command when performing administrative tasks. When using the Printers and Faxes interface, you cannot use the **Run as** command.

Estimated time to complete this lab: 10 minutes

Exercise 1
Installing Printers

In this exercise, you will install printers.

Scenario

The home office in London needs the help of all systems administrators. Northwind Traders just upgraded all print devices in the offices in London and needs your help to configure them on a print server called Glasgow. To help you create these new printers, the systems engineers have provided a table that lists the printers each systems administrator must create and specific information about the printers.

All print devices are HP LaserJet 5si, and all printers are located on the remote computer named Glasgow. Printer permissions should be configured so that:

- DL NWTraders Legal Personnel Print has Print permission for the Legal printer.
- The group Authenticated Users has Print permissions for the Exec printer.
- DL NWTraders IT Print has Manage Printer permission for both printers.

Tasks	Specific Instructions
1. Connect to the print server named Glasgow.	**a.** In the **Run** box, type **glasgow** and then click **OK**. **b.** From \\glasgow, double-click **Printers and Faxes**.
2. Create two printers on Glasgow.	▪ In the table at the end of the lab, find your student account, and then create two network printers on Glasgow with the print device port, location, and share name values in the table.
3. Configure printer permissions for the Legal printer.	**a.** Grant Print permission to the group DL NWTraders Legal Personnel Print. **b.** Grant Manage Printers permission to the group DL NWTraders IT Personnel Print. **c.** Remove the Everyone group.
4. Configure printer permissions for the Exec printer.	**a.** Grant Print permission to the group Authenticated Users. **b.** Grant Manage Printers permission to the group DL NWTraders IT Personnel Print. **c.** Remove the Everyone group.

Exercise 2
Searching for Network Printers with Locations

In this exercise, you will set printer locations.

Scenario

Your team has just installed many printers for the corporate office. You must confirm that the printers have been successfully configured for printer location tracking.

Tasks	Specific Instructions
1. Open Active Directory Users and Computers.	■ Open Active Directory Users and Computers.
2. Search for printers in the London location. (The results of your search may vary depending on the number of students in the classroom.)	a. From the root of nwtraders.msft, search for printers in the **London/Build 2** location. b. How many printers are in the **London/Build 2/FL 1/** location? _____ Your answer may vary depending on the number of students in the classroom. c. From the root of nwtraders.msft, search for printers in the **London** location. d. How many printers are in the **London** location? _____ Your answer may vary depending on the number of students in the classroom. e. From the root of nwtraders.msft, search for printers in the **Entire Directory** (Click **Browse**, and then click **Entire Directory**). f. How many printers are in the entire directory? _____ Your answer may vary depending on the number of students in the classroom.
3. Close all windows and log off.	

Student Account Table

Student account	Print device port	Location	Printer name & Share name
AcapulcoAdmin	192.168.5.13	London/Build 3	Exec Printer 13
AcapulcoAdmin	192.168.3.13	London/Build 2/Fl 1	Legal Printer 13
AucklandAdmin	192.168.5.15	London/Build 3	Exec Printer 15
AucklandAdmin	192.168.3.15	London/Build 2/Fl 1	Legal Printer 15
BangaloreAdmin	192.168.5.9	London/Build 3	Exec Printer 09
BangaloreAdmin	192.168.3.9	London/Build 2/Fl 1	Legal Printer 09
BonnAdmin	192.168.5.6	London/Build 3	Exec Printer 06
BonnAdmin	192.168.3.6	London/Build 2/Fl 1	Legal Printer 06
BrisbaneAdmin	192.168.5.4	London/Build 3	Exec Printer 04
BrisbaneAdmin	192.168.3.4	London/Build 2/Fl 1	Legal Printer 04
CaracasAdmin	192.168.5.19	London/Build 3	Exec Printer 19
CaracasAdmin	192.168.3.19	London/Build 2/Fl 1	Legal Printer 19
CasablancaAdmin	192.168.5.11	London/Build 3	Exec Printer 11
CasablancaAdmin	192.168.3.11	London/Build 2/Fl 1	Legal Printer 11
DenverAdmin	192.168.5.25	London/Build 3	Exec Printer 25
DenverAdmin	192.168.3.25	London/Build 2/Fl 1	Legal Printer 25
KhartoumAdmin	192.168.5.23	London/Build 3	Exec Printer 23
KhartoumAdmin	192.168.3.23	London/Build 2/Fl 1	Legal Printer 23
LimaAdmin	192.168.5.7	London/Build 3	Exec Printer 07
LimaAdmin	192.168.3.7	London/Build 2/Fl 1	Legal Printer 07
LisbonAdmin	192.168.5.5	London/Build 3	Exec Printer 05
LisbonAdmin	192.168.3.5	London/Build 2/Fl 1	Legal Printer 05
ManilaAdmin	192.168.5.21	London/Build 3	Exec Printer 21
ManilaAdmin	192.168.3.21	London/Build 2/Fl 1	Legal Printer 21
MiamiAdmin	192.168.5.14	London/Build 3	Exec Printer 14
MiamiAdmin	192.168.3.14	London/Build 2/Fl 1	Legal Printer 14
MontevideoAdmin	192.168.5.20	London/Build 3	Exec Printer 20
MontevideoAdmin	192.168.3.20	London/Build 2/Fl 1	Legal Printer 20
MoscowAdmin	192.168.5.18	London/Build 3	Exec Printer 18
MoscowAdmin	192.168.3.18	London/Build 2/Fl 1	Legal Printer 18
NairobiAdmin	192.168.5.24	London/Build 3	Exec Printer 24
NairobiAdmin	192.168.3.24	London/Build 2/Fl 1	Legal Printer 24
PerthAdmin	192.168.5.03	London/Build 3	Exec Printer 03
PerthAdmin	192.168.3.3	London/Build 2/Fl 1	Legal Printer 03
SantiagoAdmin	192.168.5.8	London/Build 3	Exec Printer 08
SantiagoAdmin	192.168.3.8	London/Build 2/Fl 1	Legal Printer 08

(continued)

Student account	Print device port	Location	Printer name & Share name
SingaporeAdmin	192.168.5.10	London/Build 3	Exec Printer 10
SingaporeAdmin	192.168.3.10	London/Build 2/Fl 1	Legal Printer 10
StockholmAdmin	192.168.5.17	London/Build 3	Exec Printer 17
StockholmAdmin	192.168.3.17	London/Build 2/Fl 1	Legal Printer 17
SuvaAdmin	192.168.5.16	London/Build 3	Exec Printer 16
SuvaAdmin	192.168.3.16	London/Build 2/Fl 1	Legal Printer 16
TokyoAdmin	192.168.5.22	London/Build 3	Exec Printer 22
TokyoAdmin	192.168.3.22	London/Build 2/Fl 1	Legal Printer 22
TunisAdmin	192.168.5.12	London/Build 3	Exec Printer 12
TunisAdmin	192.168.3.12	London/Build 2/Fl 1	Legal Printer 12
VancouverAdmin	192.168.5.2	London/Build 3	Exec Printer 02
VancouverAdmin	192.168.3.2	London/Build 2/Fl 1	Legal Printer 02

Microsoft®
Training & Certification

Module 6: Managing Printing

Contents

Overview

- Changing the Location of the Print Spooler
- Setting Printer Priorities
- Scheduling Printer Availability
- Configuring a Printing Pool

Introduction

As a systems administrator, you should set up a network-wide printing strategy that will meet the needs of users. To set up an efficient network of printers, you must know how to troubleshoot installation and configuration problems. Microsoft® Windows® Server 2003 helps you to perform these tasks efficiently.

Objectives

After completing this module, you will be able to:

- Change the location of the print spooler.
- Set printing priorities.
- Schedule printer availability.
- Configure a printing pool.

Additional reading

For more information about printer management, see "Print and Output Management Operations Guide" at http://www.microsoft.com/technet/ treeview/default.asp?url=/technet/prodtechnol/windows2000serv/maintain/ opsguide/pomgmtog.asp.

Lesson: Changing the Location of the Print Spooler

- What Is a Print Spooler?
- Why Change the Location of the Print Spooler?
- How to Change the Location of the Print Spooler

Introduction

This lesson introduces you to the skills and knowledge that you need to change the location of the print spooler.

Lesson objectives

After completing this lesson, you will be able to:

- Explain the purpose of the print spooler.
- Explain situations that require you to change the location of the print spooler.
- Change the location of the print spooler.

What Is a Print Spooler?

- **An executable file that manages the printing process, which involves:**
  - Retrieving the location of the correct printer driver
  - Loading that driver
  - Spooling high-level function calls into a print job
  - Scheduling the print job for printing
- **Takes files to be printed, stores them on the hard disk, and then sends them to the printer when the printer is ready**

Definition

The primary component of the printing interface is the print spooler. The print spooler is an executable file that manages the printing process. Management of the printing process involves:

- Retrieving the location of the correct printer driver.
- Loading that driver.
- Spooling high-level function calls into a print job.
- Scheduling the print job for printing.

The print spooler is loaded at system startup and continues to run until the operating system shuts down. The print spooler takes files to be printed, stores them on the hard disk, and then sends them to the printer when the printer is ready. Additionally, you can log events during this process, or you can turn off logging during high-demand periods to minimize disk space and improve the performance of the print spooler service.

Location of the spool folder

Files that are waiting to be printed are collected in a spool folder that is located on the print server's hard drive. By default, the spool folder is located at *SystemRoot*\System32\Spool\Printers. However, this hard drive also holds the Windows system files. Because the operating system frequently accesses these files, performance of both Windows and the printing functions might be slowed.

If your print server serves only one or two printers with low traffic volumes, the default location of the spool folder is sufficient. However, to support high traffic volumes, large numbers of printers, or large print jobs, you should relocate the spool folder. For best results, move the spool folder to a drive that has its own input/output (I/O) controller, which reduces printing's impact on the rest of the operating system.

Situations in which spooling should be used

The spooling solution should enable the following types of output to be delivered in a manner that is consistent with the needs of the organization:

- *Real-time business critical*. These are jobs that are typically short, but must be printed within a certain time period, with implicit financial penalties if they fail. An example is loading dock pick lists.

  Note A pick list is a printout that an employee uses to go into a warehouse and get items that are going to be shipped out.

- *Scheduled business critical*. Examples include large financial statements that print overnight. No one is at the printer waiting for them, but if they are not there by morning, it is a problem.

- *On-demand*. This category includes most typical desktop printing. The output may not be critical, but the user needs the output within a certain time period.

Why Change the Location of the Print Spooler?

- Change the location of the print spooler to:
  - Improve performance
  - Resolve disk space problems
  - Reduce fragmentation of the boot partition
  - Ensure security
  - Manage disk quotas
  - Improve reliability

Reasons to change the location of the print spooler

Change the location of the print spooler to do the following:

- Improve performance

  Print servers must have sufficient disk space and RAM to manage print jobs. Ideally, plan to have a minimum of two disks, one for the operating system, the startup files, and the paging file, and another one that holds the spool folder. This isolates the spool folder from the operating system, which improves performance and stability. To improve efficiency, add one or more drives for the paging file.

- Resolve disk space problems

  Print servers create a print queue to manage print requests. Documents may be 20 megabytes (MB) in size if they include embedded graphics. As a result, you should use disk space on a drive other than the one being used for the operating system. This helps ensure that you do not use all the free disk space on the system or boot partitions, which can cause difficulties with the swap file. If you configure the print queue on the same disk as the operating system, Windows does not have sufficient disk space to write the swap file, which can lead to problems with the overall performance of the printer.

- Reduce fragmentation of the boot partition

  When a file prints to a network printer, a spool file is created and almost immediately deleted. This process alone is repeated hundreds or thousands of times during a normal working day. If the spool folder is on a volume that is shared with other data, the volume may become fragmented. You can eliminate fragmentation if you locate the spool folder on a volume that is dedicated to the printer. After all spool files are printed, they are deleted from the volume, and new print jobs can start on a clean disk.

- Ensure security

  If print jobs are configured to not be deleted after they are printed, it is advantageous to have the print jobs on a different disk or volume so that the spool folder does not inherit any changes in the security of any parent folders. It is also advantageous to move the spool folder for printers that print sensitive data, such as payroll checks or financial reports, so that you can audit all transactions on the disk that contains the spool folder.

- Manage disk quotas

  On the disks that contain the operating system, quotas are not usually configured to increase performance. However, you may want to limit the amount of print jobs that users or groups print to the print server so that no user can fill all the available free space on a server. If this occurs, others cannot print until the print queue releases some documents.

- Improve reliability

  Typically, a boot partition is on a mirrored disk (RAID 1). For performance and recoverability, you may want to move the spool folder to a volume that has RAID 5 on it to decrease the odds of a single point of failure of a disk subsystem.

How to Change the Location of the Print Spooler

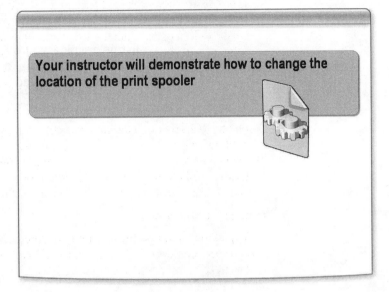

Introduction

You may want to move the location of the spool folder to increase server performance by causing less fragmentation on the boot partition or to move the spool files to another partition with greater disk space.

Procedure

To change the location of the spool folder:

1. In Printers and Faxes, on the **File** menu, click **Server Properties**.

2. In the **Print Server Properties** dialog box, on the **Advanced** tab, in the **Spool folder** box, type the path and the name of the new default spool folder for the print server, and then click **OK**.

3. Stop and restart the spooler service.

Note The location of the spool folder will be changed immediately and any documents waiting to be printed will not print. It is recommended that you wait for all documents to complete printing before changing the spool folder.

Practice: Changing the Location of the Print Spooler

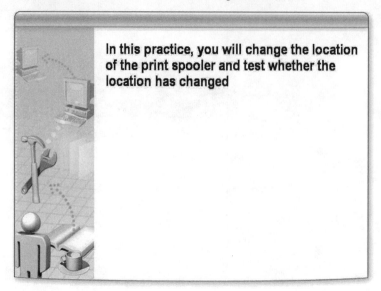

In this practice, you will change the location of the print spooler and test whether the location has changed

Objective

In this practice, you will change the location of the print spooler and test whether the location has changed.

Instructions

Before you begin this practice:

- Log on to the domain as *ComputerName*Admin.

- Ensure that you have a local printer named *ComputerName* IT Datacenter Printer.

- Review the procedures in this lesson that describe how to perform this task.

Scenario

The systems engineers at Northwind Traders have noticed that the C drive on your print server (which has the operating system on it) has been getting fragmented by the printers configured on your member server. The systems engineers have asked you to move the spool folder to the D partition so that the operating system partition will not become fragmented by the print server. You must document the current location of the spool folder and move the spooler to the D partition.

Practice

▶ **Document the current location of the spool folder**

1. In Printers and Faxes, on the **File** menu, click **Server Properties**.

2. In the **Print Server Properties** dialog box, click the **Advanced** tab.

3. Document the current location of the spool folder:

_____

▶ **Create a spool folder on the D drive**

1. Create a folder on the D drive named **Spool** (Example: D:\Spool).

2. Create a subfolder in the D:\Spool folder, named **Printers** (Example: D:\Spool\Printers).

▶ **Change the location of the spool folder**

- Change the spool folder location to D:\Spool\Printers.

▶ **Stop and start the spooler service**

1. Click **Start**, click **Run**, type **cmd** and then click **OK**.

2. From a command prompt, type **net stop spooler**

3. From a command prompt, type **net start spooler**

▶ **Test to see if the spool files are being directed to the D:\Spool\Printers folder**

1. In Printers and Faxes, right-click *ComputerName* **IT Datacenter Printer**, and then click **Pause Printing**.

   If the printer is already paused, you will not see **Pause Printing** in the list. Continue to the next step.

2. Right-click *ComputerName* **IT Datacenter Printer**, and then click **Properties**.

3. In the **Properties** dialog box, click **Print Test Page**.

4. In the message box, click **OK**.

5. In the **Properties** dialog box, click **OK**.

6. Click **Start**, click **Run**, type **D:\Spool\Printers** and then click **OK**.

7. Verify that there are two files created and close all windows.

Lesson: Setting Printer Priorities

- **What Are Printer Priorities?**
- **How to Set Printer Priorities**

Introduction

You may want to configure printer priorities for two printers that print to the same print device. This configuration guarantees that the printer with the highest priority prints to the print device before the printer with the lower priority.

This is a good strategy if the printer with the lower priority is only available to print during nonbusiness hours and has many documents waiting to print. If you must print to the print device, you can select the printer with the higher print priority, and your print job will move to the top of the print queue.

The information in this lesson presents the skills and knowledge that you need to set printer priorities.

Lesson objectives

After completing this lesson, you will be able to:

- Explain the purpose of printer priorities.
- Set printing priorities.

What Are Printer Priorities?

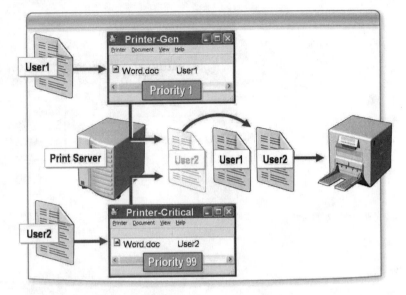

Introduction

Set priorities between printers to prioritize documents that print to the same print device. To do this, create multiple printers pointing to the same print device. Users can then send critical documents to a high-priority printer and documents that are not critical to a low-priority printer. The documents sent to the high-priority printer will print first.

Key tasks

To set priorities between printers, perform the following tasks:

- Point two or more printers to the same print device (the same port). The port can be either a physical port on the print server or a port that points to a network-interface print device.

- Set a different priority for each printer that is connected to the print device, and then have different groups of users print to different printers. You can also have users send high-priority documents to the printer with higher priority and low-priority documents to the printer with lower priority.

How to use priorities

In the illustration on the slide, User1 sends documents to a printer with the lowest priority of 1, and User2 sends documents to a printer with the highest priority of 99. In this example, User2's documents will print before User1's documents.

You can expedite documents that must be printed immediately. Documents sent by users with high priority levels can bypass a queue of lower-priority documents waiting to be printed. If two logical printers are associated with the same printer, Windows Server 2003 routes documents with the highest priority level to the printer first.

To use printer priorities, create multiple logical printers for the same printer. Assign each a different priority level, and then create a group of users that corresponds to each printer. For example, users in Group1 might have access rights to a priority 1 printer, users in Group2 might have access rights to a printer with priority 2, and so on.

How to Set Printer Priorities

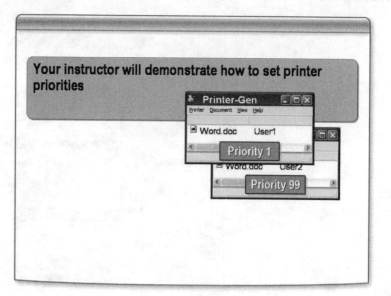

Introduction

Printer priorities are often used if two or more printers print to the same print device. Use the following procedure to set printer priorities.

Procedure

To set different print priorities for different groups:

1. In Printers and Faxes, right-click the printer you want to set, and then click **Properties**.

2. In the **Properties** dialog box, on the **Advanced** tab, in the **Priority** box, enter a priority level, where 1 is the lowest level and 99 is the highest.

3. Click **OK**.

4. Click **Add Printer** to add a second logical printer for the same physical printer.

5. On the **Advanced** tab, in the **Priority** box, set a priority higher than that of the first logical printer.

Practice: Setting Printer Priorities

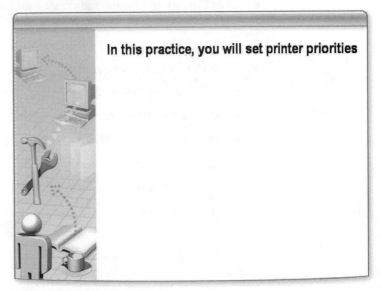

In this practice, you will set printer priorities

Objective

In this practice, you will set printer priorities.

Instructions

Before you begin this practice:

- Log on to the domain as *ComputerName*Admin.

- Review the procedures in this lesson that describe how to perform this task.

Scenario

Northwind Traders is testing printer priorities that will later be used for scheduling printer availability. You must create two printers that print to LPT2. You will name these printers Printer1 and Printer2. Printer1 will have a priority of 1, and Printer2 will have a priority of 99. You will use the default security for Printer1. You will then remove the Everyone group for Printer2 and grant Print permission to the group DL NWTraders IT Personnel Print for Printer2.

Practice

▶ **Set the priority for Printer1**

- Open Printers and Faxes, and create a printer by using the following information:

  - Port: LPT2

  - Driver: HP LaserJet 5si

  - Printer name: **Printer1**

  - Share name: **Printer1**

  - Shared printer permissions: Grant Print permission to the Authenticated Users group

  - Printer priority: 1

▶ **Set the priority for Printer2**

- Open Printers and Faxes, and create a printer by using the following information:

  - Port: LPT2

  - Driver: HP LaserJet 5si

  - Printer name: **Printer2**

  - Share name: **Printer2**

  - Shared printer permissions:

    - Remove the Everyone group

    - Grant Print permission to DL NWTraders IT Personnel Print

  - Printer priority: 99

Lesson: Scheduling Printer Availability

- When to Schedule Printer Availability
- Guidelines for Scheduling Printer Availability
- How to Schedule Printer Availability

Introduction

This lesson introduces you to skills and knowledge that you need to schedule printer availability.

Lesson objectives

After completing this lesson, you will be able to:

- Explain when to schedule printer availability.
- Describe the guidelines for scheduling printer availability.
- Schedule printer availability.

When to Schedule Printer Availability

- Schedule printer availability to print long documents or certain types of documents
- Consider scheduling printer availability:
  - To postpone printing long documents during the day by routing them to a printer that prints only during off-hours
  - To set different printers for the same print device and configure each printer to be available at different times
    For example, one printer is available from 6:00 P.M. to 6:00 A.M., and the other is available 24 hours a day

Situations in which you schedule printer availability

One way to efficiently use printers is to schedule alternate printing times for long documents or certain types of documents. Consider scheduling printer availability in the following situations:

- Schedule printer availability if printer traffic is heavy during the day, and you can postpone printing long documents by routing them to a printer that prints only during off-hours. The print spooler continues to accept documents, but it does not send them to the destination printer until the designated start time.

- Instead of dedicating an actual print device for only off-hour printing, which is not an efficient use of resources, you can set different logical printers for the same print device. You can then configure each with different times. One printer might be available from 6:00 P.M. to 6:00 A.M, and the other might be available 24 hours a day. You can then tell users to send long documents to the printer available only during off hours and all other documents to the printer available all the time.

Guidelines for Scheduling Printer Availability

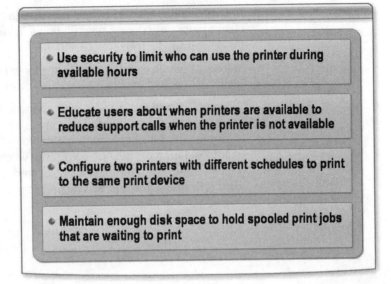

Introduction	If you schedule the availability of a printer, users and systems administrators must be aware of the security requirements and the additional support the print server needs.
Guidelines	Consider the following guidelines when scheduling printer availability:

- Use security to limit who can use the printer during available hours.

  You may want to limit when one group can use a print device, and give another group access to the same print device at all times. To do this, you must configure two printers to print to the same print device. You also must configure additional security to isolate the group that needs access to the printer at all times.

- Educate users about when printers are available to reduce support calls when the printer is not available.

  Many users are accustomed to having a printer available all the time. When they print to a printer that has a scheduling limitation, those users may try to reprint their job and then call help desk to see why their print job did not print. Educate these users that the print job is at the print server waiting to be delivered to the print device and that they should not try to reprint their job.

- Configure two printers with different schedules to print to the same print device.

  If a print device must be available to one group of people all the time and to other groups only during specific hours, configure two printers to print to the same print device.

- Maintain enough disk space to hold spooled print jobs that are waiting to print.

  When you schedule a printer to be available only for certain hours, be aware that users can still print to the printer during off hours and that the printer holds the print jobs until the available hours. Because the printer holds the print jobs during off hours, you must have enough free disk space for the printer to hold the print jobs. If this becomes a problem and you cannot get more disk space, you can set quotas on the volume that holds the print queue.

How to Schedule Printer Availability

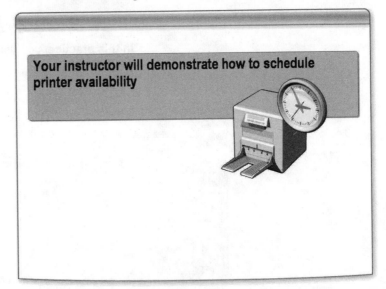

Your instructor will demonstrate how to schedule printer availability

Introduction

Use the following procedure to schedule printer availability.

Procedure

To schedule printer availability:

1. In Printers and Faxes, right-click the printer you want to configure, and then click **Properties**.

2. In the **Properties** dialog box, on the **Advanced** tab, click **Available from**.

3. In the two boxes to the right of **Available from**, enter a start and end time, such as **6:00 PM** and **6:00 AM**, and then click **OK**.

Practice: Scheduling Printer Availability

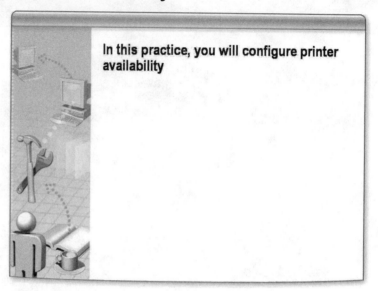

In this practice, you will configure printer availability

Objective

In this practice, you will configure printer availability.

Instructions

Before you begin this practice:

- Log on to the domain as *ComputerName*Admin.

- Ensure that you have two printers named Printer1 and Printer2 set to print to LPT2.

- Review the procedures in this lesson that describe how to perform this task.

Note You will not be able to test this practice, because there are no classroom print devices.

Scenario

Northwind Traders is testing printer priorities that will later be used for scheduling printer availability. You must configure printer availability for Printer1 and Printer2. Printer1 will have a printing schedule of 12:00 A.M. to 6:00 A.M., and Printer2 will have the default printing schedule.

Practice

▶ **Configure the printing schedule for Printer1**

- Configure Printer1 to be available from 12:00 A.M. to 6:00 A.M.

▶ **Verify that Printer2 is available 24 hours a day**

- Open the **Properties** dialog box for Printer2, and verify that the printer is always available.

Lesson: Configuring a Printing Pool

- **Multimedia: How Printing Pools Work**
- **How to Configure a Printing Pool**

Introduction

The information in this lesson presents the skills and knowledge that you need to configure a printing pool.

Lesson objectives

After completing this lesson, you will be able to:

- Explain the purpose of a printing pool.
- Explain when to configure a printing pool.
- Explain the process for configuring a printing pool.
- Configure a printing pool.

Multimedia: How Printing Pools Work

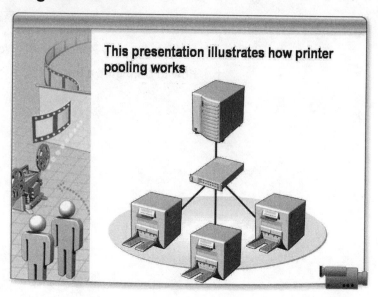

File location

To view the *How Printing Pools Work* presentation, open the Web page on the Student Materials compact disc, click **Multimedia**, and then click the title of the presentation. Do not open this presentation unless the instructor tells you to.

How to Configure a Printing Pool

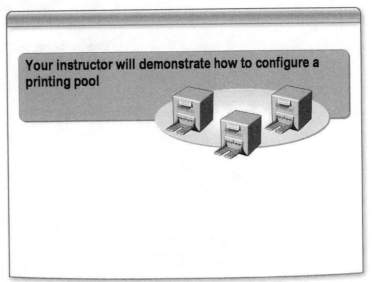

Introduction

Printing pools are very common in high volume printing areas. Use the following procedure to configure a printing pool.

Procedure

To configure a printing pool:

1. In Printers and Faxes, right-click the printer you are using, and then click **Properties**.

2. In the **Properties** dialog box, on the **Ports** tab, select the **Enable printer pooling** check box.

3. Select the check box for each port that the printers you want to pool are connected to, and then click **OK**.

Note   With printer pooling, the printers must be the same type of printer using the same printer driver.

Practice: Configuring a Printing Pool

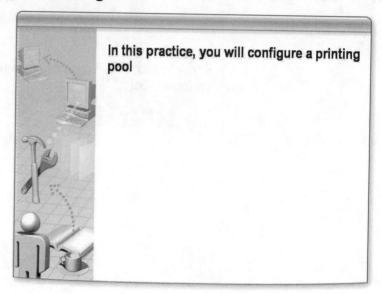

In this practice, you will configure a printing pool

Objective

In this practice, you will configure a printing pool.

Instructions

Before you begin this practice:

■ Log on to the domain as *ComputerName*Admin.

■ Review the procedures in this lesson that describe how to perform this task.

Note   You will not be able to test this practice, because there are no classroom print devices.

Scenario

Northwind Traders is testing the implementation of printing pools. You must create a printer that prints to LPT1 or LPT2 and configure it to be used in a printing pool. The printer will be called PrntPool1 and will use a HP LaserJet 5si printer driver.

Practice

▶ **Create a printer to be used in a printing pool**

1. Open Printers and Faxes, and create a printer by using the following information:

   • Port: LPT1

   • Driver: HP LaserJet 5si

   • Printer name: **PrntPool1**

   • Share name: **PrntPool1**

   • Shared printer permissions: Grant the Print permission to Authenticated Users

2. Configure PrntPool1 for printer pooling with the following ports:

   • LPT1

   • LPT2

Lab A: Managing Printing

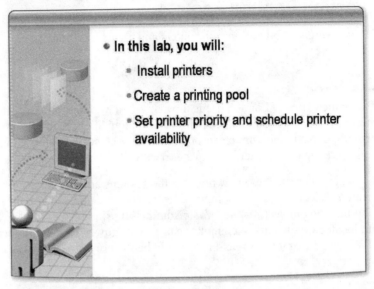

Objectives

After completing this lab, you will be able to:

- Install printers.
- Create a printing pool.
- Set printer priority and schedule printer availability.

Instructions

Before working on this lab:

- Log on to the domain as *ComputerName*Admin.
- Ensure that you have a local printer created on LPT1 called *ComputerName* Datacenter IT Printer.

Estimated time to complete this lab: 20 minutes

Exercise 1
Creating Printing Pools

In this exercise, you will install printers and create a printing pool.

Scenario

The home office in London needs the help of all systems administrators. Northwind Traders is merging with Contoso, Ltd. Because of this acquisition, many new printers must be configured as printing pools in the London corporate office. The corporate office in London needs your help to configure the new printers on a print server called Glasgow.

To help you create these new printers, the systems engineers have provided a table that lists the printers that each systems administrator must create and specific information about the printers. You must log on as *ComputerName*Admin. All print devices are HP LaserJet 5si, and all printers are located on the remote computer named Glasgow. The domain local group called DL NWTraders Legal Personnel Print should be the only group to have Print permission for these printers.

Tasks	Specific Instructions
1. Connect to the print server named Glasgow.	a. From the **Run** box, type **glasgow** and then click **OK**. b. From \\glasgow, double-click **Printers and Faxes**.
2. Create print device ports.	▪ In the student account table, find your administrator account and create two print device ports according to the table.
3. Create a printer to be used as a printing pool.	a. In the Printers and Faxes folder on Glasgow, double-click **Add Printer**. b. In the student account table, find your student account, and then create a network printer on Glasgow with the print device port, location, and shared printer name in the table.
4. Enable printer pooling and add a port to a printer.	a. Enable printer pooling. b. In the student account table, find your student account in the list, and then click the second print device port listed in the table.
5. Configure security.	a. Configure the group DL NWTraders Legal Personnel Print to have Print permission. b. Remove the Everyone group.

Student Account Table

Student account	Print device port	Location	Printer name and share name
AcapulcoAdmin	192.168.3.26 192.168.3.27	London/Build 2/Fl 1/Room 01	Legal Pool 1
BangaloreAdmin	192.168.3.28 192.168.3.29	London/Build 2/Fl 1/Room 02	Legal Pool 2
BonnAdmin	192.168.3.30 192.168.3.31	London/Build 2/Fl 1/Room 03	Legal Pool 3
BrisbaneAdmin	192.168.3.32 192.168.3.33	London/Build 2/Fl 1/Room 04	Legal Pool 4
CaracasAdmin	192.168.3.34 192.168.3.35	London/Build 2/Fl 1/Room 05	Legal Pool 5
CasablancaAdmin	192.168.3.36 192.168.3.37	London/Build 2/Fl 1/Room 06	Legal Pool 6
DenverAdmin	192.168.3.38 192.168.3.39	London/Build 2/Fl 1/Room 07	Legal Pool 7
KhartoumAdmin	192.168.3.40 192.168.3.41	London/Build 2/Fl 1/Room 08	Legal Pool 8
LimaAdmin	192.168.3.42 192.168.3.43	London/Build 2/Fl 1/Room 09	Legal Pool 9
LisbonAdmin	192.168.3.44 192.168.3.45	London/Build 2/Fl 1/Room 10	Legal Pool 10
ManilaAdmin	192.168.3.46 192.168.3.47	London/Build 2/Fl 1/Room 11	Legal Pool 11
MiamiAdmin	192.168.3.48 192.168.3.49	London/Build 2/Fl 1 Room 12	Legal Pool 12
MontevideoAdmin	192.168.3.50 192.168.3.51	London/Build 2/Fl 1 Room 13	Legal Pool 13
MoscowAdmin	192.168.3.52 192.168.3.53	London/Build 2/Fl 1 Room 14	Legal Pool 14
NairobiAdmin	192.168.3.54 192.168.3.55	London/Build 2/Fl 1 Room 15	Legal Pool 15
PerthAdmin	192.168.3.56 192.168.3.57	London/Build 2/Fl 1 Room 16	Legal Pool 16
SantiagoAdmin	192.168.3.58 192.168.3.59	London/Build 2/Fl 1 Room 17	Legal Pool 17

(continued)

Student account	Print device port	Location	Printer name and share name
SingaporeAdmin	192.168.3.60 192.168.3.61	London/Build 2/Fl 1 Room 18	Legal Pool 18
StockholmAdmin	192.168.3.62 192.168.3.63	London/Build 2/Fl 1 Room 19	Legal Pool 19
SuvaAdmin	192.168.3.64 192.168.3.65	London/Build 2/Fl 2 Room 20	Legal Pool 20
TokyoAdmin	192.168.3.66 192.168.3.67	London/Build 2/Fl 1 Room 21	Legal Pool 21
TunisAdmin	192.168.3.68 192.168.3.69	London/Build 2/Fl 1 Room 22	Legal Pool 22
VancouverAdmin	192.168.3.70 192.168.3.71	London/Build 2/Fl 1 Room 23	Legal Pool 23

Exercise 2
Setting Printer Priorities and Availability

In this exercise, you will set printer priority and availability.

Scenario

The data center in your city has been printing event logs to the printer on your member server, which is named *ComputerName* Datacenter IT Printer. These event logs are archived and are not needed on the same day that the reports are generated. You must create another printer so that the reports can print between 6:00 P.M. and 6:00 A.M. on the new printer and your IT staff can still print to the existing printer.

You will name and share the new printer as *ComputerName* Report. *ComputerName* Report will also print to LPT1. Configure *ComputerName* Datacenter IT Printer to have a priority of 50 and *ComputerName* Report to have a priority of 10. You can keep all default security settings for the new and existing printers. Because *ComputerName* Report is a printer that will be used for reports only, you do not need to implement a printer location.

Tasks	Specific Instructions
1. Create a local printer.	<ul><li>Printer name: *ComputerName* **Report**</li><li>Share name: *ComputerName* **Report**</li><li>Port: LPT1</li><li>Manufacturer and model: HP LaserJet 5si</li></ul>
2. Configure a printer schedule for *ComputerName* Report.	<ul><li>Print from 6:00 P.M. to 6:00 A.M.</li></ul>
3. Configure printer priority for *ComputerName* Report.	<ul><li>Priority: 10</li></ul>
4. Configure printer priority for *ComputerName* Datacenter IT Printer.	<ul><li>Priority: 50</li></ul>

Microsoft®
Training & Certification

Module 7: Managing Access to Objects in Organizational Units

Contents

Overview

- Multimedia: The Organizational Unit Structure
- Modifying Permissions for Active Directory Objects
- Delegating Control of Organizational Units

Introduction

The information in this module introduces the job function of managing access to objects in organizational units. Specifically, the module provides the skills and knowledge that you need to explain the permissions available for managing access to objects in the Active Directory® directory service, move objects between organizational units in the same domain, and delegate control of an organizational unit.

Objectives

After completing this module, you will be able to:

- Identify the role of the organizational unit.
- Modify permissions for Active Directory objects.
- Delegate control of organizational units.

Multimedia: The Organizational Unit Structure

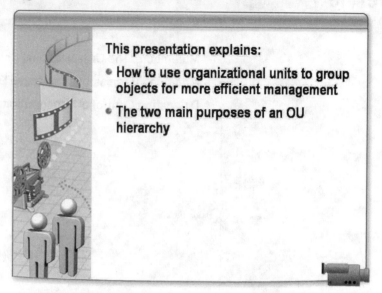

File location

To view the *The Organizational Unit Structure* presentation, open the Web page on the Student Materials compact disc, click **Multimedia**, and then click the title of the presentation. Do not open this presentation unless the instructor tells you to.

Objectives

After completing this lesson, you will be able to explain how to use organizational units to manage objects.

Lesson: Modifying Permissions for Active Directory Objects

- **What Are Active Directory Object Permissions?**
- **Characteristics of Active Directory Object Permissions**
- **Permissions Inheritance for Active Directory Object Permissions**
- **Effects of Modifying Objects on Permissions Inheritance**
- **How to Modify Permissions on Active Directory Objects**
- **What Are Effective Permissions for Active Directory Objects?**
- **How to Determine Effective Permissions for Active Directory Objects**

Introduction

Every object in Active Directory has a security descriptor that defines which accounts have permission to access the object and what type of access is allowed. The Microsoft® Windows® Server 2003 family uses these security descriptors to control access to objects.

Lesson objectives

After completing this lesson, you will be able to:

- Explain what Active Directory object permissions are.
- Describe the characteristics of Active Directory object permissions.
- Describe permissions inheritance for Active Directory object permissions.
- Describe the effects of modifying objects on permission inheritance.
- Modify permissions for Active Directory objects.
- Explain what effective permissions are for Active Directory objects.
- Determine effective permissions for Active Directory objects.

What Are Active Directory Object Permissions?

Permission	Allows the user to:
Full Control	Change permissions, take ownership, and perform the tasks that are allowed by all other standard permissions
Write	Change object attributes
Read	View objects, object attributes, the object owner, and Active Directory permissions
Create All Child Objects	Add any type of object to an organizational unit
Delete All Child Objects	Remove any type of child object from an organizational unit

Introduction

Active Directory object permissions provide security for resources by enabling you to control which administrators or users can access individual objects or object attributes and the type of access allowed. You use permissions to assign administrative privileges for an organizational unit or a hierarchy of organizational units to manage network access. You can also use permissions to assign administrative privileges for a single object to a specific user or group.

Standard and special permissions

Standard permissions are the most frequently granted permissions and consist of a collection of special permissions. Special permissions give you a higher degree of control over the type of access you can grant for objects. The standard permissions include the following:

- Full Control
- Write
- Read
- Create All Child Objects
- Delete All Child Objects

Access authorized by permissions

An administrator or the owner of the object must grant permissions for the object before users can access it. The Windows Server 2003 family stores a list of user access permissions, called the discretionary access control list (DACL), for every object in Active Directory. The DACL for an object lists who can access the object and the specific actions that each user can perform on the object.

Additional reading

For more information about Active Directory permissions, see "Best practices for assigning permissions on Active Directory objects" at http://www.microsoft.com/technet/treeview/default.asp?url=/technet/prodtechnol/windowsserver2003/proddocs/datacenter/ACLUI_acl_BP.asp.

Characteristics of Active Directory Object Permissions

Active Directory object permissions can be:

- Allowed or denied

- Implicitly or explicitly denied

- Set as standard or special permissions

  Standard permissions are the most frequently assigned permissions

  Special permissions provide a finer degree of control for assigning access to objects

- Set at the object level or inherited from its parent object

Introduction

Although NTFS permissions and Active Directory object permissions are similar, certain characteristics are specific to Active Directory object permissions. Active Directory object permissions can be allowed or denied, implicitly or explicitly denied, set as standard or special permissions, and set at the object level or inherited from its parent object.

Allowing and denying permissions

You can allow or deny permissions. Denied permissions take precedence over any permission that you otherwise allow to user accounts and groups. Deny permissions only when it is necessary to remove a permission that a user is granted by being a member of a group.

Implicit or explicit permissions

You can implicitly or explicitly deny permissions as follows:

- When permission to perform an operation is not explicitly allowed, it is *implicitly denied*.

  For example, if the Marketing group is granted Read permission for a user object, and no other security principal is listed in the DACL for that object, users who are not members of the Marketing group are implicitly denied access. The operating system does not allow users who are not members of the Marketing group to read the properties of the user object.

- You *explicitly deny* a permission when you want to exclude a subset within a larger group from performing a task that the larger group has permissions to perform.

  For example, it may be necessary to prevent a user named Don from viewing the properties of a user object. However, Don is a member of the Marketing group, which has permissions to view the properties of the user object. You can prevent Don from viewing the properties of the user object by explicitly denying Read permission to him.

Standard and special permissions

Most Active Directory object permissions tasks can be configured through standard permissions. These permissions are the most commonly used, however if you need to grant a finer level of permissions, you will use special permissions.

Inherited permissions

When permissions are set on a parent object, new objects inherit the permissions of the parent. You can remove inherited permissions, but you can also re-enable them if you want to.

Permissions Inheritance for Active Directory Object Permissions

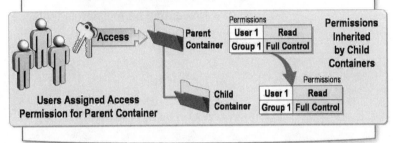

- Child containers and their objects inherit permissions set on a parent container
- Inheritable permissions propagate from a parent object to a child object when:
  - A child object is created
  - The permissions on the parent object are modified

Benefits of permissions inheritance

A parent object is any object that has a relationship with another object called a child. A child object inherits permissions from the parent object. Permissions inheritance in Active Directory minimizes the number of times that you need to grant permissions for objects.

Permissions inheritance in Windows Server 2003 simplifies the task of managing permissions in the following ways:

- You do not need to apply permissions manually to child objects while they are created.

- The permissions applied to a parent object are applied consistently to all child objects.

- When you need to modify permissions for all objects in a container, you only need to modify the permissions for the parent object. The child objects automatically inherit those changes.

Effects of Modifying Objects on Permissions Inheritance

- Permissions that are set explicitly remain the same

- Moved objects inherit permissions from the new parent organizational unit

- Moved object no longer inherit permissions from the previous parent organizational unit

- Preventing permission Inheritance

Introduction

Modifying Active Directory objects affects permissions inheritance. As a systems administrator, you will be asked to move objects between organizational units in Active Directory when organizational or administrative functions change. When you do this, the inherited permissions will change. It is imperative that you are aware of these consequences prior to modifying Active Directory objects.

Effects of moving objects

When you move objects between organizational units, the following conditions apply:

- Permissions that are set explicitly remain the same.

- An object inherits permissions from the organizational unit that it is moved to.

- An object no longer inherits permissions from the organizational unit that it is moved from.

Note   When modifying Active Directory objects, you can move multiple objects at the same time.

Preventing permissions inheritance

You can prevent permissions inheritance so that a child object does not inherit permissions from its parent object. When you prevent inheritance, only the permissions that you set explicitly apply.

When you prevent permissions inheritance, the Windows Server 2003 family enables you to:

- Copy inherited permissions to the object. The new permissions are explicit permissions for the object. They are a copy of the permissions that the object previously inherited from its parent object. After the inherited permissions are copied, you can make any necessary changes to the permissions.

- Remove inherited permissions from the object. By removing these permissions, you eliminate all permissions for the object. Then, you can grant any new permission that you want for the object.

How to Modify Permissions for Active Directory Objects

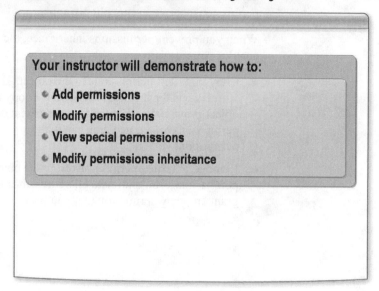

Your instructor will demonstrate how to:

- Add permissions
- Modify permissions
- View special permissions
- Modify permissions inheritance

Introduction

Windows Server 2003 determines if a user is authorized to use an object by checking the permissions granted to the user for that object, which are listed in the DACL. When you allow or deny permissions for an object, those settings override permissions inherited from a parent object.

Procedure for adding permissions

To add permissions for an object:

1. If Advanced Features is not already checked, in Active Directory Users and Computers, on the **View** menu, click **Advanced Features**.

2. In the console tree, right-click the object, and then click **Properties**.

3. In the **Properties** dialog box, on the **Security** tab, click **Add**.

4. In the **Select Users, Computers, or Groups** dialog box, in the **Name** box, type the name of the user or group to which you want to grant permissions, and then click **OK**.

Procedure for modifying permissions

To modify an existing permission:

1. If Advanced Features is not already checked, in Active Directory Users and Computers, on the **View** menu, click **Advanced Features**.

2. In the console tree, right-click the object, and then click **Properties**.

3. In the **Properties** dialog box, on the **Security** tab, in the **Permissions** box, select the **Allow** or **Deny** check box for each permission that you want to allow or deny.

Procedure for viewing special permissions

Standard permissions are sufficient for most administrative tasks. However, you may need to view the special permissions that constitute a standard permission.

To view special permissions:

1. In the **Properties** dialog box for the object, on the **Security** tab, click **Advanced**.

2. In the **Advanced Security Settings** dialog box, on the **Permissions** tab, click the entry that you want to view, and then click **Edit**.

3. To view the permissions for specific attributes, in the **Permission Entry** dialog box, click the **Properties** tab.

Procedure for modifying permission inheritance

To modify permissions inheritance:

1. In the **Properties** dialog box for the object, on the **Security** tab, click **Advanced**.

2. In the **Advanced Security Settings** dialog box, on the **Permissions** tab, click the entry that you want to view, and then click **Edit**.

3. In the **Permission Entry** dialog box, on the **Object** tab, in the **Apply onto** box, select the option that you want.

What Are Effective Permissions for Active Directory Objects?

- Permissions are cumulative
- Deny permissions override all other permissions
- Object owners can always change permissions
- Retrieving effective permissions

Introduction

You can use the Effective Permissions tool to determine what the permissions for an Active Directory object are. The tool calculates the permissions that are granted to the specified user or group and takes into account the permissions that are in effect from group memberships and any permissions inherited from parent objects.

Characteristics

Effective permissions for Active Directory objects have the following characteristics:

- Cumulative permissions are the combination of Active Directory permissions granted to the user and group accounts.

- Deny permissions override all inherited permissions. Permissions explicitly assigned take priority.

- Every object has an owner, whether in an NTFS volume or Active Directory. The owner controls how permissions are set on the object and to whom permissions are granted.

  By default, in Windows Server 2003, the owner is the Administrators group. The owner can always change permissions for an object, even when the owner is denied all access to the object.

  The current owner can grant the Take ownership permission to another user, which enables that user to take ownership of that object at any time. The user must actually take ownership to complete the transfer of ownership.

Retrieving effective permissions

To retrieve information about effective permissions in Active Directory, you need the permission to read membership information. If the specified user or group is a domain object, you must have permission to read the object's membership information on the domain. The following users have relevant default domain permissions:

- Domain administrators have permission to read membership information on all objects.

- Local administrators on a workstation or stand-alone server cannot read membership information for a domain user.

- Authenticated domain users can read membership information only when the domain is in pre-Windows 2000 compatibility mode.

How to Determine Effective Permissions for Active Directory Objects

> **Your instructor will demonstrate how to determine effective permission for Active Directory objects**

Introduction

Use the following procedure to view the effective permissions log for Active Directory objects.

Procedure

To view the effective permissions log:

1. In Active Directory Users and Computers, in the console tree, browse to the organizational unit or object for which you want to view effective permissions.

2. Right-click the organizational unit or object, and then click **Properties**.

3. In the **Properties** dialog box, on the **Security** tab, click **Advanced**.

4. In the **Advanced Security Settings** dialog box, on the **Effective Permissions** tab, click **Select**.

5. In the **Select User, Computer, or Group** dialog box, in the **Enter the object name to select** box, enter the name of a user or group, and then click **OK**.

   The selected check boxes indicate the effective permissions of the user or group for that object.

Additional reading

For more information about effective permissions, see "Effective Permissions tool" at http://www.microsoft.com/technet/treeview/default.asp?url=/technet/prodtechnol/windowsserver2003/proddocs/datacenter/acl_effective_perm.asp.

Practice: Modifying Permissions for Active Directory Objects

In this practice, you will:

- Remove the inherited permissions for your city organizational unit

- Document the security changes made to your city organizational unit

Objective

In this practice, you will:

- Remove the inherited permissions for your city organizational unit.

- Document the security changes made to your city organizational unit.

Instructions

Before you begin this practice:

- Log on to the domain by using the *ComputerName*User account.

- Open CustomMMC with the **Run as** command.

  Use the user account Nwtraders*ComputerName*Admin (Example: LondonAdmin).

- Ensure that CustomMMC contains Active Directory Users and Computers.

- Ensure that you are viewing the advanced features of Active Directory Users and Computers.

- Review the procedures in this lesson that describe how to perform this task.

Scenario

The system engineer for Northwind Traders has delegated administrative control to administrators or each *ComputerName* location. You need to determine what permissions are being inherited to your *ComputerName* organizational unit, and then remove all inherited permissions. Document the results of each step of the removal of inherited permissions.

Practice

▶ **Document the security for your city organizational unit**

1. Open Active Directory Users and Computers.

2. View the security settings for your *ComputerName* organizational unit by doing the following:

   a. Right-click your *ComputerName* organizational unit, and then click **Properties**.

   b. In the **Properties** dialog box, click the **Security** tab.

3. Document the group or users names that have inherited or explicit permissions in the following table. Write a Y for yes under Inherited or Explicit for each item in the Group or user names column.

   An explicit permission has a selected check box under **Allow** or **Deny**. Unchangeable and inherited permissions have a shaded selected check box under **Allow** or **Deny**.

Group or user names	Inherited	Explicit
Example: Account Operators	Y	
Account Operators	Y	
Administrators	Y	
Authenticated Users		Y
DL *ComputerName* OU Administrators		Y
Domain Admins		Y
Enterprise Admins	Y	
ENTERPRISE DOMAIN CONTROLLERS		Y
Pre-Windows 2000 Compatible Access	Y	
Printer Operators	Y	
System		Y

▶ **Remove inherited permissions**

1. In **Properties** dialog box for your city organizational unit, click **Advanced**.

2. In the **Advanced Security Settings** dialog box, on the **Permissions** tab, clear the **Allow inheritable permissions from the parent to propagate to this object and all child objects. Include these with entries explicitly defined here.** check box.

3. In the security dialog box, click **Remove**.

4. In the **Advanced Security Settings** dialog box, click **OK**.

▶ **Document the security changes for your city organizational unit**

1. Open Active Directory Users and Computers.

2. View the security settings for your *ComputerName* organizational unit by doing the following:

   a. Right-click your *ComputerName* organizational unit, and then click **Properties**.

   b. In the **Properties** dialog box, click the **Security** tab.

3. Document the group or users names that have inherited or explicit permissions in the following table. Write a Y for yes under Inherited or Explicit for each item in the Group or user names column.

   An explicit permission has a selected check box under **Allow** or **Deny**. Unchangeable and inherited permissions have a shaded selected check box under **Allow** or **Deny**.

Group or user names	Inherited	Explicit
Example: Account Operators	Y	
Account Operators	Y	
Administrators		
Authenticated Users		Y
DL *ComputerName* OU Administrators		Y
Domain Admins		Y
Enterprise Admins		
ENTERPRISE DOMAIN CONTROLLERS		Y
Pre-Windows 2000 Compatible Access		
Printer Operators	Y	
System		Y

Lesson: Delegating Control of Organizational Units

- **What Is Delegation of Control of an Organizational Unit?**
- **The Delegation of Control Wizard**
- **How to Delegate Control of an Organizational Unit**

Introduction

Active Directory enables you to efficiently manage objects by delegating administrative control of the objects. You can use the Delegation of Control Wizard and customized consoles in Microsoft Management Console (MMC) to grant specific users the permissions to perform various administrative and management tasks.

Lesson objectives

After completing this lesson, you will be able to:

- Describe what it means to delegate control of an organizational unit.
- Describe the purpose and function of the Delegation of Control Wizard.
- Delegate control of an organizational unit by using the Delegation of Control Wizard.

What Is Delegation of Control of an Organizational Unit?

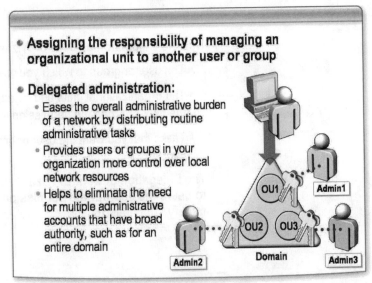

Definition	Delegation of control is the ability to assign the responsibility of managing Active Directory objects to another user, group, or organization. By delegating control, you can eliminate the need for multiple administrative accounts that have broad authority.

You can delegate the following types of control:

- Permissions to create or modify objects in a specific organizational unit
- Permissions to modify specific attributes of an object, such as granting the permission to reset passwords on a user account

Why delegate administrative control?

Delegated administration in Active Directory helps ease the administrative burden of managing your network by distributing routine administrative tasks to multiple users. With delegated administration, you can assign basic administrative tasks to regular users or groups and assign domain-wide and forest-wide administrative tasks to trusted users in your Domain Admins and Enterprise Admins groups.

By delegating administration, you give groups in your organization more control of their local network resources. You also help secure your network from accidental or malicious damage by limiting the membership of administrator groups.

Ways to define the delegation of administrative control

You define the delegation of administrative control in the following three ways:

- Change properties for a particular container.
- Create and delete objects of a specific type under an organizational unit, such as users, groups, or printers.
- Update specific properties on objects of a specific type under an organizational unit. For example, you can delegate the permission to set a password on a user object or all objects in an organizational unit.

The Delegation of Control Wizard

- **Use the Delegation of Control Wizard to specify:**
  - The user or group to which you want to delegate control
  - The organizational units and objects you want to grant the user or group the permission to control
  - Tasks that you want the user or group to be able to perform
- **The Delegation of Control Wizard automatically assigns to users the appropriate permissions to access and modify specified objects**

Introduction

You use the Delegation of Control Wizard to select the user or group to which you want to delegate control. You also use the wizard to grant users permissions to control organizational units and objects and to access and modify objects.

Delegate permissions

You can use the Delegation of Control Wizard to grant permissions at the organizational unit level. You must manually grant additional specialized permissions at the object level.

In Active Directory Users and Computers, right-click the organizational units that you want to delegate control for, and then click **Delegate control** to start the wizard. You can also select the organizational unit and then click Delegate control on the Action menu.

Options

The following table describes the options in the Delegation of Control Wizard.

Option	Description
Users or Groups	The user accounts or groups to which you want to delegate control.
Tasks to Delegate	A list of common tasks, or the option to customize a task. When you select a common task, the wizard summarizes your selections to complete the delegation process. When you choose to customize a task, the wizard presents Active Directory object types and permissions for you to choose from.
Active Directory Object Type	Either all objects or only specific types of objects in the specified organizational unit.
Permissions	The permissions to grant for the object or objects.

Note The Delegation of Control Wizard can append permissions to an organizational unit if it is run more than once. However, you must manually remove delegated permissions.

How to Delegate Control of an Organizational Unit

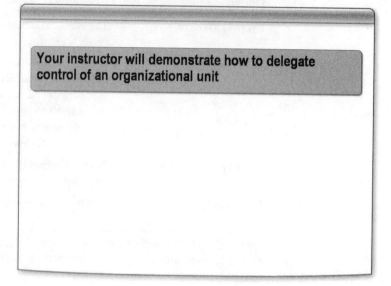

Introduction

To grant permissions at the organizational unit level, use the Delegation of Control Wizard. You can grant permissions for managing objects, or you can grant permissions for managing specific attributes of those objects. Using the Delegation of Control Wizard is the preferred method for delegating control, because it reduces the possibility of unwanted effects from permission assignments.

Procedure for delegating control for common tasks

To delegate administrative control for common tasks:

1. Start the Delegation of Control Wizard, by performing the following steps:

   a. In Active Directory Users and Computers, click the organizational unit for which you want to delegate control.

   b. On the **Action** menu, click **Delegate control**.

2. In the Delegation of Control Wizard, on the **Welcome** page, click **Next**.

3. On the **Users or Groups** page, select a user or group to which you want to grant permissions, and then click **Next**. If there are not Users or Groups displayed to select from, do the following:

   a. Click Add.

   b. In the Select Users, Computers or Groups dialog box, in the Enter the object names to select box, type the name of a user or group, and then click OK.

4. On the **Tasks to Delegate** page, specify one or more of the following tasks to delegate:

   - Create, delete, and manage user accounts
   - Reset user passwords and force password change at next logon
   - Read all user information
   - Create, delete, and manage groups
   - Modify the membership of a group
   - Manage Group Policy links

Note   You can delegate a custom task to users or groups by clicking **Create a custom task to delegate**.

---

5. Click **Next**.
6. On the **Completing the Delegation of Control Wizard** page, click **Finish**.

Procedure for delegating control for a custom task

To delegate administrative control for a custom task:

1. Start the Delegation of Control Wizard, by performing the following steps:

   a. In Active Directory Users and Computers, click the organizational unit for which you want to delegate control.

   b. On the **Action** menu, click **Delegate control**.

2. In the Delegation of Control Wizard, on the **Welcome** page, click **Next**.
3. On the **Users or Groups** page, select a user or group to which you want to grant permissions, and then click **Next**.
4. On the **Tasks to Delegate** page, click **Create a custom task to delegate**, and then click **Next**.
5. On the **Active Directory Object Type** page, click **Next**.
6. On the **Permissions** page, specify the permissions that you want to grant to the organizational unit or its objects.

   You can select the following types of permissions:

   - *General*. Displays the most commonly used permissions that are available for the selected organizational unit or the objects in the organizational unit.
   - *Property specific*. Displays all attribute permissions applicable to the type of object.
   - *Creation/deletion of specific child object*. Displays permissions that you need to create new objects in the organizational unit.

7. Click **Next**.
8. On the **Completing the Delegation of Control Wizard** page, click **Finish**.

Practice: Delegating Control of an Organizational Unit

In this practice, you will:

- Delegate control of the Computers organizational unit
- Test delegated permissions for your Computers organizational unit
- Delegate control of the Users organizational unit
- Test delegated permissions for your Users organizational unit

Objective

In this practice, you will:

- Delegate control of the Computers organizational unit.
- Test delegated permissions for your Computers organizational unit.
- Delegate control of the Users organizational unit.
- Test delegated permissions for your Users organizational unit.

Instructions

Before you begin this practice:

- Log on to the domain by using the *ComputerName*User account.
- Open CustomMMC with the **Run as** command.

  Use the user account Nwtraders*ComputerName*Admin (Example: LondonAdmin).

- Ensure that CustomMMC contains Active Directory Users and Computers.
- Review the procedures in this lesson that describe how to perform this task.

Scenario

To distribute the workload among administrators, Northwind Traders wants administrators to be able to do specific tasks in their designated organizational units. The following tasks must be delegated in the following organizational units:

- Organizational unit: Locations/*ComputerName*/Computers

  Task: Create and delete computer accounts in the organizational unit

- Organizational unit: Locations/*ComputerName*/Users

  Task: Reset user passwords and force password change at next logon

  Task: Read all user information

Practice

▶ **Delegate control of the Computers organizational unit**

1. In Active Directory Users and Computers, in the console tree, navigate to your *ComputerName* organizational unit, right-click **Computers**, and then click **Delegate Control**.

2. In the Delegation of Control Wizard, on the **Welcome** page, click **Next**.

3. On the **Users or Groups** page, add *ComputerName*User, and then click **Next**.

4. On the **Tasks to Delegate** page, click **Create a custom task to delegate**, and click **Next**.

5. On the **Active Directory Object Type** page, click **Only the Following Objects in the Folder**, and then select the **Computer objects** check box.

6. Select the **Create selected objects in this folder** and **Delete selected objects in this folder** check boxes, and then click **Next**.

7. On the **Permissions** page, select the **General** check box.

8. Under **Permissions**, select the **Read** and **Write** check boxes, and then click **Next**.

9. On the **Completing the Delegation of Control Wizard**, click **Finish**.

▶ **Test permissions for the Computers organizational unit**

1. Close CustomMMC, and then open it again without using the **Run as** command.

2. In Active Directory Users and Computers, create a computer account by using the following parameters:

   - Location: Locations/*ComputerName*/Computers

   - Computer account name: First three letters of the city and **Test** (Example: LonTest)

   You should be able to create a computer account in the Locations/*ComputerName*/Computers organizational unit.

3. Close Active Directory Users and Computers.

▶ **Delegate control of the Users organizational unit**

1. Open Active Directory Users and Computers with the **Run As** command by using the *ComputerName*Admin account.

2. Navigate to your *ComputerName* organizational unit, right-click **Users**, and then click **Delegate Control**.

3. In the **Delegation of Control Wizard**, on the Welcome page, click **Next**.

4. On the **Users of Groups** page, add *ComputerName*User and then click **Next**.

5. Delegate the following common tasks:

   - Reset user passwords and force password change at next logon

   - Read all user information

6. Click **Next**, and then click **Finish**.

▶ **Test your permissions for the Users organizational unit**

1. Close CustomMMC, and then open it again without using the **Run as** command.

2. In Active Directory Users and Computers, navigate to the Locations/ComputerName/Users organizational unit.

3. Try to delete a user account.

   You should be unsuccessful.

4. Try to enable or disable any user account.

   You should be unsuccessful.

5. Reset any user's password.

   You should be able to reset any user accounts password in the Locations/*ComputerName*/Users organizational unit.

Lab A: Managing Access to Objects in Organizational Units

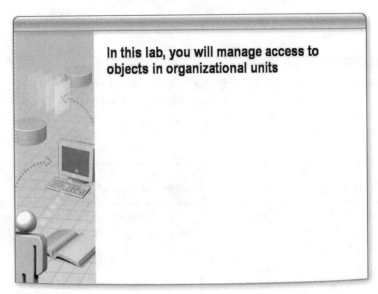

In this lab, you will manage access to objects in organizational units

Objectives

After completing this lab, you will be able to manage access to objects in organizational units.

Instructions

Before you begin this lab:

- Log on to the domain by using the *ComputerName*User account.
- Open CustomMMC with the **Run as** command.

  Use the user account Nwtraders*ComputerName*Admin (Example: LondonAdmin).

- Ensure that CustomMMC contains Active Directory Users and Computers.

Estimated time to complete this lab: 15 minutes

Exercise 1
Delegating Administrative Control

In this exercise, you will delegate administrative control of objects in an organizational unit.

Scenario

Northwind Traders wants all IT personnel to be able to create, delete, and modify groups in every city organizational unit. You must delegate authority in your *ComputerName* organizational unit to enable a global group named G NWTraders IT Personnel to have permissions to Create, delete and manage groups and to Modify membership of a group.

Tasks	Specific instructions

1. Delegate control of the *ComputerName*/Groups organizational unit.	▪ Organizational unit: nwtraders.msft/Locations/*ComputerName*/Groups
	▪ Users or Groups: G NWTraders IT Personnel
	▪ Tasks to Delegate:
	  • Create, delete, and manage groups
	  • Modify the membership of a group

Exercise 2
Documenting Security of an Active Directory Object

In this exercise, you will document the security settings of the object created in the delegated organizational unit.

Scenario

You have just created many groups in a delegated organizational unit, and you have been asked to document what permissions one of those groups has inherited. Enter information in the following table to document the permissions of the group.

Tasks	Detailed steps
1. Document the special permissions for a group created in a delegated organizational unit.	▪ Document the special permissions for the group G NWTraders IT Personnel.

Microsoft®
Training &
Certification

Module 8: Implementing Group Policy

Contents

Overview

- Multimedia: Introduction to Group Policy
- Implementing Group Policy Objects
- Implementing GPOs on a Domain
- Managing the Deployment of Group Policy

Introduction

The information in this module introduces the job function of implementing Group Policy. Specifically, the module provides the skills and knowledge that you need to explain the purpose and function of Group Policy in a Microsoft® Windows® Server 2003 environment, implement Group Policy objects (GPOs), and manage GPOs.

Objectives

After completing this module, you will be able to:

- Implement a Group Policy objects.
- Implement GPOs on a domain.
- Manage the deployment of Group Policy.

Multimedia: Introduction to Group Policy

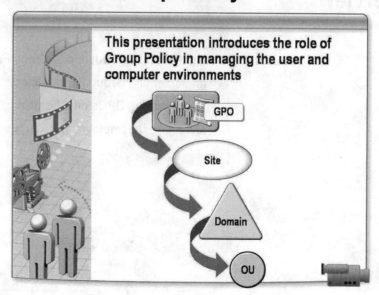

File location

To view the *Introduction to Group Policy* presentation, open the Web page on the Student Materials compact disc, click **Multimedia**, and then click the title of the presentation.

Objectives

After completing this lesson, you will be able to:

- Describe the types of settings that you can define in Group Policy.
- Describe how Group Policy is applied.

Additional reading

For more information about how clients apply Group Policy, see "Order of events in startup and logon" at http://www.microsoft.com/technet/treeview/default.asp?url=/technet/prodtechnol/winxppro/proddocs/orderofevents.asp.

Lesson: Implementing Group Policy Objects

- What Is Group Policy?
- What Are User and Computer Configuration Settings?
- How to Set Local Computer Policy Settings

Introduction

After completing this lesson, students will be able to implement GPOs.

Lesson objectives

After completing this lesson, you will be able to:

- Explain what Group Policy is.
- Describe users and computer configuration settings.
- Set local computer policy settings.

What Is Group Policy?

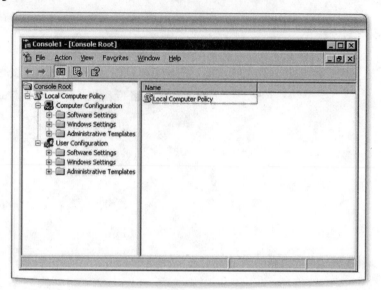

Definition

The Active Directory® directory service uses Group Policy to manage users and computers in your network. When using Group Policy, you can define the state of a user's work environment once, and then rely on the Windows Server 2003 family to continually enforce the Group Policy settings that you defined. You can apply Group Policy settings across an entire organization, or you can apply Group Policy settings to specific groups of users and computers.

Additional reading

For more information about Group Policy, see:

- "Microsoft IntelliMirror®" at http://www.microsoft.com/technet/treeview/ default.asp?url=/technet/prodtechnol/windowsserver2003/proddocs/server/ sag_IMirror_top_node.asp.

- "Group Policy settings overview" at http://www.microsoft.com/technet/ treeview/default.asp?url=/technet/prodtechnol/windowsserver2003/ proddocs/server/gpsettings.asp.

What Are User and Computer Configuration Settings?

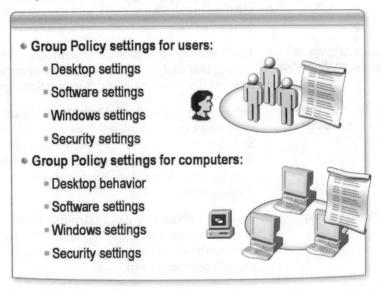

Introduction	You can enforce Group Policy settings for computers and users by using the Computer Configuration and User Configuration features in Group Policy.
User configuration	Group Policy settings for users include specific operating system behavior, desktop settings, security settings, assigned and published application options, application settings, folder redirection options, and user logon and logoff scripts. User-related Group Policy settings are applied when users log on to the computer and during the periodic refresh cycle.
	Group Policy settings that customize the user's desktop environment, or enforce lockdown policies on users, are contained under User Configuration in Group Policy Object Editor.
Software settings for user configuration	The Software Settings folder under User Configuration contains software settings that apply to users regardless of which computer they log on to. This folder also contains software installation settings, and it might contain other settings that are placed there by independent software vendors (ISVs).
Windows settings for user configuration	The Windows Settings folder under User Configuration contains Windows settings that apply to users regardless of which computer they log on to. This folder also contains the following items: Folder Redirection, Security Settings, and Scripts.
Computer configuration	Group Policy settings for computers include how the operating system behaves, desktop behavior, security settings, computer startup and shutdown scripts, computer-assigned application options, and application settings. Computer-related Group Policy settings are applied when the operating system initializes and during the periodic refresh cycle. In general, computer-related Group Policy settings takes precedence over conflicting user-related Group Policy settings.
	Group Policy settings that customize the desktop environment for all users of a computer, or enforce security policies on a network's computers, are contained under Computer Configuration in Group Policy Object Editor.

Software Settings for computer configuration

The Software Settings folder under Computer Configuration contains software settings that apply to all users who log on to the computer. This folder contains software installation settings, and it may contain other settings that are placed there by ISVs.

Windows settings for computer configuration

The Windows Settings folder under Computer Configuration contains Windows settings that apply to all users who log on to the computer. This folder also contains the following items: Security Settings and Scripts.

Security settings for user and computer configuration

Security settings are available under the Windows Settings folder under Computer Configuration and User Configuration in Group Policy Object Editor. Security settings or security policies are rules that you configure on a computer or multiple computers that protect resources on a computer or network. With security settings, you can specify the security policy of an organizational unit, domain, or site.

Additional reading

For more information about extending Group Policy, see "Advanced methods of extending Group Policy" at http://www.microsoft.com/technet/treeview/ default.asp?url=/technet/prodtechnol/windowsserver2003/proddocs/server/ sag_SPconcepts_30.asp.

How to Set Local Computer Policy Settings

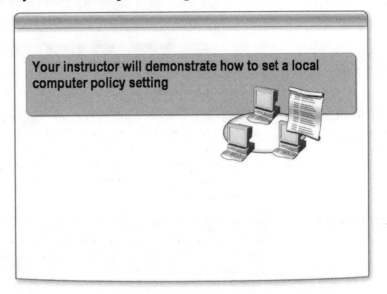

Introduction

To edit a local GPO, you must be logged on as a member of the Domain Admins group, the Enterprise Admins group, or the Group Policy Creator Owners group.

Note You can access Group Policy Object Editor from Administrative Tools or through a Microsoft Management Console (MMC) snap-in.

Procedure

To set local computer policy settings:

1. Open Group Policy Object Editor.

2. In the console tree, double-click the folders to view the policy settings in the details pane.

3. In the details pane, double-click a policy setting to open the **Properties** dialog box, and then change the policy setting.

Practice: Setting Local Computer Policy Settings

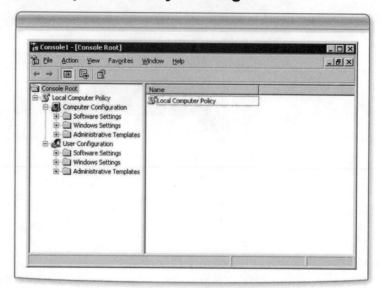

Objective

In this exercise, you will set a local computer policy setting by using Group Policy Object Editor.

Instruction

Before you begin this practice:

- Log on to the domain by using the *ComputerName*User account.

- Open CustomMMC with the **Run as** command.

  Use the user account Nwtraders*ComputerName*Admin (Example: LondonAdmin).

- Review the procedures in this lesson that describe how to perform this task.

Scenario

The systems administrators team has asked you to test some local policy settings before they deploy the policy settings to production servers. You will set some local computer policy settings on your server and test the policy settings to make sure they work.

Practice

▶ **Add Group Policy Object Editor to CustomMMC**

1. Open CustomMMC.

2. Add the snap-in Group Policy Object Editor.

3. Save CustomMMC.

▶ **Prevent users from shutting down the server by using a local policy setting**

1. In CustomMMC, expand the snap-in, **Local Computer Policy**.

2. In the console tree, expand **User Configuration**, expand **Administrative Templates**, and then click **Start Menu and Taskbar**.

3. In the details pane, double-click **Remove and prevent access to the Shut Down command**.

4. In the **Remove and prevent access to the Shut Down command Properties** dialog box, click **Enabled**, and then click **OK**.

5. Close and save all programs and log off.

▶ **Test the policy setting that prevents users from shutting down the server**

1. Log on as *ComputerName***User** with a password of **P@ssw0rd** in the NWTraders domain.

2. Click **Start** and verify that the **Shut Down** button has been removed from the **Start** menu.

3. Close and save all programs and log off.

▶ **Enable the Shut Down button on the server by using a local policy setting**

1. Log on as *ComputerName***User** with a password of **P@ssw0rd** in the NWTraders domain.

2. Open CustomMMC with the **Run as** command with the Nwtraders*ComputerName*Admin user account.

3. In CustomMMC, expand the snap-in, **Local Computer Policy**.

4. In the console tree, expand **User Configuration**, expand **Administrative Templates**, and then click **Start Menu and Taskbar**.

5. In the details pane, double-click **Remove and prevent access to the Shut Down command**.

6. In the **Remove and prevent access to the Shut Down command Properties** dialog box, click **Not configured**, and then click **OK**.

7. Close and save all programs and log off.

▶ **Test the local policy that enables the shut down option on the server**

1. Log on as *ComputerName***User** with a password of **P@ssw0rd** in the NWTraders domain.

2. Click **Start** and verify that the **Shut Down** button on the **Start** menu had been enabled.

3. Close all programs and log off.

Lesson: Implementing GPOs on a Domain

- Tools Used to Create GPOs
- What Is GPO Management on a Domain?
- How to Create a GPO
- What Is a GPO Link?
- How to Create a GPO Link
- How Group Policy Permission Is Inherited in Active Directory

Introduction

Implementing Group Policy on a domain provides the network administrator with greater control over computer configurations throughout the network structure. Also, by using Group Policy in Windows Server 2003, you can create a managed desktop environment that is tailored to the user's job responsibilities and experience level, which can decrease the amount of network support needed.

Lesson objectives

After completing this lesson, you will be able to:

- Understand the tools used to create GPOs.
- Explain what GPO management on a domain is.
- Create a GPO.
- Explain what a GPO link is.
- Explain how to configure attributes of GPO links.
- Explain how Group Policy permission is inherited in Active Directory.

Tools Used to Create GPOs

- **Default Group Policy tools**
  - **Active Directory Users and Computers**
    Domain and organizational unit GPOs
  - **Active Directory Sites and Services**
    Site GPOs
  - **Local Security Policy**
    Local computer security settings
- **Add-in tools**
  - **Group Policy Management**
    Domain, organizational unit, and site GPOs

Introduction

You can open Group Policy Object Editor from other tools to edit GPOs.

Active Directory Users and Computers

You can open Group Policy Object Editor from Active Directory Users and Computers to manage GPOs for domains and organizational units. In the **Properties** dialog box for a domain or an organizational unit, there is a **Group Policy** tab. On this tab, you can manage GPOs for the domain or organizational units.

Active Directory Sites and Services

You can open Group Policy Object Editor from Active Directory Sites and Services to manage GPOs for sites. In the **Properties** dialog box for a site, there is a **Group Policy** tab. On this tab, you can manage GPOs for the site.

Note If the Group Policy Management console is installed, the ADUC and ADSS are replaced by a button to launch the Group Policy Management console.

Group Policy Management console

The Group Policy Management console is a set of programmable interfaces for managing Group Policy, as well as an MMC snap-in that is built on those programmable interfaces. Together, the components of Group Policy Management consolidate the management of Group Policy across the enterprise.

The Group Policy Management console combines the functionality of multiple components in a single user interface (UI). The UI is structured to match the way you use and manage Group Policy. It incorporates functionality related to Group Policy from the following tools into a single MMC snap-in:

- Active Directory Users and Computers
- Active Directory Sites and Services
- Resultant Set of Policy (RSoP)

Group Policy Management also provides the following extended capabilities that were not available in previous Group Policy tools. With Group Policy Management, you can:

- Back up and restore GPOs.
- Copy and import GPOs.
- Use Windows Management Instrumentation (WMI) filters.
- Report GPO and RSoP data.
- Search for GPOs.

Group Policy Management vs. default Group Policy tools

Prior to Group Policy Management, you managed Group Policy by using a variety of Windows-based tools, including Active Directory Users and Computers, Active Directory Sites and Services, and RSoP. Group Policy Management consolidates management of all core Group Policy tasks into a single tool. Because of this consolidated management, Group Policy functionality is no longer required in these other tools.

After installing Group Policy Management, you still use each of the Active Directory tools for their intended directory management purposes, such as creating user, computer, and group objects. However, you can use Group Policy Management to perform all tasks related to Group Policy. Group Policy functionality is no longer available through the Active Directory tools when Group Policy Management is installed.

Group Policy Management does not replace Group Policy Object Editor. You still must edit GPOs by using Group Policy Object Editor. Group Policy Management integrates editing functionality by providing direct access to Group Policy Object Editor.

Note The Group Policy Management console does not come with Windows Server 2003. You must download it from http://www.microsoft.com.

Administrative Templates

There are several template files with an .adm extension that are included with Windows. These files, called Administrative Templates, provide policy information for the items that are under the Administrative Templates folder in the console tree of Group Policy Object Editor. Administrative Templates include Registry-based settings, which are available under Computer Configuration and User Configuration in Group Policy Object Editor.

An .adm file consists of a hierarchy of categories and subcategories that define how the policy settings appear. It also contains the following information:

- Registry locations that correspond to each setting
- Options or restrictions in values that are associated with each setting
- For many settings, a default value
- Explanation of what each setting does
- The versions of Windows that support each setting

What Is GPO Management on a Domain?

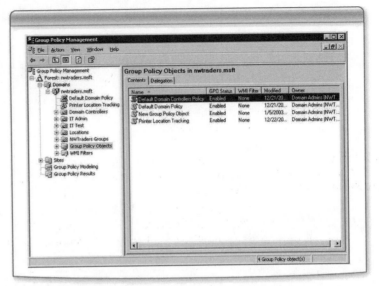

Introduction	After you create a GPO, you then configure the settings for that specific GPO. By grouping collections of settings into separate GPOs, you can specify different configurations for each GPO so that each GPO affects only the computers and users that you specify. When you place GPOs on a domain, you can manage the configuration settings on a domain-wide basis.
Group Policy container	The Group Policy container is an Active Directory object that contains GPO attributes. It includes subcontainers for Group Policy information about computers and users. The Group Policy container includes the following information:

- *Version information.* Ensures that the information in the Group Policy container is synchronized across all domain controllers.

- *Status information.* Indicates whether the GPO is enabled or disabled.

- *List of extensions.* Lists any of the Group Policy extensions that are used in the GPO.

Additional reading	For more information about Group Policy Management, see:

- "Introducing the Group Policy Management Console" at http://www.microsoft.com/windowsserver2003/gpmc/gpmcintro.mspx.

- "Enterprise Management with the Group Policy Management Console" at http://www.microsoft.com/windowsserver2003/gpmc/default.mspx.

How to Create a GPO

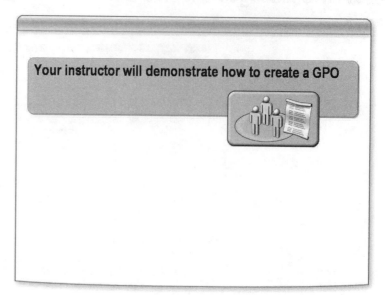

Your instructor will demonstrate how to create a GPO

Introduction

Use the following procedures to create a new GPO or link an existing GPO by using Active Directory Users and Computers and to create a GPO in a site, domain, or organizational unit.

Procedure using Active Directory Users and Computers

To create a new GPO or link an existing GPO by using Active Directory Users and Computers:

1. In Active Directory Users and Computers, right-click the Active Directory container (domain or organizational unit) for which you want to create a GPO, and then click **Properties**.

2. In the **Properties** dialog box, on the **Group Policy** tab, choose one of the following options:

   - To create a new GPO, click **New**, type a name for the new GPO, and then press ENTER.

   - To link an existing GPO, click **Add**, and then select the GPO from the list.

   The GPO that you create or link is displayed in the list of GPOs that are linked to the Active Directory container.

Procedure using Group Policy Management

To create a GPO for a site, a domain, or an organizational unit:

1. Click **Start**, point to **Administrative Tools**, and then click **Group Policy Management**.

2. In Group Policy Management, in the console tree, expand the forest containing the domain in which you want to create a new GPO, expand **Domains**, and then expand the domain.

3. Right-click **Group Policy Objects**, and then click **New**.

4. In the **New GPO** dialog box, type a name for the new Group Policy object, and then click **OK**.

Practice: Creating a GPO

In this practice, you will create a GPO by using Group Policy Management

Objective

In this practice, you will create a GPO by using Group Policy Management.

Instructions

Before you begin this practice:

- Log on to the domain by using the *ComputerName*User account.
- Open CustomMMC with the **Run as** command.

  Use the user account Nwtraders*ComputerName*Admin (Example: LondonAdmin).
- Ensure that Custom MMC contains Group Policy Management.
- Review the procedures in this lesson that describe how to perform this task.

Scenario

The systems engineers at Northwind Traders are going to test Group Policy settings in a test environment. These Group Policy settings will be used later for scalability testing. The systems engineers need your team of systems administrators to create a GPO called *ComputerName*GP in the Group Policy Objects container.

Practice

▶ **Create a GPO by using Group Policy Management**

1. In Group Policy Management, expand **nwtraders.msft**.
2. Create a GPO called *ComputerName***GP** in the Group Policy Objects container.

Additional reading

For more information about migrating GPOs, see "Migrating GPOs Across Domains with GPMC" at http://www.microsoft.com/windowsserver2003/gpmc/migrgpo.mspx.

What Is a GPO Link?

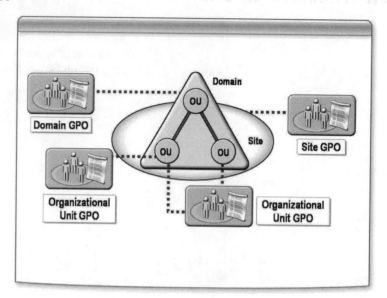

Introduction	All GPOs are stored in a container in Active Directory called Group Policy Objects. When a GPO is used by a site, domain, or organizational unit, the GPO is linked to the Group Policy Objects container. As a result, you can centrally administer and deploy the GPOs to many domains or organizational units.
Creating a linked GPO	When you create a GPO linked to a site, domain, or organizational unit, you actually perform two separate operations: creating the new GPO, and then linking it to the site, domain, or organizational unit. When delegating permissions to link a GPO to a domain, organizational unit, or site, you must have Modify permission for the domain, organizational unit, or site that you want to delegate.
	By default, only members of the Domain Admins and Enterprise Admins groups have the necessary permissions to link GPOs to domains and organizational units. Only members of the Enterprise Admins group have the permissions to link GPOs to sites. Members of the Group Policy Creator Owners group can create GPOs but cannot link them.
Creating an unlinked GPO	When you create a GPO in the Group Policy Objects container, the GPO is not deployed to any users or computers until a GPO link is created. You can create an unlinked GPO by using Group Policy Management. You might create unlinked GPOs in a large organization where one group creates GPOs, and another group links the GPOs to the required site, domain, or organizational unit.

How to Create a GPO Link

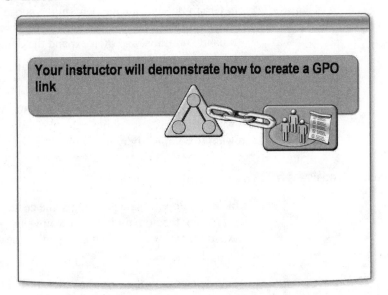

Your instructor will demonstrate how to create a GPO link

Introduction

Use the following procedures to create and link GPOs, link existing GPOs, unlink a GPO, delete a GPO link, delete a GPO, and disable a GPO.

Procedure for creating and linking a GPO

To link a GPO when you create it:

1. In Group Policy Management, in the console tree, expand the forest containing the domain in which you want to create and link a GPO, expand **Domains**, and then do one of the following:

   - To create a GPO and link it to a domain, right-click the domain, and then click **Create and Link a GPO Here**.

   - To create a GPO and link it to an organizational unit, expand the domain containing the organizational unit, right-click the organizational unit, and then click **Create and Link a GPO Here**.

2. In the **New GPO** dialog box, type a name for the new GPO, and then click **OK**.

Procedure for linking an existing GPO

To link an existing GPO to a site, domain, or organizational unit:

1. In Group Policy Management, in the console tree, expand the forest containing the domain in which you want to link an existing GPO, expand **Domains**, and then expand the domain.

2. Right-click the domain, site, or organizational unit, and then click **Link an Existing GPO**.

3. In the **Select GPO** dialog box, click the GPO that you want to link, and then click **OK**.

Important   You cannot link a GPO to containers in Active Directory like the Users and Computers containers. However, any GPO linked to the domain applies to users and computers in these containers.

Procedure for unlinking a GPO

To unlink a GPO from a site, domain, or organizational unit:

1. In Group Policy Management, in the console tree, expand the forest containing the domain from which you want to unlink an existing GPO, expand **Domains**, and then expand the domain.

2. Right-click a linked GPO, and then clear the **Link Enabled** option.

Note   Unlinking a GPO and deleting a GPO have the same effect. However, if you want to temporarily remove the GPO, you unlink it, which disables it. If you want to completely remove the GPO, then delete the link.

Procedure for deleting a GPO link

To delete a GPO link to a site, domain, or organizational unit:

1. In Group Policy Management, in the console tree, expand the forest containing the domain in which you want to delete an existing GPO link, expand **Domains**, and then expand the domain.

2. Right-click a linked GPO, and then click **Delete**.

   This deletes only the GPO link and not the GPO.

3. In the message box, click **OK**.

Procedure for deleting a GPO

To delete a GPO:

1. In Group Policy Management, in the console tree, expand the forest containing the domain in which you want to delete a GPO, expand **Domains**, expand the domain, and then expand **Group Policy Objects**.

2. Right-click the GPO that you want to delete, and then click **Delete**.

   This does not delete the link to the GPO from other domains.

3. In the message box, click **OK**.

Procedure for disabling a GPO

To disable a GPO:

1. In Group Policy Management, in the console tree, expand the forest containing the domain in which you want to disable a GPO, expand **Domains**, expand the domain, and then expand **Group Policy Objects**.

2. Click the GPO that you want to disable.

3. In the details pane, on the **Details** tab, in the **GPO status** box, click one of the following:

   • **All settings disabled**

   • **Computer configuration settings disabled**

   • **Users configuration settings disabled**

How Group Policy Permission Is Inherited in Active Directory

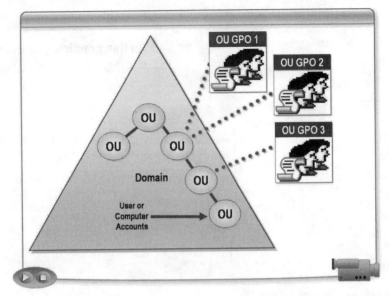

Introduction	The order in which Windows Server 2003 applies GPOs depends on the Active Directory container to which the GPOs are linked. The GPOs are applied first to the site, then to domains, and then to organizational units in the domains.
Flow of inheritance	A child container inherits GPOs from the parent container. This means that the child container can have many Group Policy settings applied to its users and computers without having a GPO linked to it. However, there is no hierarchy of domains like there is for organizational units, such as parent organizational units and child organizational units.
Order of inheritance	GPOs are cumulative, meaning that they are inherited. Group Policy inheritance is the order in which Windows Server 2003 applies GPOs. The order in which GPOs are applied and how GPOs are inherited ultimately determines which settings affect users and computers. If there are multiple GPOs that are set at the same value, by default the GPO applied last takes precedence.
	You can also have multiple GPOs linked to the same containers. For example, you can have three GPOs linked to a single domain. Because the order in which the GPOs are applied may affect the resultant Group Policy settings, there is also an order, or priority of Group Policy settings, of GPOs for each container.
Multimedia activity	The *Implementing Group Policy* activity includes multiple choice and drag-and-drop exercises that test your knowledge. To start the activity, open the Web page on the Student Materials compact disc, click **Multimedia**, and then click **Implementing Group Policy**. Read the instructions, and then click the **Effects of Group Policy Settings** tab to begin the activity.

Practice: Creating a GPO Link

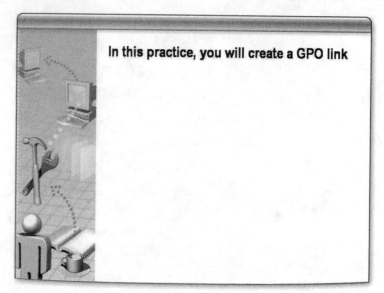

Objective	In this practice, you will create a GPO link.
Instructions	Before you begin this practice:

- Log on to the domain by using the *ComputerName*User account.
- Open CustomMMC with the **Run as** command.

  Use the user account Nwtraders*ComputerName*Admin (Example: LondonAdmin).
- Ensure that CustomMMC contains Group Policy Management and Active Directory Users and Computers.
- Review the procedures in this lesson that describe how to perform this task.

Scenario

The systems engineers at Northwind Traders are going test Group Policy settings in a test environment. These Group Policy settings will be used later for scalability testing. The systems engineers need your team of systems administrators to create GPOs for these tests.

Practice

▶ **Create an organizational unit in the IT Test organizational unit**

1. In Active Directory Users and Computers, expand **nwtraders.msft**, and then expand the **IT Test** organizational unit.
2. Create an organizational unit called *ComputerName*.

▶ **Create a GPO link to the IT Test/*ComputerName* organizational unit**

- In Group Policy Management, create a GPO called *ComputerName* **GP** and link it to the IT Test/*ComputerName* organizational unit.

Lesson: Managing the Deployment of Group Policy

- What Happens When GPOs Conflict
- Blocking the Deployment of a GPO
- How to Block the deployment of a GPO
- Attributes of a GPO Link
- How to Configure Group Policy Enforcement
- Filtering the Deployment of a GPO
- How to Configure Group Policy Filtering

Introduction

After completing this lesson, students will be able to manage the deployment of Group Policy.

Lesson objectives

After completing this lesson, you will be able to:

- Explain what happens when GPOs conflict.
- Explain what it means to block the deployment of a GPO.
- Block the deployment of a GPO.
- Describe attributes of a GPO link.
- Configure Group Policy enforcement.
- Explain what it means to filter the deployment of a GPO.
- Configure Group Policy filtering.

What Happens When GPOs Conflict

- **How conflicts are resolved**
  - When Group Policy settings in the Active Directory hierarchy conflict, the settings for the child container GPO apply
- **Options for modifying inheritance**
  - No Override
  - Block Policy inheritance

Introduction

Complex combinations of GPOs may create conflicts, which may require you to modify default inheritance behavior. When a Group Policy setting is configured for a parent organizational unit, and the same Group Policy setting is not configured for a child organizational unit, the objects in the child organizational unit inherit the Group Policy setting from the parent organizational unit.

How conflicts are resolved

When Group Policy settings are configured for both the parent organizational unit and the child organizational units, the settings for both organizational units apply. If the settings are incompatible, the child organizational unit retains its own Group Policy setting. For example, a Group Policy setting for the organizational unit that was last applied to the computer or user overwrites a conflicting Group Policy setting for a container that is higher up in the Active Directory hierarchy.

Options for modifying inheritance

If the default inheritance order does not meet your organization's needs, you can modify the inheritance rules for specific GPOs. Windows Server 2003 provides the following two options for changing the default inheritance order:

- **No Override**

  Use this option to prevent child containers from overriding a GPO with a higher priority setting. This option is useful for enforcing GPOs that represent organization-wide business rules. The **No Override** option is set on an individual GPO basis.

  You can set this option on one or more GPOs as required. When more than one GPO is set to **No Override**, the GPO set to **No Override** that is highest in the Active Directory hierarchy takes precedence.

- **Block Policy inheritance**

  Use this option to force a child container to block inheritance from all parent containers. This option is useful when an organizational unit requires unique Group Policy settings. **Block Policy inheritance** is set on a per-container basis. In the case of a conflict, the **No Override** option always takes precedence over the **Block Policy inheritance** option.

Blocking the Deployment of a GPO

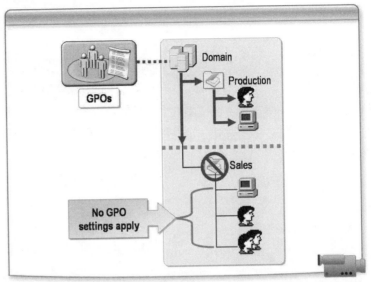

Introduction

You can prevent a child container from inheriting any GPOs from parent containers by enabling **Block Policy inheritance** on the child container.

Why use Block Policy inheritance?

Enabling **Block Policy inheritance** on a child container prevents the container from inheriting all Group Policy settings, not just selected Group Policy settings. This is useful when an Active Directory container requires unique Group Policy settings, and you want to ensure that Group Policy settings are not inherited. For example, you can use **Block Policy inheritance** when the administrator of an organizational unit must control all GPOs for that container.

Considerations

Consider the following when using **Block Policy inheritance**:

- You cannot selectively choose which GPOs are blocked. **Block Policy inheritance** affects all GPOs from all parent containers, except GPOs configured with the **No Override** option with out GPMC installed and **Enforced** with GPMC installed.

- **Block Policy inheritance** does not block the inheritance of a GPO linked to a parent container if the link is configured with the **No Override** option.

Multimedia activity

The *Implementing Group Policy* activity includes multiple choice and drag-and-drop exercises that test your knowledge. To start the activity, open the Web page on the Student Materials compact disc, click **Multimedia**, and then click **Implementing Group Policy**. Read the instructions, and then click the **Managing the Deployment of Group Policy** tab to begin the activity.

How to Block the Deployment of a GPO

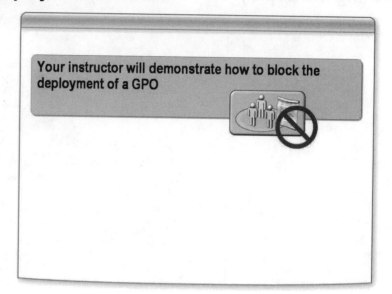

Your instructor will demonstrate how to block the deployment of a GPO

Introduction

Use the following procedure to enable **Block Policy inheritance**.

Procedure

To enable **Block Policy inheritance**:

1. In Group Policy Management, in the console tree, expand the forest in which you want to block inheritance, and then do one of the following:

   - To block inheritance of the GPO links for an entire domain, expand **Domains**, and then right-click the domain.

   - To block inheritance of the GPO links for an organizational unit, expand **Domains**, expand the domain containing the organizational unit, and then right-click the organizational unit.

2. Click **Block Inheritance**.

Attributes of a GPO Link

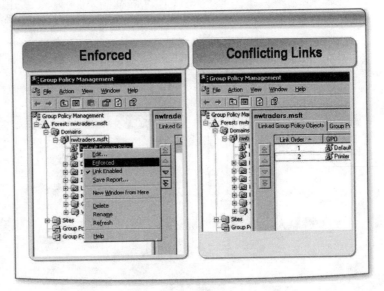

Introduction

You can enable, disable, enforce, and group GPO links. These options significantly affect the user and computers accounts in the organizational unit that the GPO is linked to.

The Enforced option

The **Enforced** option is an attribute of the GPO link, *not* the GPO itself. If you have a GPO that is linked to multiple containers, you configure the **Enforced** option on each individual container. Furthermore, if the same GPO is linked elsewhere, the **Enforced** option does not apply to that link unless you also modify that link.

All Group Policy settings contained in the GPO whose link is configured with **Enforced** apply, even if they conflict with Group Policy settings processed after them or if inheritance is blocked lower in the Active Directory tree. You should enable the **Enforced** option only for the links to the GPO that represents critical organization-wide rules. Link the GPO high in the Active Directory tree so that it affects multiple organizational units. For example, you will want to link a GPO with network security settings to a domain or site.

Important The **Enforced** option is called **No Override** in Active Directory Users and Computers before Group Policy Management is installed.

Enabling and disabling a link

Link Enabled is another attribute that you may use when you are troubleshooting a GPO. You can disable the GPO link by clearing the **Link Enabled** option, instead of deleting the GPO link. By disabling the link, you only change the effect on the user and computer accounts in the organizational unit and all child organizational units. You do not affect other links to the GPO may have.

Conflicting links

When multiple GPOs are linked to an organizational unit, the GPO with the highest link order is applied last. If Group Policy settings in the GPO conflict, the last one applied takes precedence.

How to Configure Group Policy Enforcement

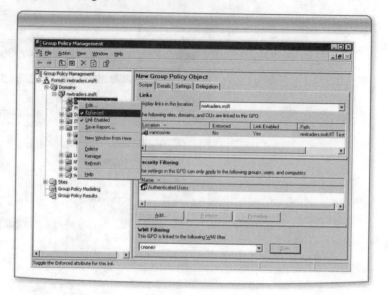

Introduction

Use the following procedure to configure the enforcement of a GPO link.

Procedure

To configure the enforcement of a GPO link:

1. In Group Policy Management, in the console tree, expand the forest with the link for which you want to configure enforcement, and then do one of the following:

   • To configure enforcement for a GPO link to a domain, expand **Domains**, and then expand the domain containing the GPO link.

   • To configure enforcement for a GPO link to an organizational unit, expand **Domains**, expand the domain containing the organizational unit, and then expand the organizational unit, which may include any parent or child organizational unit containing the GPO link.

   • To configure enforcement for a GPO link to a site, expand **Sites**, and then expand the site containing the GPO link.

2. Right-click the GPO link, and then click **Enforced** to enable or disable enforcement.

Note   Include only critical Group Policy settings in linked GPOs that are set to **Enforced**, because they take effect regardless of how other GPOs are configured. You want to be sure that you are not overriding important GPOs.

Filtering the Deployment of a GPO

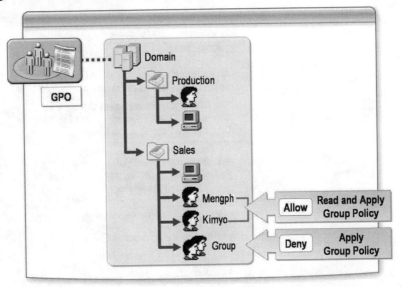

Introduction

By default, all Group Policy settings contained in the GPOs that affect the container are applied to all users and computers in that container, which may not produce the results that you desire. By using the filtering feature, you can determine which settings are applied to the users and computers in the specific container.

Permissions for GPOs

You can filter the deployment of a GPO by setting permissions on the GPO Link to determine the access of the read or deny permission on the GPO. For Group Policy settings to apply to a user or computer account, the account must have at least Read permission for a GPO. The default permissions for a new GPO have the following access control entries (ACEs):

- Authenticated Users—Allow Read and Allow Apply Group Policy
- Domain Admins, Enterprise Admins and SYSTEM—Allow Read, Allow Write, Allow Create All Child objects, Allow Delete All Child objects

Filtering methods

You can use the following filtering methods:

- Explicitly deny

  This method is used when denying access to the Group Policy. For example, you could explicitly deny permission to the administrators security group, which would prevent administrators in the organizational unit from receiving the GPO settings.

- Remove Authenticated Users

  You can omit the organizational unit administrators from the security group, which means that they have no explicit permissions for the GPO.

Class Discussion: Modifying Group Policy Inheritance

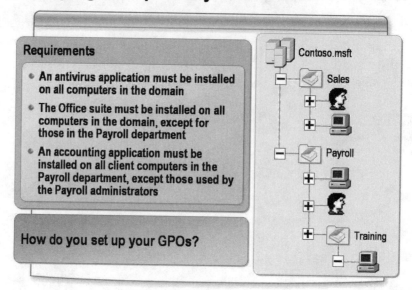

Requirements

- An antivirus application must be installed on all computers in the domain

- The Office suite must be installed on all computers in the domain, except for those in the Payroll department

- An accounting application must be installed on all client computers in the Payroll department, except those used by the Payroll administrators

How do you set up your GPOs?

Contoso.msft
Sales
Payroll
Training

Class discussion

You have determined that the following conditions must exist in your network:

- An antivirus application must be installed on all computers in the domain.

- The Microsoft Office suite must be installed on computers in the domain, except those in the Payroll department.

- A line-of-business accounting application must be installed on all computers in the Payroll department, except those that are used by administrators of the Payroll organizational unit.

How do you set up GPOs so that the above conditions are met?

How to Configure Group Policy Filtering

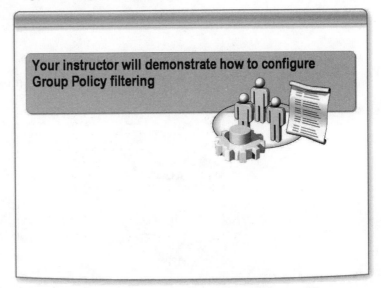

Your instructor will demonstrate how to configure Group Policy filtering

Introduction

Use the following procedure to configure Group Policy filtering.

Procedure

To filter the scope of a GPO by using security groups:

1. In Group Policy Management, in the console tree, expand the forest and domain with the GPO, expand **Group Policy objects**, and then click the GPO.

2. In the details pane, on the **Scope** tab, click **Add**.

3. In the **Select User, Computer, or Group** dialog box, in the **Enter the object name to select** box, enter the name of the security principal, and then click **OK**.

Practice: Managing the Deployment of Group Policy

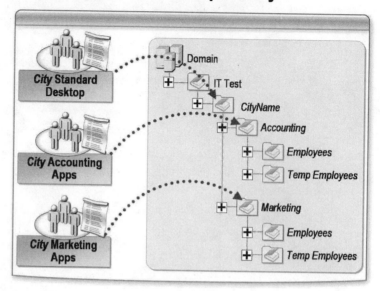

Objective

In this practice, you will manage the deployment of Group Policy.

Instructions

Before you begin this practice:

- Log on to the domain by using the *ComputerName*User account.

- Open CustomMMC with the **Run as** command.

    Use the user account Nwtraders*ComputerName*Admin (Example: LondonAdmin).

- Ensure that CustomMMC contains the following snap-ins:

    - Active Directory Users and Computers

    - Group Policy Management

- Review the procedures in this lesson that describe how to perform this task.

Scenario

Northwind Traders is testing the effect of multiple Group Policy settings on users and computers. Northwind Traders wants to implement an organizational unit that gives all users a standard desktop, except managers whose accounts are in the Employees organizational unit.

Management has asked the systems administrators team to create an organizational unit hierarchy in the IT Test organizational unit. The organizational unit hierarchy must contain an Accounting organizational unit and a Marketing organizational unit like in the diagram on the slide.

Management has also asked you to create a GPO to be used to install an Accounting and a separate Marketing application. The Accounting and Marketing applications are to be eventually installed to all Accounting and Marketing personnel; however, management wants to wait to deploy the application for the temporary employees. Management wants to maintain flexibility so when the temporary employees are ready for the applications, it can easily be enabled for them.

Practice

▶ **Create three GPOs for testing purposes**

- In Group Policy Management, create three GPOs in the Group Policy Objects container with the following names:
  - *ComputerName* Standard Desktop
  - *ComputerName* Accounting Apps
  - *ComputerName* Marketing Apps

▶ **Create an organizational unit structure that matches the slide**

- In Active Directory Users and Computers, create the organizational unit structure that appears on the slide.

▶ **Create an enforced GPO link**

1. Link the *ComputerName* Standard Desktop GPO to the IT Test/*ComputerName* organizational unit.

2. In the IT Test/*ComputerName* organizational unit, right-click the *ComputerName* **Standard Desktop** link, and click **Enforced**.

▶ **Configure a GPO security filter**

1. In Group Policy Management, in the **Group Policy Objects** container, double-click the *ComputerName* **Standard Desktop GPO** link.

2. In the details pane, on the **Scope** tab, add the following groups:
   - G NWTraders Accounting Managers
   - G NWTraders Accounting Personnel
   - G NWTraders Marketing Managers
   - G NWTraders Marketing Personnel

3. Remove Authenticated Users.

4. On the **Delegation** tab, click **Advanced**.

5. In the **Security Settings** dialog box, configure the following advanced security settings:
   - For the G NWTraders Accounting Managers group, set the Apply Group Policy permissions to Deny.
   - For the G NWTraders Marketing Managers group, set the Apply Group Policy permissions to Deny.

▶ **Configure GPOs to block inheritance**

1. Link the *ComputerName* Accounting Apps GPO to the IT Test/*ComputerName*/Accounting organizational unit.

2. Click the **Temp Employees** organizational unit in the IT Test/*ComputerName*/Accounting organizational unit.

3. List the GPOs that the IT Test/*ComputerName*/Accounting organizational unit inherits.

   _____

   _____

   _____

4. Right-click the **Temp Employees** organizational unit in the IT Test/*ComputerName*/Accounting organizational unit, and then click **Block Inheritance**.

5. List the GPOs that the IT Test/*ComputerName*/Accounting organizational unit inherits.

   _____

   _____

Lab A: Implementing Group Policy

- In this lab, you will:
  - Link a GPO to an organizational unit
  - Identify the effects of inheritance when multiple GPOs are assigned
  - Block Group Policy inheritance
  - Force a GPO to be applied to child organizational units
  - Filter a GPO so that it is applied to selected users and groups in an organizational unit

Objectives

After completing this lab, you will be able to:

- Link a GPO to an organizational unit.
- Identify the effects of inheritance when multiple GPOs are assigned.
- Block Group Policy inheritance.
- Force a GPO to be applied to child organizational units.
- Filter a GPO so that it is applied to selected users and groups in an organizational unit.

Instructions

Before you begin this lab:

- Log on to the domain by using the *ComputerName*User account.
- Open CustomMMC with the **Run as** command.

  Use the user account Nwtraders*ComputerName*Admin (Example: LondonAdmin).

- Ensure that CustomMMC contains the following snap-ins:
  - Active Directory Users and Computers
  - Group Policy Management

Estimated time to complete this lab: 25 minutes

Scenario

Northwind Traders is preparing to implement GPOs to the users and computers throughout all cities on their network. The systems engineers want the systems administrators team to create all the necessary GPOs and then link the GPOs to the appropriate organizational units. After the GPOs are created and deployed to the workstations, you must then configure the GPOs to perform the intended functions.

The systems administrators have provided you with a list of GPOs, along with their properties, that need to be created and configured. You should reuse GPOs that have already been created if you can. You also must make sure that no computer-related Group Policy settings affect laptops in your city, so you must block any GPOs from affecting the Laptops organizational unit.

GPO name	Location	Filtering	Enforcement
ComputerName Standard Desktop	Location/*ComputerName*	Default	Enforced
ComputerName Folder Redirection	Location/*ComputerName*/Users	DL Temp Employees = Deny	
ComputerName Scripts	Location/*ComputerName*/Users	Default	
ComputerName Proxy Settings	Location/*ComputerName*/Computers/ Desktops	Default	Enforced

Exercise 1
Creating and Linking GPOs

In this exercise, you will create and link GPOs to your *ComputerName* organizational unit.

Tasks	Detailed Steps
1. Link a Standard Desktop GPO.	a. Location: nwtraders.msft/Locations/*ComputerName* b. GPO Name: *ComputerName* **Standard Desktop**
2. Create and link a Folder Redirection GPO.	a. Location: nwtraders.msft/Locations/*ComputerName*/Users b. GPO Name: *ComputerName* **Folder Redirection**
3. Create and link a Scripts GPO.	a. Location: nwtraders.msft/Locations/*ComputerName*/Users b. GPO Name: *ComputerName* **Scripts**
4. Create and link a Proxy Settings GPO.	a. Location: nwtraders.msft/Locations/*ComputerName*/Computers/ Desktops b. GPO Name: *ComputerName* **Proxy Settings**

Exercise 2
Filtering the Deployment of a GPO

In this exercise, you will set Deny permissions for all temporary employees of Northwind Traders so that the *ComputerName* Folder Redirection GPO is not applied to them.

Tasks	Detailed Steps
1. Configure filtering of a GPO for a group.	a. Location: nwtraders.msft/Locations/*ComputerName*/Users
	b. GPO: *ComputerName* Folder Redirection
	c. Group: DL Temp Employees
	d. Permissions: Set the Apply Group Policy permission to Deny

Exercise 3
Configuring the Enforcement of GPOs

In this exercise, you will configure GPOs to be enforced throughout your organizational unit hierarchy.

Tasks	Detailed Steps
1. Set the **Enforced** option on a GPO link.	a. Location: nwtraders.msft/Locations/*ComputerName*. b. GPO: *ComputerName* Standard Desktop link c. Option: **Enforced**
2. Set the **Enforced** option on a GPO link.	a. Location: nwtraders.msft/Locations/*ComputerName*/Computers/ Desktops b. GPO: *ComputerName* Proxy Settings c. Option: **Enforced**

Exercise 4
Configuring the Blocking of GPOs

In this exercise, you will block inheritance of GPOs throughout your organizational unit hierarchy.

Tasks	Detailed Steps
1. Set the **Block Policy inheritance** option on an organizational unit.	a. Location: nwtraders.msft/Locations/*ComputerName*/Computers/ Laptops b. Option: **Block Policy inheritance**

Course Evaluation

Your evaluation of this course will help Microsoft understand the quality of your learning experience.

At a convenient time before the end of the course, please complete a course evaluation, which is available at http://www.CourseSurvey.com.

Microsoft will keep your evaluation strictly confidential and will use your responses to improve your future learning experience.

Microsoft®
Training &
Certification

Module 9: Managing the User Environment by Using Group Policy

Contents

Microsoft®

Overview

- Configuring Group Policy Settings
- Assigning Scripts with Group Policy
- Configuring Folder Redirection
- Determining Applied GPOs

Introduction

This module introduces the job function of managing the user environment by using Group Policy. Specifically, the module provides the skills and knowledge that you need to use Group Policy to configure Folder Redirection, Microsoft® Internet Explorer connectivity, and the desktop.

Objectives

After completing this module, you will be able to:

- Configure Group Policy settings.
- Assign scripts with Group Policy.
- Configure Folder Redirection.
- Determine Applied Group Policy objects (GPOs).

Lesson: Configuring Group Policy Settings

- Why Use Group Policy?
- What Are Disabled and Enabled Group Policy Settings?
- How to Edit a Group Policy Setting

Introduction

After completing this lesson, you will be able to configure Group Policy settings.

Lesson objectives

After completing this lesson, you will be able to:

- Explain why you use Group Policy.
- Explain what disabled and enabled Group Policy settings are.
- Edit a Group Policy setting.

Why Use Group Policy?

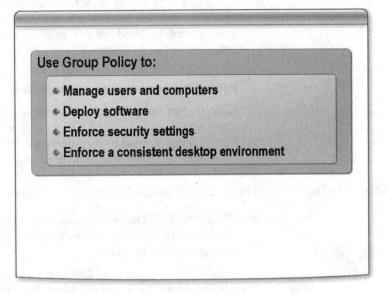

Use Group Policy to:
- Manage users and computers
- Deploy software
- Enforce security settings
- Enforce a consistent desktop environment

Introduction

Managing user environments means controlling what users can do when logged on to the network. You do this by controlling their desktops, network connections, and user interfaces through Group Policy. You manage user environments to ensure that users have what they need to perform their jobs, but that they cannot corrupt or incorrectly configure their environments.

Tasks you can perform with Group Policy

When you centrally configure and manage user environments, you can perform the following tasks:

- Manage users and computers

  By managing user desktop settings with registry-based policies, you ensure that users have the same computing environments even if they log on from different computers. You can control how Microsoft Windows® Server 2003 manages user profiles, which includes how a user's personal data is made available. By redirecting user folders from the user's local hard disks to a central location on a server, you can ensure that the user's data is available to them regardless of the computer they log on to.

- Deploy software

  Software is deployed to computers or users through the Active Directory® directory service. With software deployment, you can ensure that users have their required programs, service packs, and hotfixes.

- Enforce security settings

  By using Group Policy in Active Directory, the systems administrator can centrally apply the security settings required to protect the user environment. In Windows Server 2003, you can use the Security Settings extension in Group Policy to define the security settings for local and domain security policies.

- Enforce a consistent desktop environment

  Group Policy settings provide an efficient way to enforce standards, such as logon scripts and password settings. For example, you can prevent users from making changes to their desktops that may make their user environments more complex than necessary.

Additional reading

For more information about desktop management, see:

- "Windows 2000 Desktop Management Overview" at http://www.microsoft.com/windows2000/techinfo/howitworks/ management/ccmintro.asp.

- "Introduction to Windows 2000 Group Policy" at http://www.microsoft.com/windows2000/techinfo/howitworks/ management/grouppolicyintro.asp.

- The Group Policy newsgroup at http://www.microsoft.com/ windows2000/community/newsgroups/.

What Are Disabled and Enabled Group Policy Settings?

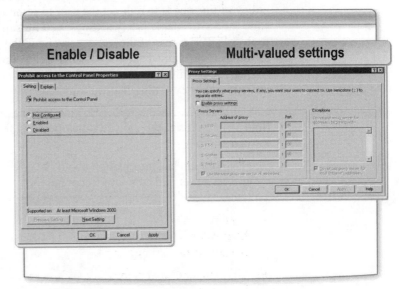

Disable a policy setting

If you disable a policy setting, you are disabling the action of the policy setting. For example, users by default can access Control Panel. You do not need to disable the policy setting **Prohibit access to the Control Panel** to allow a user to access Control Panel unless a previously applied policy setting enabled it. In this situation, you set another policy setting that disables the previously applied policy setting.

This is helpful when you have inherited policy settings, and you do not want to use filtering to apply policy settings to one group and not to another group. You can apply a GPO that enables one policy setting on the parent organizational unit and another policy setting that disables the GPO on a child organizational unit.

Enable a policy setting

If you enable a policy setting, you are enabling the action of the policy setting. For example, to revoke someone's access to Control Panel, you enable the policy setting **Prohibit access to the Control Panel**.

Not Configured

A GPO holds the values that change the registry for users and computers that are subject to the GPO. The default configuration for a policy setting is **Not Configured**. If you want to set a computer or user policy setting back to the default value or back to the local policy, select the **Not Configured** option.

For example, you may enable a policy setting for some clients, and when using the not Configured option, the policy will revert to the default, local policy setting.

Multi-valued policy settings

Some GPOs require you to provide some additional information after you enable the object. Sometimes you may need to select a group or computer if the policy setting needs to redirect the user to some information. Other times, as the slide shows, to enable proxy settings, you must provide the name or Internet Protocol (IP) address of the proxy server and the port number. If a policy setting is multi-valued and the settings are in conflict with another policy setting, the conflicting multi-valued settings are replaced with the last conflicting policy setting that was applied.

Note   The **Settings** tab indicates the operating systems that support the policy setting.

The **Explain** tab has information about the effects of the **Enabled** and **Disabled** options on a user and computer account.

How to Edit a Group Policy Setting

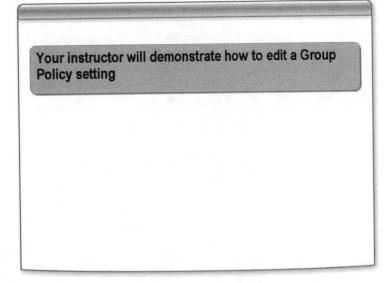

Your instructor will demonstrate how to edit a Group Policy setting

Introduction

As a systems administrator, you must edit Group Policy settings. Use the following procedure to perform this task.

Procedure

To edit Group Policy settings:

1. In Group Policy Management, in the console tree, navigate to **Group Policy Objects**.

2. Right-click a GPO, and then click **Edit**.

3. In Group Policy Object Editor, navigate to the Group Policy setting that you want to edit, and then double-click the setting.

4. In the **Properties** dialog box, configure the Group Policy setting, and then click **OK**.

Practice: Editing Group Policy Settings

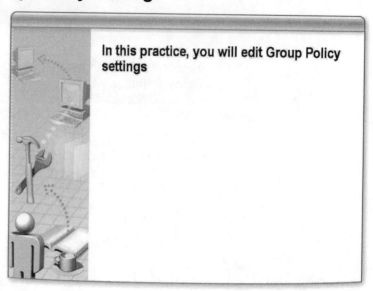

Objective

In this practice, you will edit Group Policy settings.

Instructions

Before you begin this practice:

- Log on to the domain by using the *ComputerName*User account.
- Open CustomMMC with the **Run as** command.

  Use the user account Nwtraders*ComputerName*Admin (Example: LondonAdmin).

- Ensure that CustomMMC contains the following snap-ins:
  - Active Directory Users and Computers
  - Group Policy Management
- Review the procedures in this lesson that describe how to perform this task.

Scenario

Northwind Traders must implement the *ComputerName* Standard Desktop GPO. This GPO is linked to the IT Test/*ComputerName* organizational unit for the test environment and the Locations/*ComputerName* organizational unit for the production environment. You must disable the link for the production environment first. When that is done, Northwind Traders wants to implement the following Group Policy settings in the *ComputerName* Standard Desktop GPO:

- **Remove Run menu from the Start Menu**
- **Prohibit access to the Control Panel**
- **Hide My Network Places icon on desktop**
- **Remove Network Connections from Start Menu**
- **Remove "Map Network Drive" and "Disconnect Network Drive"**

Practice

▶ **Verify that the GPO links are configured**

- Verify that the *ComputerName* Standard Desktop GPO is linked to the Locations/*ComputerName* organizational unit.

▶ **Configure security filtering**

- Location: Locations/*ComputerName*
- GPO link: *ComputerName* Standard Desktop
- Security filtering:
  - Remove all security group filtering
  - Add the Everyone group

▶ **Disable a GPO link**

- Location: Locations/*ComputerName*
- GPO link: *ComputerName* Standard Desktop

▶ **Edit a GPO**

- GPO: *ComputerName* Standard Desktop

▶ **Remove Run from the Start menu**

- Location: User Configuration/Administrative Templates/Start Menu and Taskbar
- Group Policy setting: **Remove Run menu from Start Menu Properties**
- Option: **Enabled**

▶ **Disable access to Control Panel**

- Location: User Configuration/Administrative Templates/Control Panel
- Group Policy setting: **Prohibit access to the Control Panel**
- Option: **Enabled**

▶ **Hide My Network Places icon on desktop**

- Location: User Configuration/Administrative Templates/Desktop
- Group Policy setting: **Hide My Network Places icon on desktop**
- Option: **Enabled**

▶ **Remove Network Connections from the Start menu**

- Location: User Configuration/Administrative Templates/Start Menu and Taskbar
- Group Policy setting: **Remove Network Connections from Start Menu**
- Option: **Enabled**

► **Enable Remove "Map Network Drive" and "Disconnect Network Drive"**

- Location: User Configuration/Administrative Templates/ Windows Components/Windows Explorer
- Group Policy setting: **Remove "Map Network Drive" and "Disconnect Network Drive"**
- Option: **Enabled**

► **Enable a GPO link**

- Location: Locations/*ComputerName*
- GPO link: *ComputerName* Standard Desktop

► **Create a user account**

1. Create a user account (if the user account does not already exist) with the following properties:
   - First name: *ComputerName*
   - Last name: **Test**
   - User logon name: *ComputerName***Test**
   - Password: **P@ssw0rd**
   - Organizational unit: Locations/*ComputerName*/User
2. Log off.

► **Log on**

1. Log on as *ComputerName***Test** with a password of **P@ssw0rd**.
2. Verify that the following is true:
   - **Run** has been removed menu from the **Start** menu.
   - **Control Panel** has been removed from the **Start** menu.
   - The **My Network Places** icon is hidden on the desktop.
   - **Network Connections** has been removed from the **Start** menu.
   - **Map Network Drive** and **Disconnect Network Drive** have been removed from Windows Explorer.
3. Log off.

Lesson: Assigning Scripts with Group Policy

- What Are Group Policy Script Settings?
- How to Assign Scripts with Group Policy

Introduction

You can use Group Policy to deploy scripts to users and computers. A script is a batch file or a Microsoft Visual Basic® script that can execute code or perform management tasks. You can use Group Policy script settings to automate the process of running scripts.

There are script settings under both Computer Configuration and User Configuration in Group Policy. You can use Group Policy to run scripts when a computer starts and shuts down and when a user logs on and logs off. As with all Group Policy settings, you configure a Group Policy script setting once, and Windows Server 2003 continually implements and enforces it throughout your network.

Lesson objectives

After completing this lesson, you will be able to:

- Explain what Group Policy script settings are.
- Assign scripts with Group Policy.

What Are Group Policy Script Settings?

```
Set objNetwork = Wscript.CreateObject("WScript.Network")
objNetwork.MapNetworkDrive"G:", "\\ComputerName\ComputerName Data"
msgbox "Your Script worked!!!!!"
```

Introduction

You can use Group Policy script settings to centrally configure scripts to run automatically when the computer starts and shuts down and when users log on and log off. You can specify any script that runs in Windows Server 2003, including batch files, executable programs, and scripts supported by Windows Script Host (WSH).

Benefits of Group Policy script settings

To help you manage and configure user environments, you can:

- Run scripts that perform tasks that you cannot perform through other Group Policy settings. For example, you can populate user environments with network connections, printer connections, shortcuts to applications, and corporate documents.

- Clean up desktops when users log off and shut down computers. You can remove connections that you added with logon or startup scripts so that the computer is in the same state as when the user started the computer.

- Run pre-existing scripts already set up to manage user environments until you configure other Group Policy settings to replace these scripts.

Note From Active Directory Users and Computers, you can assign logon scripts individually to user accounts in the **Properties** dialog box for each user account. However, Group Policy is the preferred method for running scripts, because you can manage these scripts centrally, along with startup, shutdown, and logoff scripts.

Additional reading

For more information about scripting, see the TechNet Script Center at http://www.microsoft.com/technet/treeview/default.asp?url=/technet/ scriptcenter/default.asp.

How to Assign Scripts with Group Policy

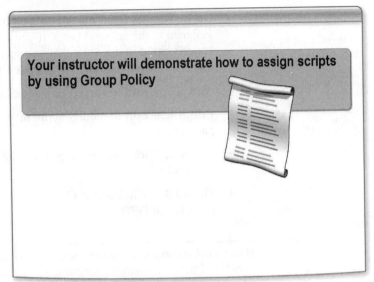

Your instructor will demonstrate how to assign scripts by using Group Policy

Introduction

To implement a script, you use Group Policy to add that script to the appropriate setting in the Group Policy template. This indicates that the script will run during startup, shutdown, logon, or logoff.

Procedure

To add a script to a GPO:

1. In Group Policy Management, edit a GPO.

2. In Group Policy Object Editor, in the console tree, navigate to User Configuration/Windows Settings/Scripts (Logon/Logoff).

3. In the details pane, double-click **Logon**.

4. In the **Logon Properties** dialog box, click **Add**.

5. In the **Add a Script** dialog box, configure any of the following settings that you want to use, and then click **OK**:

   - **Script Name**. Type the path to the script or click **Browse** to locate the script file in the Netlogon share of the domain controller.

   - **Script Parameters**. Type any parameters that you want to use in the same way that you type them on the command line.

6. In the **Logon Properties** dialog box, configure any of the following settings that you want to use:

- **Logon Scripts for**. This box lists all of the scripts that are currently assigned to the selected GPO. If you assign multiple scripts, the scripts are processed in the order that you specify. To move a script in the list, click the script, and then click either **Up** or **Down**.

- **Add**. Click **Add** to specify any additional scripts that you want to use.

- **Edit**. Click **Edit** to modify script information such as the name and parameters.

- **Remove**. Click **Remove** to remove the selected script from the **Logon Scripts** list.

- **Show Files**. Click **Show Files** to view the script files that are stored in the selected GPO.

Note   Logon scripts are run in the context of the user account and not in the context of the administrator account.

Practice: Assigning Scripts with Group Policy

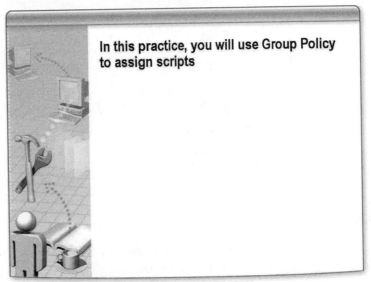

In this practice, you will use Group Policy to assign scripts

Objective

In this practice, you will use Group Policy to assign scripts.

Instructions

Before you begin this practice:

- Log on to the domain by using the *ComputerName*Admin account.

Note This practice focuses on the concepts in this lesson and as a result may not comply with Microsoft security recommendations. For example, this practice does not comply with the recommendation that users log on with domain user account and use the **Run as** command when performing administrative tasks. When using the Windows Explorer, you cannot use the **Run as** command.

- Open CustomMMC.
- Ensure that CustomMMC contains the following snap-ins:
  - Active Directory Users and Computers
  - Group Policy Management
- Review the procedures in this lesson that describe how to perform this task.

Scenario

Northwind Traders wants drive S on the computers of all personnel to be mapped to a shared folder called *ComputerName* Public on your member server. You must link a GPO named *ComputerName* Logon Scripts to the called IT Test/*ComputerName* organizational unit. You then must test the logon script.

Practice

▶ **Create a shared folder on your computer**

- Folder path: D:*ComputerName* Public

- Shared folder name: *ComputerName* **Public**

- Permissions: Grant Full Control permission to Administrators and grant Read and Write permissions to other users

▶ **Create and link a GPO**

- Location: IT Test/*ComputerName*

- GPO name: **Group** *ComputerName* **Logon Script**

▶ **Edit a GPO**

- GPO: *ComputerName* Scripts

▶ **Configure a logon script Group Policy setting**

- Location: User Configuration/Windows Settings/Scripts

- Group Policy setting: Logon

- Options:

1. In the **Logon Properties** dialog box, click **Show Files**.

2. In Windows Explorer, on the **Tools** menu, click **Folder Options**.

3. In the **Folder Options** dialog box, on the **View** tab, under **Advanced settings**, clear the **Hide extensions for known file types** check box, and then click **OK**.

4. In Windows Explorer, on the **File** menu, point to **New**, and then click **Text Document**.

5. Change the name of the file called New Text Document.txt to **Logon.vbs**.

6. In the message box, click **Yes**.

7. Right-click **Logon.vbs**, and then click **Edit**.

8. On the **File Download** dialog box, click **Open**.

9. In Microsoft Notepad, type the following:

```
Set objNetwork = Wscript.CreateObject("WScript.Network")
objNetwork.MapNetworkDrive "S:","\\ComputerName\ComputerName Public"
msgbox "Your Script worked!!!!!"
```

10. On the **File** menu, click **Save**.

11. Close Notepad, and then close Windows Explorer.

12. In the **Logon Properties** dialog box, click **Add**.

13. In the **Add a Script** dialog box, click **Browse**.

14. In the **Browse** dialog box, click **logon.vbs**, and then click **Open**.

15. In the **Add a Script** dialog box, click **OK**.

16. In the **Logon Properties** dialog box, click **OK**.

17. Close all windows and log off.

▶ **Test the logon script**

1. Log on as *ComputerName***Test** with a password of **P@ssw0rd**.

2. In the **Your Script worked!!!!!** box, click **OK**.

3. Close all windows and log off.

▶ **Delete a GPO Link**

■ Location: Locations/*ComputerName*

■ GPO: *ComputerName* Standard Desktop

■ Action: Delete the GPO Link

Lesson: Configuring Folder Redirection

- What Is Folder Redirection?
- Folders That Can Be Redirected
- Settings Required to Configure Folder Redirection
- Security Considerations for Configuring Folder Redirection
- How to Configure Folder Redirection

Introduction

Windows Server 2003 enables you to redirect folders that are part of the user profile from users' local hard disks to a central location on a server. By redirecting these folders, you can ensure that users' data is located in a central location and that users' data is available to them regardless of the computers to which they log on.

Folder Redirection makes it easier for you to manage and back up centralized data. The folders that you can redirect are My Documents, Application Data, Desktop, and Start Menu. Windows Server 2003 automatically creates these folders and makes them part of the user profile for each user account.

Lesson objectives

After completing this lesson, you will be able to:

- Explain what Folder Redirection is.
- Explain which folders can be redirected.
- Determine which settings are required to configure Folder Redirection.
- Explain security considerations for configuring Folder Redirection.
- Configure Folder Redirection.

What Is Folder Redirection?

- Folder Redirection enables users and administrators to redirect the folders to a new location
  - The new location can be a folder on the local computer or a shared folder on the network
  - Users can work with documents on a server as if the documents are located on the local drive

Introduction

When you redirect folders, you change the storage location of folders from the local hard disk on the user's computer to a shared folder on a network file server. After you redirect a folder to a file server, it still appears to the user as if it is stored on the local hard disk. You can redirect four folders that are part of the user profile: My Documents, Application Data, Desktop, and Start Menu.

Benefits of Folder Redirection

By storing data on the network, users benefit from increased availability and frequent backup of their data. Redirecting folders has the following benefits:

- The data in the folders is available to the user regardless of the client computer that the user logs on to.

- The data in the folders is centrally stored so that the files that they contain are easier to manage and back up.

- Files that are located in redirected folders, unlike files that are part of a roaming user profile, are not copied and saved on the computer that the user logs on to. This means that when a user logs on to a client computer, no storage space is used to store these files, and that data that might be confidential does not remain on a client computer.

- Data that is stored in a shared network folder can be backed up as part of routine system administration. This is safer because it requires no action on the part of the user.

- As an administrator, you can use Group Policy to set disk quotas, limiting the amount of space that is taken by users' special folders.

- Data specific to a user can be redirected to a different hard disk on the user's local computer rather than to the hard disk holding the operating system files. This protects the user's data if the operating system must be reinstalled.

Folders That Can Be Redirected

- **My Documents**
- **Application Data**
- **Desktop**
- **Start Menu**

Introduction

You can redirect the My Documents, Application Data, Desktop, and Start Menu folders. An organization should redirect these folders to preserve important user data and settings. There are several advantages to redirecting each of these folders. The advantages vary according to your organization's needs.

Redirected folders

You can use Folder Redirection to redirect any of the following folders in a user profile:

- My Documents

  Redirecting My Documents is particularly advantageous because the folder tends to become large over time.

  Offline Files technology gives users access to My Documents even when the users are not connected to the network. This is particularly useful for people who use portable computers.

- Application Data

  A Group Policy setting controls the behavior of Application Data when client-side caching is enabled. This setting synchronizes application data that is centralized on a server with the local computer. As a result, the user can work online or offline. If any changes are made to the application data, synchronization updates the application data on the client and server.

- Desktop

  You can redirect Desktop and all the files, shortcuts, and folders to a centralized server.

- Start Menu

  When you redirect Start Menu, its subfolders are also redirected.

Settings Required to Configure Folder Redirection

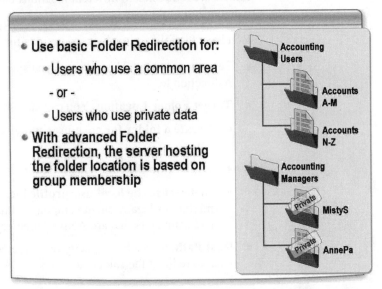

- **Use basic Folder Redirection for:**
  - Users who use a common area
  - or -
  - Users who use private data
- **With advanced Folder Redirection, the server hosting the folder location is based on group membership**

Accounting Users
Accounts A-M
Accounts N-Z
Accounting Managers
Private MistyS
Private AnnePa

Introduction

There are three available settings for Folder Redirection: none, basic, and advanced. Basic Folder Redirection is for users who must redirect their folders to a common area or users that need their data to be private.

Basic Folder Redirection

You have the following basic options for Folder Redirection:

- **Redirect folder to the following location**

  All users who redirect their folders to a common area can see or use each other's data in the redirected folder. To do this, choose a **Basic** setting and set **Target folder location** to **Redirect folder to the following location**. Use this option for all redirected folders that contain data that is not private. An example of this is redirecting My Documents for a team of Accounts Receivable personnel who all share the same data.

- **Create a folder for each user under the root path**

  For users who need their redirected folders to be private, choose a **Basic** setting and set **Target folder location** to **Create a folder for each user under the root path**. Use this option for users who need their data to be private, like managers who keep personal data about employees.

Advanced Folder Redirection

When you select **Advanced – specify locations for various user groups**, folders are redirected to different locations based on the security group membership of the users.

You have the following advanced options for Folder Redirection:

- **Select a group(s)**. This is where you specify who you want to deploy redirection to.

- **Target Folder Location**. You can choose any of the following options:

  - **Create a folder for each user under the root path**. Use this for private data.

  - **Redirect to the following location**. Use this for shared data.

  - **Redirect to the local userprofile location**. Use this for users who use a mixture of legacy client computers that are not Active Directory enabled and computers that are Active Directory enabled.

- **Root Path**. In this box, specify the server and shared folder name that you want to redirect the folders to.

Security Considerations for Configuring Folder Redirection

- NTFS permissions for folder redirection root folder
- Shared folder permissions for folder redirection root folder
- NTFS permissions for each user's redirected folder

Introduction

Folder Redirection can create folders for you, which is the recommended option. When you use this option, the correct permissions are set automatically. Usually, you do need to know what the permissions are. However, if you manually create folders, you will need to know what the permissions are. The following tables show which permissions to set for Folder Redirection.

Note Although it is not recommended, administrators can create the redirected folders before Folder Redirection creates them.

NTFS permissions required for the root folder

Set the following NTFS permissions for the root folder.

User account	Folder Redirection defaults	Minimum permissions needed
Creator/owner	Full Control, this folder, subfolders, and files	Full Control, this folder, subfolders, and files
Administrators	No permissions	No permissions
Everyone	No permissions	No permissions
Local System	Full Control, this folder, subfolders, and files	Full Control, this folder, subfolders, and files
Security group of users who need to put data on the shared network server	N/A	List Folder/Read Data, Create Folders/Append Data - This folder only

Shared folder permissions required for the root folder

Set the following shared folder permissions for the root folder.

User account	Folder Redirection defaults	Minimum permissions needed
Everyone	Full Control	No permissions (use security group)
Security group of users who need to put data on the shared network server	N/A	Full Control

NTFS permissions required for each user's redirected folder

Set the following NTFS permissions for each user's redirected folder.

User account	Folder Redirection defaults	Minimum permissions needed
UserName	Full Control, owner of folder	Full Control, owner of folder
Local System	Full Control	Full Control
Administrators	No permissions	No permissions
Everyone	No permissions	No permissions

Note When offline folders are synchronized over the network, the data is transmitted in plain text format. The data is then susceptible to interception by network monitoring tools.

Additional reading

For more information about Folder Redirection, see "Best practices for Folder Redirection," at http://www.microsoft.com/technet/treeview/default.asp?url=/ technet/prodtechnol/windowsserver2003/proddocs/server/ sag_sp_bestprac_foldred.asp

How to Configure Folder Redirection

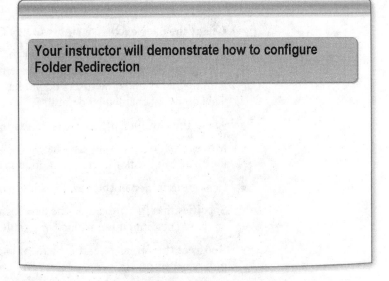

Your instructor will demonstrate how to configure Folder Redirection

Introduction   You configure Folder Redirection settings by using Group Policy Object Editor.

Procedure   To configure Folder Redirection:

1. In Group Policy Management, edit or create a GPO.

2. In Group Policy Object Editor, in the console tree, expand **User Configuration**, expand **Windows Settings**, and then expand **Folder Redirection**.

   Icons for the four folders that can be redirected are displayed.

3. Right-click the folder that you want to redirect, and then click **Properties**.

4. In the **Properties** dialog box, in the **Setting** tab, click one of the following options:

   - **Basic - Redirect everyone's folder to the same network share point.**

     All folders affected by this GPO are stored in the same shared network folder.

   - **Advanced - Redirect personal folders based on the user's membership in a Windows Server 2003 security group.**

     Folders are redirected to different shared network folders based on security group membership. For example, folders belonging to users in the Accounting group are redirected to the Accounting server, and folders belonging to users in the Marketing group are redirected to the Marketing server.

5. In the **Properties** dialog box, Click **Add**.

6. Under **Target folder location**, in the **Root path** box, type the name of the shared network folder to use, or click **Browse** to locate it.

7. On the **Settings** tab, configure the options you want to use, and then click **OK**.

The following options for settings are available:

- **Grant the user exclusive rights to My Documents.**

  Sets the NTFS security descriptor for the usernames unique folder to Full Control for the user and local system *only*. This means that administrators and other users do *not* have access rights to the folder. This option is enabled by default.

- **Move the contents of My Documents to the new location.**

  Moves any document the user has in the local My Documents folder to the shared network folder. This option is enabled by default.

- **Leave the folder in the new location when policy is removed.**

  Specifies that files remain in the new location if the GPO no longer applies. This option is enabled by default.

- **Redirect the folder back to the local user profile location when policy is removed.**

  Specifies that the folder is moved back to the local profile location if the GPO no longer applies.

The **My Documents Properties** dialog box has the following additional options for the My Pictures folder:

- **Make My Pictures a subfolder of My Documents.**

  When the My Documents folder is redirected, My Pictures remains as a subfolder of My Documents. This option is enabled by default.

- **Do not specify administrative policy for My Pictures.**

  Group Policy does not control the location of My Pictures. The location of My Pictures is determined by the user profile.

Note   You should allow the operating system to create the directory and security for Folder Redirection. Do not manually create the directory defined by username. Folder Redirection sets the appropriate permissions on the folder. If you choose to manually create folders for each user, be sure to set the permissions correctly.

Practice: Configuring Folder Redirection

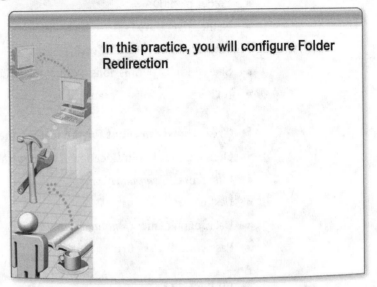

In this practice, you will configure Folder Redirection

Objective

In this practice, you will configure Folder Redirection.

Instructions

Before you begin this practice:

- Log on to the domain by using the *ComputerName*User account.
- Open CustomMMC with the **Run as** command.

  Use the user account Nwtraders*ComputerName*Admin (Example: LondonAdmin).

- Ensure that CustomMMC contains the following snap-ins:

  - Active Directory Users and Computers

  - Group Policy Management

  - Computer Management (Local)

- Review the procedures in this lesson that describe how to perform this task.

Scenario

Northwind Traders is setting up a test environment to test Folder Redirection of the My Documents folder for each city in Northwind Traders. You must create a folder called D:\\UserDataTest and share it as UserDataTest$ on your *ComputerName* server.

You also must create a GPO, linked to the IT Test/*ComputerName* organizational unit, called *ComputerName* Folder Redirection Test. This GPO should redirect the My Documents folder to *ComputerName*\\UserDataTest$. Do not give users exclusive rights to the redirected folder so that administrators can see if documents are added to it.

Practice

▶ **Create a shared folder**

- Folder path: D:\
- Name: **UserDataTest**
- Share name: **UserDataTest$**
- Shared folder permissions: Authenticated Users = Full Control
- NTFS permissions: Default

▶ **Create a user account for the test (If one does not already exist)**

- Organizational unit: Locations/*ComputerName*
- First name: *ComputerName*
- Last name: **Test**
- User logon name: *ComputerName***Test**
- Password: **P@ssw0rd**

▶ **Link a GPO**

- Organizational unit: Locations/*ComputerName*
- GPO name: *ComputerName* **Folder Redirection**
- Security filtering: Authenticated Users

▶ **Edit a GPO**

- GPO: *ComputerName* Folder Redirection

▶ **Configure Folder Redirection**

- Location: /User Configuration/Windows Settings/Folder Redirection
- Group Policy setting: My Documents
- Options:
  - Target folder setting: **Basic – Redirect everyone's folder to the same location**
  - Target folder location: **Create a folder for each user under the root path**
  - Root path: *ComputerName*\UserDataTest$
  - Redirect settings: Clear the **Grant the user exclusive rights to My Documents** check box
  - Policy Removal: **Redirect the folder back to the local userprofile location when policy is removed**
  - My Pictures Preferences: **Make My Pictures a subfolder of My Documents**

▶ **Test the Folder Redirection of My Documents**

1. Log off.

2. Log on as *ComputerName***Test** with a password of **P@ssw0rd**.

3. In the message box, click **OK**.

4. Click **Start**.

5. Right-click **My Documents**, and then click **Properties**.

6. In the **My Document Properties** dialog box, verify that the following is in the **Target** box:

   *ComputerName***userdatatest$***ComputerName*test**My Documents**

7. Click **OK**.

8. Click **Start**, and then click **My Documents**.

9. In My Documents, on the **File** menu, point to **New**, and then click **Text Document**.

10. Close all windows and log off.

▶ **Test the permissions of redirected folders**

1. Log on as *ComputerName***Admin** with a password of **P@ssw0rd**.

2. Go to: **D:\UserDataTest**.

3. In D:\UserDataTest*ComputerName*Test, double-click *ComputerName***Test's Documents**.

4. In D:\UserDataTest*ComputerName*Test*ComputerName*Test's Documents, verify that the file called New Text Document.txt was created.

5. Close all windows and log off.

Lesson: Determining Applied GPOs

- What Is Gpupdate?
- What Is Gpresult?
- What Is Group Policy Reporting?
- How to Use Group Policy Reporting
- What Is Group Policy Modeling?
- How to Use Group Policy Modeling
- What Is Group Policy Results?
- How to Use Group Policy Results

Introduction

Group Policy is the primary administrative tool for defining and controlling how programs, network resources, and the operating system operate for users and computers in an organization. In an Active Directory environment, Group Policy is applied to users or computers on the basis of their membership in sites, domains, or organizational units.

Lesson objectives

After completing this lesson, you will be able to:

- Explain what **gpupdate** is.
- Explain what **gpresult** is.
- Explain what is group policy reporting.
- Use group policy reporting.
- Explain what is group policy modeling.
- Use group policy modeling.
- Explain what is group policy results.
- Use group policy results.

What Is Gpupdate?

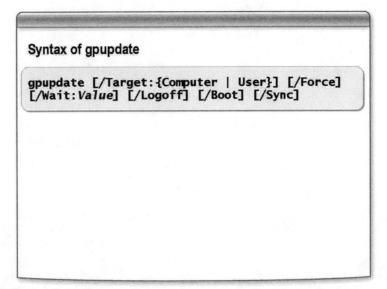

Syntax of gpupdate

```
gpupdate [/Target:{Computer | User}] [/Force]
[/Wait:Value] [/Logoff] [/Boot] [/Sync]
```

Introduction

Gpupdate is a command-line tool that refreshes local Group Policy settings and Group Policy settings that are stored in Active Directory, including security settings. By default, security settings are refreshed every 90 minutes on a workstation or server and every five minutes on a domain controller. You can run **gpupdate** to test a Group Policy setting or to force a Group Policy setting.

Examples of gpupdate

The following examples show how you can use the **gpupdate** command:

- C:\gpupdate
- C:\gpupdate /target:computer
- C:\gpupdate /force /wait:100
- C:\gpupdate /boot

Parameters of gpupdate

Gpupdate has the following parameters.

Value	Description
/Target:{**Computer** | **User**}	Specifies that only user or only computer policy settings are refreshed. By default, both user and computer policy settings are refreshed.
/Force	Reapplies all policy settings. By default, only policy settings that have changed are reapplied.
/Wait:{*Value*}	Sets the number of seconds to wait for policy processing to finish. The default is 600 seconds. The value '0' means not to wait. The value '-1' means to wait indefinitely.
/Logoff	Causes a logoff after the Group Policy settings are refreshed. This is required for those Group Policy client-side extensions that do not process policy settings during a background refresh cycle but do process policy settings when a user logs on. Examples include user-targeted Software Installation and Folder Redirection. This option has no effect if there are no extensions called that require a logoff.
/Boot	Causes the computer to restart after the Group Policy settings are refreshed. This is required for those Group Policy client-side extensions that do not process policy during a background refresh cycle but do process policy when the computer starts. Examples include computer-targeted Software Installation. This option has no effect if there are no extensions called that require the computer to restart.
/Sync	Causes the next foreground policy setting to be applied synchronously. Foreground policy settings are applied when the computer starts and when the user logs on. You can specify this for the user, computer, or both by using the **/Target** parameter. The **/Force** and **/Wait** parameters are ignored.

What Is Gpresult?

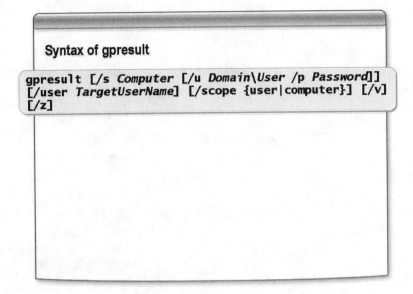

Syntax of gpresult

```
gpresult [/s Computer [/u Domain\User /p Password]]
[/user TargetUserName] [/scope {user|computer}] [/v]
[/z]
```

Introduction

Because you can apply overlapping levels of policy settings to any computer or user, Group Policy generates a resulting set of policies at logon. **Gpresult** displays the resulting set of policies that are enforced on the computer for the specified user at logon.

The **gpresult** command displays Group Policy settings and Resultant Set of Policy (RSoP) data for a user or a computer. You can use **gpresult** to see what policy setting is in effect and to troubleshoot problems.

Examples of gpresult

The following examples show how you can use the **gpresult** command:

- C:\gpresult /user targetusername /scope computer

- C:\gpresult /s srvmain /u maindom/hiropln /p p@ssW23 /user targetusername /scope USER

- C:\gpresult /s srvmain /u maindom/hiropln /p p@ssW23 /user targetusername /z >policy.txt

- C:\gpresult /s srvmain /u maindom/hiropln /p p@ssW23

Parameters of gpresult

Gpresult has the following parameters.

Value	Description
/s *Computer*	Specifies the name or IP address of a remote computer. Do not use backslashes. The default is the local computer.
/u *Domain*/*User*	Runs the command with the account permissions of the user that is specified by *User* or *Domain*/*User*. The default is the permissions of the user who is currently logged on to the computer that issues the command.
/p *Password*	Specifies the password of the user account that is specified in the /u parameter.
/user *TargetUserName*	Specifies the user name of the user whose RSoP data is to be displayed.
/scope {user|computer}	Displays either user or computer policy settings. Valid values for the /scope parameter are **user** or **computer**. If you omit the /scope parameter, **gpresult** displays both user and computer policy settings.
/v	Specifies that the output will display verbose policy information.
/z	Specifies that the output will display all available information about Group Policy. Because this parameter produces more information than the /v parameter, redirect output to a text file when you use this parameter (for example, you can type **gpresult /z >policy.txt**).
/?	Displays help in the command prompt window.

Practice: Using Gpupdate and Gpresult

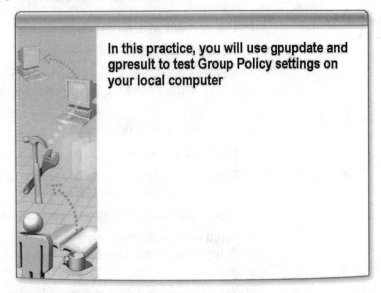

In this practice, you will use gpupdate and gpresult to test Group Policy settings on your local computer

Objective

In this practice, you will use **gpupdate** and **gpresult** to test policy settings on your local computer.

Instructions

Before you begin this practice:

- Log on to the domain by using the *ComputerName*User account.
- Open CustomMMC with the **Run as** command.

  Use the user account Nwtraders*ComputerName*Admin (example: LondonAdmin).

- Ensure that CustomMMC contains Group Policy Management.
- Open a command prompt with the Run as command.

  From Run type **runas /user:nwtraders*ComputerName*Admin cmd** and click **OK**. When prompted for a password type **P@ssw0rd**, and press **ENTER**.

- Ensure that you have a user account created named *ComputerName*Test.
- Review the procedures in this lesson that describe how to perform this task.

Scenario

You are testing some Group Policy settings on your local computer. You do not want to wait for the refresh interval to see the Group Policy update, so you must run the **gpupdate** command.

Gpupdate with no switches

▶ **Use gpupdate with no switches**

- From a command prompt, type **gpupdate**

▶ **Use gpupdate with the /force switch**

- From a command prompt, type **gpupdate /force**. If prompted to logoff, type **N** and press **ENTER**.

Scenario

You must use **gpresult** to see which Group Policy settings are in effect on your server so that you can help troubleshoot remote computers.

Gpresult with no switches

▶ **Use gpresult with no switches**

1. From a command prompt, type **gpresult**

2. Scroll up the command prompt window to see the results of the Group Policy settings that have been applied to your computer.

▶ **Use gpresult with the /scope switch**

1. From a command prompt, type **gpresult /scope computer**

2. Scroll up the command prompt window to see the results of the Group Policy settings that have been applied to your computer.

3. From a command prompt, type **gpresult /scope user**

4. Scroll up the command prompt window to see the results of the Group Policy settings that have been applied to your computer.

▶ **Send the gpresult data to a text file with the /z switch**

1. From a command prompt, type **gpresult /z >gp.txt**

2. From a command prompt, type **notepad gp.txt**

3. In Notepad, scroll through the results, and then close Notepad.

Scenario

Your boss wants you to test a Group Policy setting. The Group Policy setting removes the **Search** option from the **Start** menu and only affects your local computer. When you are done, your boss needs a report to see that the changes were applied correctly.

Testing group policy settings

▶ **Log on as *ComputerName*Test and run CustomMMC**

1. Log on as *ComputerName*Test with a password of **P@ssw0rd**.

2. Open C:\MOC\CustomMMC with the **Run as** command by using the user account nwtraders*ComputerName*Admin.

3. Type your password, and then click **OK**.

▶ **Create and link a GPO**

■ Location: Locations/*ComputerName*

■ GPO name: *ComputerName* **gpresult**

▶ **Edit a GPO**

• GPO: *ComputerName* gpresult

▶ **Remove Search menu from Start Menu Properties**

■ Location: User Configuration/Administrative Templates/Start Menu and Taskbar

■ Group Policy setting: **Remove Search menu from Start Menu Properties**

■ Option: **Enabled**

▶ **Test to see if the Group Policy setting has been applied**

1. From a command prompt, type **gpresult /z >1.txt**

2. From a command prompt, type **notepad 1.txt**

3. In Notepad, on the **Edit** menu, click **Find**.

4. In the **Find** dialog box, in the **Find what** box, type *ComputerName* **gpresult** and then click **Find Now**.

5. In Notepad, verify that the message says **Cannot find "***ComputerName*** gpresult"** and then click **OK**.

6. In the **Find** dialog box, click **Cancel**, and then close Notepad.

7. From a command prompt, type **gpupdate**

▶ **Test again to see if the Group Policy setting has been applied**

1. From a command prompt, type **gpresult /z >2.txt**

2. From a command prompt, type **notepad 2.txt**

3. In Notepad, on the **Edit** menu, click **Find**.

4. In the **Find** dialog box, in the **Find what** box, type *ComputerName* **gpresult** and then click **Find Now**.

5. In Notepad, verify that *ComputerName* **gpresult** is highlighted under **Applied Group Policy Object**.

6. In the **Find** dialog box, click **Find Next**.

7. In Notepad, verify that *ComputerName* **gpresult** is highlighted under **Administrative Templates**.

8. In the **Find** dialog box, click **Cancel**, and then close Notepad.

9. Close all windows and log off.

What Is Group Policy Reporting?

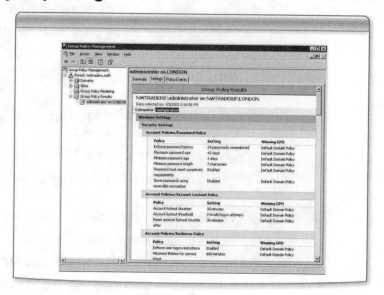

Definition

A systems administrator can make hundreds of changes to a GPO. To verify changes made to a GPO without actually opening the GPO and expanding every folder, you can generate a Hypertext Markup Language (HTML) report that lists the items in the GPO that are configured.

Settings tab

The **Settings** tab of the details pane for a GPO or GPO link in Group Policy Management shows an HTML report that displays all the defined settings in the GPO. Any user with read access to the GPO can generate this report. If you click **show all** at the top of the report, the report is fully expanded, and all settings are shown. Also, using a context menu, you can print the reports or save them to a file as either HTML or Extensible Markup Language (XML).

How to Use Group Policy Reporting

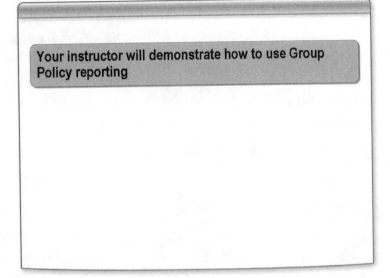

Your instructor will demonstrate how to use Group
Policy reporting

Introduction

Use the following procedure to determine applied Group Policy settings by using Group Policy reporting.

Procedure

To use Group Policy reporting:

1. In Group Policy Management, in the console tree, click the GPO that you want to generate a report for.

   You must expand the forest, domain, and domain name to locate the GPO that you want to generate a report for.

2. In the details pane, click the **Settings** tab.

Practice: Using Group Policy Reporting

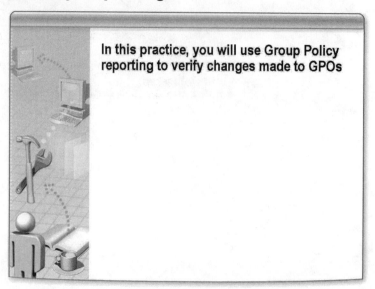

In this practice, you will use Group Policy reporting to verify changes made to GPOs

Objective

In this practice, you will use Group Policy reporting to verify changes made to GPOs.

Instructions

Before you begin this practice:

- Log on to the domain by using the *ComputerName*User account.
- Open CustomMMC with the **Run as** command.

  Use the user account Nwtraders*ComputerName*Admin (example: LondonAdmin).

- Ensure that CustomMMC contains Group Policy Management.
- Review the procedures in this lesson that describe how to perform this task.

Scenario

You have been asked to document the Group Policy settings for the Default Domain Policy GPO.

Practice

▶ **View the report for Default Domain Policy**

1. In Group Policy Management, in the console tree, expand **Group Policy Objects**.
2. Click **Default Domain Policy**.
3. In the details pane, click the **Settings** tab.
4. From the **Internet Explorer** box, click **Close**.
5. Review the Group Policy settings for Default Domain Policy.
6. Right-click anywhere in the report, and then click **Save Report**.
7. In the **Save GPO Report** dialog box, click **Save**.

What Is Group Policy Modeling?

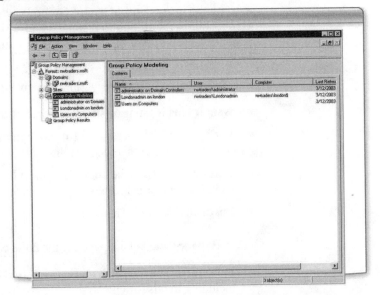

Introduction

Windows Server 2003 enables you to simulate a GPO deployment that is applied to users and computers before you actually deploy the GPO. The simulation creates a report that takes into account the user's organizational unit, the computer's organizational unit, and any group membership or Windows Management Instrumentation (WMI) filtering. It also takes into account any Group Policy inheritance issues or conflicts.

Requirements

If you want to use Group Policy modeling, there must be a Windows Server 2003 domain controller in the forest. This is because the simulation is performed by a service that is only present on Windows Server 2003 domain controllers.

Results of Group Policy Modeling

To perform a Group Policy Modeling query, the user uses the Group Policy Modeling Wizard. After the user completes the Group Policy Modeling Wizard, a new node in the console tree of Group Policy Management appears under **Group Policy Modeling** to display the results. The **Contents** tab in the details pane for Group Policy Modeling displays a summary of all Group Policy Modeling queries that the user has performed.

For each query, Group Policy Management shows the following data:

- **Name**. This is the user-supplied name of the modeling results.

- **User**. This is the user object (or the organizational unit where the user object is located) that the modeling query is based on.

- **Computer**. This is the computer object (or the organizational unit where the computer object is located) that the modeling query is based on.

- **Last refresh time**. This is the last time the modeling query was refreshed.

For each query, the details pane for the node contains the following three tabs:

- **Summary**. This contains an HTML report of the summary information, including the list of GPOs, security group membership, and WMI filters.

- **Settings**. This contains an HTML report of the policy settings that were applied in this simulation.

- **Query**. This lists the parameters that were used to generate the query.

How to Use Group Policy Modeling

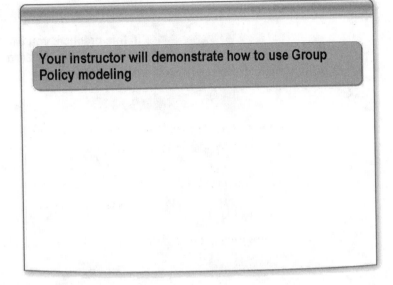

Your instructor will demonstrate how to use Group Policy modeling

Introduction

To determine the applied Group Policy settings, you use the Group Policy Modeling Wizard. This enables you to simulate the results of applying a new GPO before actually applying it.

Procedure

To use Group Policy Modeling:

1. In Group Policy Management, in the console tree, double-click the forest in which you want to create a Group Policy Modeling query, right-click **Group Policy Modeling**, and then click **Group Policy Modeling Wizard**.

2. In the Group Policy Modeling Wizard, click **Next** and then enter the following information:

   - If you want to model what the effect of a new GPO is for a user or computer, enter the name of the container for the user or computer.

   - If you want to model what the effect of a new GPO is for a specific user or computer account that will be migrated to a different organizational unit, enter the user or computer name. The wizard then prompts you for the destination of that user or computer.

3. When finished, click **Finish**.

Practice: Using Group Policy Modeling Wizard

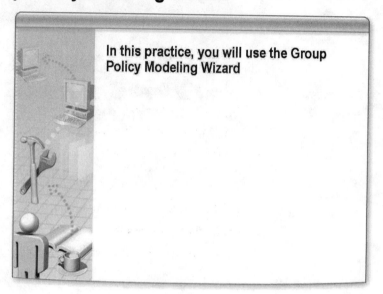

In this practice, you will use the Group Policy Modeling Wizard

Objective

In this practice, you will use the Group Policy Modeling Wizard.

Instructions

Before you begin this practice:

- Log on to the domain by using the *ComputerName*User account.

- Open CustomMMC with the **Run as** command.

  Use the user account Nwtraders*ComputerName*Admin (example: LondonAdmin).

- Ensure that CustomMMC contains Group Policy Management.

- Review the procedures in this lesson that describe how to perform this task.

Scenario

Your manager needs to know how Group Policy will be applied if your *ComputerName* computer account is moved to the IT Test/*ComputerName* organizational unit.

Practice

▶ **Generate a Group Policy Modeling report**

1. In Group Policy Management, in the console tree, right-click **Group Policy Modeling**, and then click **Group Policy Modeling Wizard**.

2. In the Group Policy Modeling Wizard, on the **Welcome** page, click **Next**.

3. On the **Domain Controller Selection** page, click **Next**.

4. On the **User and Computer Selection** page, under **Computer information**, click **Computer**, type **nwtraders***ComputerName* and then click **Next**.

5. On the **Advanced Simulation Options** page, click **Next**.

6. On the **Alternative Active Directory Paths** page, in the **Computer location** box, type **OU=**ComputerName**,OU=IT Test,DC=nwtraders, DC=msft** and then click **Next**.

7. On the **Computer Security Groups** page, click **Next**.

8. On the **WMI Filters for Computers** page, click **Next**.

9. On the **Summary of Selections** page, click **Next**.

10. Click **Finish**.

11. From the **Internet Explorer** box, click **Close**.

▶ **View the Group Policy Modeling report**

1. On the **Summary** tab, look through the report.

2. From the *ComputerName* details pane, click the **Settings** tab.

3. From the **Internet Explorer** box, click **Close**.

4. Look through the report.

5. Click the **Query** tab.

6. Look through the report.

What Is Group Policy Results?

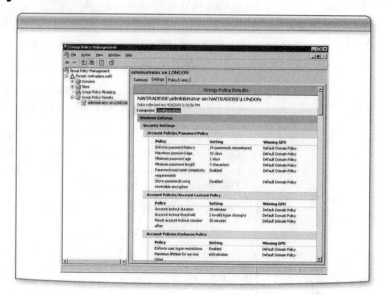

Introduction

The data that is presented in Group Policy Results is similar to Group Policy Modeling data. However, unlike Group Policy Modeling data, this data is not a simulation. It is the actual RSoP data obtained from the target computer. By default, this access is granted to all users on Microsoft Windows XP, but not on Windows Server 2003.

Requirements

Unlike Group Policy Modeling, the data in Group Policy Results is obtained from the client and is not simulated on the domain controller. Technically, a Windows Server 2003 domain controller is not required to be in the forest if you want to access Group Policy Results. However, the client must be running Windows XP or Windows Server 2003. It is not possible to get Group Policy Results data for a client running Microsoft Windows 2000.

Note By default, only users with local administrator privileges on the target computer can remotely access Group Policy Results data. To gather this data, the user performing the query must have access to remotely view the event log.

Results of Group Policy Results

Each Group Policy Results query is represented by a node under the Group Policy Results container in the console tree of Group Policy Management. The details pane for each node has the following three tabs:

- **Summary**. This contains an HTML report of the summary information including the list of GPOs, security group membership, and WMI filters.

- **Settings**. This contains an HTML report of the policy settings that were applied.

- **Events**. This shows all policy-related events from the target computer.

How to Use Group Policy Results

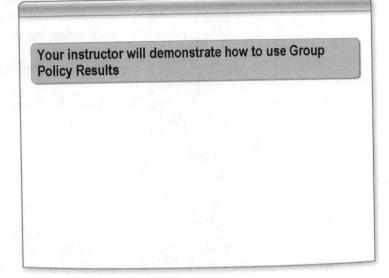

Introduction

Use the following procedure to use Group Policy Results.

Procedure

To use Group Policy Results:

1. In Group Policy Management, in the console tree, double-click the forest in which you want to create a Group Policy Results query, right-click **Group Policy Results**, and then click **Group Policy Results Wizard**.

2. In the Group Policy Results Wizard, click **Next** and then enter the appropriate information.

3. After completing the wizard, click **Finish**.

Practice: Using Group Policy Results Wizard

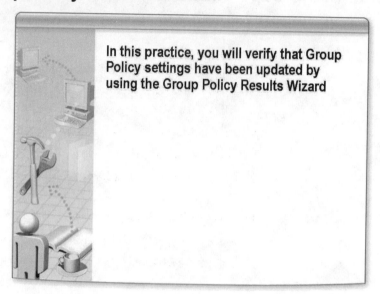

In this practice, you will verify that Group Policy settings have been updated by using the Group Policy Results Wizard

Introduction

In this practice, you will verify that policy settings have been updated by using the Group Policy Results Wizard.

Instructions

Before you begin this practice:

- Log on to the domain by using the *ComputerName*User account.

- Open CustomMMC with the **Run as** command.

  Use the user account Nwtraders*ComputerName*Admin (example: LondonAdmin).

- Ensure that CustomMMC contains Group Policy Management.

- Review the procedures in this lesson that describe how to perform this task.

Scenario

You want to verify that policy settings are being updated on your student computer. You want to look at the computer policy setting being applied to your computer with the *ComputerName*Admin account.

Practice

▶ **Generate a Group Policy Results report**

1. In Group Policy Management, right-click **Group Policy Results**, and then click **Group Policy Results Wizard**.

2. In the Group Policy Results Wizard, on the **Welcome** page, click **Next**.

3. On the **Computer Selection** page, click **Next**.

4. On the **User Selection** page, click **Select a specific user**, click **NWTRADERS**_ComputerName_**Admin**, and then click **Next**.

5. On the **Summary of Selections** page, click **Next**.

6. On the **Completing the Group Policy Results Wizard** page, click **Finish**.

7. From the **Internet Explorer** dialog box, click **Close**.

▶ **View a Group Policy Results report**

1. On the **Summary** tab look through the report.

2. On the **Policy Events** tab, double-click **Source**.

3. Scroll down to see the source labeled SceCli.

4. Double-click the first event with the source labeled SceCli.

5. In the **Event Properties** dialog box, notice the date and time the security policy setting was applied successfully.

6. Click the down arrow to see the next event, notice the date and time the security policy setting was applied successfully, and then click **OK**.

Lab A: Using Group Policies Reports

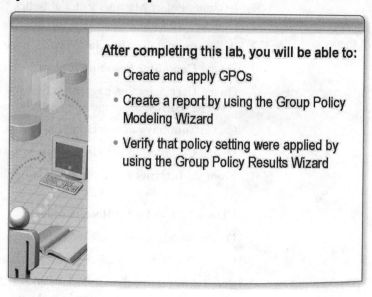

After completing this lab, you will be able to:

- Create and apply GPOs
- Create a report by using the Group Policy Modeling Wizard
- Verify that policy setting were applied by using the Group Policy Results Wizard

Objectives

After completing this lab, you will be able to:

- Create and apply GPOs.
- Create a report by using the Group Policy Modeling Wizard.
- Verify that policy settings were applied by using the Group Policy Results Wizard.

Instructions

Before you begin this lab:

- Log on to the domain by using the *ComputerName*User account.
- Open CustomMMC with the **Run as** command.

  Use the user account Nwtraders*ComputerName*Admin (example: LondonAdmin).

- Ensure that CustomMMC contains the following snap-ins:
  - Active Directory Users and Computers
  - Computer Management (Local)
  - Group Policy Management
- Ensure that you have organizational units named Laptops and Desktops in the Locations/*ComputerName*/Computers organizational unit.

Scenario

Northwind Traders has finished testing GPOs and must configure multiple GPOs that will affect many users and computers in your city. You must create and apply GPOs by using all of the properties in the following tables. After you configure all of the GPOs, you must create reports to show that the appropriate groups are not affected by certain policy settings and that the proper policy settings are applied.

Estimated time to complete this lab: 50 minutes

Exercise 1
Creating a GPO for Standard Desktop Computers

In this exercise, you will create a GPO.

Scenario

Northwind Traders has finished testing a GPO that enables the Marketing personnel to use a standard desktop computer. Create a GPO with the following properties.

Properties	Special Instructions
1. Create a GPO.	▪ GPO name: *ComputerName* **Standard Desktop 2**
2. Create a GPO link.	▪ Location: Locations/*ComputerName* ▪ GPO name: *ComputerName* Standard Desktop 2

3. Configure security filtering.	▪ Location: Locations/*ComputerName*
	▪ GPO: *ComputerName* Standard Desktop 2
	▪ Security Filtering:
	  • Remove Authenticated Users
	  • Add G NWTraders Marketing Personnel
	  • Deny the Apply Group Policy permission to G NWTraders Marketing Managers

4. Set the following Group Policy settings to **Enabled**.	▪ GPO: *ComputerName* Standard Desktop 2 ▪ Location of Group Policy setting: User Configuration/Administrative Templates/Windows Components/Application Compatibility/Prevent access to 16-bit applications ▪ Location of Group Policy setting: User Configuration/Administrative Templates/Windows Components/Windows Explorer/Remove Search button from Windows Explorer ▪ Location of Group Policy setting: User Configuration/Administrative Templates/Windows Components/ Windows Explorer/Remove Hardware tab ▪ Location of Group Policy setting: User Configuration/Administrative Templates/Start Menu and Taskbar/Remove links and access to Windows Update ▪ Location of Group Policy setting: User Configuration/Administrative Templates/Start Menu and Taskbar/Remove Network Connections from Start Menu ▪ Location of Group Policy setting: User Configuration/Administrative Templates/Start Menu and Taskbar/Remove Run from Start Menu

Exercise 2
Creating a GPO for Folder Redirection

In this exercise, you will set Deny permissions for all temporary employees of Northwind Traders so that they do not receive the *ComputerName* Folder Redirection GPO.

Scenario

Northwind Traders has finished testing a GPO for Folder Redirection. You must create a GPO that redirects folders of Accounting personnel only.

Tasks	Special instructions
1. Create a GPO.	▪ GPO name: *ComputerName* **Accounting Folder Redirection**
2. Create a GPO link.	▪ Location: Locations/*ComputerName*/Users ▪ GPO name: *ComputerName* Accounting Folder Redirection
3. Configure security filtering.	▪ Location: Locations/*ComputerName* ▪ GPO: *ComputerName* Accounting Folder Redirection ▪ Security Filtering: • Remove Everyone • Add DL NWTraders Accounting Personnel Full Control
4. Create a shared folder.	▪ Folder Path: D:\Accounting Data ▪ Share Name: *ComputerName***Accounting Data$** ▪ Permissions: Grant Full Control permission to DL NWTraders Accounting Personnel Full Control
5. Configure Group Policy settings.	▪ Location: Locations/*ComputerName*/Users ▪ GPO: *ComputerName* Accounting Folder Redirection ▪ Location of Group Policy setting: User Configuration/Windows Settings/Folder Redirection/My Documents ▪ Options: • Target folder setting: **Basic – Redirect everyone's folder to the same location** • Target folder location: **Create a folder for each user under the root path** • Root Path: *ComputerName*\Accounting Data$ • Redirection settings: • **Grant the user exclusive user rights to My Documents** • **Redirect the folder back to the local userprofile when the policy is removed**

Exercise 3
Creating a GPO for Laptop Computers

In this exercise, you will configure a GPO for laptop computers.

Scenario

Northwind Traders has finished testing a GPO for laptop computers. Create a GPO with the following properties that will be enforced on all laptop computers.

Tasks	Special instructions
1. Create a GPO	▪ GPO name: *ComputerName* **Laptop Settings**
2. Create a GPO link.	▪ Location: Locations/*ComputerName*/Computers/Laptops ▪ GPO name: *ComputerName* Laptop Settings
3. Set the following Group Policy settings to **Enabled**.	▪ GPO: *ComputerName* Laptop Settings ▪ Location of Group Policy setting: User Configuration/ Administrative Templates/System/Power Management/Prompt for password on resume from hibernation / suspend ▪ Location of Group Policy setting: User Configuration/ Administrative Templates/Network/Offline Files/Synchronize all offline files when logging on ▪ Location of Group Policy setting: User Configuration/ Administrative Templates/Network/Offline Files/Synchronize all offline files before logging off

Exercise 4
Creating a GPO for Desktop Computers

In this exercise, you will configure a GPO for desktop computers.

Scenario

Northwind Traders has finished testing a GPO for desktop computers. Create a GPO with the following properties that will be enforced on all desktop computers.

Tasks	Special instructions
1. Create a GPO.	▪ GPO name: *ComputerName* **Desktop Settings**
2. Create a GPO link.	▪ Location: Locations/*ComputerName*/Computers/Desktop ▪ GPO name: *ComputerName* Desktop Settings
3. Set the following Group Policy settings to **Enabled**.	▪ GPO: *ComputerName* Desktop Settings ▪ Location of Group Policy setting: User Configuration/Administrative Templates/Network/Offline Files/Prevent use of offline folders

Exercise 5
Generating a Group Policy Modeling Report

In this exercise, you will generate two Group Policy Modeling reports. You will generate one report for Accounting managers with laptop computers and another report for Accounting personnel with desktop computers.

Report name	Special instructions
1. Create a Group Policy Modeling report for laptop computers.	■ User Container: OU=Users,OU=*ComputerName*,OU=Locations,DC=nwtraders, DC=msft ■ Computer Container: OU=Laptops,OU=Computers,OU=*ComputerName*,OU=Locations, DC=nwtraders,DC=msft ■ User Security Groups: Authenticated Users, Everyone, NWTRADERS\G NWTraders Accounting Managers
2. Create a Group Policy Modeling report for desktop computers.	■ User Container: OU=Users,OU=*ComputerName*,OU=Locations,DC=nwtraders, DC=msft ■ Computer Container: OU=Desktops,OU=Computers,OU=*ComputerName*,OU=Locations, DC=nwtraders,DC=msft ■ User Security Groups: Authenticated Users, Everyone, NWTRADES\G NWTraders Accounting Personnel

Exercise 6
Generating a Group Policy Results Report

In this exercise, you will generate a Group Policy Results report to see what policy settings have been applied to the nwtraders\administrator account on the server named Glasgow.

Task	Special instructions
1. Create a Group Policy Results report.	▪ Computer Selection: Glasgow ▪ User Selection: NWTRADERS\administrator
2. View a Group Policy Results report.	▪ Determine when policy settings were last refreshed

Microsoft®
Training &
Certification

Module 10: Implementing Administrative Templates and Audit Policy

Contents

Overview

- Overview of Security in Windows Server 2003
- Using Security Templates to Secure Computers
- Testing Computer Security Policy
- Configuring Auditing
- Managing Security Logs

Introduction

This module will provide a broad overview of security in Microsoft® Windows® Server 2003. You will learn how to use security templates and test computer security policy. You will also learn how to configure auditing and manage security logs.

Objectives

After completing this module, you will be able to:

- Describe administrative templates and audit policy in Windows Server 2003.
- Use security templates to secure computers.
- Test computer security policy.
- Configure auditing.
- Manage security logs.

Lesson: Overview of Security in Windows Server 2003

- What Are User Rights?
- User Rights vs. Permissions
- User Rights Assigned to Built-in Groups
- How to Assign User Rights

Introduction

In this lesson, you will learn about user rights, permissions, and user rights assigned to built-in groups. You will also learn how to assign user rights.

Lesson objectives

After completing this lesson, you will be able to:

- Describe user rights.
- Distinguish between rights and permissions.
- Describe the user rights assigned to built-in groups.
- Assign user rights.

What Are User Rights?

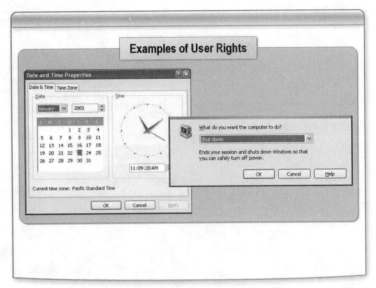

Examples of User Rights

Definition

When a user logs on, the user receives an access token that includes user rights. A user right authorizes a user who is logged on to a computer or a network to perform certain actions on the system. If a user does not have the appropriate rights to perform an action, attempts to perform the action are blocked.

Who do rights apply to?

User rights can apply both to individual users and to groups. However, user rights are best administered when they are assigned to groups. This ensures that a user who logs on as a member of a group automatically receives the rights associated with that group. Windows Server 2003 enables an administrator to assign rights to users and groups.

Common user rights

Common user rights include the following:

- *Log on locally*. Enables a user to log on to the local computer or to the domain from a local computer.

- *Change the system time*. Enables a user to set the time of the internal clock of a computer.

- *Shut down the system*. Enables a user to shut down a local computer.

- *Access this computer from a network*. Enables a user to access a computer running Windows Server 2003 from any other computer on the network.

User Rights vs. Permissions

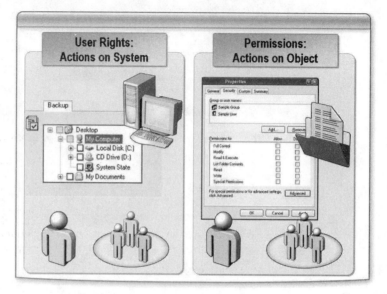

Introduction

Administrators can assign specific user rights to group accounts or to individual user accounts. These rights authorize users to perform specific actions, such as log on to a system interactively or back up files and directories. User rights are different from permissions, because user rights are attached to user accounts, and permissions are attached to objects.

What are user rights?

User rights determine which users can perform a specific task on a computer or in a domain. Although you can assign user rights to individual user accounts, user rights are best administered if they are assigned to group accounts. A user logging on as a member of a group automatically inherits the rights assigned to that group. By assigning user rights to groups rather than individual users, you simplify the task of administering user accounts. When users in a group all require the same user rights, you can assign the set of user rights once to the group, rather than repeatedly assigning the same set of user rights to each individual user account.

User rights that are assigned to a group are applied to all members of the group while they are members. If a user is a member of multiple groups, the user's rights are cumulative, which means that the user has more than one set of rights. The only time that rights assigned to one group might conflict with those assigned to another is in the case of certain logon rights. In general, user rights assigned to one group do not conflict with the rights assigned to another group. To remove rights from a user, the administrator simply removes the user from the group. The user no longer has the rights assigned to that group.

Rights apply to the entire system, rather than to a specific resource, and affect the overall operation of the computer or domain. All users accessing network resources must have certain common rights on the computers they use, such as the right to log on to the computer or change the system time of the computer. Administrators can assign specific common user rights to groups or to individual users. Additionally, Windows Server 2003 assigns certain rights to built-in groups by default.

What are permissions?

Permissions define the type of access granted to a user or group for an object or object property. For example, you can grant the Read and Write permissions to the Finance group for a file named Payroll.dat.

You can grant permissions for any secured objects such as files, objects in the Active Directory® directory service, or registry objects. You can grant permissions to any user, group, or computer. It is a good practice to grant permissions to groups.

You can grant permissions for objects to:

- Groups, users, and special identities in the domain.

- Groups and users in that domain and any trusted domains.

- Local groups and users on the computer where the object resides.

When you provide access to file resources on a computer running Windows Server 2003, you can control who has access to resources and the nature of their access by granting the appropriate permissions. Permissions define the type of access assigned to a user or group for any resource.

For example, users in the Human Resources department of an organization might need to modify the organization's document describing Human Resources policies. To facilitate this, the administrator must grant the appropriate permission to the members of the Human Resources department.

To grant permissions for individual files and folders, Windows Server 2003 uses the NTFS file system. You can also control the permissions for accessing shared folder resources and network printers.

User Rights Assigned to Built-in Groups

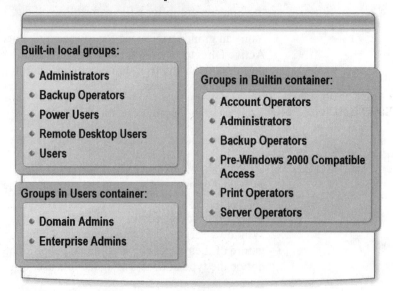

Built-in local groups:

- Administrators
- Backup Operators
- Power Users
- Remote Desktop Users
- Users

Groups in Builtin container:

- Account Operators
- Administrators
- Backup Operators
- Pre-Windows 2000 Compatible Access
- Print Operators
- Server Operators

Groups in Users container:

- Domain Admins
- Enterprise Admins

Introduction

By default, Windows Server 2003 assigns certain rights to built-in groups. The built-in groups include local groups, groups in the Builtin container, and groups in the Users container.

User rights assigned to local groups

The following user rights are assigned to local groups:

- Administrators

  Access this computer from the network; Adjust memory quotas for a process; Allow log on locally; Allow log on through Terminal Services; Back up files and directories; Bypass traverse checking; Change the system time; Create a pagefile; Debug programs; Force shutdown from a remote system; Increase scheduling priority; Load and unload device drivers; Manage auditing and security log; Modify firmware environment variables; Perform volume maintenance tasks; Profile single process; Profile system performance; Remove computer from docking station; Restore files and directories; Shut down the system; Take ownership of files or other objects

- Backup Operators

  Access this computer from the network; Allow log on locally; Back up files and directories; Bypass traverse checking; Restore files and directories; Shut down the system

- Power Users

  Access this computer from the network; Allow log on locally; Bypass traverse checking; Change the system time; Profile single process; Remove computer from docking station; Shut down the system

  ---

  Caution Members of the Power Users group can elevate their privileges to administrator.

- Remote Desktop Users

  Allow log on through Terminal Services

- Users

  Access this computer from the network; Allow log on locally; Bypass traverse checking

User rights assigned to the Builtin container

The following user rights are assigned to groups in the Builtin container:

- Account Operators

  Allow log on locally; Shut down the system

- Administrators

  Access this computer from the network; Adjust memory quotas for a process; Back up files and directories; Bypass traverse checking; Change the system time; Create a pagefile; Debug programs; Enable computer and user accounts to be trusted for delegation; Force a shutdown from a remote system; Increase scheduling priority; Load and unload device drivers; Allow log on locally; Manage auditing and security log; Modify firmware environment values; Profile single process; Profile system performance; Remove computer from docking station; Restore files and directories; Shut down the system; Take ownership of files or other objects

- Backup Operators

  Back up files and directories; Allow log on locally; Restore files and directories; Shut down the system

- Pre-Windows 2000 Compatible Access

  Access this computer from the network; Bypass traverse checking

- Print Operators

  Allow log on locally; Shut down the system

- Server Operators

  Back up files and directories; Change the system time; Force shutdown from a remote system; Allow log on locally; Restore files and directories; Shut down the system

User rights assigned to the Users container

The following user rights are assigned to groups in the Users container:

- Domain Admins

  Access this computer from the network; Adjust memory quotas for a process; Back up files and directories; Bypass traverse checking; Change the system time; Create a pagefile; Debug programs; Enable computer and user accounts to be trusted for delegation; Force a shutdown from a remote system; Increase scheduling priority; Load and unload device drivers; Allow log on locally; Manage auditing and security log; Modify firmware environment values; Profile single process; Profile system performance; Remove computer from docking station; Restore files and directories; Shut down the system; Take ownership of files or other objects

- Enterprise Admins (only appears in the forest root domain)

  Access this computer from the network; Adjust memory quotas for a process; Back up files and directories; Bypass traverse checking; Change the system time; Create a pagefile; Debug programs; Enable computer and user accounts to be trusted for delegation; Force shutdown from a remote system; Increase scheduling priority; Load and unload device drivers; Allow log on locally; Manage auditing and security log; Modify firmware environment values; Profile single process; Profile system performance; Remove computer from docking station; Restore files and directories; Shut down the system; Take ownership of files or other objects

Additional reading

For more information about user rights and upgrading operating systems, see article 323042, "Required User Rights for the Upgrade from Windows 2000 to Windows Server 2003" in the Microsoft Knowledge Base at http://support.microsoft.com/?kbid=323042.

For more information about user rights and service accounts, see article 325349, "HOW TO: Grant Users Rights to Manage Services in Windows Server 2003" in the Microsoft Knowledge Base at http://support.microsoft.com/?kbid=325349.

How to Assign User Rights

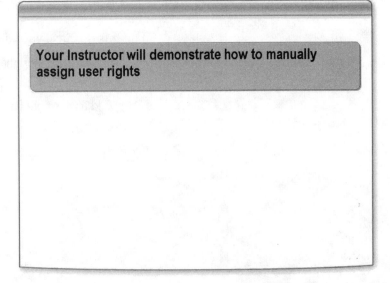

Your Instructor will demonstrate how to manually assign user rights

Introduction

Typically, administrators add users or groups to built-in groups that already have rights. In some circumstances, a built-in group might give too much or too little rights to a user, so you must assign rights manually.

Procedure

To assign user rights:

1. Click **Start**, click **Run**, type **mmc** and then press ENTER.

2. Click **Console**.

3. On the **File** menu, click **Add/Remove Snap-in**.

4. In the **Add/Remove Snap-in** dialog box, click **Add**.

5. In the **Add Standalone Snap-in** dialog box, double-click **Group Policy Object Editor**.

6. Click **Finish** to close the Welcome to Group Policy Wizard.

7. Click **Close** to close the **Add Standalone Snap-in** dialog box.

8. Click **OK** to close the **Add/Remove Snap-in** dialog box.

9. Expand **Local Computer Policy**, expand **Computer Configuration**, expand **Windows Settings**, expand **Security Settings**, and then expand **Local Policies**.

10. Click **User Rights Assignment**.

11. Add or remove a group to a user right as needed.

Practice: Assigning User Rights

In this practice, you will:

- Remove a user right and test if it was removed

- Add a user right and test if it was added

Objective

In this practice, you will:

- Remove the right to log on locally from the Users group and test if the user right is removed.

- Assign the Users group the right to log on locally and test if the user right is assigned.

Instructions

Before you begin this practice:

- Log on to the domain by using the *ComputerName*Admin account.

- Open CustomMMC

Note This practice focuses on the concepts in this lesson and as a result may not comply with Microsoft security recommendations. For example, this practice does not comply with the recommendation that users log on with domain user account and use the **Run as** command when performing administrative tasks.

- Review the procedures in this lesson that describe how to perform this task.

Scenario

The systems engineers want to test user rights by preventing users from logging on locally to your computer. After the test is successful, you will assign users the right to log on locally.

Practice

▶ **Remove the right to log on locally from the Users group**

1. Remove the group Users from the following local computer policy:

   Computer Configuration/Windows Settings/Security Settings/ Local Policies/User Rights Assignment/Allow log on locally

2. Close all programs and log off.

▶ **Test if the right was removed**

- Log on as *ComputerName*User.

  You should *not* be able to log on.

▶ **Assign the right to log on locally to the Users group**

1. Log on as *ComputerName*Admin.

2. Add the group Users to the following local computer policy:

   Computer Configuration/Windows Settings/Security Settings/ Local Policies/User Rights Assignment/Allow log on locally

3. Close all programs and log off.

▶ **Test if the right was assigned**

- Log on as *ComputerName*User.

  You should be able to log on.

Lesson: Using Security Templates to Secure Computers

- What Is a Security Policy?
- What Are Security Templates?
- What Are Security Template Settings?
- How to Create a Custom Security Template
- How to Import a Security Template

Introduction

You can create security templates to create a security policy and alter a security policy to meet the security needs of your company. You can implement security policies in several different ways. The method you use depends on your organization's size and security needs. Smaller organizations, or those not using Active Directory, can configure security manually on an individual basis. If your organization is large or requires a high level of security, consider using Group Policy objects (GPOs) to deploy security policy.

Lesson objectives

After completing this lesson, you will be able to:

- Describe a security policy.
- Describe security templates.
- Describe security template settings.
- Create a custom security template.
- Import a security template.

What Is a Security Policy?

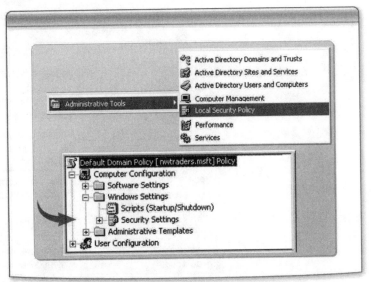

Introduction

A security policy is a combination of security settings that affect the security on a computer. You can use security policy to establish account policies and local policies on your local computer and in Active Directory.

Security policy on a local computer

You can use the security policy on a local computer to directly modify account and local policies, public key policies, and Internet Protocol security (IPSec) policies for your local computer.

With local security policy, you can control:

- Who accesses your computer.

- What resources users are authorized to use on your computer.

- Whether a user or group's actions are recorded in the event log.

If your network does not use Active Directory, you can configure security policy by using Local Security Policy, which is found on the **Administrative Tools** menu on computers running Windows Server 2003.

Security policies in Active Directory

Security policies in Active Directory have the same security settings as a security policy on local computers. However, administrators of Active Directory–based networks can save considerable administrative time by using Group Policy to deploy the security policy. You can edit or import security settings in a GPO for any site, domain, or organizational unit, and the security settings are automatically deployed to the computers when the computers start. When editing a GPO, expand **Computer Configuration** or **User Configuration** and then expand **Windows Settings** to find security policy settings.

Additional reading

For more information about default domain user rights, see article 324800, "HOW TO: Reset User Rights in the Default Domain Group Policy in Windows Server 2003" in the Microsoft Knowledge Base at http://support.microsoft.com/?kbid=324800.

What Are Security Templates?

Template	Description
Default Security (Setup security.inf)	Specifies default security settings
Domain Controller Default Security (DC security.inf)	Specifies default security settings updated from Setup security.inf for a domain controller
Compatible (Compatws.inf)	Modifies permissions and registry settings for the Users group to enable maximum application compatibility
Secure (Securedc.inf and Securews.inf)	Enhances security settings that are least likely to impact application compatibility
Highly Secure (Hisecdc.inf and Hisecws.inf)	Increases the restrictions on security settings
System Root Security (Rootsec.inf)	Specifies permissions for the root of the system drive

Definition

A security template is a collection of configured security settings. Windows Server 2003 provides predefined security templates that contain the recommended security settings for different situations.

You can use predefined security templates to create security policies that are customized to meet different organizational requirements. You customize the templates with the Security Templates snap-in. After you customize the predefined security templates, you can use them to configure security on an individual computer or thousands of computers.

How security templates are applied

You can configure individual computers with the Security Configuration and Analysis snap-in or the **secedit** command-line tool or by importing the template into Local Security Policy. You can configure multiple computers by importing a template into Security Settings, which is an extension of Group Policy.

You can also use a security template as a baseline for analyzing a system for potential security holes or policy violations by using the Security Configuration and Analysis snap-in. By default, the predefined security templates are stored in *systemroot*/Security/Templates.

Predefined templates

Windows Server 2003 provides the following predefined templates:

- Default security (Setup security.inf)

  The Setup security.inf template is created during installation of the operating system for each computer and represents default security settings that are applied during installation, including the file permissions for the root of the system drive. It can vary from computer to computer, based on whether the installation was a clean installation or an upgrade. You can use this template on servers and client computers, but not on domain controllers. You can apply portions of this template for disaster recovery.

  Default security settings are applied only to clean installations of Windows Server 2003 on an NTFS partition. When computers are upgraded from Microsoft Windows NT® version 4.0, security is not modified. Also, when you install Windows Server 2003 on a FAT (file allocation table) file system, security is not applied to the file system.

- Domain controller default security (DC security.inf)

  The DC security.inf template is created when a server is promoted to a domain controller. It reflects default security settings on files, registry keys, and system services. Reapplying it resets these settings to the default values, but it may overwrite permissions on new files, registry keys, and system services created by other applications. You can apply it by using the Security Configuration and Analysis snap-in or the **secedit** command-line tool.

- Compatible (Compatws.inf)

  Default permissions for workstations and servers are primarily granted to three local groups: Administrators, Power Users, and Users. Administrators have the most privileges, and Users have the least.

  Members of the Users group can successfully run applications that take part in the Windows Logo Program for Software. However, they may not be able to run applications that do not meet the requirements of the program. If other applications are to be supported, the Compatws.inf template changes the default file and registry permissions that are granted to the Users group. The new permissions are consistent with the requirements of most applications that do not belong to the Windows Logo Program for Software.

- Secure (Secure*.inf)

  The Secure templates define enhanced security settings that are least likely to affect application compatibility. For example, the Secure templates define stronger password, lockout, and audit settings.

- Highly Secure (hisec*.inf)

  The Highly Secure templates are supersets of the Secure templates. They impose further restrictions on the levels of encryption and signing that are required for authentication and for the data that flows over secure channels and between server message block (SMB) clients and servers.

- System root security (Rootsec.inf)

  By default, Rootsec.inf defines the permissions for the root of the system drive. You can use this template to reapply the root directory permissions if they are inadvertently changed, or you can modify the template to apply the same root permissions to other volumes. As specified, the template does not overwrite explicit permissions that are defined on child objects. It propagates only the permissions that are inherited by child objects.

Additional reading

For more information about applying security policies, see article 325351, "HOW TO: Apply Local Policies to All Users Except Administrators on Windows Server 2003 in a Workgroup Setting" in the Microsoft Knowledge Base at http://support.microsoft.com/?kbid=325351.

For more information on **secedit**, see "Secedit" at http://www.microsoft.com/technet/treeview/default.asp?url=/technet/prodtechnol/windowsserver2003/proddocs/datacenter/secedit_cmds.asp?frame=true.

What Are Security Template Settings?

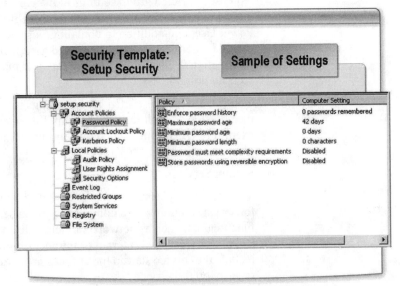

Introduction

Security templates contain security settings for all security areas. You can apply templates to individual computers or deploy them to groups of computers by using Group Policy. When you apply a template to existing security settings, the settings in the template are merged into the computer's security settings.

You can configure and analyze security settings for computers by using the Security Settings Group Policy extension or Security Configuration and Analysis.

Types of security template settings

The following list describes each of the security template settings:

- Account Policies

  You can use account policy settings to configure password policies, account lockout policies, and Kerberos version 5 (V5) protocol policies for the domain. A domain's account policy defines the password history, the lifetime of the Kerberos V5 tickets, account lockouts, and more.

- Local Policies

  Local policy settings, by definition, are local to computers. Local policies include audit policies, the assignment of user rights and permissions, and various security options that can be configured locally.

  It is important not to confuse local policy settings with setting policies locally. As with all of these security settings, you can configure these settings by using Local Security Policy and Group Policy.

- Event Log

  You use event log settings to configure the size, access, and retention parameters for application logs, system logs, and security logs.

- Restricted Group

  You use restricted group settings to manage the membership of built-in groups that have certain predefined capabilities, such as Administrators and Power Users, in addition to domain groups, such as Domain Admins. You can add other groups to the restricted group, along with their membership information. This enables you to track and manage these groups as part of security policy.

  You can also use restricted group settings to track and control the reverse membership of each restricted group. Reverse membership is listed in the **Members Of** column, which displays other groups to which the restricted group must belong.

- System Services

  You use system services settings to configure security and startup settings for services running on a computer. System services settings include critical functionality, such as network services, file and print services, telephony and fax services, and Internet or intranet services. The general settings include the service startup mode (automatic, manual, or disabled) and security on the service.

- Registry

  You use registry settings to configure security on registry keys.

- File System

  You use file system settings to configure security on specific file paths.

- Public Key Policies

  You use public key policy settings to configure encrypted data recovery agents, domain roots, trusted certificate authorities, and so on.

  Note   Public Key Policies are the only settings available under User Configuration.

- IP Security Policies on Active Directory

  You use IP security policy settings to configure IPSec.

Important   Only the Account Policies, Local Policies, Public Key Policies, and IP Security Policies on Active Directory areas are available when you use Local Security Policy.

Also, you can assign password settings, account lockout settings, and Kerberos settings at the domain or organizational unit level. However, if you configure the policy at the organizational unit level, the settings affect only the local Security Accounts Manager (SAM) databases of computer objects in the organizational unit, not the domain password policies. Windows Server 2003 does not process any changes that you make to these three settings in a GPO at the site level.

Additional reading

For more information about security template best practices, see the TechNet article "Best practices for Security Templates" at http://www.microsoft.com/technet/treeview/default.asp?url=/technet/prodtechnol/windowsserver2003/proddocs/datacenter/sag_SCEbp.asp.

How to Create a Custom Security Template

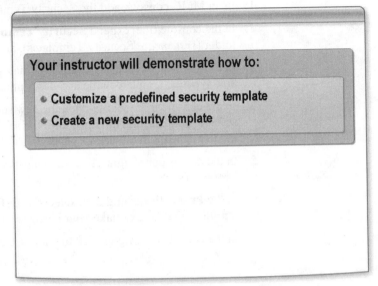

Your instructor will demonstrate how to:

- Customize a predefined security template
- Create a new security template

Introduction

If the predefined templates are insufficient for your security needs, you must create custom templates.

Procedure for customizing a predefined template

To customize a predefined security template:

1. In a Microsoft Management Console (MMC), add the Security Templates snap-in.

2. In the console tree, expand **Security Templates**, and then double-click the default path folder (*systemroot*/Security/Templates).

3. In the details pane, right-click the predefined template you want to modify, and then click **Save As**.

4. In the **Save As** dialog box, type a new file name for the security template, and then click **Save**.

5. In the console tree, double-click the new security template to display the security policies, and navigate until the security attribute you want to modify appears in the details pane.

6. In the details pane, right-click the security attribute, and then click **Properties**.

7. In the **Properties** dialog box, select the **Define this policy setting in the template** check box, make your changes, and then click **OK**.

8. In the console tree, right-click the new security template, and then click **Save**.

Procedure for creating a new security template

To create a new security template:

1. In an MMC console, add the Security Templates snap-in.

2. In the console tree, expand **Security Templates**, right-click the default path folder (*systemroot*/Security/Templates), and then click **New Template**.

3. In the *systemroot*/**security**/**templates** dialog box, in the **Template Name** box, type the template name and description and then click **OK**.

4. In the console tree, double-click the new security template to display the security policies, and navigate until the security attribute you want to modify appears in the details pane.

5. In the details pane, right-click the security attribute, and then click **Properties**.

6. In the **Properties** dialog box, select the **Define this policy setting in the template** check box, make your changes, and then click **OK**.

7. In the console tree, right-click the new security template, and then click **Save**.

How to Import a Security Template

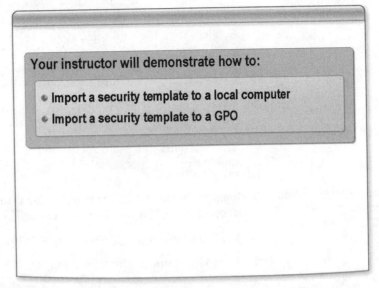

Introduction

When you import a security template to a local computer, you can apply the template settings to the local computer. When you import a security template into a GPO, the settings in the template are applied to computers in the containers to which the GPO is linked.

Procedure for importing a template to a local computer

To import a security template to a local computer:

1. Open Security Configuration and Analysis.

2. In the console tree, right-click **Security Configuration and Analysis**, and then click **Import Template**.

3. (Optional) To clear the database of any template, select the **Clear this database before importing** check box.

4. In the **Import Template** dialog box, click a template file, and then click **Open**.

5. Repeat these steps for each template that you want to merge into the database.

Procedure for importing a template to a GPO without GPMC installed

To import a security template into a GPO when Group Policy Management is not installed:

1. Open Active Directory Users and Computers or Active Directory Sites and Services from the **Administrative Tools** menu.

2. Edit the appropriate GPO.

3. Expand **Computer Configuration**, and then expand **Windows Settings**.

4. Right-click **Security Settings**, and then click **Import Policy**.

5. Click a template, and then click **Open**.

   The template settings are applied to the GPO and will be applied the next time the computer is started.

Procedure for importing a template to a GPO with GPMC

To import a security template into a GPO when Group Policy Management is installed:

1. In Group Policy Management, edit the appropriate GPO.

2. Expand **Computer Configuration**, and then expand **Windows Settings**.

3. Right-click **Security Settings**, and then click **Import Policy**.

4. Click a template, and then click **Open**.

   The template settings are applied to the GPO and will be applied the next time the computer is started.

Practice: Using Security Templates to Secure Computers

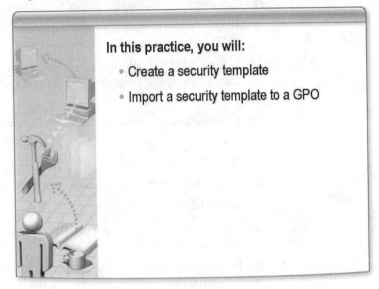

In this practice, you will:
- Create a security template
- Import a security template to a GPO

Objective

In this practice, you will:

- Create a security template.

- Import a security template to a GPO.

Instructions

Before you begin this practice:

- Log on to the domain by using the *ComputerName*User account.

- Open CustomMMC with the **Run as** command.

  Use the user account Nwtraders*ComputerName*Admin (Example: LondonAdmin).

- Open a command prompt with the Run as command.

  From the **Start** menu click **Run**, and then type **runas /user:nwtraders*ComputerName*Admin cmd** and click **OK**. When prompted for a password, type **P@ssw0rd** and press **ENTER**.

- Review the procedures in this lesson that describe how to perform this task.

Practice: Creating a custom template on a local computer

▶ **Check the local group membership of the Power Users local group**

1. To verify that NWTraders\\G IT Admins is not a member of the Power Users group from a command prompt type **net localgroup "power users"**

2. There should be no members listed under Members.

3. With a default installation of the operating system, the Power Users group should not contain any members.

4. Leave the command prompt open.

▶ **Create a new security template called *ComputerName***

1. In CustomMMC, add the Security Templates snap-in.

2. In Security Templates, in the console tree, right-click
   C:\WINDOWS\cecurity\templates, and then click **New Template**.

3. In the **C:\WINDOWS\security\templates** dialog box, in the **Template
   Name** box, type *ComputerName* and then click **OK**.

▶ **Edit the *ComputerName* custom security template**

1. In Security Templates, in the console tree, expand *ComputerName*, and then
   click **Restricted Groups**.

2. Right-click **Restricted Groups**, and then click **Add Group**.

3. In the **Add Group** dialog box, type **Power Users** and then click **OK**.

4. In the **Power Users Properties** dialog box, under **Members of this group**,
   click **Add Members**.

5. In the **Add Member** dialog box, type **NWTRADERS\G IT Admins** and
   then click **OK**.

6. In the **Power Users Properties** dialog box, click **OK**.

7. In the console tree, right-click *ComputerName*, and then click **Save**.

▶ **Import and apply the *ComputerName* custom security template**

1. In CustomMMC, add the Security Configuration and Analysis snap-in.

2. Right-click **Security Configuration and Analysis**, and then click **Open
   Database**.

3. In the **Open database** box, type *ComputerName* and then click **Open**.

4. In the **Import Template** dialog box, click *ComputerName*.**inf**, and then
   click **Open**.

5. Right-click **Security Configuration and Analysis**, and then click
   Configure Computer Now.

6. In the message box, click **OK**.

7. Right-click **Security Configuration and Analysis**, and then click **View
   Log File**.

8. In the details pane for **Security Configuration and Analysis**, verify that the
   NWTRADERS\G IT Admins group was added to the Power Users group by
   looking for the following log file entry:

   ----Configure Group Membership...
   Configure Power Users.
   add NWTRADERS\G IT Admins.

▶ **Check the local group membership of the Power Users local group**

1. To verify that NWTraders\G IT Admins is a member of the Power Users
   group, from a command prompt type **net localgroup "Power Users"**

2. NWTraders\G IT Admins should be listed under Members.

3. Leave the command prompt open.

▶ **Remove the imported custom security template**

1. From a Command prompt type **net localgroup "power users" /delete "g it admins"**

2. Leave the command prompt open.

▶ **Check the local group membership of the Power Users local group**

1. To verify that NWTraders\G IT Admins is not a member of the Power Users group from a command prompt type **net localgroup "power users"**

2. There should be no members listed under Members.

3. Leave the command prompt open.

Practice: Importing a custom template to a GPO

▶ **Import a security template to a GPO**

1. In Group Policy Management, create a GPO called *ComputerName* **Restricted Users**.

2. Link the *ComputerName* Restricted Users GPO to the Locations/*ComputerName*/Computers organizational unit.

3. Edit the *ComputerName* Restricted Users GPO.

4. Import the custom security policy named *ComputerName*.inf.

▶ **Move your *ComputerName* computer account**

1. Search for your *ComputerName* computer account in the nwtraders.msft domain.

2. Move your *ComputerName* computer account to the Locations/*ComputerName*/Computers organizational unit.

3. From a command prompt, type **gpupdate /force**

4. If prompted to logoff, type **N** and then press **ENTER**.

▶ **Check the local group membership of the Power Users local group**

1. To verify that NWTraders\G IT Admins is a member of the Power Users group, from a command prompt type **net localgroup "power users"**

2. NWTraders\G IT Admins should be listed under Members.

3. Close the command prompt

Lesson: Testing Computer Security Policy

- What is the Security Configuration and Analysis tool?
- How to Test Computer Security

Introduction

Before deploying a security template to large groups of computers, it is important to analyze the results of applying a configuration to ensure there are no adverse effects on applications, connectivity, or security. A thorough analysis also helps you identify security holes and deviations from standard configurations. You can use the Security Configuration and Analysis snap-in to create and review possible scenarios and adjust a configuration.

Lesson objectives

After completing this lesson, you will be able to:

- What is the Security Configuration and Analysis tool?
- Test computer security with the Security Configuration and Analysis tool.

What is the Security Configuration and Analysis tool?

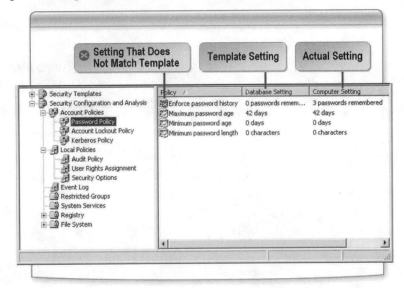

	Introduction	The most common tool that is used to analyze computer security is the Security Configuration and Analysis tool.

Introduction

The most common tool that is used to analyze computer security is the Security Configuration and Analysis tool.

Security Configuration and Analysis tool

The Security Configuration and Analysis tool compares the security configuration of the local computer to an alternate configuration that is imported from a template (an .inf file) and stored in a separate database (an .sdb file). When analysis is complete, you can browse the security settings in the console tree to see the results. Discrepancies are marked with a red flag. Consistencies are marked with a green check mark. Settings that are not marked with either a red flag or a green check mark are not configured in the database.

Why use Security Configuration and Analysis tool?

After analyzing the results by using the Security Configuration and Analysis tool, you can perform various tasks, including:

- Eliminate discrepancies by configuring the settings in the database to match the current computer settings. To configure database settings, double-click the setting in the details pane.

- Import another template file, merging its settings and overwriting settings where there is a conflict. To import another template file, right-click **Security Configuration and Analysis**, and then click **Import Template**.

- Export the current database settings to a template file. To export another template file, right-click **Security Configuration and Analysis**, and then click **Export Template**.

Additional reading

For more information about the security tools, see:

- "Security Configuration Manager" at http://www.microsoft.com/technet/ treeview/default.asp?url=/technet/prodtechnol/windowsserver2003/ proddocs/server/SEconcepts_SCM.asp.

- "Best Practices for Security Configuration and Analysis" at http://www.microsoft.com/technet/treeview/default.asp?url=/technet/ prodtechnol/windowsserver2003/proddocs/server/sag_SCMbp.asp.

How to Test Computer Security

> Your instructor will demonstrate how to analyze security settings on a computer by using Security Configuration and Analysis

Introduction

Sometimes you must analyze a computer to see what security settings on a server are different from the settings in a base security template. To do this, you run the Security Configuration and Analysis tool.

Procedure

To analyze security by using Security Configuration and Analysis:

1. Add the Security Configuration and Analysis snap-in to an MMC console.

2. Right-click **Security Configuration and Analysis**, and then click **Open database**.

3. In the **Open database** dialog box, select an existing database file or type a unique name to create a new database, and then click **Open**.

   Existing databases already contain imported settings. If you are creating a new database, the **Import Template** dialog box appears. Select a database, and then click **Open**.

4. Right-click **Security Configuration and Analysis**, and then click **Analyze Computer Now**.

5. In the **Perform Analysis** dialog box, choose a location for the analysis log file, and then click **OK**.

6. In the console tree, expand **Security Configuration and Analysis**.

7. Navigate through the security settings in the console tree, and compare the **Database Setting** and the **Computer Setting** columns in the details pane.

Practice: Testing Computer Security

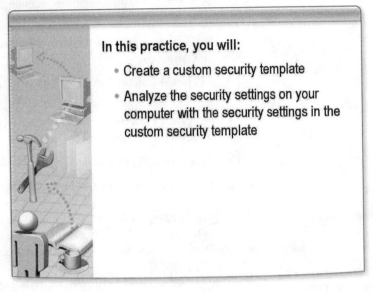

In this practice, you will:

- Create a custom security template
- Analyze the security settings on your computer with the security settings in the custom security template

Objective

In this practice, you will:

- Create a custom security template.
- Compare the security settings on your computer to the settings in the custom security template.

Instructions

Before you begin this practice:

- Log on to the domain by using the *ComputerName*User account.
- Open CustomMMC with the **Run as** command.

  Use the user account Nwtraders*ComputerName*Admin (Example: LondonAdmin).

- Review the procedures in this lesson that describe how to perform this task.

Scenario

You are a systems administrator for Northwind Traders. You must implement the following security settings on your member servers:

- Passwords must be at least 10 characters.
- A dialog box must be displayed during the logon process, informing users that unauthorized access is not allowed.
- The alerter service, which is set to start manually, must be disabled.

Practice: Creating security templates

▶ **Create a custom security template**

1. In the Security Template snap-in, change the following policies in the securews template:

   • Set **Account Policies/Password Policy/Minimum password length** to 10 characters.

   • Set **Local Policies/Security Options/Interactive Logon/Message text for users attempting to log on** to **Authorized Access Only**.

   • Set **Local Policies/Security Options/Interactive Logon/Message title for users attempting to log on** to *ComputerName*.

   • Set **System Services/Alerter** to **Disabled**.

2. Save the custom security template as *ComputerName*Secure.

Scenario

Now that you have configured the template and the appropriate policy settings, you want to perform a security analysis to create a baseline for future security analysis and to verify the current configuration.

Practice: Testing computer security

▶ **Import and clear the current security configuration and analysis baseline database**

• In Security Configuration and Analysis, import the *ComputerName*Secure template and clear the database.

▶ **Perform the security analysis**

1. Right-click **Security Configuration and Analysis**, and then click **Analyze Computer Now**.

2. From **Perform Analysis** dialog box, click **OK**.

3. In Security Configuration and Analysis, expand **Local Policies**, and then click **Security Options**.

4. Notice the **Interactive logon: Message text for users attempting to log on** and the **Interactive logon: Message title for users attempting to log on** policies.

5. In the details pane, notice the system settings that have a red flag.

   A red flag indicates that the security template is different than the current computer settings.

Lesson: Configuring Auditing

- What Is Auditing?
- What Is Audit Policy?
- Types of Events to Audit
- Guidelines for Planning an Audit Policy
- How to Enable an Audit Policy
- How to Enable Auditing for Files and Folders
- How to Enable Auditing for Active Directory Objects
- Best Practices for Configuring Auditing

Introduction

No security strategy is complete without a comprehensive auditing strategy. More often than not, organizations learn this only after they experience a security incident. Without an audit trail of actions, it is almost impossible to successfully investigate a security incident. You must determine as part of your overall security strategy what events you need to audit, the level of auditing appropriate for your environment, how the audited events and collected, and how they are reviewed.

Lesson objectives

After completing this lesson, you will be able to:

- Describe auditing.
- Describe what an audit policy is.
- Describe types of events to audit.
- Identify the guidelines for planning an audit policy.
- Enable an audit policy.
- Enable auditing for files and folders.
- Enable auditing for an organizational unit.
- Apply best practices while configuring auditing.

What Is Auditing?

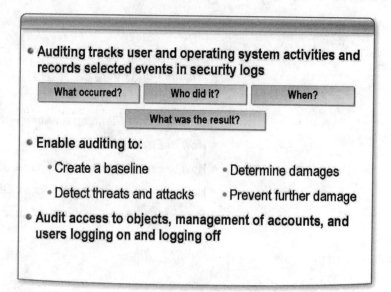

Definition

Auditing is the process that tracks user and operating system activities by recording selected types of events in the security log of a server or a workstation. Security logs contain various audit entries, which contain the following information:

- The action that was performed

- The user who performed the action

- The success or failure of the event and when the event occurred

- Additional information, such as the computer where the event occurred

Why perform auditing?

Enable auditing and monitor audit logs to:

- Create a baseline of normal network and computer operations.

- Detect attempts to penetrate the network or computer.

- Determine what systems and data have been compromised during or after a security incident.

- Prevent further damage to networks or computers after an attacker has penetrated the network.

The security needs of an organization help determine the amount of auditing used. For example, a minimum-security network may choose to audit failed logon attempts to monitor against potential brute force attacks. A high-security network may choose to audit both successful and failed logon attempts to track any unauthorized users who successfully gain access to the network.

Although auditing may provide valuable information, excessive auditing fills the audit log with unnecessary information. This can potentially affect the performance of your system and make it extremely difficult to find relevant information.

Types of events to audit

The most common types of events to audit are when:

- Objects, such as files and folders, are accessed
- Managing user accounts and group accounts
- Users log on to and log off from the system

Additional reading

For more information about auditing, see the TechNet article "Auditing overview" at http://www.microsoft.com/technet/treeview/default.asp?url=/technet/prodtechnol/windowsserver2003/proddocs/server/sag_SEconceptsAudit.asp.

What Is Audit Policy?

- **An audit policy determines the security events that will be reported to the network administrator**

- **Set up an audit policy to:**

  - **Track success or failure of events**

  - **Minimize unauthorized use of resources**

  - **Maintain a record of activity**

- **Security events are stored in security logs**

Introduction

Establishing an audit policy is an important part of security. Monitoring the creation or modification of objects gives you a way to track potential security problems, helps to ensure user accountability, and provides evidence in the event of a security breach.

Definition

An audit policy defines the types of security events that Windows Server 2003 records in the security log on each computer. Windows Server 2003 writes events to the security log on the specific computer where the event occurs.

Why set up an audit policy?

Set up an audit policy for a computer to:

- Track the success and failure of events, such as attempts to log on, attempts by a particular user to read a specific file, changes to a user account or group membership, and changes to security settings.

- Minimize the risk of unauthorized use of resources.

- Maintain a record of user and administrator activity.

Use Event Viewer to view events that Windows Server 2003 records in the security log. You can also archive log files to track trends over time. This is useful to determine trends in the use of printers, access to files, and attempts at unauthorized use of resources.

How can you implement an audit policy?

You can set up an audit policy on any single computer, either directly by using the Local Policy snap-in or indirectly by using Group Policy, which is more commonly used in large organizations. After an audit policy is designed and implemented, information begins to appear in the security logs. Each computer in the organization has a separate security log that records local events.

When you implement an audit policy:

- Specify the categories of events that you want to audit. Examples of event categories are user logon, user logoff, and account management. The event categories that you specify constitute your audit policy. There is no default audit policy.

- Set the size and behavior of the security log. You can view the security log with Event Viewer.

- Determine which objects you want to monitor access of and what type of access you want to monitor, if you want to audit directory service access or object access. For example, if you want to audit attempts by users to open a particular file, you can configure audit policy settings in the object access event category so that successful and failed attempts to read a file are recorded.

Default audit policies

The default auditing settings for servers are configured by administrative templates. The following security templates configure default auditing settings:

- Setup security.inf
- Hisecdc.inf
- Hisecws.inf
- Secuerdc.inf
- Securews.inf

To view the policy settings that each security template configures, in the Security Templates snap-in, navigate to Local Policies\Audit Policy for each administrative template.

Additional reading

For more information about audit policies, see the TechNet article "Auditing policy" at http://www.microsoft.com/technet/treeview/default.asp?url=/ technet/prodtechnol/windowsserver2003/proddocs/server/APtopnode.asp.

Types of Events to Audit

- Account Logon
- Account Management
- Directory Service Access
- Logon
- Object Access
- Policy Change
- Privilege Use
- Process Tracking
- System

Introduction

The first step in creating a strategy for auditing the operating system is to determine what type of actions or operations that you need to record.

Determining what events to audit

What operating system events should you audit? You do not want to audit every event, because auditing all operating system events requires enormous system resources and may negatively affect system performance. You should work with other security specialists to determine what operating system events to audit. Only audit events that you believe will be useful for later reference.

An effective way to begin determining what events to audit is to gather the relevant group of people and discuss:

- What actions or operations you want to track.

- On what systems you want to track these events.

For example, you may decide to track:

- All domain and local logon events on all computers.

- The use of all files in the Payroll folder on the HR server.

The success and failure events

In Windows Server 2003, audit events can be split into two categories:

- Success events

  A success event indicates that the operating system has successfully completed the action or operation. Success events are indicated by a key icon.

- Failure events

  A failure event indicates that an action or operation was attempted, but did not succeed. Failure events are indicated by a padlock icon.

Failure events are very useful for tracking attempted attacks on your environment, but success events are much more difficult to interpret. The vast majority of success events are indications of normal activity, and an attacker who accesses a system also generates a success event.

Often, a pattern of events is as important as the events themselves. For example, a series of failures followed by a success may indicate an attempted attack that was eventually successful.

Similarly, the deviation from a pattern may also indicate suspicious activity. For example, suppose the security logs show that a user at your organization logs on every workday between 8 A.M. and 10 A.M., but suddenly the user is logging on to the network at 3 A.M. Although this behavior may be innocent, it should be investigated.

Events that Windows Server 2003 can audit

The first step in implementing an audit policy is to select the types of events that you want Windows Server 2003 to audit. The following table describes the events that Windows Server 2003 can audit.

Event	Example
Account Logon	An account is authenticated by a security database. When a user logs on to the local computer, the computer records the AccountLogon event. When a user logs on to a domain, the authenticating domain controller records the Account Logon event.
Account Management	An administrator creates, changes, or deletes a user account or group; a user account is renamed, disabled, or enabled; or a password is set or changed.
Directory Service Access	A user accesses an Active Directory object. To log this type of access, you must configure specific Active Directory objects for auditing.
Logon	A user logs on to or off of a local computer, or a user makes or cancels a network connection to the computer. The event is recorded on the computer that the user accesses, regardless of whether a local account or a domain account is used.
Object Access	A user accesses a file, folder, or printer. The administrator must configure specific files, folders, or printers for auditing.
Policy Change	A change is made to the user security options (for example, password options or account logon settings), user rights, or audit policies.
Privilege Use	A user exercises a user right, such as changing the system time (this does not include rights that are related to logging on and logging off) or taking ownership of a file.
Process Tracking	An application performs an action. This information is generally only useful for programmers who want to track details about application execution.
System	A user restarts or shuts down the computer, or an event occurs that affects Windows Server 2003 security or the security log.

Events edited by default

The Setup security.inf template includes default settings that enable auditing of successful account logon events and successful logon events. No other events are audited by default.

Guidelines for Planning an Audit Policy

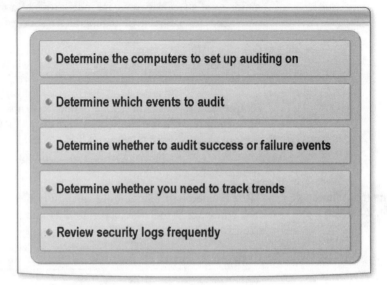

- Determine the computers to set up auditing on
- Determine which events to audit
- Determine whether to audit success or failure events
- Determine whether you need to track trends
- Review security logs frequently

Introduction

Auditing too many types of events may create excess overhead, which may result in diminished system performance.

Guidelines

Use the following guidelines when planning an audit policy:

- Determine the computers to set up auditing on. Plan what to audit for each computer, because Windows Server 2003 audits events on each computer separately. For example, you may frequently audit computers used to store sensitive or critical data, but you may infrequently audit client computers that are used solely for running productivity applications.

- Determine the types of events to audit, such as the following:

  - Access to files and folders

  - Users logging on and off

  - Shutting down and restarting a computer running Windows Server 2003

  - Changes to user accounts and groups

- Determine whether to audit success or failure events, or both. Tracking success events can tell you how often Windows Server 2003 or users access specific files or printers. You can use this information for resource planning. Tracking failure events can alert you to possible security breaches.

- Determine whether you need to track trends of system usage. If so, plan to archive event logs. Some organizations are required to maintain a record of resource and data access.

- Review security logs frequently and regularly according to a schedule. Configuring auditing alone does not alert you to security breaches.

How to Enable an Audit Policy

> **Your instructor will demonstrate how to:**
>
> - Configure an audit policy on a local computer
> - Configure an audit policy on a domain or organizational unit

Introduction

There are two procedures for enabling an audit policy, depending on whether the computer is in a workgroup or a domain.

Procedure for an audit policy on a local computer

To enable an audit policy on a local computer:

1. From the **Administrative tools** menu, click **Local Security Policy**.

2. In the console tree, expand **Local Policies**, and then double-click **Audit Policy**.

3. In the details pane, double-click the policy that you want to enable or disable.

4. Do one or both of the following, and then click **OK**:

   - To audit success events, select the **Success** check box.

   - To audit failure events, select the **Failure** check box.

   For example, suppose you select the **Success** and **Fail** check boxes for logon and logoff events. If a user successfully logs on to the system, it is logged as a success audit event. If a user tries to access a network drive and fails, the attempt is logged as a failure audit event.

Note   If you are a member of a domain, and a domain-level policy is defined, domain-level settings override the local policy settings.

Procedure for an audit policy on a domain or organizational unit

To enable an audit policy on a domain or an organizational unit:

1. In Group Policy Management, create or browse to a GPO linked to an organizational unit, and then edit it.

2. In the console tree, navigate to Computer Configuration/Windows Settings/ Security Settings/Local Policies/Audit Policy.

3. In the details pane, double-click the policy that you want to enable or disable.

4. Do one or both of the following, and then click **OK**:

   • To audit success events, select the **Success** check box.

   • To audit failure events, select the **Failure** check box.

How to Enable Auditing for Files and Folders

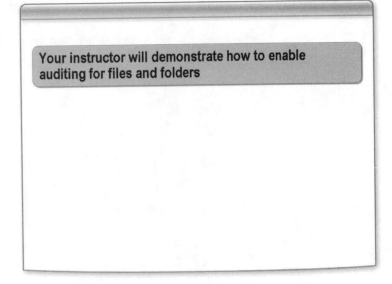

Your instructor will demonstrate how to enable auditing for files and folders

Introduction

You enable auditing to detect and record security-related events, such as when a user attempts to access a confidential file or folder. When you audit an object, an entry is written to the security log whenever the object is accessed in a certain way.

After you enable auditing, you can keep track of users who access certain objects and analyze security breaches. The audit trail shows who performed the actions and who tried to perform actions that are not permitted.

Procedure

To enable auditing for files and folders:

1. In Windows Explorer, locate the file or folder that you want to audit.

2. Right-click the file or folder, and then click **Properties**.

3. In the **Properties** dialog box, on the **Security** tab, click **Advanced**.

4. In the **Advanced Security Settings** dialog box, on the **Auditing** tab, do one of the following:

   - To enable auditing for a new user or group, click **Add**. In the **Enter the object name to select** box, type the name of the user or group, and then click **OK**.

   - To view or change auditing for an existing group or user, click the name, and then click **Edit**.

   - To disable auditing for an existing group or user, click the name, and then click **Remove**.

5. Under **Access**, click **Successful**, **Failed**, or both **Successful** and **Failed**, depending on the type of access that you want to audit.

6. If you want to prevent child objects from inheriting these audit entries, select the **Apply these auditing entries to objects and/or containers within this container only** check box.

Practice: Enabling Auditing for Files and Folders

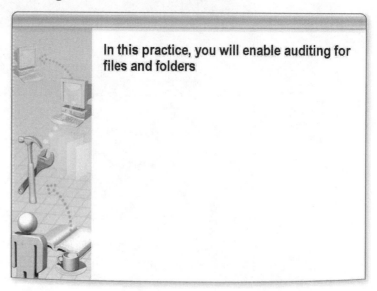

In this practice, you will enable auditing for files and folders

Objective

In this practice, you will enable auditing for files and folders.

Instructions

Before you begin this practice:

- Log on to the domain by using the *ComputerName*User account.

- Open CustomMMC with the **Run as** command.

  Use the user account Nwtraders*ComputerName*Admin (Example: LondonAdmin).

- Ensure that the D:\\HR Reports folder is created and shared from a previous practice or lab.

- Review the procedures in this lesson that describe how to perform this task.

Scenario

You get a call from the Human Resources manager, who tells you that files are being deleted. The Sales manager wants to know which user is deleting files. You must enable auditing on your server for the HR-Reports folder.

Practice

▶ **Create a GPO that enables an audit policy**

- Tool: Group Policy Management

- GPO name: *ComputerName* **Audit Policy**

- GPO link to the following location: Locations/*ComputerName*/Computers

- Enable auditing of the success and failure of the following security policy: Computer Configuration/Windows Settings/Security Settings/ Local Policies/Audit Policy/Audit object access

▶ **Verify the location of the computer account**

1. Ensure your computer is in the Locations/*ComputerName*/Computers organizational unit.

   If your computer is not in this organizational unit, search for it and move it.

2. From a command prompt, type **gpupdate /force**

3. If prompted to logoff, type **N** and press **ENTER**.

▶ **Audit the HR-Reports folder**

- Enable auditing for the folder D:\HR Reports by using the following criteria:

  - Audit the group G NWTraders HR Personnel.

  - Audit **Successful - Delete of Subfolders and Files**.

  - Audit **This folder, subfolders and files**.

  - Prevent child objects from inheriting these audit entries.

How to Enable Auditing for Active Directory Objects

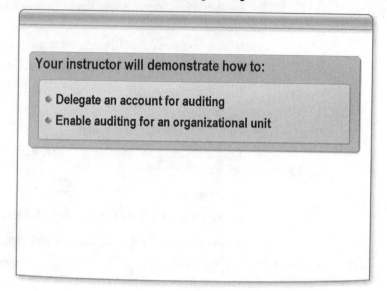

Introduction

When you enable auditing for an organizational unit, you audit the event generated when a user accesses an Active Directory object that has permissions. By default, auditing is set to Success in the Default Domain Controller GPO, and it remains undefined for workstations and servers where it does not apply.

Note By default, only members of the Administrators group have privileges to configure auditing. You can delegate the task of configuring auditing for server events to another user account by assigning the Manage auditing and security log user right in Group Policy.

Procedure for delegating an account to enable auditing

To enable nonadministrators to manage and view audit logs on a member server, you must first delegate the authority to a user or group. To do this:

1. In Group Policy Object Editor, in the console tree, navigate to the following:

    Computer Configuration/Windows Settings/Security Settings/ Local Polices/User Rights Assignment

2. Click **Manage auditing and security log**.

3. On the **Action** menu, click **Properties**.

4. In the **Manage auditing and security log** dialog box, select the check box, **Define these policy settings**, and then click **Add User or Group**.

5. Type the name of the appropriate user or user group from the list, and then click **OK**.

6. Click **OK**.

Procedure for enabling auditing for an organizational unit

To enable auditing for an organizational unit:

1. In Active Directory Users and Computers, right-click the organizational unit that you want to audit, and then click **Properties**.

2. In the **Properties** dialog box, on the **Security** tab, click **Advanced**.

   To view the security properties, you must click **Advanced Features** on the **View** menu of Active Directory Users and Computers.

3. In the **Advanced Security Settings** dialog box, on the **Auditing** tab, do one of the following:

   - To enable auditing for a new user or group, click **Add**. In the **Enter the object name to select** box, type the name of the user or group, and then click **OK**.

   - To remove auditing for an existing group or user, click the group or user name, click **Remove**, and click **OK**. Skip the rest of this procedure.

   - To view or change auditing for an existing group or user, click the group or user name, and then click **Edit**.

4. In the **Apply onto** box, click the location where you want auditing to take place.

5. Under **Access**, indicate what actions you want to audit by selecting the appropriate check boxes:

   - To audit success events, select the **Successful** check box.

   - To stop auditing success events, clear the **Successful** check box.

   - To audit failure events, select the **Failed** check box.

   - To stop auditing failure events, clear the **Failed** check box.

   - To stop auditing all events, click **Clear All**.

6. If you want to prevent child objects from inheriting these audit entries, select the **Apply these auditing entries to objects and/or containers within this container only** check box.

Practice: Enabling Auditing for an Organizational Unit

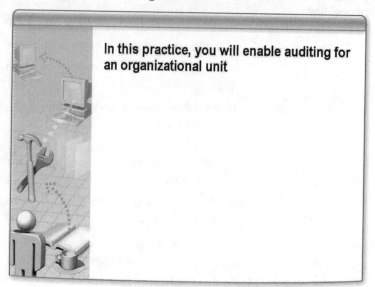

In this practice, you will enable auditing for an organizational unit

Objectives

After completing this practice, you will be able to configure an audit policy that audits the creation and deletion of objects in an organizational unit.

Instructions

Before you begin this practice:

- Log on to the domain by using the *ComputerName*User account.

- Open CustomMMC with the **Run as** command using Nwtraders*ComputerName*Admin (Example: LondonAdmin).

- Review the procedures in this lesson that describe how to perform this task.

Scenario

You are concerned that someone is adding and removing user, computer, and group objects in your *ComputerName* organizational unit. You want to configure an audit policy that audits the successful and unsuccessful creation and deletion of those objects in your *ComputerName* organizational unit.

Practice

▶ **Enable auditing for the organizational unit *ComputerName***

- Enable auditing by using the following criteria:

  - Audit the Everyone group.

  - Audit the *ComputerName* organizational unit and all child objects.

  - Audit the following access properties for success and failure events:

    - Create Account Objects

    - Delete Account Objects

    - Create Computer Objects

    - Delete Computer Objects

    - Create Group Objects

    - Delete Group Objects

Best Practices for Configuring Auditing

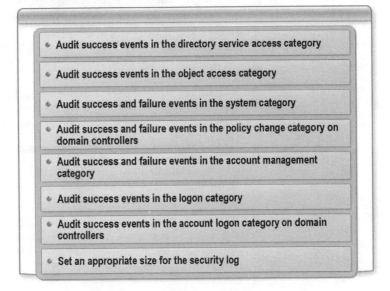

Best practices

Apply the following best practices while performing auditing:

- Audit success events in the directory service access category.

  By auditing success events in the directory service access category, you can find out who accessed an object in Active Directory and what operations were performed.

- Audit success events in the object access category.

  By auditing success events in the object access category, you can ensure that users are not misusing their access to secured objects.

- Audit success and failure events in the system category.

  By auditing success and failure events in the system category, you can detect unusual activity that indicates that an attacker is attempting to gain access to your computer or network.

- Audit success and failure events in the policy change category on domain controllers.

  If an event is logged in the policy change category, someone has changed the Local Security Authority (LSA) security policy configuration. If you use Group Policy to edit your audit policy settings, you do not need to audit events in the policy change category on member servers.

- Audit success and failure events in the account management category.

  By auditing success events in the account management category, you can verify changes that are made to account properties and group properties. By auditing failure events in the account management category, you can see if unauthorized users or attackers are trying to change account properties or group properties.

- Audit success events in the logon category.

    By auditing success events in the logon category, you have a record of when each user logs on to or logs off from a computer. If an unauthorized person steals a user's password and logs on, you can find out when the security breach occurred.

- Audit success events in the account logon category on domain controllers.

    By auditing success events in the account logon category, you can see when users log on to or log off from the domain. You do not need to audit events in the account logon category on member servers.

- Set an appropriate size for the security log.

    It is important to configure the size of the security log appropriately, based on the number of events that your audit policy settings generate.

Additional reading

For more information about audit policy best practices, see the TechNet article "Best practices" at http://www.microsoft.com/technet/treeview/ default.asp?url=/technet/prodtechnol/windowsserver2003/proddocs/ server/sag_SEconceptsImpAudBP.asp.

For more information about managing audit logs see:

- TechNet article "Microsoft Operations Manager 2000" at http://www.microsoft.com/technet/treeview/default.asp?url=/technet/ prodtechnol/mom/evaluate/mom2k.asp.

- Article 325898, "HOW TO: Set Up and Manage Operation-Based Auditing for Windows Server 2003, Enterprise Edition" in the Microsoft Knowledge Base at http://support.microsoft.com/?kbid=325898.

Lesson: Managing Security Logs

- What Are Log Files?
- Common Security Events
- Tasks Associated with Managing the Security Log Files
- How to Manage Security Log File Information
- How to View Security Log Events

Introduction

You can configure the security logs to record information about Active Directory and server events. These events are recorded in the Windows security log. The security log can record security events, such as valid and invalid logon attempts, as well as events that are related to resource use, such as creating, opening, or deleting files. You must log on as an administrator to control what events are audited and displayed in the security log.

Lesson objectives

After completing this lesson, you will be able to:

- Describe the types of security log files and the information contained in each log file.

- Identify common security events.

- Describe tasks associated with managing the security log files.

- Manage security log file information.

- View security log events.

What Are Log Files?

The following logs are available in Event Viewer:

- Application
- Security
- System
- Directory service
- File Replication service

Introduction

The security log records events, such as valid and invalid logon attempts, and events related to resource use, such as creating, opening, or deleting files or other objects. For example, if logon auditing is enabled, attempts to log on to the system are recorded in the security log. After an audit policy is designed and implemented, information begins to appear in the security log.

Each computer in the organization has a separate security log that records local events. Domain controllers hold the security log information about Active Directory.

Logs available in Event Viewer

You can view the following logs in Event Viewer, depending on the type of computer that you are using and the services that are installed on that computer:

- Application

   Contains events generated by applications installed on the computer, including server applications, such as Microsoft Exchange Server or Microsoft SQL Server™, and desktop applications, such as Microsoft Office.

- Security

   Contains events generated by auditing. These events include logons and logoffs, access to resources, and changes in policy.

- System

   Contains events generated by components and services in Windows Server 2003.

- Directory service

  Appears only on domain controllers. The directory service event log contains, for example, Active Directory replication.

- File Replication service

  Appears only on domain controllers. The file replication service event log contains, for example, events that are related to the replication of Group Policy.

Tip If you decide to use auditing extensively, increase the size of the security log in the Event Log section of the security policy for the Default Domain Controllers GPO.

Security log files format

Security log files are also stored in the *systemroot*/system32/config directory. Security logs can be exported and archived in the following file formats:

- Event log files (.evt) (Default)

- Comma delimited (.csv)

- Text file (.txt)

Common Security Events

Logon	Event Description
Event ID 528	Successful logon
Event ID 529	Unsuccessful logon attempt
Event ID 539	Attempts to log on to a locked out account
File Ownership	**Event Description**
Event ID 578	Change in file ownership
Security Log	**Event Description**
Event ID 517	Security log cleared
Shutdown	**Event Description**
Event ID 513	System is shut down

Introduction

Many events appear in the security log. The following are some common scenarios that may be cause for concern and suggestions for diagnosing problems by using the event log.

Invalid logon attempts and account lockout

A successful logon generates an Event ID 528. When a user attempts to guess another user's password, they will likely make several incorrect guesses. Each incorrect guess generates an Event ID 529, which is also generated by a misspelled user name. If an account becomes locked out, subsequent attempts generate an Event ID 539.

Notice that one or two of these events might occur when a user types incorrectly, does not realize that the CAPS LOCK key is on, or forgets a password.

Change of file ownership

The owner of a file in the NTFS file system can modify the file's permissions to read and modify the file. A user who has the user right to take ownership can access any file by first taking ownership of that file. This change of ownership constitutes the use of a user right and generates an Event ID 578.

Clearing the security log

An unscrupulous administrator with the user right to clear the security log from Event Viewer can clear the log to hide his or her security-sensitive activities.

The security log must always be cleared according to a well-planned schedule and only immediately after a full copy of the log is archived. If the log is cleared under any other circumstances, the administrator must justify his or her actions. Clearing the security log generates an Event ID 517, which is the first event generated in the new log.

System shutdown

Ordinarily, mission-critical servers must be shut down only by administrators. You can prevent others from shutting down a server by assigning or denying the Shut down the system user right in the local security policy or by using Group Policy.

To identify if the **Shut down the system** right was mistakenly assigned, audit the system Event ID 513, which indicates who shut down the computer.

Additional reading

For more information about security events, see:

- Article 299475, "Windows 2000 Security Event Description (Part 1 of 2)" in the Microsoft Knowledge Base at http://support.microsoft.com/ ?kbid=299475.

- Article 301677, "Windows 2000 Security Event Description (Part 2 of 2)" in the Microsoft Knowledge Base at http://support.microsoft.com/ ?kbid=301677.

- The TechNet article "Security Operations Guide for Windows 2000 Server" at http://www.microsoft.com/technet/treeview/default.asp?url=/ TechNet/security/prodtech/windows/windows2000/staysecure/ DEFAULT.asp.

Tasks Associated with Managing the Security Log Files

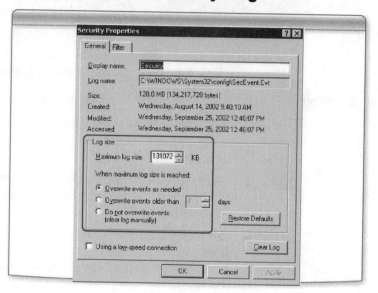

Introduction

All events related to operating system security in Windows NT, Windows Server 2003, and Microsoft Windows XP are recorded in the security log in Event Viewer. Security-related events may also be recorded in the application and system logs.

Evaluate the configuration of the log file

Before you enable audit policies, you must evaluate whether the default configuration of the log files in Event Viewer is appropriate for your organization.

To view the log files settings in Event Viewer:

1. From the **Administrative Tools** menu, open Event Viewer.
2. Right-click the security event log, and then click **Properties**.

Log file location

By default, the security log is stored in the *systemroot*/System32/config directory in a file named SecEvent.evt. In Windows Server 2003, you can change the log file location in the security log properties. In Windows NT 4.0 and Windows Server 2000, you must edit the registry to change the location of each log file.

By default, only the System account and the Administrators group have access to the security log. This ensures that nonadministrators cannot read, write, or delete security events. If you move the log to a new location, ensure that the new file has the correct NTFS permissions. Because the Event Viewer service cannot be stopped, changes to this setting are not applied until the server is restarted.

Maximum log file size

By default, the maximum size that the security log can grow to before the overwrite behavior is initiated is 512 KB. Because hard disk space is much more readily available now than it was in the past, you will likely want to increase this setting. The amount by which you increase this setting depends on the overwrite behavior configured for the log file, but a good general guideline is to set the maximum size to at least 50 MB. You can change the maximum size of the log file on individual computers in the security log properties or on many computers by using security templates or editing the registry.

The maximum size that you should set for the combined total size of all event logs is 300 MB. Each security event is 350 to 500 bytes, so a 10-MB event log contains approximately 20,000 to 25,000 security events.

Log file overwrite behavior

When you configure the security log settings, you must define the overwrite behavior when the maximum log file size is reached. The following list describes the overwrite event options.

- **Overwrite events as needed**

  New events continue to be written when the log is full. Each new event replaces the oldest event in the log.

- **Overwrite events older than [x] days**

  Events are retained in the log for the number of days you specify before they are overwritten. The default is seven days.

- **Do not overwrite events**

  New events are not recorded, and the event log must be cleared manually.

Delegate the right to manage the file

To delegate the rights to manage the security log file, configure the Group Policy setting **Manage auditing and security log**. This is found in Computer Configuration/Windows Settings/Security Settings/Local Policies/User Rights Assignment.

How to Manage Security Log File Information

Your instructor will demonstrate how to:

- Manage security log files by using Computer Management
- Manage security log files by using Group Policy

Introduction

The more security information you capture, the bigger the security log file you need. You want a log file to track what security events have occurred since the last archival of the events.

Procedure for using Computer Management

To manage security log file information through Computer Management:

1. In Computer Management, in the console tree, expand **System Tools and Event Viewer**.

2. Right-click a log file, and then click **Properties**.

3. In the **Properties** dialog box, you can do the following:

   - Configure the maximum log file size

   - Configure overwrite behavior

   - Clear the log file

Procedure for using a GPO

To manage security log file information through a GPO:

1. Edit a GPO.

2. In Group Policy Object Editor, in the console tree, expand **Computer Configuration**, expand **Windows Settings**, expand **Security Settings**, and then expand **Event Log**.

3. Define a parameter for the following Group Policy settings:

   - **Log size**

   - **Prevent local guest from accessing logs**

   - **Retain Log**

   - **Retention method for Log**

How to View Security Log Events

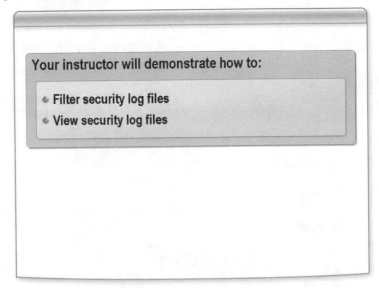

Your instructor will demonstrate how to:

- Filter security log files
- View security log files

Introduction

Security logs can get rather large, and viewing large logs or finding specific types of events in the log may be difficult. You can set a filter on the log to view specific types of events or events from specific users or groups.

Procedure for filtering the security logs

To filter the security logs:

1. In Event Viewer, in the console tree, right-click **Security**, click **View**, and then click **Filter**.

2. In the **Security Properties** dialog box, define your filter criteria, and then click **OK**.

Procedure for viewing security logs

To view security logs:

1. In Event Viewer, in the console tree, click **Security**.

2. The details pane lists individual security events.

   If you want to see more details about a specific event, in the details pane, double-click the event.

Practice: Managing Log File Information

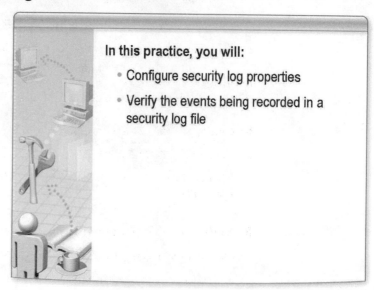

In this practice, you will:

- Configure security log properties
- Verify the events being recorded in a security log file

Objective

In this practice, you will:

- Configure security log properties.
- View security log events.

Instructions

Before you begin this practice:

- Log on to the domain by using the *ComputerName*User account.
- Open CustomMMC with the **Run as** command.

  Use the user account Nwtraders*ComputerName*Admin (Example: LondonAdmin).

- Review the procedures in this lesson that describe how to perform this task.

Scenario

The network security team at Northwind Traders tells you that the security log file must have the following properties on your *ComputerName* server:

- The maximum log size must be 30,016 KB.

- The overwrite behavior is **Do not overwrite events (clear log manually)**.

They also ask you to review your security log file to determine if the security events are being logged for the folder D:\HR Reports.

Practice

▶ **Configure the security log properties**

1. Change the maximum log size to 30,016 KB.

2. Change the overwrite behavior to **Do not overwrite events (clear log manually)**.

▶ **Verify that security events are being logged for D:\HR Reports**

1. Create a security log filter that filters the following types of events:

   - Success events and failure events

   - Security

   - Object access

2. Browse through the security log to see success and failure events for D:\HR Reports.

Lab A: Managing Security Settings

In this lab, you will:

- Create a custom security template

- Test your computer configuration against the custom security template

- Deploy the custom security template by using Group Policy

- Audit security of an organizational unit

Objectives

After completing this lab, you will be able to:

- Create a custom security template.
- Test your computer configuration against the custom security template.
- Deploy a custom template by using a GPO.
- Configure and test security auditing of organizational units.

Instructions

Before you begin this practice:

- Log on to the domain by using the *ComputerName*User account.
- Open CustomMMC with **Run as** command.

  Use the user account NWTraders*ComptuerName*Admin (Example: LondonAdmin).

- Ensure the CustomMMC has the following snap-ins:
  - Security Templates
  - Group Policy Management
  - Security Configuration and Analysis
  - Active Directory Users and Computers
  - Computer Management (Local)
  - Computer Management (London)

**Estimated time to
complete this lab:
35 minutes**

Exercise 1
Creating a Custom Template

In this exercise, you will create a custom security template.

Scenario

The security team has finished testing the security requirements for Northwind Traders. They have given you security requirements that you must use to create a custom security template called *ComputerName* Server Policy.

Tasks	Special instructions
1. Create a new custom security template.	▪ Security template name: *ComputerName* **Server Policy**
2. Enable audit policies.	▪ Enable the following audit policies for failure: • **Audit account logon events** • **Audit logon events** ▪ Enable the following audit policies for success and failure: • **Audit account management events** • **Audit object access events** • **Audit policy change events** • **Audit privilege use events** • **Audit system events**
3. Set event log properties.	▪ Set the following event log properties: • Set maximum application log size to 99,840 KB • Set maximum security log size to 99,840 KB • Retain security log for 7 days • Retain system log for 7 days
4. Save the template.	▪ Save the template *ComputerName* Server Policy.

Exercise 2
Testing a Custom Template

In this exercise, you will compare a custom security template to your server's current security policy.

Tasks	Special instructions
1. Create a new configuration and analysis baseline database.	▪ Database name: *ComputerName* **Security Test** ▪ Template: *ComputerName* **Server Policy Settings.inf**
2. Analyze your server.	▪ Analysis log name: *ComputerName* **Security Test.log**

3. Review the results of the audit policy analysis.	▪ Circle Y if your computer setting matches the database. Circle N if your computer setting differs from the database.
	   • **Audit account logon events** (Y / N)
	   • **Audit account management events** (Y / N)
	   • **Audit logon events** (Y / N)
	   • **Audit object access events** (Y / N)
	   • **Audit policy change events** (Y / N)
	   • **Audit privilege use events** (Y / N)
	   • **Audit system events** (Y / N)

4. Review the results of the event log analysis.	▪ Circle Y if your computer setting matches the database. Circle N if your computer setting differs from the database.
	   • **Maximum application log size** (Y / N)
	   • **Maximum security log size** (Y / N)
	   • **Retain security log** (Y / N)
	   • **Retain system log** (Y / N)

Exercise 3
Deploying a Custom Template Using a GPO

In this exercise, you will import a custom template to a GPO and deploy the template to your computer. You will then test your computer to determine if you received the GPO.

Tasks	Special instructions
1. Create and link a GPO.	▪ Organizational unit to link to GPO: Locations/*ComputerName*/Computers ▪ GPO name: *ComputerName* **Security Settings**
2. Import a security template to a GPO.	▪ Template name: *ComputerName* Server Policy.inf
3. Disable **Block Policy inheritance**.	▪ Expand all organizational units of **Locations/*ComputerName*** and remove any blocking of inheritance of all sub organizational units.
4. Verify that the computer account is in the proper organizational unit.	▪ Verify that the computer named *ComputerName* is in the organizational unit Locations/*ComputerName*/Computers. ▪ If *ComputerName* is not in the Locations/*ComputerName*/Computers organizational unit, move it there.
5. Update your Group Policy settings.	▪ Run **gpupdate /force**.
6. Analyze the local computer security policy.	▪ Run **Analyze Computer Now** in Security Configuration and Analysis.

7. Review the results of the audit policy analysis.	▪ Circle Y if your computer setting matches the database. Circle N if your computer setting differs from the database.
	
	  • **Audit account logon events** (Y / N)
	  • **Audit account management events** (Y / N)
	  • **Audit logon events** (Y / N)
	  • **Audit object access events** (Y / N)
	  • **Audit policy change events** (Y / N)
	  • **Audit privilege use events** (Y / N)
	  • **Audit system events** (Y / N)

8. Review the results of the event log analysis.	▪ Circle Y if your computer setting matches the database. Circle N if your computer setting differs from the database.
	
	  • **Maximum application log size** (Y / N)
	  • **Maximum security log size** (Y / N)
	  • **Retain security log** (Y / N)
	  • **Retain system log** (Y / N)

Exercise 4
Configuring and Testing Security Audits of Organizational Units

In this exercise, you will configure and test security audits of organizational units.

Scenario

Northwind Traders wants to configure security on the Location/*ComputerName* organizational units to monitor the G IT Admins group. You must configure and test auditing for failed attempts to delete user and computer accounts.

Tasks	Special instructions
1. Enable auditing for an organizational unit.	▪ Audit the organizational unit Locations/*ComputerName* ▪ Remove inheritable auditing entries ▪ Remove all noninherited auditing entries ▪ Audit the Everyone group ▪ Audit the access of **Delete Computer Objects** for **Failed** access ▪ Apply policy to **This object and all child objects**

2. Try to delete computer account with an unauthorized account.	▪ Tool: DSRM
	   a. Open a command prompt with runas
	   b. runas /user:nwtraders*ComputerName*User cmd
	   c. Password: P@ssw0rd
	 ▪ Use DSRM to try and delete the computer *ComputerName*
	   • Dsrm CN=*ComputerName*,OU=Computers,OU=*ComputerName*,OU=Locations,DC=nwtraders,DC=msft
	 ▪ You should get an access is denied error message

3. Filter the London security log.	▪ Tool: Computer Management (London)
	 ▪ Filter security policy for:
	   • Event types: **Failure audit**
	   • Event source: **Security**
	   • Category: **Directory Service Access**
	   • User: *ComputerName***User**

❓ What was *ComputerName*User trying to do?	

Course Evaluation

Your evaluation of this course will help Microsoft understand the quality of your learning experience.

To complete a course evaluation, go to http://www.CourseSurvey.com.

Microsoft will keep your evaluation strictly confidential and will use your responses to improve your future learning experience.

Microsoft® Windows® Server 2003 Enterprise Edition 180-Day Evaluation

The software included in this kit is intended for evaluation and deployment planning purposes only. If you plan to install the software on your primary machine, it is recommended that you back up your existing data prior to installation.

System requirements

To use Microsoft Windows Server 2003 Enterprise Edition, you need:

- Computer with 550 MHz or higher processor clock speed recommended; 133 MHz minimum required; Intel Pentium/Celeron family, or AMD K6/Athlon/Duron family, or compatible processor (Windows Server 2003 Enterprise Edition supports up to eight CPUs on one server)
- 256 MB of RAM or higher recommended; 128 MB minimum required (maximum 32 GB of RAM)
- 1.25 to 2 GB of available hard-disk space*
- CD-ROM or DVD-ROM drive
- Super VGA (800 × 600) or higher-resolution monitor recommended; VGA or hardware that supports console redirection required
- Keyboard and Microsoft Mouse or compatible pointing device, or hardware that supports console redirection

Additional items or services required to use certain Windows Server 2003 Enterprise Edition features:

- For Internet access:
  - Some Internet functionality may require Internet access, a Microsoft Passport account, and payment of a separate fee to a service provider; local and/or long-distance telephone toll charges may apply
  - High-speed modem or broadband Internet connection
- For networking:
  - Network adapter appropriate for the type of local-area, wide-area, wireless, or home network to which you wish to connect, and access to an appropriate network infrastructure; access to third-party networks may require additional charges

Note: To ensure that your applications and hardware are Windows Server 2003–ready, be sure to visit **www.microsoft.com/windowsserver2003**.

* Actual requirements will vary based on your system configuration and the applications and features you choose to install. Additional available hard-disk space may be required if you are installing over a network. For more information, please see **www.microsoft.com/windowsserver2003**.

Uninstall instructions

This time-limited release of Microsoft Windows Server 2003 Enterprise Edition will expire 180 days after installation. If you decide to discontinue the use of this software, you will need to reinstall your original operating system. You may need to reformat your drive.

Microsoft®

Notes

Notes

Notes

Notes

MSM2274BCPN/C90-02024